The October War

Memoirs of Field Marshal El-Gamasy of Egypt

Translation by
Gillian Potter
Nadra Morcos
Rosette Frances

The October War

Mohamed Abdel Ghani El-Gamasy

The American University in Cairo Press

First published in Arabic in 1989 as *Mudhakkarat al-Gamasi: harb Uktubar 1973.*

This translation is published by arrangement with the author.

Dar el Kutub No. 3195/93
ISBN 977 424 316 1

Printed in Egypt by International Press

To my son Medhat, my daughters Magda and Maha, and to the coming generations, who will be facing difficult and complex times. May this testimony help you on your journey to a better future.

– Mohamed Abdel Ghani El-Gamasy

CONTENTS

Introduction

A number of momentous events shook Egypt and the Arab world between October 1973 and October 1978. Their repercussions are still being felt.

On 6 October 1973 I was at the Operations Department, changing into my field uniform, when the fourth war between the Arabs and Israel broke out. At the time, I was participating in my capacity as chief of the Operations Department of the Egyptian Armed Forces, and this latest war was part of the long-drawn-out conflict between the Arabs and Israel.

Five years later to the day, on 6 October 1978, my services as commander in chief of the armed forces had come to an end, along with my functions as deputy prime minister and minister of war and military production. On that occasion, I was a civilian once more and was watching on television at home the annual military parade commemorating the war.

October 1973 marked a new chapter in the contemporary history of Egypt and the Arabs with a war that shook the Middle East, upsetting the existing political, military, and economic balance of the region. Immediately after hostilities had ended, a military disengagement was brokered on both the Egyptian and Syrian fronts, followed by a second disengagement on the Egyptian fronts. The Suez Canal was reopened to navigation and the Friendship Treaty between Egypt and the Soviet Union was abrogated. By the end of 1977, President Sadat had visited Jerusalem in what is now known as the 'peace initiative,' and by

September 1978, he had signed the Camp David Accords in the United States, following stalemated political and military negotiations between Egypt and Israel on the ground.

Two weeks after Camp David, President Sadat told me personally that it was his conviction that Egypt was now going through a new phase which required a complete change in its state institutions and administrative apparatus. For this reason, he had decided to replace the present cabinet headed by Mamduh Salem, and in which I was deputy prime minister and minister of war, and to appoint a new speaker to the People's Assembly. The military leadership was to change, including the commander in chief and the chief of staff, and the Ministry of War would be renamed the Ministry of Defense. There would also be additional negotiations with Israel to implement the Camp David Accords in the form of a peace treaty between Egypt and Israel.

Thirty years of conflict (1948–1978) had elapsed when I left the armed forces in October 1978. The period had witnessed four wars: the 1948 Palestine war, the 1956 aggression on Egypt by Britain, France, and Israel, the June 1967 war, and six grim years of protracted hostilities which became, in effect, a war of attrition. I had lived through all of these and taken part in all but the first war, during which I was abroad on a training mission.

Notwithstanding the serious concern and attention paid to these events and their consequences, I have always felt that we, the Arabs, have not ascribed sufficient importance to understanding in depth the fundamental causes of the Arab–Israeli conflict. We have not been mindful enough of the purposes and goals of the international Zionist movement, nor of those of the great powers; we were not sufficiently aware of their underlying strategies until the state of Israel was carved out of the land of Palestine; nor did we attend to Israel's continued manipulations since its establishment, backed by the major powers and with the support of world Zionism. But we have learned what to expect in the future and the outcomes to anticipate in this conflict, and must prepare to deal with these—taking into account the larger framework of international rivalries in which the Middle East plays a prominent role.

Zionism created Israel by armed force. Very early on in Palestine, it had already set up a paramilitary organization which it named the Haganah, later to become the nucleus of the Israeli army. The existence of this force was announced immediately after Israel was proclaimed a state. At the time, David Ben-Gurion, founder of the state, had declared that "Judaism was destroyed by blood and fire, and by blood and fire it will rise again," appearing to confirm the Zionist's article of faith that "war is the only means by which a nation can be created."

The establishment of a Hebrew state in Palestine was not an end in itself, but only one step in a process by which it would expand territorially at the expense of the Arabs and extend its military, economic, and political domination over the region. To this end, Israel built up a powerful military machine which was to become a major source of danger to the Arab countries. In this context, Ben-Gurion was quoted as saying that "the state of Israel is just one step in the fulfillment of the Zionist dream. It is a means to an end, and as such an unfinished expression of the original Zionist vision."

The 1967 war had dire consequences for the Arabs. Israel's 'armed prophet' Ben-Gurion was now able to express more openly the need for a powerful army to achieve the state's expansionist ambitions, declaring, "We must use our military conquests as a basis for the establishment of settlements, thereby 'creating facts' on the ground which the Arabs will be compelled to acknowledge and accept." To a question on Israel's boundaries, he replied that "Israel's borders are where its soldiers stand."

An analysis of the first three wars (1948, 1956, and 1967) shows clearly that Israel is in a state of continuous military preparedness. Its military and political wherewithal are in a constant state of alert and readiness and public morale is always highly mobilized, whereas we Arabs disperse our energies and efforts, wasting our enormous potential through our obstructive political practices and thereby limiting our effectiveness.

In 1948, Israel was able to seize over 33 percent more Palestinian land than was stipulated in the United Nations Partition Resolution of November 1947 one year earlier. It was also able to obtain, as a result of its participation in the invasion of Egypt in 1956, the right to navigation in the Gulf of 'Aqaba. In 1967 Israel expanded into Arab territory once more, occupying Sinai, the Syrian Golan Heights, the West Bank of the Jordan River, and the Gaza Strip, and imposed by force of arms (with the compliance of outside powers) a fait accompli on the region. More than twenty years later, the Golan Heights, the West Bank, and Gaza remain under a military occupation which continues the fait accompli.

The three wars each had their individual and particular political circumstances, strategic goals, and specific repercussions and took place within the framework of superpower interests and rivalries in the Middle East. From a military perspective, however, the capabilities of the two antagonists are not reflected in the outcomes of the wars, although the decisive factor in 1967 was military strength. Then came the October 1973 war which was conducted very differently. A better understanding and knowledge of our enemy enabled us to locate with greater precision its sources of strength and areas of weakness, and this was a major positive contribution to our success.

Our armed forces fought the same enemy both in 1967 and in 1973, the first time in defeat and the second time in victory. Most of the men who participated in the June 1967 war were the same men who took part, six years later, in the October 1973 war. This lapse of time was not sufficient for one generation of soldiers to have replaced another. Strategically, conditions were also more complex in 1973. Yet our armed forces were able to achieve victory under circumstances which even in the political arena were more complicated than those of June 1967. It is interesting that in 1967, when Israel won the war, it had not considered its borders to be secure. In 1973 the Arabs were able to claim victory from borders the Israelis believed were secure.

This change is what encouraged me to write an objective assessment of the October 1973 war. My intention was to highlight the positive and negative factors of the war for the benefit of the coming generations, which may find my experience useful when their turns come to bear the burdens of responsibility in a difficult and complex world. At that time, the rivalry between the superpowers was not likely to abate, and now the conflict between the Arabs and Israel is not likely to cease.

Following my departure from military and government service, I had written about the 1973 war under the title "Thoughts of a Solider in the October War." This title was chosen deliberately to indicate that I was not writing a military history but a broad review of events which would provide useful lessons rather than the tactical detail required by military professionals.

I found that this did not fully meet my purpose and that I must include the June 1967 war. The two wars are clearly linked, particularly at the levels of military operations and superpower conflict in the Middle East. I must emphasize that the 1967 experience had important repercussions on the military operations of October 1973, and the lessons gained were of major strategic importance to Egypt. I could not ignore the events of the six-year interval between wars either. During this time, Egypt sustained a strong will to fight and our armed forces initiated a series of clashes against Israel, escalating them into a war of attrition. This was a necessary preliminary to the 1973 war. I did not publish my writings at this time, waiting for the opportune moment according to the law.

The years went by. I read widely on the two wars in political and military memoirs, articles, scholarly works, studies, and research reports. Most of these were published outside of Egypt, a few in Egypt. I was struck by the fact that the Israeli perspective had become the main reference point for writers, historians, and researchers on the subject. Often much of what was written was neither objective nor precise, for one reason or another, and gave a misleading impression of the 1973 war. I was offered the opportunity to speak at a symposium on "The Egyptian and the October War" at the University of Manufiya. I participated in a discussion group on the October War with members of Alexandria University's Teacher's Association. A third encounter took place with members of the Egyptian Press at the Press Syndicate. Finally, at the invitation of the Gisra Cultural Association, I attended a conference in Qatar on "The October War in the Arab Strategic Balance." I was faced at these conferences and symposia with a number of questions of both a military and political nature and felt that the upcoming generation was entitled to know the facts and the truth.

I noticed at these gatherings that the literature on the October War published outside of Egypt had been available to Egyptians and had affected them powerfully, prompting them to probe and to seek the reasons behind the facts. This pleased me greatly.

The influence of foreign publications on the war could equally be seen in the research carried out by foreign universities. It so happened that two academics from universities in the United States, a Pakistani and an American, came to Cairo to investigate the Egyptian outlook on the October War. They were familiar with the Israeli point of view through the numerous published memoirs of Israeli military commanders, personal interviews with Israeli military personnel, and other Israeli publications. My three-hour meeting with the Pakistani scholar was balanced, objective, and candidly covered all the issues he was researching. I believe it corrected any distortions in his research resulting from his initial exposure to Israeli references and his meetings with the Israeli leaders.

I hesitated and delayed the publication of this book for many months, even though it had been over twenty-one years since June 1967 and sixteen years since the October 1973 war. Then the prominent author and writer Hilmi Sallam addressed an open letter to me on the pages of *Akhir Sa'a* magazine under the title "A Letter to Field Marshal El-Gamasy: Silence is Not Always Golden." In it he wrote:

> For many years, the October War has been open to discussion by those with inside knowledge, but equally by those observing from the outside. . . . All of them have spoken up, except for yourself.

> You cannot—you ought not to—overlook the importance of open discussion on this war, its execution, and its secrets. It allowed us to overcome defeat and to raise our heads. . . . You have a duty to speak out, both to history and to the generation which fought this war and may have to fight the next one. . . .

I decided then to abbreviate my notes and to focus on the events I had lived through. Consequently I began with the June 1967 war, which I cover in part one, and I explain how Egypt was drawn into war at a time when we were not prepared for it. It was a foolhardy venture, perhaps a trap, which ended in a painful defeat for Egypt and the Arabs.

We then started to rebuild our armed forces and engaged in an increasing number of skirmishes and raids which escalated into a war of attrition and led to a state of limbo somewhere between war and peace, but which was neither. Politically we were at a dead end, with no solution in sight for the Middle East. Part two covers this period.

War became inevitable. It came about with the military engagement of October 1973. Part three covers this period and includes several chapters on the planning stages and the implementation of the war, as well as a daily chronicle of events at operations headquarters from the first day, 6 October, to the ceasefire on 28 October.

Politics now stepped in, with the new postwar conditions serving as a point of departure. US Security Advisor and Secretary of State Henry Kissinger began his step-by-step diplomatic initiative, and this led to a first disengagement between Egyptian and Israeli forces, negotiated at Kilometer 101 on the Suez desert road. This was followed by the disengagement between Syrian and Israeli forces on the Golan front. Part four covers these issues, since I had headed the military delegation for Egypt at Kilometer 101.

President Sadat's visit to Jerusalem occurred towards the end of 1977. Negotiations between the Egyptian and Israeli foreign ministers came soon after, along with military negotiations in Cairo with Israel's minister of defense in which I participated as minister of war. Some months later, all talks—both political and military—had reached a stalemate and were finally discontinued. I have reserved part five for a discussion of the military aspect of the negotiations.

The Camp David talks took place in September 1978. These were held at the presidential level by the presidents of Egypt, Israel, and the United States, and were concluded with the signature of the Camp David Accords by President Sadat and Prime Minister Begin, with President Carter of the United States acting as a witness. As I had no part in these negotiations, I have not included them in this book.

Immediately following Camp David, President Sadat decided that Egypt had shifted into a new phase which required a complete transformation of its institutions and state organizations. He was resolved to act on this belief, so I requested to be relieved of my duties and resigned from the armed forces and the government. Part six covers this period.

I am well aware that war is an extension of politics, using different means. I am also quite sure that politicians are better qualified than I am to discuss the policies of Egypt during the period 1967–73 and then after the war through to 1978. In my writings, therefore, I have given priority to the military dimension, introducing political commentary only insofar as it relates to military issues. I have tried as much as possible to cover my subject from the strategic rather than the tactical perspective. The latter would have been useful only to the military tactician.

I hope it is evident that this book is an expression of my personal point of view, and does not express an official position either of the Egyptian government or of the Egyptian armed forces. I am neither seeking approval nor criticism. This book is my testimony, and a gift to Egypt.

PART I

THE JUNE 1967 WAR

There is no doubt in my mind that the armed forces were among the victims of the 1967 defeat and not one of the reasons for it.

—President Sadat

1

The Roots of the June 1967 War

During May 1967, I was stationed with the armed forces in Sinai, scheduled to return tc Cairo in June. During this time I witnessed a rapid succession of events, beginning with the disinformation that Israeli forces were mobilizing for an attack on the Syrian border and leading in turn to an informal show of force by the Egyptian armed forces in Sinai. Events escalated into a real war for which Egypt and the Arab countries, unlike Israel, were unprepared.

The circumstances behind the events were a combination of faulty political and military evaluations, acts of political opportunism with little regard for consequences, and a conspiracy to draw Egypt, Jordan, and Syria into war and ultimately to defeat. The war in June 1967 resulted in the Israeli occupation of Sinai, the Gaza Strip, the West Bank, and the Golan Heights, as well as in the deaths of thousands of men on the battlefield.

It is important to keep the right perspective on the war and the invaluable lessons it provided. Distinguished journalist Ahmad Baha' al-Din expressed this sentiment when he said that we must view the war

> without giving in to the psychological warfare waged against us in hundreds of books and articles which have ascribed larger dimensions to the reality of defeat, in other words, which attempt to show that the causes of the defeat were inherent in the nature and abilities of our peoples. On the other hand, the defeat should not be played down or excused. There is a middle ground between self-blame and

hiding one's head in the sand, and this is where the most useful lessons can be drawn for our young people. The history of every nation is made up of defeats and victories, but the important thing, always, is to draw the right conclusions.[1]

What went on in 1967? How did it happen? Why did it happen? With the revolution of 23 July 1952 in Egypt, the Middle East began a new phase in its history. The repercussions of this event were deeply felt in the political, economic, and social lives of all the peoples of the Arab world. They touched the interests of the competing great powers, particularly of the United States and the Soviet Union, in their struggle for dominance in this vital region—a struggle which dates back to the end of the Second World War. No matter how historians differ in their assessment of the impact of the revolution on internal and external policies, there is no doubt that it marked a turning point in the Arab–Israeli conflict.

Egypt's revolutionary government pursued a foreign policy which led to national independence in 1954, bringing seventy-four years of British colonialism to an end; it broke for the first time in the history of Egypt a Western arms monopoly through an arms agreement with the Soviet Union in 1955, thereby antagonizing the West; it supported the Algerian Revolution both politically and economically (to France's dismay); in 1956 it nationalized the Suez Canal, which represented British and French interests in Egypt and which was administrated with no regard for Egypt's sovereignty; that same year it stood firm against the triple aggression of England, France, and Israel, marking a political victory against these three countries; finally—in the crowning achievement of its foreign policy—it effected a union with Syria, announcing the creation of the United Arab Republic in 1958, to the consternation of the great nations, West and East.

Egypt's foreign policy goals were clear: Arab nationalism, Arab unity, and non-alignment. It stood against foreign-brokered military pacts and aided Arab and African countries in their struggles towards independence. It worked to halt Israel's regional ambitions and strove to regain the rights of the Palestinian people.

The United States and the nations of Western Europe reacted with hostility, developing a personal animosity towards President Gamal 'Abd al-Nasir who had now become the uncontested nationalist leader in the Arab world. Under his leadership, Egypt posed a threat to their interests in the region and jeopardized the balance of power as the influence of the Soviet Union increased yearly.

The policy of the United States in the Middle East was to endorse and support Israel politically, militarily, and economically at the expense of the Palestinian people. It also aimed to encircle the Soviet Union through a chain of military bases and military pacts or agreements with those countries of the region with strategic or economic value. Hence the discord with Egypt. With Britain, the United States made an attempt to draw Egypt and other Arab neighbors into a military pact known as the Baghdad Pact. President Nasir persistently refused to participate and exerted his influence to prevent other Arab states from joining, arguing that the collective security pact between the Arabs ensured the defense of the region within an Arab security framework. This created tense relations between Egypt and the United States, especially since the US secretary of state at the time, John Foster Dulles, had declared that "those who are not with us are against us." However, the political tug of war ended when Iraq, which had been the only Arab country to join the Baghdad Pact in 1955 under its prime minister at the time, Nuri al-Sa'id, withdrew following the overthrow of the government in the revolution of 1958.

THE SOVIET ARMS DEAL WITH EGYPT

Egypt's announcement that it had concluded, for the first time, an arms deal with the Soviet Union through Czechoslovakia was a substantial political victory for the Soviet Union. The news came as a shock to United States, Britain, France, and Israel, and tension rose in the region. Egypt needed to equip its army against recurring attacks from Israel and President Nasir had tried, without success, to obtain arms from the United States. He concluded a deal with the Soviet Union, breaking the West's arms monopoly, and this was seen as a dangerous development. US Secretary of State Dulles, in a meeting with our ambassador to Washington, said that he was greatly perturbed by this development, which had been described by some analysts as the United States' biggest foreign policy defeat since the "loss of China." Israel's representatives, he said, had told him that they would not wait until the Arabs had completed their preparations to destroy them. He added that the arms deal with the Eastern bloc had placed the US government in a critical position with regard to continued US economic aid to Egypt now that its prestige was in the balance.[2]

Similarly, the British chief of staff, Marshal Templar, in a preliminary report on 15 October 1955, acknowledged that "the deal has upset our defense system in the Middle East. The Soviet Union has disregarded the Baghdad Pact and now has an effective presence in the heart of the region, that is, Cairo."[3] Templar based his evaluation on several factors, notably that a re-equipped Egyptian army would create an imbalance amongst the regional powers and would give Egypt a bigger role in the Middle East—ensuring that neither now or in the future would it ever join a Western defense pact—and that this would set a precedent. He believed that it would lead to an arms race with Israel, and it was not far-fetched, in his opinion, that Israel would decide to attack Egypt before the Egyptian army was able to adjust to its new weapons. Therefore, his conclusion was that the region would probably remain unstable for the foreseeable future.

France took a hostile attitude towards Egypt because of Egyptian aid to Algeria in its struggle against French occupation. It was believed that a destabilized Egypt would be less likely to help Algeria.

Israel's reaction to the arms deal was that it was imperative to attack Egypt, with an eye to opening the straits leading to the port of Eilat, and to support the overthrow of President Nasir. The withdrawal of British troops from the Suez Canal zone and a newly-equipped Egyptian army were both seen as serious threats.

And so, the goals of the United States, Britain, France, and Israel coincided: to keep an upper hand in the region as a way to protect their various interests.

The Tripartite Attack of Egypt

Egypt's nationalization of the Suez Canal in July 1956 provided an opportunity for Britain, France, and Israel to attack Egypt, with the hope of occupying the canal zone and overthrowing President Nasir. The terms of the secret Treaty of Sevres were put into effect on 29 October 1956, and called for the Israeli forces to strike on that day, their goal being to reach the canal zone by the following day, 30 October, when both the British and French governments would issue an appeal to the Egyptian and Israeli governments for a ceasefire and the withdrawal of all forces to a distance of ten miles from the Suez Canal. Egypt would accept British and French troops in key positions on the canal to ensure freedom of navigation for all nations until a formal agreement was signed. If Egypt refused to comply or delayed its response beyond twelve hours, then Anglo–French forces would attack in the early hours of the morning of 31 October. It was also stipulated that Israel would occupy the coastline of the Gulf of 'Aqaba, as well as the islands of Tiran and Sanafir, to guarantee freedom of navigation in the gulf.

Israel's role was to launch a land attack against our forces in Sinai at Abu 'Uwigla, and to parachute troops into the region east of the Mitla Pass, sixty-five kilometers from the canal. The Anglo–French forces would follow with an air attack against Egyptian airports to wipe out our air power. Wide-scale airdrops and naval landings would lead to an occupation of the canal zone. World public opinion would be told that the intervention was necessary to disengage the Egyptian and Israeli forces and to guarantee freedom of navigation on the Suez Canal.

It is obvious that the intention was to draw the bulk of the Egyptian forces into Sinai to face a diversionary Israeli attack, thereby facilitating the occupation of the canal zone by the main Anglo–French forces. The destruction of Egypt's army in Sinai was to be accomplished in collaboration with the Israeli forces.

The aggression against Egypt ended in political and military defeat for Britain and France. Israel was clearly to provide an advance position in the great powers' plans for domination of the Arab world. But the Anglo–French forces, while tactically succeeding in occupying the town of Port Said, failed strategically in occupying the canal zone. Israeli forces were defeated at the battles of Abu 'Uwigla and Mitla in Sinai. However, the withdrawal of Egyptian troops from Sinai in compliance with the political realities and international pressures enabled Israel to achieve a political victory, which was the opening of the Straits of Tiran.

The Egyptian forces were tactically successful in the battles of Abu 'Uwigla and Mitla, and evacuated Sinai in compliance with a political decision to discourage its occupation and destruction in the event that Britain and France came into the canal zone. Port Said had to be evacuated under pressure of superior strength. Strategically, we were not able to protect Egypt in the east or the north.

Britain, France, and Israel were forced to yield to international, US, and Soviet pressure and withdraw from Egyptian territory. The United States had opposed the aggression, which had been planned and executed without its knowledge. The Soviet Union had threatened military action against the three belligerents.

When the firing came to a stop in Sinai, Ben-Gurion had immediately announced to the Israeli Knesset that "Egypt has lost its sovereignty over Sinai, which has now become an integral part of Israel," thereby clearly demonstrating one of Israel's expansionist goals. It came as a shock to Israel to be forced to withdraw from Sinai and Gaza following the withdrawal of the Anglo–French forces from Port Said.

By the end of this adventure against Egypt, Israel had gained access to the Straits of Tiran at the entrance of the Gulf of 'Aqaba, following a United Nations resolution placing international peacekeeping forces in Sharm al-Shaykh, on our eastern front, and in the Palestinian sector of Gaza under Egyptian jurisdiction. Egypt, in its handling of the crisis, won significant political advantage internationally, regionally, and at home, which overshadowed its military shortcomings in the eyes of the Egyptian public.

It became important for Egypt's political and military leadership to analyze this war and learn practical lessons in order to secure Egypt's eastern borders, particularly after Israel had officially announced its intention to annex Sinai. What was needed was a military presence able to deter Israel effectively and defend Sinai without ever needing to resort to an evacuation—as had happened during the Tripartite Aggression. It was also essential to use the war experience to upgrade and maximize the efficiency of the air force and the air defense system against air attacks and prevent any recurrence of the damages of this war. Broadly speaking, an intensive and precise analysis of military operations should have been initiated at all levels, but this was not done with enough urgency or seriousness. As a result, a series of political and military errors was committed leading to the defeat in June 1967, when events closely paralleled those of 1956 with an Egyptian withdrawal from Sinai and the destruction of the air force on the ground. Israel, on the other hand, had used its 1956 experience to reorganize its armed forces and this was a factor in its success in June 1967.

THE UNION BETWEEN EGYPT AND SYRIA

The volatile mood of the region increased with the announcement of the union between Egypt and Syria and the creation of the United Arab Republic on 22 February 1958. The repercussions of this union had not been carefully studied or anticipated—especially its effects on the balance of power in the Middle East. The United States, the Soviet Union, Britain, and France expressed deep reservations, and some Arab neighbors, each for its own reasons, reacted with great caution.

Israel's interests coincided with those of the great powers and it perceived the union as a dangerous development, with the creation of a combined political and military front on its northern and southern borders.

THE REVOLUTION IN IRAQ

A second major upheaval took place a few months later when on 14 July 1958 the Iraqi army toppled the pro-British government then in power, replacing it with a strongly Arab nationalist government which—under the banner of Arab unity and freedom from foreign influence—withdrew from the Baghdad Pact, a link in the chain of Western treaties against the Soviet Union. This treaty was seen not only by Iraq but equally by Egypt as a symbol of Western domination.

The Iraqi revolution came as a blow to the West's hold on the region, but it understandably had Egypt's full backing since as it would spread Arab nationalism and weaken the West's influence in this part of the world. The Soviet Union applauded the revolution because it had shattered the Western-brokered chain of military alliances against it. Israel saw Iraq's new orientation as a threatening addition to Arab power.

LEBANON AND JORDAN

The union between Egypt and Syria and the revolution in Iraq inflamed public passions in the Arab world, and Lebanon and Jordan saw popular uprisings against their governments which threatened to destabilize both countries. Lebanese president Camille Chamoun turned to the United States for help and US marines landed on Lebanon's shores. Jordan's King Husayn turned to Britain and was sent airborne British troops.

The natural reaction to these events was anger at more Western meddling in the region. President Nasir spoke up strongly against it and the Soviet Union, in line with its strategic interests, also criticized what it saw as military interference, so that British and US troops withdrew when internal conditions in both Lebanon and Jordan had stabilized.

THE SEPARATION OF SYRIA FROM EGYPT

This period was a critical and sensitive one for the region. Perhaps the most significant development was the growing influence of Arab nationalism, coupled with the struggle for independence, which led to the diminishing role of the West and an increase in Soviet influence. It is clear that Egypt played a major and highly effective part in these new developments. President Nasir enjoyed tremendous popularity with the peoples of the Arab world, and his astute handling of political affairs with the West enhanced his prestige even further.

The United States and Western Europe were challenged to respond, and this called for a plan which would allow them to regain hegemony and secure their vital interests in the region once more. A limit needed to be imposed on growing Arab nationalism and on any idea or form of unity, and Egypt's role and influence in the region had to be checked, partly by undermining President Nasir's popularity and standing.

The great powers, with the collusion of a few Arab countries, took advantage of a number of policy errors by the government of Syria to stir up dissent among the Syrian people, who were becoming increasingly unhappy because their expectations from a union with Egypt remained unfulfilled. A military coup took place on 28 September 1961, during a visit to Damascus by Field Marshal 'Abd al-Hakim 'Amer. The union with Egypt was severed. This event had powerful repercussions in Egypt, but President Nasir declared that Syria had made a choice which must be respected.

Without going into the reasons for Syria's decision to break away, its outcome was evident: it weakened the idea of Arab unity and, regretfully, Arab nationalism, diminishing Egypt's influence and decreasing Nasir's popularity.

A struggle emerged within the political leadership. As recorded by General Muhammad Fawzi, "President Nasir placed moral and military responsibility for the split on the shoulders of Field Marshal 'Amer. The disagreement between them was never publicly declared, nor was it well known."[4] This falling out had consequences which were amplified over time, eventually obstructing development of a national military strategy.

One result of the separation from Syria was an attempt by President Nasir to restructure the organizational framework of the leadership and the state. A suggestion was made for the armed forces to be absorbed into the state administration, and that members of the Revolutionary Council be divested of any executive power or function to be able to focus on military planning and execution. Field Marshal 'Amer turned these proposals down, believing that President Nasir wanted to take charge of the armed forces himself, and that his competence and leadership abilities were being questioned. The power struggle between Nasir and 'Amer began in earnest from this point onwards.

The Yemen War

In the following year, 1962, a revolution broke out in North Yemen and the new revolutionary leadership turned to Egypt for help. Egypt provided military aid in the belief that it was helping Yemen free itself from a backward and retrograde system of government. This was interpreted as an unfriendly act by the Kingdom of Saudi Arabia, which declared publicly that it had had a major hand in Syria's breakaway from the union with Egypt.

Military aid to Yemen was limited at first. Slowly, Egypt became more involved until approximately a third of its armed forces was fighting there. This posed a threat to Saudi Arabia, which opposed the new Yemeni republican government and supported, both morally and materially, the Yemeni tribesmen fighting the Egyptian forces. The intention was to drain Egypt economically, weaken it militarily, and undermine morale amongst its troops.

The United States and other Western nations were concerned that the presence of Egyptian forces in North Yemen could expand Egypt's influence and threaten oil interests in the region. If these forces were to remain in North Yemen indefinitely, this would give the Soviet Union, via Egypt, a new and unacceptable strategic advantage. The British forces, which then occupied South Yemen, also felt vulnerable.

And so, the interests of the United States, Britain, Saudi Arabia, and a number of other Western and Arab nations coincided to prevent a conclusive military victory by Egypt. Conditions were created whereby the war became a long-drawn-out struggle, intended to deplete and weaken our army, until the time came to make a counter-offensive against Egypt which could destroy its credibility in the Arab world and reduce Nasir's influence to domestic affairs.

Israel was best suited to administer a military blow against Egypt, given its own regional ambitions and its intentions since the Tripartite Aggression for a total war, for which it had been preparing. Furthermore, the international political climate had been slowly shifting against Egypt during its five-year involvement in Yemen, and international and Arab public opinion were now being mobilized against it.

Realizing the dangers of a prolonged war, Lieutenant General Anwar al-Qadi (who headed the Egyptian forces in Yemen from October 1962 to November 1963) requested a meeting with President Nasir in May 1963, at which he gave a full and complete picture of the situation. He is quoted as saying, "We have more than accomplished our duty and must withdraw from this trap as soon as possible." President Nasir replied, "Withdrawal is impossible. . . . It would mean the disintegration of the revolution in Yemen. . . . This is more a political operation than a military one. . . . I consider it to be a counter-response to the separation from Syria. We cannot leave Yemen." Lieutenant General al-Qadi tried once more, warning, "Most of the tribes of al-Guf and Sa'da have for years owed allegiance to Saudi Arabia. We must come to an understanding with Saudi Arabia, otherwise this situation will continue indefinitely." Al-Qadi reports that he understood, from the tone of the conversation, that President Nasir was clear on the need for an arrangement with Saudi Arabia to end the war, with the proviso that a republican system would be retained, and said that he would try to reach a settlement with King Sa'ud for the army to return before the end of 1963.[5] The settlement was not achieved until Faysal became king of Saudi Arabia, very much later.

ISRAEL PREPARES FOR WAR

While Egypt remained tied down in Yemen, and successive Arab summit conferences passed resolutions that were politically and militarily impossible to implement, Israel continued to prepare for war. It had learned an important political lesson from the Tripartite Aggression: its total dependence on Britain and France for its defense needs inhibited its policy of expansion in the region. Therefore it was important for it to develop an independent and autonomous military force, capable of defeating neighboring Arab states without any reliance on outside help. Had it not been for the Anglo–French operation, it is doubtful that Israel could have carried out the Sinai campaign.

A second lesson for Israel was the importance of its relationship with the United States. Up until 1956, it had had a 'special relationship' with Britain and France, especially with regard to the supply of arms and equipment. Between 1957 and 1966, it obtained weapons from the West under the pretext that its superiority guaranteed the balance of power in the region. Particular attention was given to the air force and the armored and paratroop forces, which could strike quickly and decisively. Israel's success at establishing a 'special relationship' with the United States was cemented by the so-called 'Hawk deal' for Hawk anti-aircraft missiles, which made the United States Israel's main arms supplier and major political supporter, especially during President Johnson's time in office.

By the end of 1966, Israel felt confident that it was ready for war with the Arabs. It believed that it would continue to have political and military support from the United States, with whom it now enjoyed strong relations. In the meantime, the relationship between Egypt and the United States had deteriorated sharply, mainly as a result of President Johnson's unqualified support of Israel and his intransigence towards Egypt's policies. Despite the several Arab summit conferences, inter-Arab relations had also grown progressively worse until they were on the point of disintegration. The 'Arab Unified Command' created by a summit resolution in January 1964 was now a rigid, crippled, and ineffectual body. Summit resolutions were not implemented because neither the will nor the capacity was there. The largest and strongest Arab force capable of challenging Israel, the Egyptian army, had been tied down in Yemen for several years. Israel felt that it was more powerful than all the Arab armies combined. International and local conditions were now in its favor. All that remained was to find a plausible reason to start a war.

A Pretext for War

On 13 November 1966, Israeli units raided the Jordanian village of al-Semou under the pretext of destroying Palestinian resistance bases. Over seventy Jordanians were left dead or wounded. Jordan expressed its disillusion with Egypt and Syria for not having met their commitments to help in the event of such an occurrence. In fact, the Israeli raid was deliberately provocative and violent because it was meant not only as a deterrent to Jordan, but also to test Egypt's and Syria's reactions and those of the Arab world. The raid confirmed Israel's belief that an Arab response to its military efforts would be negligible.

Israel's plans took on a certain seriousness by the beginning of 1967. In the spring of that year, Palestinian resistance activities had targeted Israeli attempts to divert the waters of the Jordan river to the Negev, which was being settled by Jewish immigrants. The Israeli government blamed Syria for encouraging this and other Palestinian activities in the occupied territories and whipped up an international hate campaign against Syria in the media.

On 10 May 1967, the Israeli foreign minister instructed all Israeli ambassadors abroad to brief their host nations on Syria's "dangerous" intentions on the Syrian–Israeli borders and to insist that Palestinian "terrorist" activities were sponsored and encouraged by Syria. In preparing the world psychologically for the war, Prime Minister Levi Eshkol of Israel also saw fit to condemn guerrilla warfare as "unacceptable for all of us, so we cannot allow it to exist in Israel," pointing to Syria as "the source of . . . terrorism and destruction . . . and of those terrorists who come to our country to perpetuate terrorism." Eshkol conveniently ignored the many and repeated condemnations by the United Nations Security Council and General Assembly of Israel's bloody and aggressive conduct towards the Arab inhabitants of Palestine. He also seemed to have overlooked the words of Menachem Begin when on a tour of Arab Israel in 1948: "Had it not been for the slaughter of Deir Yasin, Israel would not have existed."

On 7 April 1967, an exchange of fire took place on the Syrian borders followed by an air engagement. Syria lost six planes and Egypt faced a critical dilemma because of its joint defense agreement with Syria. The truth is that the air battle that day had one purpose for Israel: to probe Egypt's degree of readiness and defensive capacity by provoking Egypt into coming to Syria's assistance. Eventually of course the aim was to lure Egypt into battle, if it took the bait.

Israel continued to escalate matters on the Syrian borders. Israeli leaders threatened Syria repeatedly and publicly until General Yitzhak Rabin actually announced on Radio Israel on 12 May 1967 that "we will make a lightning attack against Syria and occupy Damascus to overthrow the government there. Only then will we withdraw. . . . "

Egypt took these threats seriously and President Nasir found himself obliged to stand by Syria. The concentration of Egyptian forces in Sinai was a concrete demonstration of this. The focus of military tension moved from the Syrian to the Egyptian borders with Israel. This was the first step in a process by which Egypt would be drawn into a full war for which Israel knew it was unprepared, but for which Israel itself was completely ready.

2

On the Road to War

On the evening of 13 May 1967, General Muhammad Fawzi, chief of staff of the Egyptian armed forces, received a message from Major General Ahmad Sweidan, chief of staff of the Syrian army. It said that Israel had called up the greater part of its reserve forces and was mobilizing around fifteen brigades on the Syrian front with plans to attack, using largely paratroop forces. The attack was expected to take place between 15 and 22 May 1967. President Sadat reported the following exchange with regard to this information. "On my return from [a trip to] Moscow, Seminov, the Soviet foreign minister and the head of the Soviet Assembly, accompanied me to the airport, and our conversation centered on the situation in Syria and how Israel had mobilized ten brigades on the frontiers. When I arrived in Egypt, I found that they had communicated the same information to President Nasir."[1]

Similarly, Lieutenant General Anwar al-Qadi, who at the time was chief of the operations department of the armed forces, reports that

> on 14 May 1967, everything was proceeding quite normally at the Operations Command Center when we were surprised to learn that Field Marshal 'Abd al-Hakim 'Amer had held a meeting in his office with Chief of Staff General Muhammad Fawzi and had issued orders for the army to be placed on full alert. When I asked for the reasons for this, the reply was unclear—reports from our political leadership indicated that Israel was preparing to attack Syria, there were Israeli troop concentrations on the Syrian borders, the Golan front was expected to explode, Egypt must get ready to meet the provisions

of the joint defense pact with Syria, and so forth. This of course came as a complete surprise to me particularly since in my position as chief of operations I was fully aware of the capability and strength of our armed forces at this time, and our degree of military readiness. I was therefore alarmed at this situation which seemed dangerous, but Field Marshal 'Amer reassured me, saying that this was no more than a 'demonstration' in response to Israeli threats against Syria.[2]

Thus at midday on 14 May, when matters seemed to be following their normal course, the armed forces were unexpectedly informed of a state of maximum alert, with a general mobilization to be completed before 17 May. Troops were to be reinforced and take up new positions in Sinai before 6:00 A.M. of that day. All training programs in the military institutes and academies were suspended. Naval forces were to take up their strategic positions and joint offensive and defensive plans drawn up in agreement with the Syrian general command.

These directives were issued by Chief of Staff Fawzi on 14 May 1967 in the form of official 'military operations instructions' which said that "information from the various services confirm Israel's intention to attack the Arab Republic of Syria. In accordance with the joint defense agreement between Egypt and Syria, the armed forces high command has decided on land and air action if Israel attacks Syrian territory with the intent of occupying it, or any part of it, or destroying the Syrian air force." I say once more that these instructions came as a surprise to the armed forces because we could see no obvious reason to warrant such measures.

A second more detailed directive was issued to clarify matters. This said:

> Reliable sources indicate a large concentration of Israeli forces on the border with Syria since the beginning of May. The intention appears to be an offensive inside Syria with the purpose of overthrowing the progressive government there, replacing it with a reactionary body and bringing to an end the movement for the liberation of Palestine. Field Marshal 'Abd al-Hakim 'Amer, deputy supreme commander of the armed forces, believes that Israel has been encouraged to take on a belligerent role in response to America's hostility towards progressive movements in the Arab world, the failure of Britain and America to halt the Yemen revolution, the lack of success of Britain's policy in occupied South Yemen, the vulnerable positions of King Faysal of Saudi Arabia and King Husayn of Jordan, and fears in the West of the growing progressive Arab revolutionary tide.

> Based on our understanding of world events and the international configuration behind the present circumstances, knowing full well the support given to Israel by the colonial powers, and also taking into account Israel's belief that we can be drawn into battle at a time unsuitable for us, we have nevertheless decided to take a clear stand against any military threat, and will intervene immediately in the event of an Israeli attack against Syria.

Our armed forces began to implement these directives with troop concentrations in Sinai according to the so-called Kaher Defense Plan. The general mobilization required that various measures be taken to get regular units onto a war footing and to create new units as required by the plan. On 14 May, Chief of Staff Fawzi went to Syria, on Field Marshal 'Amer's orders, to see the Israeli troop concentrations for himself and to coordinate between Syria and Egypt. After visiting the Syrian front, he was able to comment on the veracity of the reports which had reached us via Syrian and Soviet sources. He said, "I did not find any concrete evidence to support the information received. On the contrary, aerial photographs taken by Syrian reconnaissance on 12 and 13 May showed no change in normal military positions."[3]

On his return to Cairo on 15 May, General Fawzi presented his report to Field Marshal 'Amer. It rejected the claim that there were Israeli concentrations on the Syrian front. Recalling his meeting with 'Amer, he says, "I noticed no reactions from the field marshal with regard to the negative situation on the Syrian front. Consequently, I began to believe that from his perspective the business of troop concentrations was not the principal reason for the mobilization or the troop movements which we had been asked to undertake in such a hurry."[4]

Despite General Fawzi's report, troop concentrations in Sinai continued. Political factors were playing their part in these events, of which the general command of the armed forces had no knowledge. Indeed, despite the intense military activity taking place, no orders were issued for any military operation. This led to some confusion as to the purpose of these preparations. Questions were raised among the troops regarding the nature of these large-scale movements. What was our mission? Was it a demonstration of strength simply to deter Israel from attacking Syria?

We must stop here to examine the extent to which political goals are related to military action. My position is that in cases where the former depends on the latter, the political leadership should be more frank and not conceal anything from the military leadership, within the limits imposed by security. The chief of staff of the armed forces and his principal advisors and services must be given the opportunity early on to think about and analyze the consequences of a given political goal as it relates to the military, and to take appropriate measures. This is the essence of reliable planning, which links political strategy to military capacity.

PULLOUT OF THE INTERNATIONAL PEACEKEEPING FORCES

The real reasons for the continued military buildup in Sinai began to appear. On 16 May, two days following the order for troop concentrations—and before this had been completed—Egypt requested the withdrawal of the United Nations peacekeeping forces from the eastern border with Israel, from Sharm al-Shaykh in southern Sinai, and from the borders of the Gaza Strip under Egyptian administration. On the instructions of Field Marshal 'Amer, General Fawzi sent the following message to General Rickie, commander of the UN forces, in which he wrote:

> I inform you that I have issued orders to the armed forces of the United Arab Republic (Egypt) to be ready for immediate action against Israel should this country aggress any Arab country. As a result, we have moved forces into Sinai and the eastern border. As we are concerned for the safety of your troops in Sinai and on our eastern borders, I ask you to order an immediate pullout of these forces from their positions. I have requested that the commander of the eastern military sector inform me of the implementation of these orders.[5]

General Rickie replied promptly that this request was of a political nature and had to be referred back to U Thant, secretary-general of the United Nations.

President Nasir agreed to send the request to the United Nations, through the Foreign Ministry. Egypt asked only for the peacekeeping forces on the eastern border to be pulled out. However, Secretary-General U Thant raised a controversial point: he believed that either all the peacekeeping forces should be withdrawn together, including those on the eastern border, in Sharm al-Shaykh, and the Gaza Strip, since they were an integral unit, or that they should all remain in their positions. Egypt decided that all the peacekeeping forces should be withdrawn, and orders for this were issued by U Thant on 18 May.

Mahmud Riyad, our foreign minister at the time, has commented:

> The request was very clear. It asked for a limited pullout of the peacekeeping forces on the Egyptian frontier with Israel. We did not ask for the withdrawal of this force from Gaza or Sharm al-Shaykh. When U Thant refused a partial pullout, Egypt could not go back and

the only choice before us was a total pullout of United Nations forces, which of course included those in Gaza and Sharm al-Shaykh. This meant a return of our own military forces in Sharm al-Shaykh, which, in turn, resuscitated the old problem over Israel's navigation in the Gulf of 'Aqaba.[6]

At the time, the presence of the UN peacekeeping forces in Sinai was being used by a hostile international media to demonstrate what it judged to be Egypt's inability to defend itself—hiding, as it were, behind the presence of these troops. This had obviously rankled Egypt's leadership, and had made it susceptible to accusations that it was indeed out to get rid of these forces. It is worth mentioning that Field Marshal 'Amer, on a visit to Pakistan in 1966, felt sufficiently pressured to send a telegram to President Nasir asking for the withdrawal of these forces from Sinai, so as to put a stop to the virulent propaganda directed against Egypt. The wire was sent at a time when 'Amer had only recently, before his departure for Pakistan, been given an evaluation of the situation and had been advised to avoid military confrontation with Israel as long as a third of Egypt's army remained tied down in Yemen. This recommendation had come from the general command of the armed forces.

The UN forces in 'Aqaba had during the eleven years since 1956 kept the Straits of Tiran open to Israeli navigation, allowing Israel access to the Red Sea and to Africa from the port of Eilat with no interference from Egypt. This had been a major Israeli gain following the Tripartite Aggression. When Egyptian forces took over Sharm al-Shaykh, Israel viewed this as a dangerous development which could lead to the closing of the straits to its shipping once more. It therefore shifted the focus from the Syrian border to an entirely different issue: freedom of Israeli navigation in the Gulf of 'Aqaba. This took place under the umbrella of a powerful media campaign over Egypt's request for a UN pullout, which was orchestrated by the United States, Britain, and Canada. The confrontation became one between Egypt and Israel, and the front pages of the world's newspapers were now preoccupied with the issue of freedom of navigation for Israel and the new military threat on the Egyptian–Israeli borders.

Regardless of the nationalist motives behind the Egyptian request for a UN pullout, the decision was rash and precipitate. Not enough consideration was given to its consequences nor to alternative political and military strategies which might have brought about a successful outcome. It was clear from the start that a pullout would be followed by the entry of Egyptian troops into Sharm al-Shaykh. This inevitably leads to the question of whether Egypt should have been guided by a broader national strategy in which well-defined political and military goals, together, would have better served the higher national purpose.

There was enough time to develop such a strategy. The political leadership did not at the time face a pressing situation which justified hasty action. Nor was the military engaged in any activity which might have required the removal of the UN peacekeeping forces from the borders with Israel in the east. An ill-conceived political gesture became, after the concentration of Egyptian troops in Sinai, another step towards a war Israel was actively trying to provoke. I would have thought that a meeting of the National Defense Council would have been a necessary precondition for the request for a UN pullout; a meeting between senior foreign ministry officials, various specialists, and the general command of the armed forces would have resulted in a realistic evaluation of the political and military situation and would have provided a number of alternative options for the head of state.

CLOSURE OF THE STRAITS OF TIRAN

Events continued to move Egypt and Israel closer to war. Egypt had to make an important political decision when Nasir met with some members of the Revolutionary Command Council and Prime Minister Sidqi Suliman: to control the entrance to the Gulf of 'Aqaba with troops in Sharm al-Shaykh, and either to allow navigation for all nations in the Gulf, including Israel, or to close the Straits of Tiran to Israeli navigation.

President Sadat has described this meeting.

> Towards the end of May 1967, Nasir called for a 'Higher Executive Committee' meeting which included 'Amer, Zakaria Muhi al-Din, Husayn al-Shaf'i, myself, 'Ali Sabri, and Sidqi Suliman, then prime minister. Nasir told us that our forces in Sinai created a 50 percent possibility of war, while if we closed the straits, then war was 100 percent certain. He then turned towards 'Amer and asked, 'Are our armed forces ready 'Abd al-Hakim?' 'Amer placed his hand on his throat and said, 'My neck is at stake. Everything is completely ready.' We understood from this that there was no doubt that our army was fully prepared. Therefore when Nasir asked for our opinion, we all agreed to the closure of the straits except for Sidqi Suliman, who asked for more time to deliberate, given our economic situation and our ambitious development plans, most of which were not implemented yet. Nasir paid no attention to Suliman's objections. He appeared to favor the closure of the straits

as a means to end Arab opposition to him, and to maintain his popularity and high esteem in the Arab world. He issued orders to close the straits.[7]

Nasir issued the order on the eve of 17 May, and the following day the general command of the armed forces took steps to organize the land, air, and naval units needed to carry out the order. The nature of the task required the participation of the three branches and the opening up of a new axis.

Field Marshal 'Amer decided to fly a paratroop unit into Sharm al-Shaykh. The general command was forced to use paratroops from the general command reserve to carry out the mission while an infantry brigade designated for the same mission and in position since 14 May was not used. 'Amer also placed Brigadier General 'Abd al-Mun'im Khalil, commander of the sector, directly under the orders of the armed forces general command rather than under orders of field command in Sinai.

Brigadier General Khalil was not clear as to how he should close the entrance to the Gulf of 'Aqaba, and this led to much uncertainty and questioning because any military action against international shipping in the straits could become highly sensitive and have repercussions on the political and military situation.

On 22 May 1967, Field Marshal 'Amer issued instructions to bar entrance to the Gulf of 'Aqaba to any vessel flying the Israeli flag and to oil tankers sailing to Eilat, regardless of their flag, effective twelve o'clock noon on 23 May. Ships sailing out of the gulf were allowed to proceed, vessels under the protection of a warship were to be allowed through, even if they flew an Israeli flag, and no such vessel was to be intercepted or engaged. Directives for interception and warning were also given.

Political and military tension reached a peak when President Nasir announced the closure of the Gulf of 'Aqaba commencing 23 May at a meeting with officers of the air force at Abu Suwayr Airport. The United States reacted strongly, President Johnson declaring the gulf an international waterway and its closure to Israeli navigation illegal and a grave threat to peace. Israel naturally claimed that the closure was a violation of international law and worked hard through diplomatic channels and through the media at winning European and US support for an eventual war when the time was ripe. It expected that the close military cooperation between Israel and the United States would continue to their mutual advantage. Now that Israel had an excuse for war, President Johnson was being given the opportunity to destroy President Nasir's image as an influential leader in the Arab world.

In the ten years following the 1956 Tripartite Aggression, commercial shipping to and from the Israeli port of Eilat had in some months reached sixty ships. Throughout these years, Israel continued to link the issue of freedom of navigation to the issue of Israeli national security, meaning, in fact, that it would go to war if its shipping route were threatened. The Egyptian leadership during that same period was waiting for an opportunity to wipe out the effects of 1956 and regain sovereignty over territorial waters at the entrance of the Gulf of 'Aqaba. The crisis in May 1967 made war inevitable. Measures were hastily taken, but these were such that the focus was unclear. Troops poured into Sharm al-Shaykh and south Sinai, but responsibilities were being continuously modified—eight naval vessels were made available but were not placed under sector command, air support was to be from Hurghada, the South Sinai sector commander received several experienced senior officers for opinions on the military plan—as decisions were made and then changed.

Judging by the manner in which preparations were made, it becomes obvious that no serious or objective thinking had gone into the issue of regaining sovereignty over Egypt's territorial waters, despite its weight and importance. No coherent plan had emerged in ten years, and it was as though the problem—both militarily and politically—had just come into being.

Convening the National Defense Council and the cabinet was imperative in conditions where the political leadership knew that certain choices would undoubtedly lead to war. This did not happen.

A MILITARY DEMONSTRATION

Our troops were deliberately marched through the streets of Cairo on their way to Sinai, in full view and for all to see—citizens and foreigners alike. The mass media covered these movements, contrary to all principles and measures of security. And while we were openly mobilizing in an atmosphere of hostile foreign propaganda, and before our men had settled into their positions in Sinai with specific assignments to fulfill, Israel quietly prepared for war under optimal conditions.

Israeli intelligence reported that our forces were crossing the Suez Canal and heading in the direction of Sinai. The Israeli high command learned this in the late hours of 14 May, the evening of the first day of troop movements.[8] Israel began mobilizing in progressive stages and called up a reserve armored brigade on 16 May, the day Egypt asked for the pullout of the UN forces from Sinai and the Gaza Strip. On 18 May it raised the level of alert for its land, air, and naval forces. This was the day UN Secretary-General U Thant ordered a pullout of UN forces from Egypt.

When Nasir announced the closure of the Straits of Tiran, Prime Minister Eshkol went in person at eight o'clock that same evening to Israeli command headquarters to communicate the message—received from President Johnson—not to open fire or take any measures before consulting with the United States.

On 22 May Eshkol told the Knesset that before 14 May, Egyptian forces in Sinai consisted of less than two infantry divisions and a few armored vehicles. By 22 May, they had reached approximately four infantry divisions with armored vehicles, plus a large number of artillery units. Egypt had also reinforced its air force in Sinai. According to Israeli estimates, the number of Egyptian troops had risen from thirty-five thousand to eighty thousand men—the first time that this concentration has been reached in Sinai—and therefore Israel was now looking seriously at Egypt's movements in east Sinai and its intentions.

Our troop concentrations continued in Sinai, in the hostile political atmosphere generated by the UN pullout and the closure of the Straits of Tiran. The United States and some Western nations expressed anger at Egypt and President Nasir. Support for Israel was total, as was opposition to the closure of the straits. Some Western nations even considered the creation of a joint naval force to open the straits forcibly. However, this was not followed up. On 29 May, fifteen days after the mobilization had begun, Field Marshal 'Amer issued instructions to the effect that the field army in Sinai and in the Palestinian sector of Gaza, with the assistance of the air force and air defense, was to prevent enemy forces from penetrating our defense lines, breaking through our borders, or attempting to reach the Suez Canal. Some units were to prepare for limited offensive action against defined targets within Israeli territory.

On that same day, the prime minister of Israel, Levi Eshkol, declared to the Knesset that "any interference with our freedom of navigation in the gulf and the straits is a violation of international law and will be considered a hostile act against Israel. We have ordered the mobilization of our reserves, and the Israeli Defense Forces are prepared and ready to face any belligerent act in all sectors and on all frontiers. . . . Israeli forces will remain mobilized, under arms, and ready for any test. If the need arises, Israel has the power to defeat its attackers."

Israel's Green Light

While our forces were taking up defensive positions in Sinai, while the mobilization continued through to 30 May, and while our forces were yet to complete their preparations for war, successive meetings of the military were taking place in Israel to launch a rapid offensive against us. Political coordination with the United States proceeded apace as well as consultations with France and Britain during Israeli Foreign Minister Abba Eban's visit to all these countries starting on 24 May.

A crucial meeting with Eban was held at the Pentagon on 26 May in the presence of the secretary of defense, the chairman of the Joint Chiefs of Staff, and the director of the CIA. In their evaluation, Israel would easily win a war no matter when it began and which side started hostilities. They estimated that a war would not last a week.[9] Israel pressed the United States to declare its support openly. It had two choices: either to give Israel a free hand in the use of force, with the knowledge that its success was assured, or to confront Nasir, thereby increasing his standing and popularity in the Arab world. It appeared wiser to back the Israeli option.

Israel now had completed preparations for war, including calling up the reserves. In his memoirs, General Rabin, then Israeli Chief of Staff, describes the situation at the time: "If Nasir was waiting for Rabin, then Rabin was waiting for Eshkol, and Eshkol was waiting for the cabinet, the cabinet was waiting for Eban, and Eban was waiting for President Johnson. In all cases, we had to wait before taking any measures."

On 30 May, Meir Amit, head of Israeli intelligence, was sent on a secret mission to Washington to get a clear and precise confirmation of Eban's impressions from his recent visit to the United States Amit met with Secretary of Defense McNamara and with CIA Director Helms and concluded from these meetings that Israel had been given a 'green light' to act, and that a victory would not be contested.[10]

KING HUSAYN IN CAIRO

On 30 May, King Husayn of Jordan arrived unexpectedly in Cairo. An Egyptian–Jordanian joint defense agreement was signed. Lieutenant General 'Abd al-Mun'im Riyad was appointed to coordinate operations between the two forces. Immediately following this, some Egyptian commando units were airlifted to Jordan, to operate against targets within Israeli territory from the Jordanian borders.

It appeared that the Arab states had now encircled Israel on three fronts—Egyptian, Jordanian, and Syrian. Iraq had also announced its intention to reinforce the eastern front with a number of units. However, the truth of the matter is that no serious plans for joint military cooperation had, in the real sense, been made between Egypt and Syria despite an agreement dating back to 1966. The June 1967 war started and ended without any coordinated military effort between the Egyptian and Syrian fronts, and Israel was able to deal with each separately. As for Jordan, events overtook hopes for military cooperation since war broke out five days following the signature of the joint defense agreement. King Husayn's decision at the time needs to be examined. Was he the victim of a political deception aimed at propelling his army, unprepared, into war? Or did he at the time misjudge military and political conditions? Or was his evaluation correct but overtaken by events?

The Political Bluff

During this tense time when the United States and Israel had already coordinated their positions and Israel had been given the green light for war, the United States, through a stream of envoys and an exchange of letters with President Nasir, tried to convey that it was keen on preventing a military confrontation. President Nasir, in reaction to the communications from the United States, made it clear that "Egypt would not be first to attack." By revealing his intentions, he made it politically possible for Israel to pick and choose its own time for war.

On 23 May, the US ambassador in Cairo delivered a message from President Johnson to Foreign Minister Mahmud Riyad. In this message the president of the United States spoke of his good intentions towards Egypt and the importance of averting a military confrontation. Disagreements should not, in his view, be resolved by the unlawful crossing of borders by the armed forces. He suggested that in the absence of open hostilities, Vice President Hubert Humphrey should visit the Middle East for negotiations between President Nasir, other Arab leaders, and Israel.[11]

The spoken message which accompanied this letter expressed US fears that the hasty pullout of UN troops had made the question of the borders between Egypt and Israel even more difficult. The United States also believed that the mobilization and concentration of troops by both Egypt and Israel should stop, and expressed the hope that the two sides would withdraw their forces back to their bases. The message ended with a US commitment to the principle of free navigation for all nations in the Gulf of 'Aqaba, asserting that any violation of international law could have dangerous international consequences. However, the government of Egypt and other Arab governments could depend absolutely at this time on the United States' firm opposition to any form of attack, whether open or covert, and whether undertaken by regular or irregular forces.

In his capacity as UN Secretary-General, U Thant arrived in Cairo to try to restore calm to an explosive situation. Following President Nasir's agreement to a list of proposals, he asked Nasir a question: "Mr. President, the Israelis fear an attack against them. Will you give an assurance that Egypt will not attack Israel?" Nasir replied, "At no time have we said that we would attack Israel. It is Israel which has publicly threatened an invasion of Syria. The measures we have taken are defensive, to prevent such a threat from becoming a reality. Therefore we will never initiate an attack."

As a result, U Thant was optimistic when he left Cairo on 25 May. I must make clear that he was not party to the US deception, but his visit served to convey the message that Egypt would not attack first.

In the early hours of 27 May, the Soviet ambassador to Cairo woke up President Nasir with an urgent message from the Soviet leadership asking Egypt not to open fire first. This was the result of a message from President Johnson to the Kremlin that Egypt would attack Israel at dawn that same day. President Nasir had received a similar message from President Johnson. As mentioned by Mahmud Riyad, this was openly threatening in tone, warning that Egypt would have to bear the consequences of its action if it opened fire.

On June 1967, two US envoys arrived in Cairo, the first officially and the second unofficially. Ambassador Charles Post, in his official capacity, met with Foreign Minister Mahmud Riyad to warn that the United States would not support the party which opened hostilities. Riyad replied, "We have officially assured you, in accordance with your request, that we will not begin an attack." An unofficial envoy, Robert Anderson, met with Nasir to assure him that the United States would try to find a peaceful solution to the crisis. Nasir repeated Egypt's position: "We will not initiate an armed aggression."[12]

On 3 June 1967, President Johnson announced that he was ready to meet with Egyptian Vice President Zakaria Muhi al-Din, and a date was set for 5 June. This was the day Israel had chosen to launch the war. This situation is reminiscent of a similar configuration of events in 1956. A conference was to be held in Geneva on 29 October of that year, when Egypt, Britain, and France would discuss the consequences of the nationalization of the Suez Canal Company. However, it was on 29 October that Britain and France, with Israel, attacked Egypt in the Tripartite Aggression.

US deception had uncovered Nasir's intentions and inhibited him from taking the initiative while the United States gave itself time to complete its coordination with Israel.

It is interesting to consider that the Soviet Union was moving in the same direction as the United States to prevent Nasir from starting a war, even though it was surely aware that Israel was preparing an imminent attack on Egypt and that Egypt was not prepared for this. Yet the Soviet Union, during the second week of May, was the source of information about the concentration of Israeli forces on the Syrian border which precipitated the crisis.

We can also reflect on the fact that neither the United States nor the Soviet Union, either jointly or separately, took serious measures to prevent the closure of the Straits of Tiran. Neither of them tried to diffuse the ensuing conflict by proposing a peaceful solution. It is my opinion that they stood to gain from military escalation and war, since this eventually would provide new opportunities to penetrate the region ideologically and strategically.

As for the conduct of the United States, Mahmud Riyad in his memoirs comments that during this period of crisis—when the United States was sending out signals that it supported a peaceful resolution; while Undersecretary of State Eugene Rostow was in his official capacity assuring the Egyptian ambassador to Washington that Israel would never begin hostilities and that the United States would strongly oppose any such action; and at a time when President Johnson specifically set 5 June as the date at which he would meet Zakaria Muhi al-Din—during all of this time, the United States knew that Israel would launch a war on 5 June, and indeed discussed the course of that war with Israeli intelligence.

THE BRINK OF WAR

On 2 June the situation deteriorated sharply. Israel, in an ominous sign, had announced the formation of a new national coalition cabinet, headed by Levi Eshkol and with General Dayan as minister of defense, in what the world press now referred to as Israel's war cabinet. After having completed war preparations in the past fortnight, there was nothing left to do but to set the date of the attack. Furthermore, international public opinion was now very supportive of Israel's case. International diplomatic efforts had not (and would not) be taken to prevent a war.

Israeli Chief of Staff General Rabin, along with the military command, believed that a war against Egypt should be short and quick, with Israel immediately taking the initiative in order to assess its length, its outcome, and the losses Israel expected to bear. During the discussions to fix a date, which took place on 2 June, Rabin quotes Prime Minister Eshkol as saying,

> We will still need Johnson's help and support. I hope we won't need it during the fighting, but we shall certainly need it if we are victorious in order to protect our gains. I want to make it clear to the president, beyond a shadow of a doubt, that we have not misled him; that we've given the necessary time for any political action designed to prevent the war. Two days more or less won't sway the outcome of a war![13]

On this basis, Israel decided not to launch hostilities before Monday 5 June. On 4 June, the Israeli cabinet set the date for the commencement of hostilities. This definitely would be 5 June.

In Cairo on that same day, 2 June, President Nasir met with the Egyptian high command at general headquarters. His evaluation was that Israel would launch an offensive in the next forty-eight to seventy-two hours. He expected Israel to start with an air attack against the Egyptian air force and air defense system, to gain control of the air. He asked for arrangements to be taken to face this situation and minimize losses, explaining that Israel would rely on the elements of surprise and flexibility, and that the battle would be short.

President Nasir made it clear that he had decided to allow this first aggression—the air attack—for political reasons. It was important that it should be seen that Egypt had not begun hostilities. Field Marshal 'Amer then issued directives to our forces in the eastern military sector (the field army in Sinai) to respond defensively to any incursions or penetration of our borders, and to repel or destroy enemy forces. Our capabilities for such defensive action, following the radical changes which had been made to the original Kaher Defense Plan, were not discussed at the meeting. President Nasir then, under pressure from the United States, was unwilling to initiate the war, thereby giving the initiative to Israel.

AN ADVENTURE AND A CONSPIRACY

An analysis of the events taking place between 14 May and 4 June 1967 raises questions about the interpretation given to them by Egypt's political leadership.

The crisis had been precipitated by intelligence from Syria and the Soviet Union on Israeli troop concentrations on the Syrian borders. This intelligence was not accurate, but despite the personal disclaimer by Egypt's chief of staff, General Fawzi, after a visit to Syria, Egyptian troops were rushed into Sinai for the stated purpose of helping Syria in the event of an Israeli attack.

The political leadership in Egypt took this opportunity to demand a pullout of the UN peacekeeping forces from Sinai. This was followed by the closure to Israeli navigation of the Straits of Tiran, which provided Israel with both a reason and an excuse to launch a war against Egypt. The focus of the crisis shifted from the issue of an Israeli threat on the Syrian borders to the issue of freedom of navigation for Israel in the Gulf of 'Aqaba.

Since Egypt had been mired in a five-year war in Yemen with no settlement in sight, and since Israel enjoyed military supremacy over neighboring Arab countries, and since Egypt, through a series of political choices, had mobilized international opinion against itself, the time was clearly ripe to drag it into another decisive war for which Israel had been preparing for ten years.

Given these conditions, one could say that Egypt's political leadership embarked on a political and military adventure, first to demonstrate that it was able to defend Syria, and then to regain a sovereignty lost in the Tripartite Aggression. Intended to raise President Nasir's standing in the Arab world, it was an uncalculated response to a negative international propaganda campaign against Egypt. However, the leadership found itself sucked into a cleverly-planned war to inflict a defeat and destroy President Nasir's standing in the Arab world.

3

Was Egypt Prepared for War?

With great biterness, I must admit that Egypt was not at the time ready for war. Several senior commanding officers had been seriously concerned about the poor state of the army, which by 1967 had become a victim of the difficult conditions and circumstances in which it had to operate. If I admit this quite frankly, it is because I see no reason to play down the factors which led to the defeat. They provided the impetus for the October 1973 strategy and must serve as a lesson to future generations. As a member of the armed forces, having spent all of my active years in the army, I personally witnessed the events and developments of the 1967 war. However, I intend here to concentrate on only those reasons which were directly responsible for the defeat, as a detailed analysis would require a full study in its own right.

Five Years of Fighting in Yemen

The military operations in the Yemen, which go under the name of 'The Yemen War,' are an important component of the history of modern Egypt.

In 1962, the political leadership in Egypt decided to send a small force to help the revolution in Yemen, which had just started. We were gradually drawn in more deeply until, five years later, nearly a third of our land forces, supported by our air force and navy, were engaged in an operation approximately two thousand kilometers away from Egypt, with no prospects for either a political or a military settlement.

We incurred heavy losses in manpower, our military budget was drained, discipline and training suffered, weapons and equipment deteriorated, and fighting capability was seriously affected. Soldiers returning from Yemen were given furloughs during which weapons were overhauled, but levels of training consequently declined. Planes and technical equipment belonging to the air force were subjected to heavy wear and tear as a result of airborne operations and troop movements. Five years had gone by without the construction of a single hanger, although this was considered essential following the 1956 Tripartite Aggression on Egypt, when the British and French were able to destroy not only our airports but our planes on the ground. The navy was also heavily involved in troop transportation, as well as keeping communication lines open in the Red Sea. This gradually wore away at the technical efficiency of our fleet.

Military discipline also deteriorated because of the unconventional nature of the fighting. The Yemen War was more like a police operation. We were facing irregular guerrilla forces in mountainous terrain. However, the fact that in Yemen we naturally had complete superiority in the air and in firepower led some of our men to draw the wrong conclusions about a war against Israel in open desert terrain and under completely different conditions, particularly as in the case of Israel the enemy was militarily superior.

One dangerous outcome of the Yemen War was that the high command of the armed forces had concentrated its attention almost exclusively on this field of operation for over five years. Consequently, there was no preparation or training for a war against Israel. Our lines of defense were not integrated in a systematic manner; thus in Sinai, the first defense lines on the eastern borders of Egypt were well-equipped and prepared whereas other lines—including the Straits of Tiran, which is considered Egypt's last defense in the east—were not.

Continuous obligations in Yemen distracted our high command from what should have been its main task. One could justify the shift from one battlefield to another if it were part of a positive plan, but the command was unable to settle the Yemeni conflict militarily and at the same time neglected to plan for the defense of Sinai, with obvious results in June 1967.

Realizing the dangerous configuration, the staff of the operations department of the armed forces prepared a report for Field Marshal 'Amer. This was in fact a warning, recommending that military operations against Israel be suspended for as long as the size of our fighting forces in Yemen remained high.

The chief of the operations department staff, General Anwar al-Qadi, said in an interview commemorating twenty-one years since the June 1967 war,

> The general military strategy was purely defensive; that is, a defense of Sinai in the event of an Israeli attack. All the defense lines, according to this strategy, were directed at preventing the Israeli forces from reaching the Suez Canal and destroying any forces which might reach the first defense zone. The total size of the armed forces, including those in Yemen, were barely sufficient to accomplish this limited mission.[1]

The elements of the Kaher Plan for the defense of Sinai were completed by the beginning of December 1966, and by 16 December the armed forces operations staff began to compile a general report on the plan and the complicated factors behind its implementation. The most important of these were that the greater part of our forces—estimated at two-thirds of the total Egyptian forces—were in Yemen, that combat formations and units were weak, that there was a shortage of men, and that equipment and weapons were showing signs of wear because of their intensive use in Yemen.

The operations staff made a report—and I say this again—warning against any confrontation with Israel for some time to come. This was submitted to Chief of Staff General Muhammad Fawzi, who wholeheartedly supported its recommendations and passed it on to the high command. The operations staff had also added a warning against any action, however small, before the return of the main body of our forces from Yemen.

It appears that Field Marshal 'Amer ignored the report and did not take its recommendations into account when, in May 1967, he agreed to the closure of the Straits of Tiran, which led to war.

The War's Political Resolution

It is clear that a proper political decision to engage in war is always taken with the understanding that the armed forces are fully prepared; it is not enough just to consider internal or external political factors, economic or social issues, or problems of morale. Such a grave and dangerous decision, taken at the highest level of government, cannot be left to one individual, but like any other major political, military, or economic issue must be the outcome of in-depth study and the careful judgment of specialized agencies. All the facts and conditions surrounding it must first be fully analyzed and understood.

When President Nasir had inquired as to the readiness of the armed forces, emphasizing that "if we close them [the straits], then war is 100 percent certain," it is regrettable that Field Marshal 'Amer replied, "I stake my neck on it. Everything is perfectly ready." This was the decisive evaluation, superficial as it was, on our fighting capability, and was entirely unfounded. Furthermore, the way in which this critical decision was made was not right. The armed forces were about to be thrown into a war against an enemy whose first priority had always been to be stronger and more powerful than the Arab countries.

It was common knowledge that nearly a third of our active army was in Yemen, along with part of our air and naval forces. The political leadership was of course following developments very closely, but it was to be expected that Israel and the great powers were equally well-informed. It was therefore known that our forces were operating at a peacetime level of reduced draft conscription when the decision was taken to close the straits.

In an effort to reduce the armed forces budget in line with a general belt-tightening taking place, the minister of war had discharged large numbers of reservists two months ahead of schedule. A three-month freeze on new recruits was in effect. This applied from March until June 1967, which meant that no allowance had been made for any political and military escalation like that of May 1967.

The armed forces were therefore taken aback when the political crisis exploded on 14 May. We had a shortage of manpower on the order of 37 percent for the officer ranks and nearly 30 percent for other ranks. To compensate for this, it became necessary not only to recall officers and reservists but to create new units. Furthermore, our land forces lacked the weapons and equipment needed for war. Generally speaking, this translated into a 30 percent shortage in small arms, 24 percent in artillery weapons, 45 percent in support tanks, and 40 to 70 percent for the motorized detachments.

Our call-up system was also deficient from the start. Years had passed without any practical training in the mobilization of the reserve force. One unit had been called up in 1965 to test the response. No actual plan existed for regular and periodic combat training of the reserve forces. The confusion and inadequacy of the system became obvious when men arrived in Sinai in their civilian clothes, having been sent as they were from the various mobilization centers. Some men were posted to units which were not of their specialization. New units were created from men who had not seen any training in years, if at all.

The field army command in Sinai had to bear the consequences of units with little or no technical or professional training, a lack of familiarity with weapons and equipment, and a general standard which fell well below the expected norm.

Until the breakout of war, the size of the reserve forces in Sinai was more than half the total of the men in the field of operations.

For years before the June 1967 war, we had boasted that we had the largest air force in the Middle East. The truth was that our air force had been inferior to the Israeli air force in number, kind, and training for the last ten years before the war, so that the Israelis were able to destroy the greater part of our aircraft on the ground in the first strikes during the first three hours of the war.

Our air force lacked trained fighter pilots, who were fewer than the number of planes available. Our airports had not taken the measures needed to protect the aircraft, nor was the air defense system adequate. It goes without saying that a highly efficient air force requires a highly capable and experienced senior command. Its role as a major branch of the armed forces must be fully understood, and this was not the case before 1967. In May 1967, appearances overcame substance.

With regard to air defense, which at the time was the responsibility of the air force, the means at its disposal were insufficient and it was unable to provide protection for the airports, for our troops on land and sea, or for vital national targets. Radar detection was limited and unable to pick up enemy aircraft flying at altitudes lower than 500 meters. So it was unable to provide early warning, which helped Israel succeed in its first air strike on the morning of 5 June.

It is impossible to imagine that the high command under Field Marshal 'Amer was unaware of the problems facing both our air force and our air defense system when the decision was taken in May to close the Straits of Tiran. It is equally obvious that Israel was fully aware of the real situation when it decided to launch a war against us.

As for levels of training, 1967 was one of the worst years and witnessed the lowest standards yet, according to the command. Training was one of the responsibilities Field Marshal 'Amer shared with Minister of War Shams Badran. However, the field marshal was occupied by other responsibilities of state, and his inspection visits to various units were more for morale than for anything else. In a period of five years, from 1962 to 1967, he visited the units in Sinai only three times and under normal peacetime conditions. Under these circumstances, it would have been difficult for the field marshal to gauge their combat readiness or their fighting skills.

This became clear when it was decided to engage in small raids into Israel during the period of troop concentration in Sinai. Field Marshal 'Amer was surprised to learn from Lieutenant General Salah Muhsin, commander of the field army, that his forces were not trained for offensive action. The commander in chief was obviously ignorant of his troops' capabilities.

Egypt's Internal Situation

President Sadat in his memoirs describes the internal situation before the war:

> The power struggle at the top, which began in the early sixties, widened and became increasingly divisive because of the bad feelings between Nasir and 'Amer, between 'Amer and the others, and between Nasir and the others. This situation was a first step towards the defeat of 1967.
>
> In 1965, the internal situation was bleak. Everything had been made the responsibility of either the armed forces or the military police. Public transport, for example, was in very poor shape, so it was up to the armed forces to rehabilitate it; even the fisheries were under the supervision of the forces.
>
> By the end of 1966, the power struggle between Nasir and 'Amer had reached a peak, with each lying in wait for the other. 'Amer was tightening his grip on power and was fast becoming master and despot, ruler of the people's destiny and of every event taking place in Egypt. We started the year 1967 in an atmosphere of gloom. The country was insolvent as a result of ambitious planning and insufficient funding to finance it. On a Friday in February 1967 I saw Nasir, who told me, 'Frankly, the picture is bad, and I feel we are moving towards disaster.'

Egypt's High Strategy

Before and during the period of escalation in May 1967, a strategy should have been developed with clearly-defined political goals to guide military strategy and to coordinate all sectors of national activity.

What was in question—and remained in question—was the political reasoning behind the troop buildup in Sinai. It was said that it was needed because of a possible Israeli attack on Syria. If this were true, then the military strategy should have been offensive. Our forces would have taken up positions for offensive operations against Israel, in coordination with Syria. And if the troop concentrations in Sinai were a backup to the closure of the Straits of Tiran then the mode should have been defensive, with the forces taking up defensive positions in line with the Kaher Plan, a strategy which would not have prevented troops from shifting from a defensive to an offensive mode should the need have arisen.

When at noon of 14 May the order was given to move from a state of alert to a state of high readiness for war, the armed forces began to implement a series of consecutive political directives issued by the political leadership. These measures extended over a period of twenty-three days and were not completed when the enemy attacked on the morning of 5 June.

The eastern military sector (the field army in Sinai) until 17 May proceeded with troop concentrations in Sinai according to the Kaher Plan. When the political decision for a pullout of the UN peacekeeping forces was made, followed by a second decision to close the Gulf of 'Aqaba to Israeli navigation commencing on 23 May, it became necessary to move into the Sharm al-Shaykh sector and hold al-Tor–Sharm al-Shaykh. Following the closure of the straits, we had to protect Gaza and to reinforce Sinai in anticipation of an Israeli military response. The decision to close the straits marked the beginning of a fundamental change in the defense plans for Sinai with an increase in the number of troops assigned to this. It also saw the beginning of limited raids into al-Naqab.

Our presence in Sharm al-Shaykh opened up a new axis for the land, naval, and air forces. Troop reinforcements followed in quick succession, military missions multiplied, and the forces in Sharm al-Shaykh lost their uniformity and combat efficiency. These multiple activities were indicators that Egypt had not given enough objective thought to the contingencies involved in regaining sovereignty over territorial waters in the Gulf of 'Aqaba, despite the fact that ten years had elapsed since the UN forces had first been posted there.

Political interest in the Gaza sector began on 25 May, when a meeting was held at general headquarters attended by President Nasir, Field Marshal 'Amer, the chief of staff, the commanders of the land, air, and naval branches of the armed forces, the chief of operations staff, the commander of the field army, and the head of military intelligence. The idea of an offensive operation to isolate Eilat was put forward. President Nasir was not convinced. He drew attention to the importance of the Gaza sector. There were not enough troops there to withstand an attack and its fall to Israel would be a great blow to Egypt's prestige. He thought it would be necessary first to build up strength in order to make

Israel think twice before attacking. The president then moved to the subject of Sharm al-Shaykh, saying that the western sector needed protection, and that al-Tor had to be held in case of an attack.

On the following day, 26 May, we began to strengthen the Rafah zone so that Gaza would not become isolated from Sinai. This mission was assigned to a newly-formed division of brigades from other formations. These had been taken from their assigned positions in the Kaher Defense Plan. An infantry brigade from al-'Arish, which had spent several months in training to defend this zone, was shifted to Rafah and replaced by another brigade which had no experience in al-'Arish.

With the reinforcement of Rafah, the principal defense lines for Sinai in the northern axis were shifted several kilometers to the east, which in turn required a chain of new measures to defend the new positions and new orders and assignments for the troops.

Limited operations against Israel were considered, and the field army commander was ordered to put plans forward for this. However, the plans were destined never to see the light of day.

Then orders from general command were issued for the Fourth Armored Brigade—which was the country's strategic reserve—to be stationed east of the passes in Sinai. Meantime, other troops continued to pour into Sinai.

In this manner, fundamental and radical changes were grafted onto the Kaher Defense Plan.

The commander of the field army, Lieutenant General Salah Muhsin, saw that the situation was becoming increasingly complex and confused. Continual changes and modifications were being made to duties and missions, relatively few formations were being assigned to offensive missions within Israel, the Fourth Armored Brigade (the strategic reserves), now in Sinai, could not be used except by direct order of Field Marshal 'Amer—too many questions were being raised and needed to be clarified. The chief of army operations was therefore sent to Cairo, to seek answers from the operations staff of the armed forces.

The following questions were raised: What was the exact overall mission of the field army? How did the high command plan to use it? What were the plans for offensive missions and what was their duration? What was the mission of Fourth Armored Brigade? What were the conditions and troop concentrations of the enemy forces, and did we know their possible intentions?

That the commander of the field army should need to raise such questions indicates the vagueness and confusion which prevailed. This obviously had repercussions on army command and on the troops under its orders.

Field Marshal 'Amer issued directives defining the duties of the field army in Sinai and Gaza, which were to prevent enemy forces from penetrating our defense lines and to prevent enemy forces from reaching the Suez Canal. The army was to prepare some of its forces to carry out limited offensives in south Naqab. This would be undertaken with the participation of the general reserves, the air force, and air defense.

Thus by 31 May, directives were being issued which were a complete deviation from the original Kaher Plan.

Other changes to the plan occurred later, as a result of an Israeli deception which fooled general command and military intelligence. In brief, it was believed that Israel planned to attack from a direction other than the one anticipated, and forces were therefore moved to new positions. This shifting around of troops affected the general condition of our forces.

On the evening of 2 June, President Nasir called for a meeting at general headquarters. This was attended by Field Marshal 'Amer, Minister of War Shams Badran, the chief of staff, the chief of operations staff, the head of military intelligence, General Sidqi Mahmud, the commander of the air force and air defense, and others. President Nasir reviewed the situation. He said that he expected Israel to attack within forty-eight to seventy-two hours, and that the aggression would begin with an air attack against our air force, to gain air supremacy. He asked for steps to be taken to minimize losses. The president also said that Israel always depended on the element of surprise and on short battles. The outcome of the meeting was that the armed forces now had to put on a defensive mode and absorb a first offensive air attack.

In short, in the period preceding war the field army in Sinai had its mission changed more than once. During the first days of the crisis, it was asked to defend Sinai within the framework of the Kaher Plan. Then it had to defend against an enemy attack while at the same time undertaking limited offensive operations within Israel itself. Then it was to repulse an enemy attack while agreeing to absorb a first air strike.

The concepts behind the defense of Sinai had been changed fundamentally. All the land forces were moved to Sinai, including the strategic reserves of the country. The structure of our forces was modified at a technical level, the range and extent of our major defenses shifted, and the defense lines for the straits were not equipped for their task, despite the fact that they represented our last line of defense in Sinai. Our defense system lost its equilibrium and our forces were less prepared for war than they should have been, considering that by 4 June three weeks had passed since troop buildups began.

In my judgment, there was a complete disconnection between political and military perceptions from the beginning of the crisis on 14 May until the morning of 5 June. There is no question that Field Marshal 'Amer was aware of all the developments on the political front, but as commander in chief of the armed forces he should have clearly defined military goals and strategy, and their implementation, to general command. This failing, in my opinion, was a result of a lack of coordination in the absence of a higher national strategy. Consequently, there was no focus and a dangerous lack of proper preparation for war.

Israel's gain after the Tripartite Aggression in 1956 was navigation through the Gulf of 'Aqaba, guaranteed by presence of UN forces in Sharm al-Shaykh. After this, for ten years Israeli shipping there became a regular feature. In the meantime, the political leadership in Egypt was waiting for an opportunity to reestablish sovereignty over the waters at the entrance to the gulf. But Israel had now linked freedom of navigation to its national security and this meant that it would go to war if it were threatened. The elements of a confrontation between Egypt and Israel were evident and there for all to see.

Ten years passed since this problem began and yet Egypt's political leadership did not develop a national strategy to regain sovereignty over gulf waters or be in a position to seize an opportunity to implement it. The sequence of events starting on 18 May and leading to war suggests that political decisions were products of the moment. The consequences for the military were disastrous.

Command and Control

Methods of command and control in the armed forces were inefficient. The command of the air and naval forces was independent of and separate from that of the land forces. This weakened the armed forces general command. A basic spirit of cooperation did not exist, even though a modern war can only be a joint effort.

Two figures representing two centers of power stood at the top of the system: Field Marshal 'Amer, deputy supreme commander of the armed forces, who was responsible for operations, training, and organization; and Shams Badran, minister of war, who was responsible for all matters of personnel, such as appointments, promotions, termination of service, medical and health treatment (for officers), intelligence operations, military police, legal affairs, and morale, or psychological well-being. This made him a powerful influence on both senior officers and the ranks. Badran had headed Field Marshal 'Amer's bureau before his appointment as minister of war.

Field Marshal 'Amer had numerous political and executive state duties. He was not always available for his military responsibilities in operations and training. These usually require specialized skills and complete devotion.

Security matters were given top priority, and loyalty was placed ahead of competence in the armed forces. The concept of allegiance was visibly applied in the transfer notices (publications, decrees, and circulars) distributed among senior officers and commanders before and following the mobilization period, such that some of the field units were placed under the command of men of confidence rather than men of competence.

Security was a major concern and preoccupied both Field Marshal 'Amer and Shams Badran. There were multiple services devoted to the security of the armed forces and this became the focus of military intelligence, which consequently did not pay proper attention to gathering information about the enemy, its capabilities, its fighting methods, or its intentions.

Information was therefore limited and intelligence was not able to detect the misinformation on Israel's planned attack, issuing a report on 1 June 1967 saying that Israel's main thrust was expected to be in the direction of the southern axis of the front, using armored forces. It was discovered later that this axis was secondary and a decoy. Military intelligence was also unable to collect any genuine information about the Israeli air force, estimate its real capabilities, or provide details on the expected air attack. A report on 2 June discounted an Israeli attack on Egypt. On that same day, President Nasir warned army command that he expected an Israeli attack within forty-eight to seventy-two hours.

On the other hand, Israeli intelligence was able to obtain reliable information on the size, ability, conditions, and intentions of our armed forces over the years before the outbreak of war and during the period of troop buildups in Sinai. This ensured not only its war successes but, specifically, contributed towards the successes of the initial air attacks against Egypt, Jordan, and Syria in 1967.

It can be said then that the energy and efforts required to ensure security within the armed forces effectively prevented adequate information-gathering on the Israeli enemy, the main task at hand. In contrast, in 1973, military intelligence accomplished its task well, focusing on the enemy and contributing to the success of the October War.

The Advance Command in Sinai

When a state of maximum alert was declared in mid-May, the high command decided to set up an 'advance command center' in Sinai. This was not part of the Kaher Plan. The command was hurriedly pulled together and consisted of General 'Abd al-Muhsin Murtagi, commander of the land forces, Major General Ahmad Isma'il, myself, and a small group of other senior officers.

The command moved to Isma'iliya on 17 May, and then to a position in Sinai behind the field army command under Lieutenant General Salah Muhsin. It was understood that the war would be directed by the high command in cooperation with field army command. Thus when the advance command center was created and General Murtagi appointed commander of the Sinai front, it was important to clarify the role of this extra link in the chain of command. General Murtagi commented on this later:

> Among Field Marshal 'Amer's instructions was the creation of an 'advance command center' in Sinai, which had not existed before in the Kaher Defense Plan. . . . I was appointed commander of the front, a position which had also previously not existed. It was known that the war would be directed by the high command and the field army command. Until that time, I had held the position of political military commander for the Yemen theater of operations. At the same time, I held the position of commander of the land forces and planning of operations was not among my responsibilities. This fell on the shoulders of the armed forces operations command center which was the planning arm of the chief of staff and the deputy supreme commander of the forces. Operations instructions are issued from the operations staff to the eastern military zone command (the field army command) who review the plan with their people and make decisions accordingly, then present the result to the chief of staff and his services for study. Then it is presented to the deputy supreme commander of the forces, for ratification, in the presence of those responsible for the plan.
>
> When I communicated my opinion that responsibilities outlined for the front command would not enable it to command battles or control them, and that it was an extra link in the chain of command

> and was not needed, Field Marshal 'Amer justified himself by saying that he himself would be present at the advance command center (which was the front command at the same time) sometime before operations. He would oversee battles in cooperation with the front command. In this case, the front commander would be the equivalent to his chief of staff. Even though this was not convincing, the common feeling at the time was that there would be no war, and therefore matters were taken at face value without any consideration of the dangers of a war breaking out.[2]

While we were in Sinai, we were worried about the nature of the task of the advance command center and its responsibilities in the command and control of the forces. Decisions on troop concentrations and operations instructions were issued out of general command in Cairo, and Lieutenant General Salah Muhsin and his command were in direct and continuous contact with them. It became clear that the advance command center was a useless link between general command in Cairo and field army command. When troops were sent to Sharm al-Shaykh to close the straits to Israeli navigation starting 23 May, they were placed under direct orders of the general command in Cairo. The advance command center had nothing to do with these forces nor with what was going on in the Sharm al-Shaykh region. Thus the center was not what its name suggested, either practically or theoretically.

I witnessed at the center itself a discussion between Major General Ahmad Isma'il and General Murtagi on its purpose. The conclusion they came to was that there was one general commander, Field Marshal 'Amer, and that the war would be directed from general command. We were therefore not required to make decisions which could affect general command plans or to issue orders, as we were not able to follow up on their implementation and we had no reserve forces which could affect the battle, since field army command directed all the forces in Sinai. Therefore, the center was created as a Sinai base for 'Amer to use when he was there.

In the interests of truth and for the historical record, the advance command center did not perform anything of value, from the moment of its creation to the end of the war. The most important and crucial decision of the war—the general withdrawal from Sinai—was issued by the commander in chief to the commander of the field army, and was implemented without the knowledge of the advance command center, and without General Murtagi's participation either in that decision or in its implementation.

The Military Situation Before the War

As stated earlier, it became clear to us that the condition of the armed forces completely ruled out entering a war against Israel at the time. Only Field Marshal 'Amer was of the opinion that the forces were ready and prepared to implement the closure of the Straits of Tiran.

From this perspective, the political decision to close the straits obviously did not take military considerations into account nor did it weigh the capabilities of Egypt and Israel realistically. One might ask if the political leadership was fully aware of the situation when it asked for a pullout of UN forces and closed the straits, since both actions clearly and inevitably led to war. Could the political leadership have been ignorant of facts known to Israel and the big powers? And if those facts were known, was it right or acceptable for the armed forces to be pushed into a war for which they were unprepared?

As a result of rash and uncalculated political action and a war which was imposed on them, the armed forces found themselves facing a critical situation.

- The absence of a higher national strategy to coordinate politics with military capabilities meant that the armed forces were pushed into a war at a time that did not suit them.
- They had to take part in a war even though the armed forces command had, in 1966, strongly recommended avoiding such an involvement for as long as a large part of the active army remained in Yemen.
- The war in Sinai was against a major and militarily superior enemy—Israel—but a third of the active army was still in Yemen, so the armed forces had to rely on untrained reserves for more than half the total number of troops on the front.
- This was a war to achieve political goals, and these changed from one moment to the next. Consequently, strategies and missions were being continuously modified and the defense plan for Sinai lost its strategic equilibrium.
- The military leadership was unable to plan or direct operations because of disruptions in the system of command and control.
- On an Arab level, there was no military coordination between Egypt, Syria, and Jordan, which allowed Israel to treat each front as a separate entity.
- All of this took place against a backdrop of international and regional conditions unfavorable to Egypt and in the absence of a political strategy—let alone a military one.

Could the armed forces have faced worse conditions than these during the second half of May and the first days of June 1967?

A CANCELED VISIT

In this depressing atmosphere, with unstable and changing military conditions and incomplete preparations for a war which might break out at any moment, we were informed on June 4 that Field Marshal 'Amer would arrive in Sinai the following day to inspect and coordinate the troops at the front.

On the morning of Monday, 5 June 1967, I was at the advance command center with some colleagues. General Murtagi and Major General Ahmad Isma'il had gone to Tamada Airport to meet the commander of the field army, Lieutenant General Salah Muhsin, along with a number of senior officers. They were to receive Field Marshal 'Amer, who was expected to arrive at 8:30 in the morning.

Shortly before his expected arrival, I heard nearby explosions. I quickly found out that it was enemy aircraft bombing the airports of Tamada and al-Maliz. From the top of a hill, I watched enemy planes attack Tamada. I pitied the troops without commanding officers at a time like this. My heart went out to those officers at the airport. I was very anxious about what was happening to them, asking myself how long it would take for each to regain his command post or if any had been hurt or wounded.

I immediately got in touch with the armed forces operations center in Cairo to notify them of the bombings. And this is how I came to learn that the rest of the airports in the canal zone and in Cairo were also being bombarded by Israeli planes at that very moment. War had begun.

4

War

The Israeli plan was first to strike the Egyptian forces in Sinai—considered a principal threat—then attack Jordan and seize the West Bank, and follow this with an attack against Syria to take the Golan Heights. The war would begin with an intensive air strike against Egyptian bases and airports, followed by a land attack, and the weaknesses of the three fronts would be exploited.

Israel's idea, in brief, was to avoid a dispersal of its strength by avoiding an attack on more than one front at a time. The main effort would be concentrated against the Egyptian forces to destroy the larger part of these, occupy the Sharm al-Shaykh sector, and open up the Straits of Tiran to Israeli shipping. In the meantime, the Jordanian and Syrian fronts would be immobilized using the smallest number of troops possible until Israel could turn to each individually after defeating the Egyptians. The plan required that Israel take the initiative, establish air supremacy, keep the war short, and settle it in a few days.

General Rabin, Israeli chief of staff at the time, in his memoirs recalls that in the original plan "we would concentrate on dealing a crushing blow to Egypt's air and armored forces and occupying the Gaza Strip and areas further south, without deciding now on the depth of our penetration." However, the plan was modified on 25 May to include preparations for an advance towards the Suez Canal. According to Rabin, "Dayan instructed us not to occupy the Gaza Strip during the first phase of fighting in order to avoid having to cope with a densely populated area right from the beginning of the war. Moreover, he insisted that . . . we take Sharm al-Shaykh earlier than we had originally planned." Rabin "assumed that the dimensions of our offensive would be dictated by the outcome of the air force strike against the enemy's airfields. If we gained absolute air superiority and succeeded in the first phases of our plan, we could extend ourselves beyond the confines of northern Sinai and destroy the Egyptian army throughout the peninsula. . . . If, as I expected, the Syrians and the Jordanians joined in, I doubted whether we would be able to occupy the whole of Sinai. But I was convinced that we were capable of dealing the Egyptian army a crushing blow."

He notes that "before the tanks began to roll, we would place our fate in the hands of the air force, whose pre-emptive strike was to destroy Egypt's planes on the ground and give us control of the skies. . . . Prior to the launch of the attack, and long after the Six-Day War, I often wondered what would have happened if the air battle against Egypt had lasted more than three hours and Syrian and Jordanian planes attacked Israel while most of our fighters were away over Egypt."[1] It was this total reliance on snatching the initiative which gained the advantage for Israel and which facilitated the task of its land and sea forces.

THE ARAB PLANS

At no time since 1948 did any joint Arab plan exist, nor any arrangement made in the full military sense, for cooperation in the struggle against Israel.

In 1948 during the Palestine War, King 'Abdallah of Jordan, aided by the British general Glubb, was appointed to command the Arab armies, but only in name and not in actual practice. Each Arab country, in fact, fought individually and issued separate orders to its own army in Palestine. The result was that instead of the Palestinians being able to reestablish their rights as legal owners of their land, Israel was able to consolidate as a state and extend beyond the boundaries provided by the partition resolution.

In 1956, Egypt on its own faced a triple aggression from Britain, France, and Israel, carried out according to well-laid plans. However, we should not forget that the Arab states and their peoples gave non-military support to Egypt in this war.

When the 'United Command of the Armies of the Arab States' was created in 1964 by a resolution of the Arab summit conference and was placed under the command of General 'Ali 'Amer, it was immediately crippled by the sensitivities and distrust of individual Arab states and was unable to coordinate Arab military efforts to face an Israeli aggression. Thus it became one more gesture without substance, unable to fulfill any serious military operation until 1967. Israel and the great powers were well aware of this. Indeed, this gave Israel the confidence to fight each front separately, with no interference expected from other Arab fronts.

In Egypt, the Kaher Plan was defensive, designed to prevent enemy penetration of the borders and stop enemy forces from reaching the Suez Canal, while absorbing a first air strike by Israel with minimal losses.

Jordanian and Syrian plans were also defensive, with no cooperation between each other or with Egypt.

The War on the Egyptian Front

War broke out at 8:45 A.M. Cairo time on Monday 5 June, when Israel hit at our air force and air defense system.

At that hour, Field Marshal 'Amer, accompanied by Lieutenant General Sidqi Mahmud, air force and air defense commander, and several senior officers were flying out to Tamada Airport to review the troops on the front. Their plane was forced to return to Cairo, as all airports in Sinai and the canal zone were under bombardment. This was their first warning that war had begun.

Meanwhile, General Murtagi, chief of the advance command center and commander of the Sinai front, Major General Ahmad Isma'il, his chief of staff, Lieutenant General Salah Muhsin, commander of the field army, and a number of other senior officers were not at their command posts but at Tamada Airport to greet Field Marshal 'Amer. The airport was attacked while they were waiting, and this was their first inkling that war had begun.

General Murtagi later described the events as follows.

> At forty-five minutes past eight, Cairo summer time, Israeli planes attacked the airport, destroying all aircraft and bombing runways to render them inoperational. . . . At first, we had not identified the planes flying over us as Israeli, because they looked very much like our own . . . we did not expect a betrayal, nor did the general situation lead us to believe that Israel would attack so soon. . . . We were sure that our Egyptian fighters would soon appear in the sky and take matters in hand, but we waited for some time in vain. . . . We were forced to return as quickly as possible by land to our command centers, notwithstanding the continued air strikes and the dense cloud of Israeli planes in our skies.[2]

It so happened that Vice President Husayn al-Shaf'i and Iraqi Prime Minister Taher Yahya were on a visit to the canal zone. Their plane landed in Fayed while the airport there was being bombed. Shaf'i later described what happened.

> We arrived over the Fayed airport at 8:45 A.M. and came face to face with the Israeli planes, almost as though fate had arranged for an appointment. . . . Our plane was able to land, and two bombs exploded nearby. We came down, scattered, taking shelter on the ground, and watched events unfold minute by minute.
>
> Enemy planes came at ten- to fifteen-minute intervals in groups of three to four planes, targeting specifically the planes which stood motionless on the ground, their wings touching each other as though carefully arranged to be destroyed in the shortest time possible, with no effort or trouble. Every sortie ended with one or two planes going up in flames. . . . Enemy aircraft met with no resistance of any kind either from aircraft or from air defense. If the radar could not spot low-flying planes, then that explains the first sortie. But what about the successive waves which lasted till about 11:30 A.M.?
>
> All along the return to Cairo with the Iraqi delegation, we observed the same picture—columns of smoke rising in the air at each of the airports of Abu Suwayr, Inshas, Belbeis, and finally Almaza, until we arrived at Manshiet al-Bakri to meet with President Nasir and report on what we'd seen.[3]

It was a bad beginning to a war. The commander in chief, the commander of the air force and air defense, the commander of the advance command center, the commander of the field army, several commanders of field formations and units—not one of these men was at his center of command, and a return to positions would take more time than the military situation could afford.

The sequence of events was as follows.

8:40 A.M: The commander of the Israeli southern command in Beersheba sent a message to general command claiming (falsely) that Egyptian forces were advancing to al-Naqab and that enemy planes had been observed on radar near the borders. Israeli positions in the Gaza Strip were reported to be heavily strafed by Egyptian artillery.

8:50 A.M: An official communiqué from the Israeli army command announced that Egypt had started its land and air attack against Israel. Air raid sirens went off in Tel Aviv to warn against an air raid against the city (false).

9:00 A.M: Israel declared that it was at war with Egypt.

9:10 A.M: Israel's permanent delegate to the United Nations notified the head of the UN Security Council of the (fictitious) Egyptian aggression.

In this way, Israel not only kindled the fires of war but placed the blame on Egypt and pleaded self-defense—to win over world public opinion. The truth became obvious soon after when Abba Eban at the United Nations admitted that Israel started the war in self-defense as a reaction to the closure of the straits.

The First Air Strike

The first Israeli air strike was echeloned into two attacks on bases and airports. 185 aircraft took part in a series of consecutive waves which hit ten airports and radar installations and destroyed runways and planes on the ground. The airports were Tamada, al-Maliz, al-Sirr and al-'Arish in Sinai; Abu Suwayr, Fayed, and Kabrit in the canal zone and Inshas, Cairo West, and Beni Suef in the Delta. The second attack (165 planes) then struck in waves, hitting remaining air bases and airports, with more runways and aircraft destroyed on the ground.

In the first attack, planes flew at very low altitudes, keeping radio silence to evade the radar. By the second attack, it was no longer necessary to take these precautions. Priority was given to runways, which were bombed with time bombs (able to detonate even after repairs had begun) in order to delay their repair, after which all manner of firepower (rockets, automatic and cannon fire) was used against planes and remaining targets.

Israeli intelligence had been able to collect the vital information needed for a successful air strike—information about airports and air bases, their size and type of operation, the condition and capabilities of the air defense system, air paths not covered by the air defense network, etc. Brigadier General Mordechai Hod, commander of the Israeli air force, said at a press conference in the middle of June that

> the plan to annihilate the Egyptian air force was based on solid and precise intelligence on the enemy. Our intelligence services were able to pinpoint almost all squadron positions for us and this played a large part in the success of our air attacks. We were informed of the number and types of aircraft expected at each base and airport, which allowed us to prioritize and strike first at the bombers then at other aircraft

according to their importance, so that MiG-21s and Sokhoy 7s came next, followed by MiG-19s and MiG-17s, then transport aircraft and helicopters last, to be hit when the opportunity presented itself.

General Hod explained that flight routes from Israel to Egypt were set from the west (the sea) at altitudes ranging between twenty and thirty meters. On approaching Egyptian territorial waters between al-'Arish and Dumyat, the planes split up into three groups. From north of al-'Arish, the first group would proceed to the airports of al-'Arish, al-Sirr, al-Maliz, and Tamada simultaneously. From Port Said, the second group would hit simultaneously the airports of the canal zone, that is Abu Suwayr, Fayed, and Kabrit. The third group would attack Cairo West, Cairo International, Almaza, Beni Suef, Inshas, Quwisna, Mansura, and Luxor airports.

All airports, radar, and anti-aircraft batteries were to be put out of action on the first day of fighting, and the success of the plan was to some extent predicated on the number of pilots available—double the number of planes—and the efficiency of ground services and maintenance at the airports and bases. Planes were to return to Israeli skies in the event of an unforeseen reaction, such as Egyptian air cover, if the plan became known.

He added that the air strike had lasted for nearly three hours during which time Egypt lost all of its heavy and light bombers and 85 percent of its fighter planes.

The Egyptian air force was therefore put out of action in the first three hours of the first day of fighting, giving Israel freedom of the sky, leaving our land and naval forces without air cover or air support—vulnerable to continuous enemy attacks—and giving the Israeli land forces an unqualified advantage.

In the face of this disastrous situation, the general command and the air force command went into a state of paralysis and were unable to think or plan a response. The effect on the troops in Sinai was terrible, as we learned the following day, and as we listened with growing horror to the military communiqués on Cairo radio, reporting fictitious enemy casualties and the downing of huge numbers of enemy aircraft, while we could see Israeli planes fly in complete freedom over Sinai.

The political leadership was naturally devastated at the extent of the losses. President Sadat has described their reactions on the morning of 5 June.

When I arrived at general headquarters that day, Nasir was coming out of the reception area with 'Amer, who was blaming it all on the Americans, saying that it was the American air force and not Israel

> that had hit us. Nasir replied, 'I am not prepared to believe this, nor to issue an official communiqué that America was the aggressor—not unless you can produce the wing of a single aircraft with American markings on it.' But later, realizing the extent of the catastrophe, he retracted and issued a communiqué to that effect. It was a cover-up in the face of his people. Another extraordinary thing on that fateful day was that 'Amer, on his return to Cairo, and fully aware of the disaster, sent for the Soviet ambassador to ask for a ceasefire one hour after hostilities had begun. That is why the Soviet ambassador was to be found at general headquarters on the morning of that day.[4]

In his memoirs, Vice President 'Abd al-Latif Bughdadi describes the situation in Field Marshal Amer's office that day.

> We went to the army's general headquarters and met with 'Abd al-Hakim 'Amer, asking for an explanation. It was nearly 1:00 P.M. He told us that we had brought down seventy-three enemy planes so far. He would not give us any figures on our own losses, but said that almost all our aircraft were gone. During the conversation, we noticed that Sidqi Mahmud, commander of the air force, had gotten in touch with him by telephone several times. Sidqi was saying that there must be American and British participation because Israel did not own the large number of planes needed to sustain the continuous waves of raids we were experiencing on our airports. 'Abd al-Hakim 'Amer asked him for proof . . .
>
> 'Amer then phoned Nasir to inform him that the raids were very dense, and that Israel did not have this number of planes, and that American planes were hitting Luxor . . .
>
> Nasir asked about our losses, but 'Abd al-Hakim evaded the question, replying that a list of our losses had not yet reached him. When Nasir insisted, 'Abd al-Hakim looked at a list on his desk and said, 'We have forty-seven planes left, thirty-five of which are in usable condition. The rest are in repair and can be used after being fully equipped.

It Was Unavoidable

After our air force had been exposed to this destruction and knocked out of the war, the Israeli air force turned its attention to Jordan, striking at the airports of Amman and al-Mafrik. Having finished with these, it turned to Syria and the airports there. All the Jordanian aircraft were destroyed, and half of Syria's, and their airports were crippled. The air strikes against the aviation of Egypt, Jordan, and Syria were a major factor in the June 1967 defeat.

On analyzing the air attack against Egypt, we find that the timing was no surprise because the armed forces as a whole were in a state of maximum alert. At the meeting held on 2 June and attended by Field Marshal 'Amer, Lieutenant General Sidqi Mahmud, and other senior commanders, Nasir had clearly said that he expected a war to break out within forty-eight to seventy-two hours and that the enemy would begin with an air strike against our air force and air defense system. The decision that day had been to absorb a first air strike for political reasons, but to work at reducing losses as much as possible. The surprise came from the devastating impact of the air attack and the lack of preparation, with no serious measures taken for over ten years to prepare the air force.

To begin with, the air defense system was deficient and unable to pick up aircraft flying at low altitudes. This allowed enemy aircraft to reach their targets undetected despite their large numbers and despite the distance flown—across Sinai, the canal zone, the Delta, Hurghada, and Luxor. This weakness had been identified by air and defense command, and was known to the general command and Field Marshal 'Amer long before the war. The deficiency, although dangerous, had not been corrected by recourse either to new equipment from the Soviet Union or other resources. This can only be described as irresponsible.

Furthermore, a wide-range radar station in 'Ajlun, Jordan, had been installed as part of an early warning system. It was in radio contact with the air force and air defense operations center in Cairo, with a backup receiver in the office of Shams Badran, minister of war.

General Fawzi reports that

> at 7:00 Israeli time, and 8:00 Cairo time, the station at 'Ajlun using the code word 'Enab' warned of consecutive waves of Israeli aircraft moving southwest. The message was sent to air force command headquarters and to Shams' office.
>
> The main receiving station never received the message. The signals corporal on duty said at the inquest that he had changed the receiving frequency for better reception. On a second occasion, he said that operating time on the old frequency had ended (according to the code timetable) and so he had changed it to the next frequency. In any case, the message was not received and the air force command was not given the early warning.
>
> As for the backup receiver in Shams' office, it got the message, there was no problem there . . . a definite signal announcing the start of an enemy attack. However, the officer on duty failed to inform the minister (who was not in his office) of this. About forty-five

minutes after receiving the message, the officer, during a telephone conversation with a colleague at the air force and air defense center, mentioned this and the code word 'Enab,' which indicated an attack. At that point in time, Israeli planes were actually bombing our airports. It was 8:45 A.M., Cairo time.[5]

This was how matters stood at air defense during the most critical moments. They were completely irresponsible and neglected their duties entirely. One can only imagine what could have happened if our planes had been able to take off to repel the air strike.

Secondly, no precautions were taken by the air and defense command either to contain the expected attack or to try to limit losses. At the 2 June meeting at general headquarters, President Nasir had said that a first strike by Israel would be absorbed for political reasons. Lieutenant General Sidqi Mahmud had objected at the time, saying, "This means we lose the initiative which could cripple our air force," using the English word "cripple." He estimated that losses would stand at 15 to 20 percent.[6]

At the end of the meeting, it was agreed that protective measures must be taken to limit the damage of an Israeli first strike, in order to be able to make a retaliatory strike. Field Marshal 'Amer gave his orders to Sidqi Mahmud for the necessary steps to be taken. In any case, air power would be used defensively and a 20 percent loss was better than having to face a combined US and Israeli enemy.

The question is obvious: What were the precautionary measures taken by the commander in chief and the commander of the air defense forces?

- We needed air cover over Sinai and other sectors where a strike was expected. This would have allowed some of our planes to stall the enemy and enable others to take off and repulse them. Starting on 3 June, it was no longer adequate to follow the basic flight maneuvers established since the crisis began because these were now familiar to the enemy.
- Squadron and bomber bases needed to be shifted around, but the only measure taken here was to transfer one squadron from Sinai to the Kabrit base.
- Air defense procedures needed closer supervision and review. The 'Ajlun early warning may have not come through because of orders to restrict activities between Cairo and Sinai as Field Marshal 'Amer was on his way to Sinai, and Husayn al-Shaf'i to Fayed, both between eight and nine o'clock in the morning. This should not have prevented opening fire in the case of a direct aggression.

- Command and control for air defense was not up to standard at the critical time. Five TU16 heavy bombers were on a daily training exercise from Beni Suef (the base) to Aswan. They were not warned until half an hour after enemy aircraft had been in Egyptian airspace, and then they were ordered to land at Luxor civil airport. Would it not have been better for them to continue to Aswan, or Khartoum?

Thirdly, enemy air capability had not been properly assessed before the war. Planning had been based on poor and inadequate information. The number of planes estimated to be available to Israel was lower than the number actually used in the air strike. Furthermore, the ability of the Israeli Mirages to fly for long distances at low altitudes was incorrectly calculated. It was believed that their range precluded an in-depth penetration, but on 5 June, they were able to reach Luxor and Cairo West airports. This kind of information is the joint responsibility of military intelligence and air and defense command. Without it, there can be no effective planning or action.

Fourthly, measures taken to protect our fleet of aircraft, such as providing camouflaged hangers, were inadequate. The need for camouflaged facilities and hangers had become evident after the Tripartite Aggression in 1956. Ten years later, nothing had been done to implement this lesson. This can only be ascribed to a lack of will and perseverance on the part of command. One cannot accept the argument that budget constraints were to blame. After the June War, funds were allocated for such a project and this was accomplished with commitment and responsibility by the new air force command.

Fifthly, runway 'parachute' bombs used by Israel caught military intelligence by surprise. It had not known that this type of bomb existed. Slow to detonate, the bomb blew out craters nearly three meters wide and over a meter and a half deep. Repairing damage to the runway took some time, giving enemy planes ample time and opportunity to destroy grounded aircraft. Naturally, this type of bomb was especially effective at airports with just one runway, which was the case at a great many of our airports. Furthermore, there were no on-the-spot engineering field units to repair the craters.

The five reasons given for our failings in no way excuse them. They are mentioned to illustrate some of the principal factors behind our loss of air power and to serve as a lesson. During the six lean years after June 1967, these weaknesses were attended to, as were problems of organization, training, weapons, and equipment. Our air force gave proof of its abilities in October 1973.

Several questions must necessarily be raised in this context. On what grounds did air force command request to be given the initiative to strike first? How did General Sidqi Mahmud come up with an estimate of 15 to 20 percent losses in the event of a first air strike by Israel—given that our losses were of a magnitude of 100 percent for some types of aircraft and 85 percent for others? And on what basis were air force command and the forces' commander in chief able to imagine that our air force could absorb a first strike, and then proceed to retaliate?

The Land Attack on Sinai, 5 June 1967

At around ten o'clock in the morning of that day, Israel launched a land assault on the forces of the northern axis (Rafah–al-'Arish) to break through Rafah's defenses and open up the coastal road to al-'Arish. This was to isolate the Gaza Strip from Sinai. Fighting continued throughout the day with heavy losses on both sides, and the sector commander and the chief of staff both lost their lives in a violent and sustained attempt to hold their position. The haste with which our forces had first occupied the position and a consequent lack of mechanical equipment undoubtedly helped the Israelis succeed, and by seven o'clock in the evening nearly twenty Israeli tanks were advancing towards al-'Arish.

In the Gaza Strip, towns and refugee camps were shelled and bombed by Israeli artillery and aviation. Deir al-Balah was captured and fighting continued to nightfall in Khan Yunis and Gaza.

In the central axis (Umm Qatf–Abu 'Uwigla), the Israelis attacked Abu 'Uwigla itself, which is the gateway to central Sinai. Because of its strategic importance, fighting was fierce there throughout the day. By midnight, helicopters had landed Israeli troops behind the defensive positions and these had engaged with artillery units, depriving the Egyptian forces of their firepower. Despite this, our forces held on stubbornly and the Israelis were able to penetrate the defense line only in part the following day.

On the southern axis (al-Kuntala–Nakhl), an Israeli force made a limited attack to contain our units at al-Kuntala, a secondary route, and tie them down, but were forced to withdraw back into enemy territory.

The sector of Sharm al-Shaykh was relatively lightly touched, with no ground attack and scattered air strikes of no real consequence.

Throughout, we were fighting with no air support or protection, which gave the Israeli land forces greater flexibility and firepower. They also were effectively supported by their air force.

By the end of the day, we can be said to have performed acceptably, from a strategic perspective, and our condition was not desperate, despite the absence of the air force. Fighting was continuing in the first defense belt. As mentioned, the coastal axis (Rafah–Gaza) had failed to hold up, but the attack against Abu 'Uwigla and al-Kasima had not achieved its goal, and the attack on the southern axis (al-Kuntala–Nakhl) had not directly affected the situation. In the Gaza Strip, the battle continued at Khan Yunis and at Gaza, while the forces at Sharm al-Shaykh had not been exposed to a land attack.

However, the first tactical belt had not been attacked, the army reserves had suffered no losses and were available, and the general command reserve (the Fourth Armored Division) had not been used, although it had been hit by Israeli fighter planes.

I must repeat that on the evening of 5 June, despite the presence of enemy troops on our territory and despite the great loss of the air force, the front had not collapsed and we were not in a position where we were unable to use the land forces in Sinai to protect the next defensive lines the following day.

6 June 1967

The sixth of June arrived with all its painful events. The enemy had occupied al-'Arish and gone into Abu 'Uwigla. At this point, general command in Cairo ordered the Fourth Armored Division to carry out a counteroffensive on Abu 'Uwigla–al-Kasima and restore the first defense belt firmly into our hands.

As a representative from the advance command center, I was there when the order was issued by Lieutenant General Salah Muhsin, commander of the army, to Major General Sidqi al-Ghul, Fourth Division commander. On my way back to the center after this, I saw one of our armored brigades under attack. It was heartbreaking. The Israeli planes had complete freedom of the skies. The tanks were moving across open desert in daylight, which made them easy targets with no effective means of defense.

When I arrived at the center on the afternoon of 6 June, I found that it had been destroyed in repeated air attacks. I was notified that the decision to use the Fourth Armored Division in a counterattack had been annulled. Field Marshal 'Amer subsequently issued orders to General Salah Muhsin in the evening of that same day, 6 June, for a general withdrawal of all the forces from Sinai to the west of the canal.

War on the Jordanian and Syrian Fronts

The Jordanian front was the second front to be attacked by Israel. Fighting began with an artillery barrage at around 11:00 on the morning of 5 June. About thirty Jordanian planes were destroyed in an air attack and two military air bases at al-Mafrik and Amman were hit.

Israel now had air supremacy and land forces were able to occupy the West Bank and the eastern sector of Jerusalem. A ceasefire was declared on 7 June. In his memoirs, Dayan has remarked that the speedy termination of fighting on the Jordanian front stopped the Palestinians on the West Bank from participating in the war.

There was now an opportunity to attack Syria. Activity on the Syrian front had, for the first four days of the war, been limited to artillery engagements and some land raids. Chief of Staff General Fawzi comments:

> At around eleven o'clock on the morning of 5 June, Field Marshal 'Amer asked me to get in touch with the Syrian command to inform them of developments, and to ask them to put into effect part of a plan I had worked out with the Syrian army chief of staff, Major General Ahmad Sweidan, and bomb Israel's northern airports. I got in touch by radio and asked Sweidan to go ahead with the 'Rashid' plan, but got no positive response beyond the one sentence 'We will try, sir.' Later, I discovered that no orders were ever issued on the Syrian side for any offensive action or indeed for any operation against Israel whatsoever.
>
> Lieutenant General 'Abd al-Mun'im Riyad, who was in Amman, had made the same request about an hour earlier, but the Syrian command had responded negatively.[7]

To contain the Syrian front and prevent it from making any wide-scale attack, on 5 June Israel destroyed approximately half of the Syrian air force in an air strike which consequently limited activity on this front. A ceasefire had come into effect on 8 June, but Israeli forces had nevertheless attacked on the morning of 9 June, and the Syrian general command had ordered a withdrawal from the Golan Heights that same day, concentrating their forces outside of Damascus.

On all fronts—Jordanian, Syrian, and Egyptian—the outcome was defeat. It must be remembered that although their participation differed in size and form, these differences are only technical. A great many men were lost, to no strategic advantage or purpose.

Jordan accepted a ceasefire on 7 June, having lost the West Bank. Egypt accepted a ceasefire on 8 June while Israel was consolidating its control over Sinai, and troops continued to pour into the Suez Canal on 9 June and the coastline of the Gulf of Suez on 10 June. Syria accepted a ceasefire on 8 June, but the Israelis occupied the Golan Heights on 10 June. The June 1967 war ended with Egypt losing Sinai and the Gaza sector, Jordan losing the West Bank, and Syria losing the Golan Heights.

It was a disaster for the Arabs.

5

The General Withdrawal From Sinai

Considering the developments of 6 June, General Murtagi asked Field Marshal 'Amer to approve the transfer of the advance command center to a position west of the Giddi Pass. 'Amer gave his consent and army field command was notified.

We moved on the evening of 6 June. To our consternation, we noticed a flow of vehicles, weapons, and equipment westward in the direction of the Suez Canal. We had not yet received the orders from general command for a general withdrawal from Sinai. This would have been transmitted through Lieutenant General Salah Muhsin, commander of the field army.

We arrived at the new advance command center at around one o'clock in the morning. Soon after, at about three o'clock, the chief of military police notified us that there were orders for a general withdrawal from Sinai, and that this was actually now taking place. We were amazed, and became even more so when we heard that field army command had also withdrawn, that Lieutenant General Salah Muhsin was now west of the canal, and that pontoons had been provided for the troops to cross to the west.

General Murtagi, with Major General Ahmad Isma'il, hurried back in the direction of the canal to find out what exactly was going on. Murtagi relates that

> when we reached west of the canal and south of the lakes, we found the field army commander on the phone to the commander in chief

of the armed forces, who was instructing him to provide shelter for the troops returning from Sinai. . . . I asked Lieutenant General Salah Muhsin why he had not asked for my permission to move his command, and why he had not notified the advance command center of the orders for withdrawal? His answer to both questions was unconvincing, especially as he attributed it to a breakdown in the line connecting him to the command center.[1]

At the advance command center, I watched a heavy flow of troops move westward. It was completely disorganized. Could this be happening? Could a withdrawal take place in this manner, when it normally required extreme discipline and precision and, according to the doctrine of war, should take place while fighting continued? Why had the troops been sent to Sinai only to pull back two days later in such a haphazard way?

The questions I kept turning over in my mind were: Where were the senior officers who should be leading the troops? Where was the army commander? How had the retreat been organized? I discovered later that Lieutenant General Salah Muhsin and his command, with Field Marshal 'Amer's approval, had moved west of the canal on the evening of 6 June. The command had given up control of its forces at the most critical time during the withdrawal. It should have been the absolute duty of the army commander and his senior officers to remain in Sinai to keep the fighting going while organizing a retreat. A field commander cannot forsake this kind of responsibility. The situation was completely confused, with the army commander and his men in Isma'iliya, the advance command center remaining in the Giddi area of Sinai, and the troops withdrawing from Sinai. I repeat that the inability of the operational army command in Sinai at the very least to control the situation can neither be explained nor excused.

I waited and watched on the morning of 7 June and saw the troops withdraw in the most pathetic way from Giddi and Mitla under continuous enemy air attacks, which had turned the Mitla Pass into an enormous graveyard of scattered corpses, burning equipment, and exploding ammunition. Then a message reached me at advance command center to return to Isma'iliya.

There I found everybody in a desolate state. A large proportion of the forces had now pulled out of Sinai and the rest were on their way west. As for Sharm al-Shaykh, I learned that the troops there had withdrawn and that the Israelis had come in without a fight.

RETREAT OR SUICIDE?

When Field Marshal 'Amer had issued the order to withdraw in the afternoon of 6 June, effective the following day, the armed forces operations staff had suggested that this take place over three nights and four days to avoid the brunt of enemy air bombardment and to allow time for some organization. 'Amer did not accept this. It seems that he was still under the influence of President Nasir's 1956 decision to withdraw from Sinai during the Tripartite Aggression, when Egypt had directed its efforts mainly against Britain and France and not Israel, which was then considered the cat's paw. It had slipped Field Marshal 'Amer's mind that 1967 was a completely different set of circumstances.

It had also escaped his attention that the size of the forces in Sinai was enormous in 1967, and that the roads were limited and could not carry the movement of such large numbers of troops in so short a time. A disorganized retreat would make the troops totally vulnerable to an enemy with complete freedom of the skies and losses would be very heavy, not to mention that the troops would be exposed to pressure from enemy land forces.

According to military science, a withdrawal is an acceptable strategy for field troops under pressure from a superior enemy in order to regroup, defend on other lines, or to extend and exhaust enemy lines of communication until a stronger defense and counterattack becomes possible. In all cases, the withdrawal must be well-planned and orderly, and enforced by a strong command according to a set timetable which would allow some fighting to continue so that the withdrawal does not turn into a rout.

The closest contemporary example from military history is the confused withdrawal to al-Alamein in July 1942 of the Eighth Army under pressure from Rommel after the battle of al-Ghazala. The British were in disarray, but their command imposed order on the scattered and exhausted troops, forcing them to stand fast and defend al-Alamein until conditions became right for an offensive and ultimately led to victory in the battle of al-Alamein.

When Rommel's forces withdrew from al-Alamein, they were organized so that fighting continued in a delaying tactic to allow the bulk of the forces to move behind the next defensive line. In this way, Rommel's withdrawal became one of the most successful operations of its kind.

Without referring to other examples, it had been absolutely essential for the June 1967 withdrawal to be planned with delaying tactics and a determined hold on the passes, despite Israeli air supremacy. The nature of the territory around the passes provides excellent opportunities for resistance to a superior attacking force.

Field Marshal 'Amer's order to withdraw was given after less than two days of fighting, which had remained concentrated on the first defense belt. This meant that we had enough depth and sufficient troops to defend the passes if the determination and will had been there. Regardless of enemy air or firepower, the outcome would have been preferable, militarily, politically, and morally.

Who Decided to Withdraw?

The question of whether the decision for a withdrawal was taken unilaterally by Field Marshal 'Amer or with President Nasir's approval has often been raised. Frankly, this did not preoccupy us in Sinai. We were more concerned with why it had been decided, and why it had been implemented so poorly with such obviously disastrous results.

General Fawzi, then chief of staff, comments:

> Field Marshal 'Amer's intention to withdraw the troops from Sinai first came to light when a radio message was sent from high command to the commander of the Sharm al-Shaykh sector at 5:50 on the morning of 6 June, asking him to submit a plan for a full withdrawal of his forces to west of the canal.
>
> The field marshal called me on the afternoon of 6 June and said, 'I want you to make a quick plan for troop withdrawal from Sinai to west of the Suez Canal.' Then he added, 'You have only twenty minutes to do this.'
>
> I was astounded by the request. This was the first order Field Marshal 'Amer had given me, personally. The field marshal was psychologically worn out and seemed on the verge of nervous collapse, and the situation did not allow for any discussion or argument. The land forces in Sinai—except for the Seventh Division—were holding out steadily, and there seemed to be no reason whatsoever to consider a withdrawal.
>
> I rushed into the operations room where I called Lieutenant General Anwar al-Qadi and his assistant, Major General al-Tohami. We sat down to think. Then we briefly set out some very broad and general lines for a withdrawal, and Major General Tuhami wrote this down on a piece of paper. It provided a framework for a withdrawal and a schedule.
>
> The three of us went to Field Marshal 'Amer. Tuhami began reading out that the forces were to withdraw to line so-and-so, on such-and-such a date, to line so, and that the retreat would be

conducted so that each line would replace the other until the last line west of the Suez Canal, four days from the beginning of the withdrawal. This meant that it would be completed in four days and three nights.

When Field Marshal 'Amer heard the last part, on the timing, he raised his voice a little and addressing me, said, 'Four days and three nights, Fawzi? I have already given the order to withdraw, and that's that.' His face had become very red and he left, looking somewhat hysterical, to his bedroom, situated behind his office. The three of us were left completely taken aback by his condition.

General 'Abd al-Muhsin Murtagi has had this to say about the withdrawal:

> During a visit to Field Marshal 'Amer immediately after the war, I asked him how much the president had known of his decision, whether he had agreed to it, or if the decision had been his ('Amer's) alone. Such a decision had grave strategic repercussions and would have needed a shared political perspective. Field Marshal 'Amer replied that he had been in agreement with President Nasir, and had gotten his approval and could not possibly have made the decision without his knowledge.[2]

As a member of the Committee for the Historical Record, where I followed the military statements and testimonies on the 1967 June War, I learned from the statement of Brigadier 'Abd al-Sattar Amin (who headed Field Marshal 'Amer's office during the war), that 'Amer had called President Nasir on 6 June and informed him of the decision to withdraw, saying,

> Al-'Arish has fallen. All we have left in Abu 'Uwigla is the equivalent of a battalion. In Umm Qatf the artillery has been destroyed. Al-Kasima is besieged and a gap of about half a kilometer is all that separates us. . . . The area of al-Kuntala is intact. I have decided to withdraw the armed forces to west of the canal. We have to free ourselves of the responsibility and open up the way for the next generation to shoulder it.

'Abd al-Latif Bughdadi's memoirs also speak of the withdrawal. He says that on Tuesday 6 June

> we returned to Field Marshal 'Amer's office in the evening and found Zakaria Muhi al-Din there. I asked for news . . . and he surprised me by saying that we had decided on a pullout to west of the Suez Canal.

The effect of this information was like thunder. It shocked me, and I could not believe what I had heard. I asked for the reasons behind this grave decision. He replied, 'The planes are hunting our tanks down in the open desert. They have to withdraw to agricultural areas to hide.'

Spontaneously, I exclaimed, 'It's a disgrace.' He replied, 'It is not a matter of honor or bravery, but a matter of saving our boys. The enemy has destroyed two of our divisions.'

I asked what Nasir's opinion was on the withdrawal. He replied, 'He is the one who took this decision to save our boys.' I kept repeating 'the shame, the disgrace . . . ' and he said, 'It's over. It's become part of history.'

Bughdadi continues:

'Abd al-Hakim was in continuous touch with front command and issued the orders to withdraw although it seems that there was no plan. His orders, which he gave to anyone who got in touch with him, was to pull out during the night and try to reach west of the canal before dawn, abandon heavy weapons and carry only light arms, and to move in small, scattered groups.

We sat watching the disaster unfold . . . our hearts heavy, until we decided to leave the room in which the future of a nation and the destiny of its people were being played out.[3]

According to Mahmud Riyad, who was foreign minister at the time, 'Abd al-'Aziz Bouteflika, the Algerian foreign minister, arrived in Cairo on a private plane on the afternoon of 7 June. His message was that Algeria was ready to do all that it could and that President Houari Boumediene would send planes, asking for pilots to return with him to take possession of these. Riyad records the following:

When I accompanied Bouteflika to Nasir's home, he said that Algeria's view was not to accept a ceasefire. Nasir then asked for a map of Sinai and pointed to the major landmarks. He stopped at the line of the passes and said that Egypt was going to withdraw to that line and hold it to halt the Israeli advance. . . .

Later on . . . I discovered that while Gamal 'Abd al-Nasir had been talking of resisting at the line of the passes, 'Abd al-Hakim 'Amer had already issued orders on the evening of 6 June for a general withdrawal of our forces to the west of the canal.

It is clear that none of these quoted passages show what really went on between Field Marshal 'Amer and President Nasir, nor do they reveal any actual discussion between them on the withdrawal from Sinai. However, this was a grave political and military decision to make and they undoubtedly must have examined it together. I cannot imagine that Field Marshal 'Amer could have been so naive as to think he could come to such a decision on his own, nor would President 'Abd al-Nasir have been so simple as to allow Field Marshal 'Amer to make a decision such as this without his knowledge and approval. Perhaps the words of Field Marshal 'Amer's bureau chief and those of 'Abd al-Latif Bughdadi suggest this.

My opinion is that the decision to pull out of Sinai was wrong, and that the manner in which it was implemented was wrong and contrary to all military practice. Politically, the situation required continued fighting for as long as would have been possible. There seems to have been no reason for Sinai to be abandoned.

Strategically, our military position on 6 June did not call for a general withdrawal to west of the canal. Lieutenant General Salah Muhsin, commander of the field army, issued orders to Major General Sidqi al-Ghul, commander of the Fourth Armored Division, to hold the line of the passes until noon of 7 June to cover the withdrawal of the troops. For the record, I was not directly involved in the orders issued by field army command or general command regarding the role of this division in the general withdrawal, and cannot therefore discuss it in detail or comment on how the mission was carried out.

Nevertheless, I must make clear that using the army during the withdrawal necessarily meant holding the passes with all of the men available to the army commander. That the line had not been fully prepared or equipped before or during preparations for war does not justify abandoning it. Militarily, there exists a 'hasty' defense mode to allow for a change in tactics and a move to a stronger position. The geography of the area around the passes is in fact favorable to an effective defense in a variety of ways.

In any case, whatever the circumstances, it is the responsibility of the military command alone to organize a retreat and to direct it in an acceptable military manner, and not in the improvised way in which it was done. Because of command errors from above, the regular soldiers found the retreat turning into a defeat. A great many men were killed and we lost large quantities of weapons and equipment. The retreat—along with other military and political mistakes—became a major cause of the defeat.

History will not be merciful to those men responsible for the June 1967 general withdrawal, and it will remain a notorious example of a fatal military error.

President Nasir had announced the closure of the Straits of Tiran to Israeli navigation on 23 May. With the retreat, Israel had occupied Sharm al-Shaykh without a fight. Dayan, in his memoirs, says,

> At the end of the second day of war, Egyptian forces in the advanced positions, which had not been encircled, began to retreat. Orders had been issued from Cairo to withdraw. When we found out that Egyptian forces were pulling out of their positions in Sharm al-Shaykh, we hastily put forward the time scheduled for its seizure and sent a paratroop unit, without waiting for the land forces to get there. The unit arrived at Sharm al-Shaykh in helicopters at 1:00 in the afternoon of 7 June. From the air, two Israeli torpedo boats could be seen already in the port. They had arrived at 11:30 to find the port empty of Egyptian troops, and had landed two platoons. Three-quarters of an hour later, the Israeli flag was flying over the international hospital vacated by the UN peacekeeping forces on Nasir's orders. The first Egyptian prisoners in the area were taken by the Israeli navy—they were thirty-three commandos, with their weapons, on the island of Tiran.

This is how Israeli shipping returned to the Gulf of 'Aqaba; not under the United Nations' flag, but by force of arms.

The Ceasefire

At the UN Security Council, consultations were going ahead for a ceasefire and an Israeli withdrawal to the lines of 4 June. The United States opposed this, insisting that Israeli withdrawal from Arab territory should not be a condition. The resolution was then limited to a ceasefire because of US pressure and a sustained diplomatic effort by President Johnson inside and outside of the Security Council. Israel was, in this way, encouraged to continue its occupation of Arab land.

In his memoirs, Foreign Minister Mahmud Riyad describes the moments leading up to the ceasefire:

> At nine o'clock on the evening of 8 June, President Nasir called me on the telephone. It was a conversation I shall never forget. His voice was desolate, full of pain, and his tone was enough to describe the situation. He told me that the collapse of the armed forces was total, was beyond imagination. We could no longer continue fighting, and we must notify al-Kuni, our ambassador at the United Nations, to inform the Security Council of our acceptance of a cessation of military activity.
>
> When I called al-Kuni at ten o'clock, I realized from his response that this was the biggest shock of his life. I had over the past few

days been giving him the communiqués from military command, and these had described a situation which was far from true, but al-Kuni had refused to believe the other information from foreign ambassadors in New York that the front had collapsed.

Now, we were both discovering, at the same moment, the world of make-believe we had been living in.

Nasir Resigns

An uninterrupted chain of reactions took place in Egypt.

On 9 June, President Nasir announced his resignation, entrusting the presidency to Zakaria Muhi al-Din. The decision was a way of taking on the historic responsibility for the defeat. Demonstrations took place in the streets of Cairo on 9 and 10 June in support of Nasir, and the People's Assembly and the cabinet turned down his resignation. On 10 June, President Nasir declared that he would stay on, saying, "I will remain until we are able—all of us—to wipe out the consequences of the aggression. After this, the matter will revert to the people in a general referendum. I am convinced of the reasons behind my decision, but the voice of the people is to me something I cannot ignore, and for this reason, I have postponed my decision."

We listened in Isma'iliya to this broadcast from Cairo while our forces now on the west bank of the canal were still in confusion and incapable of defending the canal zone. Our principal concern was to bring some order back, reassemble, and somehow compensate for our heavy losses so as to be able to take up new positions as quickly as possible with the few remaining available weapons.

Israeli troops now stood on the east bank of the canal. We felt a grief that bordered on tears. Impossibly harsh political and military conditions had been imposed on the armed forces and had made it a victim to dreadful circumstances.

Those were hard and terrible days, impossible to describe, bitter days I will never forget. Only those of us who lived through them in Sinai and in the canal zone can understand the extent of the feeling of crisis.

Nasir Takes Control

The eleventh of June was a decisive day. Following the announcement of the resignations of Field Marshal 'Amer and Shams Badran, President Nasir took over command and control of the armed forces. He immediately appointed General Muhammad Fawzi commander in chief of the armed forces, Lieutenant General 'Abd al-Mun'im Riyad chief of staff, and Lieutenant General Madkur Abu'l-'Izz (at the time governor of Aswan) commander of the air force and air defense.

On that same day, resignations were accepted from General Murtagi (land forces), General Sidqi Mahmud (air force), General Suliman 'Izzat (naval forces), as well as from the chief of the armed forces operations staff and from all aides to the deputy supreme commander. It was also decided to retire any other senior officer in close touch with Field Marshal 'Amer, effective immediately.

Nasir felt that both the military and the internal situation required his direct input and control. At a cabinet meeting, he explained this, saying,

> I will never be able to forget the first days after the June War. I felt a bitterness beyond description. The June events have had a profound psychological, moral, and material effect on us all. . . . On some days, I wished that I had in fact resigned and distanced myself from all the responsibilities, but I kept in mind that the days we were facing were very difficult internally and externally, because our adversaries were strong, organized, and . . . had the funds necessary to destroy us.
>
> When I went back on my decision to resign on 11 June, I was in very bad shape, to the point where I sent my family out of Cairo and kept a gun beside me to use at the last minute. On that day, I was told that we only had seven tanks left in Cairo. I spoke with Lieutenant General Fawzi every night before retiring, and then once again at six o'clock in the morning to review conditions of the armed forces, the commands, and names of the officers responsible for each command. If I had not done this, the situation would have escaped me.[4]

The Aftermath of War

Slowly, as things began to fall into place again in Cairo, on the canal front the forces after the withdrawal began to be reorganized, first into small units and then into larger units, and to take up position gradually, despite the low morale and the lack of the most basic weapons.

I was at the command center for the canal region, under the command of Lieutenant General Salah Muhsin. I stayed there for nearly two weeks, and then returned to Cairo to join the armed forces operations command, where I learned from general headquarters that Major General Ahmad Isma'il had been retired with a number of other officers. It was sad news, especially as he could in no way be held responsible for any of the mistakes made since the state of emergency in May.

I went home for an hour or so, my head bowed. My eyes swam in tears as I faced my wife and children and saw the questions on their faces and felt the shock and bewilderment that kept them from speaking.

I decided then to leave the service after this catastrophe. My feeling was that my generation had to make way for future generations better able to serve the armed forces and raise the flag high once more. When I told my family that I was thinking of this, my youngest daughter burst into tears, crying, "No, no, no."

On my return to headquarters, where like my colleagues I lived and worked, I handed in my resignation. According to the rules, I had to continue service until it was accepted.

Fate would have it that my despair was brought to a head with the death of my father in our village—al-Batanun—in Manufiya governorate. This was the climax to a disastrous month and a miserable year. I left for the village still in uniform to attend the funeral, after which I came immediately back to Cairo.

AHMAD ISMA'IL IS APPOINTED COMMANDER

The darkness in which we had found ourselves began to recede. Major General Ahmad Isma'il was returned to the service and appointed commander of the eastern military zone (the Suez Canal front), to replace Lieutenant General Salah Muhsin. This was the command from which the Second Army and the Third Army were later to emerge. It was never made clear to me why Ahmad Isma'il had been retired and reinstated in such a short period of time.

Major General Isma'il came to see me in my office shortly after his appointment. He looked outwardly composed, but seemed to be holding back an inner dissatisfaction. We talked briefly of the need for a new start for both Egypt and the armed forces. He spoke of his new responsibilities at this difficult stage, then asked me to work with him as chief of staff of the canal front. We had successfully cooperated together before the war in the land forces' command.

I turned the offer down after thanking him. I explained that I had presented my resignation and was waiting for a reply to this. If it was not accepted, then he would surely find me with him at the canal front.

A few days later, the minister of war issued an official statement of my appointment as chief of staff for the front. I left to the canal zone by car, and on the way remembered the many instances in the Second World War when defeat was turned to success and victory. I thought of previous wars between Egypt and Israel and the Arab–Israeli conflict, the positive and the negative factors.

When I arrived at front command, I found Major General Isma'il seated on a field chair, under some trees. He was alone, and had a collection of maps spread out on a rough table in front of him. Command officers were busy elsewhere on various assignments in the dugouts and trenches.

Our eyes met; we were both very moved. We sat together talking for a while, reviewing the military situation, analyzing and forecasting, discussing how the forces could be speedily reconstructed to face an arrogant enemy, conceited by a victory won as a result of our own mistakes, and not because of any special military accomplishment.

A couple of months later, I finally received a reply to my resignation. It had been refused.

FIELD MARSHAL 'AMER'S SUICIDE

One evening as I was reviewing as usual the day's events with Major General Isma'il, the phone rang just as we were about to retire to our bunkers. It was General Fawzi from Cairo, and he was calling to tell us that Field Marshal 'Amer had committed suicide at his home. He had taken a potent poison hidden on his body beneath his underclothes. The medical examination had been undertaken at a very high level by a special medical committee. He said the suicide would be treated like any other, and his body would be turned over to his family. This meant that there would be no ceremony whatsoever at his funeral and burial.

Major General Isma'il and myself discussed the potential reaction this could have among the troops, and came to the conclusion that it would be minimal. The loss of Sinai, the death of thousands of men, and the role played by the field marshal in the defeat were too fresh in their memories for the reaction to be otherwise.

The report on the suicide from the public prosecutor's office was published on 10 October 1967. It said, "In view of the evidence, it is established that Field Marshal 'Amer took in his own knowledge and of his own free will a poisonous substance with the intention of committing suicide while he was at his home and among his family on 13 September 1967, by which he died the following day, and therein there is no legal crime. We therefore ask for this to be registered and filed."

This was the fate of Field Marshal 'Amer, who had held the rank of major when the revolution came about on 23 July 1952, was promoted to major general in less than a year, and became commander in chief of the armed forces in June 1953. Less than five years later, in February 1958, he was promoted to the rank of field marshal and became deputy supreme commander of the armed forces.

THE TRIAL OF SHAMS BADRAN

Minister of War Shams Badran was tried and in February 1968 was asked by the presiding judge what in his opinion were the reasons for the June defeat. Badran replied,

> As the situation developed, we found that we had to get rid of the international police (the UN peacekeeping forces) to show that we were ready to attack. . . . They pulled out and we went into Sharm al-Shaykh, then closed the Gulf of 'Aqaba.
>
> The opinion was that our army was ready to carry out operations against Israel. We were 100 percent sure that Israel would not dare to attack or take a first step or the initiative for a first strike. Any action by Israel would mean a suicidal operation because it was certain to be defeated.

When the court asked his opinion on Nasir's decision to close the Gulf of 'Aqaba following the green light from the commander of the forces, Badran said, "The commander in chief [Field Marshal 'Amer], gave the OK, saying he could back it up. But later, implementation was difficult."

Commenting on this, the presiding judge said, "Frankly, if matters are conducted in this way and evaluated on this kind of a basis, with no responsibility for the words spoken and the actions undertaken, then we deserve what has happened to us."

6

Lessons From the June War

When the firing had stopped and this third round between Arabs and Israelis had come to an end, Israel was at an advantage, with major political, military, and economic gains and a tremendous boost in morale. The Arabs had lost on nearly all fronts.

Israel had occupied Sinai, which was later liberated through a peace treaty between Egypt and Israel. The Golan Heights, the West Bank of the Jordan River, and the Gaza Strip are still occupied by Israel. It used these cards, with some help from the United States, to impose a peace. Twenty-six years later, the Arabs are still living under the pressure of some of the war's consequences, especially the Palestinians after many years of occupation in what remained of their land, including the West Bank and Gaza. Today, in 1993, the United States and Russia are making efforts in an international peace conference, held in the United States, to find a solution to the Palestinian question and the Golan Heights.

Israel, as a result of this war, was in a stronger strategic position militarily. It felt confident that it was more powerful than the Arab states, and this gave it the impetus to impose the fait accompli and draw maximum political advantage from the war. Its forces, in positions on the new lines of the Suez Canal in the south, the Jordan River in the east, and the Syrian Golan Heights in the north, could follow a strong defensive strategy using a limited number of men while at the same time making it virtually impossible for an Arab attack to succeed. On the other hand, Israel was in a position of advantage from which to attack neighboring Arab countries.

Israel had been in recession, and the war gave its economy a powerful push. We might remember that the deputy speaker of the Knesset, Arieh Ben Eliazer, had said in a speech on 10 May 1967 that "Israel is about to celebrate the creation of the state when there are 250,000 Israeli citizens who have been forced to leave this country for want of a job because life has become unbearable without an income. . . . " Such were the consequences of the economic situation in Israel before the war, but this was to change radically afterwards.

Morale was high and Israel felt absolutely certain of its military might; its senior officers were confident to the point of arrogance and conceit.

For the Arabs it was a catastrophe, with more land lost and long years needed to rebuild armies and regain political credibility in a world which looked at them with pity after a defeat which had split and humiliated them.

The truth is that the defeat was rejected. It was never accepted by the Arabs, who refused to submit politically to Israel. They came to believe instead that the land which had been taken by force of arms could only be regained by force of arms, and committed themselves to a military struggle to return the lost territories to their rightful owners. This policy was clearly stated in the Khartoum summit conference of 1967: "No negotiations, no peace, no recognition of Israel." Egypt, Syria, and Jordan began to rebuild their armed forces, intending to make the price of occupying Arab land a high one.

On the international level, we can say that the outcome of the war in this strategically important region represented a political victory for the United States and a defeat for the Soviets in their struggle for influence. Each began to refashion strategy to suit the new circumstances in the Middle East. The region had already witnessed a struggle between the great powers in the fifties and early sixties with the gradual decline of Western influence and an increase in the influence of the Eastern bloc. Then came June 1967 and a settling of accounts with President Nasir after he had become a national hero and a symbol of defiance to the West.

As a result of the war, Egypt, Syria, and Jordan became vulnerable to pressure from the United States, which was a firm friend of Israel, providing both political and military assistance to keep it ahead of the Arabs militarily. Together, Israel and the United States worked at consolidating the 'facts' which had been created on the ground. In the long term, this was to the United States' advantage in that having the upper hand meant creating a peace which would serve its interests in the region and diminish Soviet influence.

The reasons for the defeat have to be carefully studied in Egypt for useful lessons. We lost Sinai and Gaza. Over 9,800 men died or were missing in action. The greater part of our weapons and equipment was lost. The economy was hit very hard and the people had to bear the brunt of the burden.

In more detail, we lost 17 percent of the land forces and 4 percent of our pilots; 85 percent of the equipment was lost to the air force, air defense, and army. The air force lost 85 percent of its fighters and all of its bombers. The volume of losses betrays the immensity of the disaster. Objectively, the defeat was the natural outcome of many mistakes which had added up since the Tripartite Aggression in 1956. It was an outcome of the separation of Syria from Egypt in 1961 and its consequences. It was an outcome of the 1962 war in Yemen which lasted for five years. It came from the absence of effective state organizations for defense. It came from shortcomings and confusion in the command and control of the armed forces.

A Higher National Strategy

The escalation of the crisis with Israel during 1967 took place without due consideration of great power rivalries and their struggle for strategic advantage in the region. It was natural that the United States, with the support of some Western European countries, would try to limit the growth of Arab nationalism, reject the idea of Arab unity, attempt to confine Egypt's influence within its borders, and undermine President Nasir and his system of government. Nasir was a major actor in the events of the region and his influence was effective and visible. This the United States and some in Europe believed to be contrary to their interests.

Similarly, within this broader framework, the escalation in May 1967 of Syria, Jordan, and Egypt on the one hand, and Israel on the other, took no account of consequences or timing. For Egypt, the timing was inappropriate for war and it was for this reason that Israel, in coordination with the United States, carefully planned all its political moves to provoke a war.

Probably the most significant weakness was the lack of a higher strategy of state which would have identified political goals and balanced these against the available military, economic, and social capabilities.

Three major political actions were taken: the concentration of troops in Sinai, the withdrawal of the international peace forces, and the closure of the Straits of Tiran to Israeli navigation without consultation with the armed forces general command, despite the fact that President 'Abd al-Nasir had in May 1967 foreseen that the closure of the straits would certainly lead to war. If we analyze events in May and June, we come to the conclusion that the political leadership in Egypt had tried a political bluff and supported it with a demonstration of military power for political gain. The situation developed into a real war for which Egypt was not prepared. The use of a military threat to support a political strategy is not uncommon, but the military side of the operation must be well-planned and capable of genuinely enforcing the political decision. War is after all an extension of politics by force of arms. The truth is that the political leadership was progressively lured into a war for which the Israelis had been preparing for a long time.

For a military strategy to fulfill its purpose, that purpose must first be identified within the context of an overall political goal. A political decision for war inevitably depends on military capability as well as on political, economic, and psychological preparation. The armed forces were wrongly estimated to be prepared for war. On this judgment, the decision to close the Straits of Tiran was wrongly taken, as was the hasty decision to push the armed forces into a war. The consequences were not calculated. Could there have been any worse an evaluation than that given by Shams Badran, when at his trial he said that the opinion was that an operation by Israel would be suicidal and would meet with certain defeat?

My opinion is that there was no higher strategy of state when the crisis began in May 1967. This can be attributed to the absence of an organization with the specific purpose of defending the state. The defense of a state—any state—cannot be entrusted to one person because of the complexities involved in preparing for a war.

From a military perspective, the armed forces must be equipped with plans, fighting competence, weaponry appropriate to the operation, etc. These needs are identified through specialized services and organizations and cannot be left to the judgment of one man. Every country, east or west, has developed its own system to provide for this and all of them have a specialized body responsible for this work.

In Egypt, the National Defense Council was created for the defense of the state. It never met in May or in June and consequently was not able to contribute its specialized services or suggest alternatives and options. The outcome was a strategic vacuum in the face of political and military developments. For all practical purposes, politics were directed and administered by the head of state, President Nasir, alone. Military strategy became the domain of the deputy supreme commander, Field Marshal 'Abd al-Hakim 'Amer, who directed and administered matters on his own, a dangerous precedent for the security of the state.

Given that the National Defense Council did not meet during the crisis and the subsequent war, it was still essential for the cabinet of ministers to meet in a situation where political choices could lead to war. In fact, the cabinet should have remained in continuous session to follow developments throughout the war and to provide the necessary political guidance.

If either the National Defense Council or the cabinet, or both, had met, this would surely have averted faulty political decisions from the start. It would certainly have prevented the withdrawal from Sinai.

In my mind, the first lesson of the June 1967 war was the need for a higher strategy of state to define a program of national goals. From this master plan would have come well-considered and coordinated political, military, economic, and social policies.

State defense and matters related to this are a primary concern, as 1967 demonstrated. A National Defense Council should by law and constitutionally be responsible for this. It should be mandatory to convene this body in times of national crisis, and the council should remain in permanent session from the moment a mobilization is proclaimed.

Command and Control of the Armed Forces

A second lesson from the war was the need to identify the shortcomings in the system of command and control of the armed forces, which at the time was a major factor contributing to the defeat. A system of control had gradually evolved with the appointment of Major 'Abd al-Hakim 'Amer as commander in chief, his promotion to field marshal in June 1953, and finally when he was given the title of deputy supreme commander, becoming more and more autocratic with time. The armed forces now fell outside of the normal executive framework of the state, and this was exacerbated by the absence of a national defense council or any other such body responsible for state defense. Executive power became centered in the hands of one individual, Field Marshal 'Amer, and the president of the republic (the supreme commander) became increasingly distanced from the armed forces. A national military strategy did not exist.

Another characteristic was the distribution of responsibility between two unequal bodies, the general staff of the armed forces and the office for general affairs of the deputy supreme commander, which later was named the Ministry of War, without recourse to any system or principal or reference to examples from other countries, west or east.

'Abd al-Hakim 'Amer had been appointed commander in chief as way to safeguard the revolution in its early stages. The political victory in the Tripartite Aggression of 1956 encouraged a reliance on politics and drew attention away from our military deficiencies and their causes. The armed forces exploited this political success in the worst possible way, using it as a cover for irresponsible and negligent behavior. Many imagined that victory could be achieved by methods other than armed struggle.

The command began to neglect its responsibilities. Training, discipline, and preparations for war were abandoned for other interests up until the June 1967 defeat, which swept away military man and politician alike in its wake.

Colonel Shams Badran ran the Ministry of War. He had been Field Marshal 'Amer's bureau chief before taking on this position. The minister gave very little of his time to field operations and war. This would have required too much specialized effort and knowledge. Instead, he tightened his grip on the armed forces by controlling appointments and promotions, medical services, retirement, and paying special attention to security matters and political 'guidance.' Decrees were issued dividing power and responsibility between Field Marshal 'Amer and Minister of War Badran. Consequently, general command functions became fragmented and this had serious repercussions on the capabilities of the armed forces.

General command was made responsible for training, planning, and operations while the Ministry of War became responsible for appointing and/or promoting those officers assigned to carry out the training exercises or implementing plans. The Ministry of War took charge of reconnaissance, a cornerstone of strategic planning requiring high precision and accuracy. This now became dependent on information from the ministry. The Ministry of War alone became responsible for morale, while the general command remained in charge of combat training, despite the close link between moral and combat training.

Then came security considerations which were manipulated by the ministry to obstruct the general command in the performance of its duty, namely the training and preparation of the armed forces for war. The two bodies were now issuing conflicting instructions and it was natural that security took priority. In fact, security was a subject which preoccupied both Field Marshal 'Amer and Minister of War Badran.

Field Marshal 'Amer neglected his principal duties. He had no time to spare for building up the forces, for planning operations, or for training exercises. These needed proper military thinking and a commitment to responsible follow-up. It was only during the May crisis and the June War that it became obvious that he was ignorant of his own forces' strength and capabilities and knew even less about those of his enemy. As for Shams Badran, he had no role to play either during the crisis or in the war.

The net result of this system of command and control was that the armed forces went to war without a military strategy, without a proper operations plan, and failed in their operations.

AN HONEST WORD

There are many reasons for the political and military defeat, and we need only to look at events as they unfolded between the crisis in May and the end of military operations in June to find them. I have focused on two major failings which I consider important enough to provide a lesson and a warning for the future: the matter of state defense and the control and command over and within the armed forces. These are areas which require good planning and meticulous execution.

The truth is that the difficult circumstances confronting the armed forces—indeed, into which they had been placed—were the natural outcome of ten years of accumulated political and military errors.

Following the Tripartite Aggression on Egypt in 1956, it was necessary to analyze this war and to draw practical lessons. This was not done. The record of military operations for 1956 was only published in 1969, thirteen years later. This war had exposed 'Abd al-Hakim 'Amer's inadequacies and his inability to command operations. The normal response would have been to place the command in the hands of a professional soldier rather than leave it with a political man whose system of command was based on security considerations. This was not done and 'Amer was promoted the following year (1958) to the rank of field marshal. Furthermore, the performance of other commanders and senior officers should have been reviewed. It was unacceptable to allow Lieutenant General Sidqi Mahmud to continue to head the air force after it had been destroyed on the ground in 1956. It was destroyed once again in 1967 when the air force was still under his command. The mistake was President Nasir's, who had both the constitutional authority and the right to make changes in the command structure.

Field Marshal 'Amer's military shortcomings and blunders preceded the breakup of the union between Syria and Egypt. The military revolt took place during his presence in Damascus with the participation of his senior Syrian aide and bureau chief. President Nasir then had the opportunity to replace 'Amer with a more capable military professional, but a massive struggle for power had developed between them which was to continue until the June War. Even then, President Nasir did nothing until after the defeat.

Testifying before the Committee for the Historical Record, General Muhammad Fawzi, then armed forces commander in chief, replied to questions about Field Marshal 'Amer in the following way.

> *Question:* "What were the responsibilities of Field Marshal 'Amer, deputy supreme commander, towards the supreme commander, the president of the republic?"
>
> *Answer:* "There were no responsibilities."
>
> *Question:* "What were Field Marshal "Amer's responsibilities towards the legislature [the National Assembly] at that time?"
>
> *Answer:* "There were no responsibilities."

Then General Fawzi added:

> At the time, no one in the country could question 'Abd al-Hakim 'Amer. The president of the republic could not do so, and the National Assembly could not invite him to take the executive seat in the assembly, and answer any questions put to him. This of course never happened. . . . The armed forces were under the command and control of one individual who was answerable to no one.

With regard to Shams Badran, minister of war at the time, he had been a key figure in the Free Officer's Movement, which is why he had been made head of 'Amer's bureau. He was very close to 'Amer, thereby acquiring extensive power in the armed forces, but his military education and his experience in the field were not adequate for the task given him. Since July 1952, when he had held the rank of captain, he had not attended a single course of military study, if only to keep up with developments, and his knowledge remained limited. He could not be expected to be of active help in technical or related activities such as training, combat preparation, or planning.

General Muhammad Fawzi came third in the chain of command, after Field Marshal 'Amer and Shams Badran. His testimony following the June War has shed some light on the factors of the defeat. Among other things, he has said:

• All commanders of the armed forces—myself included as chief of staff—were removed from the political discourse which shapes a military strategy. The reason for this complete break lies at the most senior level of political and military leadership [Nasir and 'Amer]. There was a divergence of thought between the political leadership and the military leadership and the armed forces as one of the institutions of the state.

• Following the separation from Syria on 29 September 1961, a powerful struggle began to take place. President Nasir put the blame on Field Marshal 'Amer, but this was never openly acknowledged, nor was it widely known. The conflict between them can be traced back to this point.

• The creation of a National Defense Council was just ink on paper even though it was the only body constitutionally responsible for decisions on state defense. The Ministry of War was next in line, and was headed by Field Marshal 'Amer . . . but Field Marshal 'Amer did not create a body which could follow up and implement council decisions and recommendations, and no guidelines were issued to the armed forces general command. All these activities were in the hands of one person.

• Field Marshal 'Amer cut himself and the armed forces off from the government, taking over all of the authority without a state agency for national defense. That is why no national strategy or state policy was ever formulated.

• The armed forces became involved in land reclamation, housing, the national transport system, state security, the Aswan High Dam, and many other activities. Their agents could be found in the administration of most of these organizations, representing the field marshal and Shams. . . . For the record, I would like to repeat that the growing power and presence of the armed forces in civilian life was detrimental to its main responsibility, which was to be a fighting force, ready for battle.

• If we are to say that the two revolutionary leaders heading the state politically and militarily—that is, President Nasir and Field Marshal 'Amer—were united in spirit and in nationalism, then we must also say that they were rivals and competing for control of the armed forces.

• There was no solidarity between the Arabs and consequently no united policy views on the enemy . . . no meeting of minds on the issue—even between two countries when matters were concluded with bilateral agreements there was no real united front, as we can see from the agreements between Egypt and Syria, Egypt and Iraq, Egypt and Jordan, and Egypt and Yemen. For the Arab nation, 'bilateral' does not have the same power as 'united,' stopping short, as it does, at coordination. And let me point out that coordination plus distrust equals nothing.

In this context, a joint defense agreement was signed with Syria in 1966. Trust was nonexistent, but despite this, the agreement was concluded. In my opinion, this was not a military agreement but the expression of a political emotion, if that. . . . There was no mutual trust between the armed forces, and there was no unified command for both. Each acted independently because of the lack of trust.

• Preparing a country for war falls under the jurisdiction of the National Defense Council. According to the constitution, it is chaired by the president of the republic. This was not to be. Neither did there exist a collective council or body to follow up and implement council decisions. Nor was there a supreme council headed by the minister of war.

We had no consensus on how to prepare the country for war. . . . How could we begin to talk of preparations when the two principal bodies for this did not exist in our country? How could the leadership dare threaten to initiate or pretend to be able to carry out acts of aggression against another country?

The records and documents will eventually give us the details on the long years of negligence suffered by the armed forces before the June 1967 war. Then historic responsibility for the political and military defeat will become clearer.

It is obvious, however, that President Nasir carried the burden of the bitterness of those critical days when he came to realize that whatever the reasons or mistakes, he alone bore the historic responsibility for the defeat.

I have found no truer words than these of President Sadat, spoken to the People's Assembly on 16 October, during the October War of 1973: "There is no doubt in my mind that our armed forces were among the victims of the 1967 defeat, and not one of the reasons for it. The forces were not given a chance to fight, to defend the homeland, its honor, and its soil. They were not defeated by the enemy but overpowered by conditions which did not give them the opportunity to fight."

Part II

SIX LEAN YEARS

What was taken by force can only be recovered by force.

—Gamal 'Abd al-Nasir

7

Rebuilding the Armed Forces

Shortly after my conversation with Major General Ahmad Isma'il, who had just been appointed commander of the Suez Canal front (extending from Port Said in the north to Suez in the south), a decree was issued appointing me chief of staff for the front.

I left Cairo for the canal zone and, driving along in the jeep, thought of the Second World War when some armies were at first defeated but were later able to rebuild their forces and triumph.

I focused my attention on the mistakes which had led to the 1967 June defeat with all its bitter consequences. Israel had completed its occupation of whatever remained of Palestinian land—the West Bank and the Gaza Strip—and had taken the Sinai Peninsula and the Golan Heights. The Arab countries, which had had to deal with a Palestinian 'problem' since the establishment of the state of Israel, now found themselves having to face Israel's occupation of the rest of Palestine and a new occupation of Egyptian and Syrian territory.

As I walked into the front command, I found Major General Ahmad Isma'il seated on a stool looking at maps in front of him. Command officers were at work in trenches and dugouts.

As our eyes met, our feelings rose. We sat together and discussed the military situation on the front and forecasts on enemy action and intentions. We agreed on the need to speed up reconstruction and training. We had to be able to face an enemy which was conscious of its military superiority and victorious in a war it thought had put an end to all wars, that is, a war which had left the Arabs with no option but to surrender.

Egypt had to respond to this situation with sound political and military principles that had to be developed to deal with the hard times ahead. Israel obviously intended to remain indefinitely in the Arab territories occupied in June, and was politically backed by the United States.

And so we began to move into a new stage of action which required Egyptian and Arab commitment and preparation for the inevitable battle to regain our land and our rights. We had to concentrate on reorganizing and rebuilding our armed forces and to set ourselves the task of "total dedication to the defense of Egypt's soil and the liberation of the occupied lands," on the principle that "what was taken by force could only be recovered by force."

The starting point—immediately after the June War—was to rebuild the armed forces. The forces had lost not only the greater part of their weapons and equipment but also any confidence in their leadership, and they were very demoralized. The population had also lost confidence after Israel had occupied Sinai and raised its flag on the east bank of the canal, much to our humiliation. Furthermore, our forces on the west bank of the canal were neither sufficiently organized nor adequately equipped to defend it nor, ultimately, to defend the country.

The process of rebuilding our forces had to take place in exceptionally difficult conditions given the shock of defeat on the army and the people. The military command, the backbone of the armed forces, was tackled first. Nasir relieved Field Marshal 'Amer of his duties and appointed General Muhammad Fawzi commander in chief in his place. Lieutenant General 'Abd al-Mun'im Riyad was appointed chief of staff. Commanders of the air, naval, and land forces were relieved of their duties and new men with proven records replaced them. This new leadership started immediately to apply the lessons learned from the June War to build a new army.

The choice of General Fawzi and Lieutenant General 'Abd al-Mun'im Riyad was opportune. General Fawzi was a strict disciplinarian to the point of cruelty, a much-needed quality at this bleak time when military discipline had collapsed as a result of the war in Yemen, the heavy involvement of the armed forces in non-military activities, and the June War. On the other hand, 'Abd al-Mun'im Riyad had both extensive military experience and the broad strategic vision needed for the creation of sound policies. In other words, the two men complemented each other in the task of rebuilding and upgrading the combat ability of the forces.

Naturally enough, reconstruction involved healing the psychological wounds. The forces had been made to bear the brunt of the defeat, although they too were victims of a situation rather than its cause. The buildup of the mens' morale and confidence was among the hardest and most important tasks for the new military leadership after the war, but general command had a firm belief that with determination and high morale they could recover what they had lost and rebuild what the war had destroyed.

DEFINING COMMAND AND CONTROL

The next step in the process of rebuilding the armed forces was the issuing of a new law defining the command and control of state defense affairs and the armed forces. This also aimed at correcting an imbalance that had existed prior to the June War and which was a major cause of the defeat.

Chief among the causes of the 1967 political and military defeat had been the lack of a clear definition of the authority of the president over the armed forces. Consequently, his ability to exercise any influence over them was limited. Effective authority was in the hands of the deputy supreme commander, Field Marshal 'Amer.

Another reason for the defeat lay in the division of responsibility between two unequal bodies, namely the armed forces general staff and the deputy supreme commander's office for general affairs. The latter had been transformed—without due thought or consideration—into the Ministry of War just before war broke out, an unprecedented step in the experience of both western and eastern countries.

It had become imperative to reconsider the system of command and control over the armed forces after the 1956 Tripartite Aggression, and to appoint a professional military leadership capable of handling responsibilities starting from the level of general commander through to all command levels of the land, naval, and air forces. However, this was not done. Indifference and irresponsibility became the order of the day with regard to military planning, training, organization, and discipline, the command choosing instead to turn to marginal concerns. Consequently, when the June War broke out, the result was a wide-scale defeat.

Despite the overriding importance of preparing the country for war and despite the fact that this matter lies within the jurisdiction of the

National Defense Council—which never exercised its prerogative—a grave flaw in the organizational structure of defense affairs led to the failure to prepare for war or to put the armed forces on a war footing.

Accordingly, a new law was drawn up to define responsibilities and competencies, notably those of the National Defense Council, the Supreme Council of the Armed Forces, and the armed forces command. The task was assigned to the minister of war who became, by virtue of his position, the general commander in chief. The post of deputy supreme commander was abolished given that the reasons and circumstances which had led to the creation of this post had ceased to exist.

Thus matters proceeded, and the new chosen path eventually led to the realization of our national objectives and our readiness for war.

Before the June War, we had three commands each for the land, naval, and air force (which was also in charge of air defense). The commands tended to be isolated and independent of each other, each hoping to increase its influence and authority under a weak general command. This attitude had effectively prevented the spirit of cooperation and the teamwork required, and its reform was handled with some rigor so that the general command came to be the central authority for all the branches of the armed forces, and able once more to concentrate its efforts on one objective: the armed conflict with Israel. In this way, correct military practice which had in fact prevailed before the June War was restored, and the armed forces were reorganized in a new spirit.

After analyzing both the enemy's capabilities and our own, it was decided to set up a new and separate air defense force given Israel's air supremacy, which was expected to continue for some years. This meant that air force command needed to restructure its organization, reassess its weapons and its training for combat, and review its equipment needs. We now had two bodies operating against the Israeli air force and this proved successful in the October 1973 war, when the air defense force performed remarkably well in the face of Israel's principal strike force—its air force—in close cooperation with the air force. It also became imperative to recall our troops from Yemen after a five-year war; we now needed these forces in Egypt, and at the same time their presence in Yemen became incompatible with Egypt's new policy of cooperation with the Arab states—particularly with Saudi Arabia. The question of Yemen was finally settled and Egyptian forces started gradually withdrawing, thereby removing the tension in Egyptian–Saudi relations.

MILITARY PROFESSIONALISM

The third major step in the reconstruction process was to end the participation of the armed forces in civil works. Officers working in non-military sectors either reverted to their military posts or took on permanent civilian posts. Non-combat units entrusted with civil works which lay within the jurisdiction of various ministries were removed. In this way, the armed forces were shaped into a professional organization dedicated exclusively to military activities.

This was one of the most useful and effective steps taken by the political and military leadership at that stage. The armed forces supreme command had embarked on civil works to such an extent that at one point, Field Marshal 'Amer headed a 'Committee for the Liquidation of the Wealth of Land-Owning Classes' at a time when he should have devoted himself entirely to military matters in his capacity as general commander of the armed forces. Within the framework of the new policy, decrees were issued transferring guards on customs duty to the Ministry of the Interior and the supply control units to the Ministry of Supply. The decrees also canceled the 'agriculture units,' which comprised more than three brigades with their officers, men, and vehicles and which had been assigned to cultivate fifty thousand feddans in al-Tahrir province. The job was transferred to the Ministry of Agriculture. The public transport units in Cairo, which used men and material from the military vehicles section and the military police, were canceled and services reverted to the Public Transport Authority.

One of the major reforms during this period was the reorientation of all military intelligence operations back to their principal task of collecting and analyzing data on the enemy. National security, a major concern before the June War, had been given minimum attention and intelligence had been used to protect the armed forces from espionage and to implement measures taken for military security. In this respect it must be stressed that intelligence was a weak point before the June 1967 war; it became a point of strength after reform following the war and a factor in the victory of October 1973.

As for military discipline, this was re-established according to normal practice. It had been totally missing before the June War. There is no doubt that restoring an authentic military 'spirit' helped develop precise, efficient, and timely performance and behavior. This was subsequently very noticeable in all activities and on the canal front in particular.

Weapons

Re-arming was important at this stage. The Soviet Union was the main source of arms supplies to Egypt and without them we could not have rebuilt our forces. They wasted no time in providing Egypt with arms and equipment to make up for what was lost in the June War. Arms were transported to Egypt by air and sea, and priority was given to aircraft and air defense weapons. Artillery, tanks, and other equipment to boost the defenses of the canal zone ranked next in priority.

On the canal front, we were eagerly looking forward to the arrival of much-needed supplies to enhance our defensive capabilities. When weapons began to reach the front, training on them immediately took place at a time when our forces were in defensive positions and were engaging with the enemy on the eastern side of the canal. It should be said, in the interest of truth, that these activities were conducted in a spirit of great cooperation, which gradually boosted and helped to restore self-confidence in the military command.

A large Soviet military delegation led by General Lashinkof arrived in Egypt during June 1967 to help reorganize, arm, and train the armed forces. This marked the beginning of the stream of Soviet 'experts' (later redesignated 'advisors') to be posted with units, formations, and commands. It is worth mentioning that the advisors headed by Lashinkof were highly efficient and experienced and were held in high esteem.

On 21 June 1967, Soviet Chairman Podgorny arrived in Egypt accompanied by a second military delegation headed by Soviet Chief of Staff Marshal Zakharof. This was an expression of political support for Egypt. Arms and equipment needs were discussed, and Marshal Zakharof stayed in Egypt for almost a month.

Mahmud Riyad, then foreign minister, has reported the following on the Nasir–Podgorny talks:

> The following day—22 June 1967—talks started with the participation of Marshal Zakharof and the Soviet ambassador to Cairo. Attending with Nasir were Zakaria Muhi al-Din, 'Ali Sabri, General Muhammad Fawzi, and myself.
>
> The importance of the first session of official talks lies in the fact that it marked the beginning of a new stage in Egyptian–Soviet relations and later led to a strong Soviet presence not only in Egypt but in other parts of the Arab world. Consequently, this led to a gradual change in Egypt's policy of non-alignment. The Soviet

presence increased as the United States continued to support the Israeli military occupation. During his talks with Podgorny on 22–23 June 1967, Nasir asked for military parity between Egypt and Israel. This would require reinforcing the armed forces and a new supply of arms and Soviet expertise, especially for air defense. Nasir explained that the June War had severely shaken the forces' confidence and that it was imperative to replace lost weaponry. This would certainly raise the morale of the officers and the men.

As for the air force, Nasir explained that following the battle, twenty-five MiG-21s and ninety-three MiG-17s had been received. Agreement had also been reached on the dispatch of forty MiG-21 planes. Technically, MiGs had a shorter range than the Mirage and the Mystere aircraft which Israel possessed. From bases inside Israel, these could reach as far as Marsa Matruh and strike deep into Egyptian territory while we were unable to do likewise. Nasir asked for a new type of long-range fighter–bomber with which to face Israel's superiority and strike back. He also requested an urgent dispatch, by air, of a number of MiG-21 fighters for the defense of Egypt, as we had pilots but no planes.

As for air defense, Nasir preferred to build this up within the framework of a joint Egyptian–Soviet defense system, thereby providing our officers and our men with direct experience from the Soviet cadres. Podgorny, however, was of the view that it was more appropriate to have an Egyptian air defense with some Soviet aid.

Expanding on Egypt's position at this critical stage, Nasir also said, 'Egypt faced an aggression in 1956 and once again in 1967 because the West considers us aligned to the Eastern bloc because of our refusal to fall into the orbit of US policy. Our foreign policy has been prompted by our commitment to non-alignment. But now we find Israel attacking us and occupying our land in collusion with the United States. During the war, people in Egypt were asking, 'Where are our Soviet friends?'

'Obviously, you could not have cooperated with us militarily before concluding an agreement on the necessary military arrangements. I know that such an agreement would antagonize the US side even further but I'm also well aware that the United States has sided with Israel in the Security Council and has rejected any draft resolution requiring Israel to return to the 4 June lines. I also know that the United States will continue with its aggressive policy against us in the near future.

'Therefore, it is illogical for Egypt to remain neutral either towards those who strike at us or towards those who help us. We want to deepen and consolidate Egyptian–Soviet cooperation with the priority of liquidating the consequences of the Israeli aggression on us.'

At this point Podgorny commented, 'It is difficult to find a country which is 100 percent non-aligned.' Nasir added, 'As we have asked you to be with us in times of war we must also be with you in war and in peace. We are facing hard times and we cannot overcome them alone. This time our struggle is to liberate our land by force of arms and we must reciprocate with the Soviet Union. We are ready to offer facilities for your ships from Port Said to al-Sallum. Naturally some people in Egypt will tell us, 'you got the British out through the door to let the Soviets in through the window.' But we have to put up with this to liberate our land.'

The outcome of the talks was visible in a Soviet response on 29 June welcoming the growing ties between the two countries, the increased military cooperation, and approving the dispatch of military advisors, including air defense experts, to Egypt. As for the question of non-alignment, the Soviet Union supported Egypt's decision to adopt policies which served the national interest. Foreign Minister Mahmud Riyad notes:

> This round of talks between Nasir and Podgorny in June was decisive in many ways. On his part, Nasir wanted to know where he stood so as to be able to remove the consequences of the aggression. For him, military considerations took top priority to the extent that our independence in foreign policy—for which Nasir had fought tremendous battles over long years—had to be adapted to fit the requirements of a new set of circumstances. The policy of non-alignment which he had championed along with Nehru and Tito had to be reviewed for the first time and perhaps sacrificed after we had seen the total US bias towards Israel.[1]

The armed forces started to receive arms and equipment from the Soviet Union. This had a tremendous impact on combat ability and morale.

Starting in 1968, new arms deals were concluded in the form of agreements and financial loans on easy terms. The agreements provided for a ten-year grace period. The installments were to be paid over many years with a low interest rate of about 2.5 percent. Egypt sought Soviet military advisors for training and for maintenance. Gradually, these advisors rose in number and were to be found in every command from the Ministry of War down to the level of the units themselves. Their presence in such large numbers created a sensitive situation, sometimes provoking friction and difference of opinion between the Egyptian commanders and their advisors. In these instances, however, discretion always prevailed. The fact remained that we needed their help in the years following the war, and they performed their military duties with efficiency and dedication.

Since Egypt was facing hard times, Nasir agreed to offer facilities to the Soviet fleet in the ports of Alexandria and Port Said. Consequently, the Soviet Union came to have a naval presence in the two ports. These facilities remained available to them during Sadat's time and with his approval.

On the canal front, we were well aware both of the efforts exerted by the political leadership and of the aid extended by the Soviet Union to rebuild the armed forces and to supply us with arms and equipment to reconstruct our defenses in the canal region. The results were clearly visible on the front and contributed daily to the defense effort and to troop combat readiness.

8

The Armed Struggle During the Buildup

While the armed forces were being rebuilt, planning for combat action proceeded at a rapid pace. The Supreme Council of the Armed Forces held frequent meetings to ensure coordinated action and policy agreement and to hear the views of senior commanding officers. Nasir made an enormous effort to speed up the reconstruction of the forces, and his meetings with the Supreme Council gave momentum to the process. He was remarkably well-informed on developments in all areas. Despite his many other preoccupations, he gave top priority to raising the forces' combat ability and refused to allow the front to remain quiescent.

The canal front was in a state of constant motion. We were concerned with the enemy's activities, movements, and intentions in Sinai. Training was the order of the day. Planning for defense or for engagement with the enemy never ceased. Our forces overcame the many difficulties facing them, one by one, and made intensive and forceful efforts towards the defense of the canal region. Faced with an enemy which was militarily superior, it was essential to continue to fight and to make Israel pay a high price for its continued occupation of Sinai. The day would come when it would be liberated by force.

We believed that our land would be restored only by the use of force against an enemy so sure of its own strength that its command had come to believe that the Arabs would not recover for many years. Some foreign specialists suggested that this would take a whole generation, basing their predictions on the performance in the June 1967 war—which did indeed demonstrate a decline in combat ability when compared to 1956. However, these military specialists had miscalculated, mainly because they had not analyzed in depth the factors behind the Israeli success and the reasons for the defeat of the Arab forces.

The armed struggle against Israel began with a stage of 'resistance.' Then, our forces moved into a stage we called 'active defense' and later fighting developed into what became known as the War of Attrition.

Resistance focused on a speedy reconstruction of the armed forces and the building of defensive fortifications on the west bank of the Suez Canal. This required a quiet front to allow for implementation, especially of the engineering and technical work. This stage of preparation extended from June 1967 to August 1968.

As for active defense, in the light of our growing arms supplies, it was decided that this should aim at activating the front to engage by fire with the enemy in order to restrict their movements to the front lines on the east bank of the canal. It also aimed at inflicting casualties and damaging equipment. This stage lasted from September 1968 to February 1969, when fighting escalated to a new stage, the War of Attrition, which aimed at inflicting maximum losses in life and equipment. The purpose was to demonstrate the high cost of staying in Sinai. It was also a practical and moral preparation for battle. This stage lasted from March 1969 to August 1970.

The fourth stage, which followed the ceasefire after the War of Attrition, was to prepare for full war and lasted from August 1970 to October 1973, during which time we drew up detailed plans to launch an attack, storm the Suez Canal, and destroy the Bar-Lev line on the east bank. At this time, we had completed all the training and preparation needed for the armed forces to accomplish their assigned tasks in the October War.

RESISTANCE

The UN Security Council's adoption of Resolution 234 on 8 June 1967 did not mean that the war was over. However, political and military conditions were not favorable for the resumption of fighting on the canal front. An initial period of resistance provided the political leadership with an opportunity to correct for the errors which had led to the defeat. It also provided the military leadership with the time needed to build defenses in the canal area as completely as the successive shipments of arms from the Soviet Union would allow.

During this period, radical changes were made in the armed forces leadership, including the appointment of Major General Ahmad Isma'il as commander of the canal front.

Action at this stage was limited to negative defense which meant keeping the front calm. Nevertheless, this stage witnessed a number of battles starting on the first day Major General Isma'il assumed command of the front, 1 July 1967. On that day, an Israeli force advanced north from the city of al-Qantara East, east of the canal, in the direction of Port Fuad, east of Port Said, with the intention of occupying it, as this was the only part of Sinai not occupied during the June War. Our forces repelled them in the battle of Ras al-'Ish.

The Battle of Ras al-'Ish

The Ras al-'Ish area, south of Port Fuad, was defended by a small Egyptian force of thirty men from a commando unit. The Israeli force—ten tanks backed by a mechanized infantry unit in half-tracks—launched an attack, but our men held fast to their position and managed to destroy three enemy tanks. The enemy launched a second attack but failed to penetrate the position, either head-on or by out-flanking it, with further losses in half-tracks and men.

The Israelis had to withdraw, and the Port Fuad sector remained the only part of Sinai under Egyptian control up to the outbreak of the October War. It was the first battle in which Egyptian fighters showed that despite the bitterness of defeat they had nevertheless not lost the will to fight with skill, hold their positions, and defend their land.

The Air Force in the Battle

Immediately following the battle at Ras al-'Ish, a squadron of Israeli fighters bombed the artillery positions on the west bank, which had supported the commandos with shelling.

Major General Ahmad Isma'il asked the general command in Cairo to respond with an air strike against the enemy. This would be a morale booster and also proof that we had not lost combat ability despite enemy air superiority. At front command, we were confident that our force, under Air Marshal Madkur Abu'l-'Izz, would perform well. On 14 July 1967 we were informed that ten Egyptian MiG-17 fighter–bombers supported by ten fighter aircraft had attacked enemy tank and armored vehicle concentrations in the southern sector of the front. Two Israeli planes were hit in the ensuing air battle. This was a practical response and a clear signal to Israel that our air force—with whatever means remaining to it after the June War—had not lost its combat ability. Another sortie took place on 15 July, when our pilots once again proved their battle mettle. Troop morale on the front rose correspondingly and the action had deep and positive repercussions at all levels.

During this period, Israel tried to take advantage of its access to the eastern half of the Suez Canal by launching small craft into the water, for so-called 'recreation activities.' Egypt would not allow this, given the hidden political agenda behind these activities, and orders were issued to fire on any craft or person in the canal waters.

We had left an ammunition depot behind in Sinai when our forces had withdrawn during the June War. A small contingent of men from the commandos crossed the canal by night and blew it up, starting a fire which lasted for three days and preventing the enemy from making use of the huge quantities of arms stockpiled there.

SINKING THE DESTROYER *EILAT*

On 21 October 1967 a third engagement, this time naval, took place. I arrived at the front command center after field leave to find Major General Ahmad Isma'il and Brigadier Hasan al-Geredli (head of front operations) following the movements of the Israeli destroyer *Eilat* close to Egyptian territorial waters, north of Port Said. The enemy destroyer would enter our territorial waters, stay for a while, then withdraw to sea, repeating this provocation several times in a transparent attempt to demonstrate that our naval forces would not confront it.

The commander of the naval forces ordered its destruction on re-entry into our territorial waters, and two launches armed with missiles were sent out from the base at Port Said. The first launch scored a direct hit and the destroyer started to tilt. A second missile sank the *Eilat* with all crew on board northeast of Port Said, one nautical mile inside Egyptian territorial water just after 5:00 P.M. on 21 October 1967.

The launches returned safely to base after an operation which had been carried out swiftly and efficiently and had achieved spectacular results. The sinking of the *Eilat* by two naval surface-to-surface missiles marked the beginning of a new stage in naval combat and weaponry. 21 October is duly observed as Egyptian Navy Day.

Israel informed the UN Observation Forces of its desire to send rescue planes for the men who had gone down with the destroyer. Egypt responded positively to this request, relayed through the UN forces, and abstained from interfering with the rescue operation, which was carried out at night using flares dropped from planes.

The three encounters—the land battle of Ras al-'Ish (1 July), the air engagements (14 and 15 July), and the naval engagement (21 October

1967)—were practical proof and evidence that all branches of our forces were willing and able to fight. This bore immediate fruit with our men. Morale rose at a time when circumstances were especially difficult; units were still in the process of reorganizing themselves and taking on defensive positions with very few weapons available. The defensive lines west of the canal had not been completed yet.

The three engagements had been sparked off by aggressive acts from an enemy consumed with arrogance. The success of the engagements in lifting the spirits and confidence of our forces was far greater than any material success they may have scored.

Escalation of Military Action

In response to the sinking of the destroyer *Eilat*, Israel shelled the oil refineries and depots in Suez on 24 October, using artillery concentrated east of the canal in the southern sector of the front line. The depots caught fire and we lost about 60 percent of the oil stored there. We did not at that time have the capability to fire back or to silence enemy artillery. After this incident, the government promptly moved the oil refineries and depots to other areas deep inside the country.

In this respect, we note that Egypt had acted against an Israeli military target—the destroyer *Eilat*—which had violated our territorial waters. Egypt had also allowed the subsequent rescue operations to proceed undisturbed. Israel's response was to strike at a civilian target when Egyptian military targets west of the canal were within range of its artillery.

The Israeli mentality appeared to condone the bombing of civilian targets, despite its pretense of being a victim of the Arabs, whom it claimed hit at its civilian population. And in a subsequent exchange of fire, Israel shelled the cities of Isma'iliya and Suez for a second time, directing its fire at civilians although military targets were within its firing range. Its purpose seems to have been to put the Egyptian government under the pressure of the daily losses sustained by its citizens to force it to stop the firing. But Egypt decided instead to move over a million citizens away from the cities and villages in the canal region, especially from Suez, Isma'iliya, and Port Said, for there to be no constraints on the forces at the front.

We witnessed the evacuation, which was jointly coordinated by a number of government bodies and organizations. It was painful to watch. The people of this region had suffered immensely from repeated Israeli aggressions before and after its establishment as a state. The population of the canal zone had shown the kind of courage, forbearance, and patriotism which words cannot describe.

After the evacuation of the canal zone, our forces resumed the bombing of enemy positions in response to repeated aggressions. We meant to send a signal to Israel that we—the people and the army—were determined to continue fighting until the results of its aggression were erased.

Israel then turned to hitting barrages and dams in Upper Egypt, hoping to draw attention away from the canal front and divide Egypt's military efforts. We responded by setting up 'popular defense organizations' made up of local squadrons and battalions to defend vital targets inside the country.

Mahmud Riyad, in his memoirs, describes international reactions to these events in New York, where he was attending consultations on UN Security Council Resolution 242.

> From the very beginning, members of some delegations expressed their surprise to me at our determination to resist following the tremendous military defeat. But gradually their surprise turned to admiration as the resistance we put up became visible in the practical results achieved on the battlefield. Our forces sank the *Eilat,* and on 21 October Israel retaliated by bombing oil refineries and civilians. Accordingly, Egypt decided to evacuate the entire canal zone population so that they would not remain pawns to Israeli blackmail. On that very day, the United States announced its decision to deliver another batch of bombers to Israel. This was further evidence of how far the United States was willing to go to confirm the Israeli occupation and to condone barbaric acts.
>
> All these developments influenced the turn of events at the Security Council in November. They were a radical factor in transforming Israel's image in the eyes of the international community. After posing as the 'meek lamb' surrounded by Arab 'wolves,' the image was reversed. The wild beast was obviously Israel which had occupied the lands of three Arab countries and bombarded civilian targets, while it was the Arabs who were fighting a war of liberation, determined not to surrender to Israel's terms.

Political Action in the Resistance Period

Egyptian and Arab political efforts began to face a deteriorating situation began after the June War. Israel now occupied even more Arab land—equal to three times its own size—and had revealed its true identity: a colonial power which depended on military superiority to occupy more and more Arab land, rendering in the process about one million Palestinians homeless and stateless. The confrontation states—

Egypt, Jordan, and Syria—had been obliged to accept a ceasefire in June 1967 without any provision in the relevant Security Council resolution for the withdrawal of Israeli forces to the 4 June lines, thanks to a powerful US political initiative. In this way, the United States, which had protected Israel before the war, came to support its occupation of Arab lands after the war.

Arab political action was of special significance at that time because military action was not possible, and in 1967 two major political events took place. The first, at the Arab level, was the Arab summit conference in Khartoum, and the second, at an international level, was the adoption of UN Security Council Resolution 242. Both events had a direct bearing on the developments of Egyptian and Arab action at subsequent stages of the conflict.

The Khartoum Conference

The Arab summit conference was held in Khartoum in August 1967. It was a landmark in inter-Arab cooperation. The conference agreed to extend 135 million pounds sterling of annual economic aid to Egypt and Jordan, of which 95 million pounds would go to Egypt to make up for losses due to the closure of the Suez Canal and the loss of the Sinai oil fields. Jordan was to be given 40 million pounds to meet various commitments. Nothing was earmarked for Syria because it did not attend the conference. Saudi Arabia committed itself to contributing 50 million, Kuwait 55 million, and Libya 30 million pounds of the total sum. On the political side, President Nasir clarified his position as follows.

> We must take two basic points into account when we deal with the subject of political action to remove the consequences of the aggression, namely military preparation and economic resistance. There is no doubt that the decision made during the previous session on economic support will be a great help. We must also keep in mind that there is an agreement between the United States and the Soviet Union to solve the problem along the lines of the draft text presented to the General Assembly. This is based on two major goals: an end to the state of war, and Israel's withdrawal from the occupied Arab lands.
>
> I hope it is clear to all of us that when we speak of political action this does not mean that we will take without giving in return. We should look into what we will give or, in other words, what we can offer.
>
> The international situation is totally different from what it was in 1956. At that time, the United States and the Soviet Union agreed

to oppose the Tripartite Aggression. But now, in 1967, the United States and the Soviet Union have agreed on Israel's right to exist. They have also agreed on ending the state of war.

Nasir added:

The political situation for us in Egypt has also greatly changed after today's decision to support the confrontation states economically. The Americans thought we would surrender after six months, but this support will enable us to stand fast. Our situation in Egypt is very different from that of King Husayn in Jordan because Egypt can stand fast for a year or two or even more. We in Egypt can wait until we complete our military preparations, then we can take the only kind of action Israel understands, which is to liberate our land by force.

Therefore, I am not worried as far as the situation in Egypt is concerned, but frankly I am worried about the situation on the West Bank. At this point we should ask ourselves: Will the element of time in the case of the West Bank be in our favor or not? I personally believe that it will not be in our favor. We have to move quickly to recover Jerusalem and the West Bank with whatever means available to us at present, because even if we are a little slow, neither Jerusalem nor the West Bank will return.

Here we have to ask ourselves another question: Is it possible to recover the occupied land by military means? I think the answer is clear. This approach is not possible at present. Hence, we have only one alternative now, which is political action for the West Bank and Jerusalem.

The Khartoum Conference ended with an unanimous resolution for "no negotiations, no recognition, and no peace with Israel," a commitment to the full rights of the Palestinian people, and agreement on annual financial support for Egypt and Jordan.

RESOLUTION 242

In November 1967, the UN Security Council adopted Resolution 242, in which the superpowers tried to reconcile Arab demands—which at the time focused on Israeli withdrawal and the non-acceptance of the principle of the occupation of land by force—with Israeli demands, which centered on recognition of its existence within secure borders, and the principles of sovereignty and territorial integrity.

Egypt accepted the resolution partly because of unfavorable military conditions following the June War and partly to gain time to rebuild its military capability to place it in a stronger position. Egypt's acceptance of the resolution also showed political flexibility and a readiness to accept a just and peaceful solution in response to Zionist propaganda, which tried relentlessly to demonstrate that the Arabs did not want peace. Furthermore, the resolution did not support Israel's demand for direct negotiations with the Arabs. It was decided to appoint a UN envoy—Ambassador Jarring—to report on the implementation of the resolution by all parties.

Resolution 242 marked the beginning of a new stage of political and diplomatic action for Egypt, aimed at exploring all of the possibilities for a just and comprehensive settlement to the Middle East problem and at promoting an international climate in favor of the Arabs.

After Foreign Minister Mahmud Riyad had presented a report to the cabinet on 18 February 1968, Nasir commented,

> We will cooperate with Jarring even though we believe that he will fail in his mission. We will listen to the United States even though it now wants us to enter the dark area of negotiations on Resolution 242. We will even cooperate with the devil himself simply to prove our good intentions. But we know from the very beginning that it is we ourselves who will liberate our land by force of arms, which is the only language Israel understands. Let the United States support Israel in its aggressions and let them both try to wipe out the Palestinian problem, but they both know that we cannot be defeated in war as long as we neither negotiate with Israel, nor make peace with it, nor agree to liquidate the Palestinian cause.[1]

The stage of resistance ended in August 1968. During this period, the armed forces concentrated on building defenses west of the Suez Canal against the continued danger of an Israeli canal crossing. The defense plan took clearer shape, along with our growing combat ability, after the arrival of successive arms shipments from the Soviet Union.

Israel consolidated its defenses in Sinai using the least possible number of troops to avoid having to call in its reservists. The Israeli 'mobile defense' system was designed to use the smallest number of men and depended on speed and mobility according to defense needs.

Active Defense

In order to prevent the military situation on the front from freezing into a status quo, and having now recovered partial combat ability and strengthened the defense positions west of the canal, our armed forces shifted into an active defense mode in September 1968.

On 8 September 1968, Egyptian artillery simultaneously opened fire—from Port Said in the north to Suez in the south—on all frontline enemy positions on the east bank of the canal. The shelling continued for several hours with heavy enemy losses in life, weapons, and equipment. Reports indicated that ten Israelis were killed and eighteen wounded. On that day our artillery achieved remarkable success because of efficient planning and execution. In reply, Israel shelled the cities of Isma'iliya and Suez with heavy artillery. During this period of active defense, fighting between Egypt and Israel developed to include raids and ambushes in addition to artillery exchanges.

Faced with Egypt's determination to continue fighting—despite the cost—and with growing casualties, Israel hastily began to build shelters and fortified positions, erecting a high sand barrier to protect troops and hide their movements. The strongpoints or forts became the skeleton on which the Bar-Lev defense line was later built.

In brief, during this stage the Egyptian forces completed their defensive capabilities on the canal front and the west coast of the Gulf of Suez and the Red Sea. Meanwhile, various combat operations were initiated to show our ability to inflict losses, thereby demonstrating to Israel the high cost of remaining in Sinai.

We met several goals during this period. Chief among them was boosting morale and erasing the negative psychology of the June 1967 defeat by directly confronting the enemy. The continuance of combat activity on the front contributed positively to the political situation. Israel tried at this stage to distract and dilute the Egyptian military effort by carrying out raids deep inside Egypt so as to reduce pressure on the canal front, while continuing to engage our forces and hit at civilian targets in the canal area.

This mode of combat continued till February 1969, when Egypt decided to destroy the defense line Israel had set up on the east bank of the canal and to embark on a new stage of highly intensive engagements which became known as the War of Attrition.

9

The War of Attrition

The War of Attrition started on 8 March 1969 and ended with US Secretary of State Rogers' initiative in 1970. Egypt's purpose was to inflict enough damage on the Israeli forces in Sinai in arms, equipment, and to its fortifications—in addition to losses in life—to convince it that its stay in the occupied Arab lands would be at a very high cost, not only in terms of the actual losses sustained—with all the negative psychological impact this would have on the Israeli forces and people—but also in terms of the size of the forces it would have to commit to Sinai and with the need for continuous mobilization over long periods, which would inevitably have detrimental economic consequences on Israeli society.

As for the immediate psychological objective, which was one of the main cornerstones of the War of Attrition, this was to restore confidence to the Egyptian fighting man—in himself, in his leadership, and in his weapons—as well as to raise standards of combat ability and field performance; in other words, to 'inoculate' the troops for battle by instilling in them an aggressive spirit and giving them practical training in crossing the canal and fighting and overpowering the enemy.

The War of Attrition—and its persistence over some time—was a living political message to the entire world that Egypt and the confrontation states would not abandon the occupied lands and would use everything in their power to liberate them, if not through political channels then by force of arms.

The attrition stage was inaugurated on 8 March 1969 with concentrated fire from Egyptian artillery on enemy fortifications and positions on the east bank of the canal. These were conceived and erected by the Israeli chief of staff, General Chaim Bar-Lev. Engagement continued for about five hours during which the Egyptian forces destroyed part of the enemy positions and silenced some of its artillery.

On the following morning, 9 March 1969, Chief of Staff Lieutenant General 'Abd al-Mun'im Riyad traveled to the front to inspect the outcome of the previous day's fighting and to be visibly present among the troops. He was accompanied by the commander of the Second Army, Major General 'Adli Hasan Sa'id, of the frontlines north of Isma'iliya. During his tour, Lieutenant General Riyad was fatally wounded by Israeli artillery, and Commander Sa'id received a lesser injury though he had to undergo surgery several times. Riyad died as both men were rushed to Isma'iliya hospital. His death was a great loss to the armed forces and to Egypt. He was a distinguished military commander and we were in dire need of his skills.

The ninth of March has since become Martyrs' Day in symbolic expression of the military spirit which requires every senior officer, whatever his rank, to set an example to his men even in death. At the end of the October 1973 war, when I was chief of staff, a proposal was made to name the day on which the largest number of men had fallen 'martyrs' day.' I objected and marked the October celebrations instead with a visit to the Tomb of the Unknown Soldier, symbol of all martyrs in all wars. As for 9 March, I insisted on keeping this date as an expression of the true Egyptian military spirit.

Major General Ahmad Isma'il was appointed chief of staff to succeed Lieutenant General Riyad. The War of Attrition steadily escalated and crossings of the canal and the Gulf of Suez by small groups of our men became commonplace. Raids and ambushes increased in scale and intensity, and the firing continued unabated. Fighting had at first been concentrated on the canal front, but it now extended to the Red Sea zone. The military situation was becoming more volatile day by day, and both sides lived in a continuous state of combat .

Hostilities escalated gradually along the front as combat action expanded and intensified. A variety of weapons was used and different targets and operational styles selected. We continued artillery bombardment of Israeli positions on the east bank of the canal, inflicting heavy losses. This forced Israel to speed up the fortification of its frontline defenses, which it accomplished according to an integrated plan, setting up a powerful line of strong fortress points and fortifications known as the Bar-Lev Line.

Apart from firing engagements, and to increase the effectiveness of our strikes and develop the combat spirit of the men, the command coordinated canal crossings and raids to coincide with artillery barrages, using special infantry and engineering units. The size of these special raiding units gradually grew and crossings operations reached their peak on the night of 9 July 1969, when a commando battalion crossed the canal to the east bank facing Suez, wiping out the enemy units positioned at Port Tewfik, destroying their equipment, and returning safely to base with some casualties but no deaths.

The growing success of the Egyptian forces and the increasing losses of the Israeli forces as a result of the continuous pounding by our artillery and the accompanying raids across the canal were instrumental in making Israel reconsider its military strategy in June 1969. The Israelis decided to escalate the course of the war radically by using their air force in a policy of counter-attrition against Egypt, striking at both military and civilian targets.

The Air Force in the Battle

Egypt's combat performance in the first five months of the War of Attrition was perceived by Israel as sufficiently threatening to require a review of military strategy and strategic objectives. In the first place, it wanted to reduce its ever-increasing losses as these were now becoming a serious problem. In the second place, it did not want to call in too many reservists because of the impact this would have on the country's economy. Naturally enough, losses in men and equipment are always a determining factor in any decision about military action.

Israel realized that the continuance of this situation would help restore confidence to the Egyptian side, which suffered few losses compared to the relatively greater losses of the Israeli forces. Besides, the escalation on the front was bound to have an impact on the political situation.

Israel needed then to find an effective means to end the War of Attrition, and to check the growing effectiveness of the Egyptian forces so as to be in a position to take the military initiative once more. It decided to use its air force. This meant a shift from 'limited deterrence' with ground weapons to 'great deterrence' with air power, which had always been its main striking force and which it had not used since the June War.

Judging by the course taken in the fighting, it would seem that the Israeli command had set itself the strategic objective of disrupting the

Egyptian war machine and paralyzing it, as well as exerting psychological pressure on the Egyptian people to weaken the home front until it collapsed.

The Israeli air force chose to launch raids on selected targets in an extensive air war stretching over a prolonged period. This approach suited Israel best because it already possessed sophisticated Mystere and Mirage fighters and had been receiving since March 1969 advanced US Skyhawks, which were part of a twenty-eight-plane deal. As of September 1969, the United States had also agreed to send Israel the more sophisticated Phantom A-4s at a rate of four planes a month .

The Egyptian air defense force and air force were unable at the time to confront the Israeli air force because since the June War the Soviet Union had refrained from providing Egypt with offensive weapons which could give it a military edge over Israel. We may recall that during his talks with Podgorny in July 1967, Nasir had compared Israeli and Egyptian air power in terms of range and capacity. At the time, Nasir had requested Soviet aircraft able to reach deep into Israel to counterbalance Israel's range and capacity. However, our air capacity remained unchanged, even during President Sadat's presidency, until we entered the October 1973 war.

One can imagine the military situation on the front at the time. Starting from 20 July 1969, the Israeli air force began strafing our positions west of the canal, concentrating heavily on anti-aircraft missile and artillery positions. Neither Egyptian air defense nor the air force could stop these raids despite intense efforts and despite air sorties in defense of the front and against enemy positions and targets in Sinai. Until the end of 1969, clashes continued using all ground force weapons on hand, with intermittent air battles and constant air raids on military targets on both sides. Air defense guns and missiles blasted fire back and forth. Our naval forces actively defended our coasts, and naval bombardment of enemy land targets in Sinai was relentless. Raiding expeditions increased, using land, sea, and air for the transport of our men. Fires were set ablaze in Sinai and west of the canal, sending up plumes of black smoke over vast areas. Unexploded bombs were scattered everywhere and explosions created craters across the landscape. On both sides, the number of dead or wounded grew daily. It was war with all its implications in sacrifice and heroism.

While the war continued to rage violently on, and after the air force came into the battle, international political efforts were underway for a solution to the Middle East problem. It was clear that the stands taken by the United States and the Soviet Union were affected by developments on the canal front. On 19 September 1969, Israel's ambassador to Washington, General Rabin, reported back to his country that the Soviet Union was not ready to make concessions to reach an agreement with the United States on the Middle East problem. The US National Security Council was taking into consideration the impact of Israeli military operations against Egypt and was carefully considering their effect on the stability of Nasir's rule.

Rabin, evaluating the US stance at the time, said that the "continuation of Israeli military operations, including air attacks, is likely to lead to far-reaching results. Nasir's standing could be undermined, and that would in turn weaken the Soviet position in the region." Rabin further noted that one "would have to be blind, deaf, and dumb not to sense how much the [US] administration favors our military operations, and there is a growing likelihood that the United States would be interested in an escalation of our military activities with the aim of undermining Nasir's standing."[1] Rabin also remarked that the United States' readiness to provide Israel with additional weapons depended largely on an escalation.

The Za'farana Raid

At dawn on 9 September 1969, the enemy landed a squadron of ten tanks on the west bank of the Gulf of Suez in a deserted area. The tanks proceeded by land in the direction of al-Za'farana, where five men were stationed at an outpost. After killing them, the tanks then destroyed a radar position about a hundred kilometers south of Suez. The raiding force—the tanks, supported by a mechanized infantry unit—remained on the west bank of the Gulf of Suez for six hours under the protection of the Israeli air force, then returned to the east bank of the gulf. In preparation for the raid, Israeli frogmen had sunk two Egyptian torpedo launches moored at Marsa al-Sadat on the west bank of the gulf.

The sinking of the launches became a matter of serious investigation. The general command reacted immediately to determine why the raiding force had not been detected on the east side of the gulf even before it was able to cross over, why the raiding party was not repulsed after it had landed on the west coast, and why it had been able to remain there for several hours. Israel had filmed the raid and shown it to the Israeli public for propaganda purposes.

On that very day, a training maneuver was taking place in the desert east of Cairo and President Nasir was scheduled to attend it. I was at the maneuvers in my capacity as deputy director of military intelligence for reconnaissance when I received a note from Major General Muhammad

Sadeq, director of military intelligence in Cairo, informing me of the raid and asking me to relay the information to the minister of war.

I left to inform General Fawzi and Chief of Staff Major General Ahmad Isma'il, who were both with President Nasir and on their way to the maneuvers area, north of the Cairo–Suez desert road. When Nasir heard the news (he was in his car with General Fawzi), he looked deeply angry and this showed on his face. Major General Isma'il and I returned to Cairo to follow up on the situation while Nasir and General Fawzi continued towards the training area.

As a result of this raid, it was decided to relieve Major General Ahmad Isma'il of his functions. He had hardly held the post for six months. Major General Muhammad Sadeq was appointed in his place. Vice Admiral Fuad Zikri was also relieved of his command of the naval forces and Vice Admiral Mahmud Fahmi was appointed in his place. Other drastic measures were taken at lower levels.

A RAID ON THE PORT OF EILAT

Soon after, a special unit known as Group 39, led by Colonel Ibrahim al-Rifa'i, sank three Israeli naval vessels in the port of Eilat on 16 November 1969.

Colonel Ibrahim al-Rifa'i was a member of the elite commandos and had a reputation for extraordinary courage and leadership, having personally led numerous commando operations against the enemy. His group of men had not only had high combat experience but the morale and spirit to undertake any mission, however dangerous or difficult.

The group usually undertook operations 'of a special nature' and Eilat was such an operation, requiring long hours of preparation, complete secrecy, and great courage. Repercussions of the raid in Israel were powerful in view of the extensive material and human losses. More important, it was a sign of Egypt's ability to penetrate an Israeli naval port and successfully complete a daring operation. Fate would have it that Colonel Ibrahim al-Rifa'i fell as a martyr during a commando operation in the October 1973 war. He was posthumously awarded the Sinai Star, the highest military decoration at the time. He remains an example of tremendous courage and his name was given to a graduating class of the military academy after the October War.

COMBAT ACTS AFTER 1969

On the evening of 6 January 1970, the Supreme Council of the Armed Forces held a meeting under President Gamal 'Abd al-Nasir when General Fawzi presented a report on the condition of the armed forces. This was to give the president a clear and true picture of the military situation.

The report revealed a shortage of pilots and long-range bombers for air deterrence. It also pointed to a marked air defense shortage in troops and equipment, especially in medium-range SAM missiles. The report covered the combat ability and morale of the frontline troops. The statistics for 1969 were as follows.

- About 3500 enemy air strikes at our air defenses and frontline troops, using the most advanced aircraft in air battles with our planes. Our losses in life were sixteen officers and 150 men killed, and nineteen officers and 299 men wounded.
- Enemy losses were eleven planes of various types (five helicopters, two Mirages, three Skyhawks, one Mystere), and one Israeli officer taken prisoner. An unspecified number of the enemy were killed or wounded, but figures could be computed from official communiqués and foreign broadcasting services. According to Moshe Dayan's memoirs, 133 Israelis were killed and 320 wounded from April 1969 to November 1969.
- Our air force carried out 2900 defensive sorties; 170 were against land targets and 70 were for reconnaissance purposes. Twenty-two air battles took place in which 110 Egyptian fighters engaged 130 Israeli aircraft. Our losses were twenty-three planes and the enemy's were fourteen planes.

During three sessions on 6, 7, and 10 January, Nasir listened to reports from commanders of the armed forces. All of these communicated a readiness to continue escalating military operations and reported high combat spirit. The president came to the conclusion that it was necessary to pressure the Soviet Union for help in overcoming the chronic shortages in air defense equipment, especially missiles, to increase the number of pilots, and to acquire more advanced types of aircraft, including some for defense.

Air Raids Deep into Egypt

A major and serious development in the War of Attrition came on 7 January 1970 when Israel began to bombard military and civilian targets deep inside Egypt. Israeli planes would approach their targets at very low altitudes thereby neutralizing the anti-aircraft missiles. At that time, the air force was unable to prevent Israeli planes from reaching their targets or to destroy them once they did.

The year 1969 came to an end and the Egyptian armed forces continued to be exposed to the Israeli air strikes which had commenced in July 1969. Egypt had become vulnerable to strikes deep within the country after the damage inflicted on canal front air defense units in the

1967 war. The Egyptian air force had not yet completed reconstruction and was not equipped with sophisticated aircraft to match those of the Israelis. We did not have any fighters or bombers capable of threatening Israel's interior—we could not even reach east Sinai. Israel was aware of this.

The Egyptian command at the time realized that its assessment of the expected Israeli response to the War of Attrition was over-optimistic. It had not expected Israel to put its entire air potential into the war, a move which quickly gave the Israelis a tremendous advantage. However, in the long run Israel's action led directly to Egypt's decision to set up the missile barrier which played such a decisive role in the October War.

There is no doubt that the Israeli raids inflicted heavy losses in life and equipment, but in spite of this we neither stopped nor scaled down the fighting. Israel's raids deep into Egypt marked a major turning point because they led President Nasir to adopt countermeasures to cope with the situation and to insist on finding a solution with the Soviet Union.

Israel's raids on military and civilian targets used US-made Skyhawk and Phantom planes, concentrating on military targets near Cairo and on a number of Delta cities. In January 1970, the areas of al-Tall al-Kibir, Inshas, Dahshur, and al-Ma'adi were hit. In February, Israel struck at Abu Za'bal and Helwan. In Abu Za'bal alone, seventy civilians were killed. In April, Israeli planes hit a school at Bahr al-Baqar, killing thirty children.

The aim was to put the Egyptian people under heavy psychological pressure and make the political leadership appear weak, forcing it to halt the War of Attrition. The raids carried the implicit message that since the Egyptian armed forces could not see the futility of fighting, the raids might demonstrate this directly to the Egyptian people. Golda Meir said openly on 13 January 1970 that she saw no opportunity for peace as long as Nasir remained in office. Therefore, getting rid of him and the regime he represented should precede any talks about peace. Consequently, the political objective was to create instability within Egypt. This backfired. The Egyptian people became all the more determined to resist. From the military point of view, Israel wanted to show that the Egyptian forces were unable to protect their country and prevent them from setting up anti-aircraft missile bases on the canal so that our land forces would remain constantly exposed to air attack. The ultimate goal was to inflict maximum damage on the Egyptian war machine.

Despite all of this, military action against Israel did not stop. On 22 January 1970, our forces fought a successful battle at Shedwan, a Red Sea island opposite Hurghada. Several combat operations took place on the command front, with ground raids and ambushes in Sinai to destroy specific enemy positions and take prisoners. The enemy continued to have marked air superiority, so there was an urgent need for weapons and equipment to cope with the situation, particularly with regard to air defense.

In an attempt to limit losses and complete military installations, the general command drew up a plan code-named 'Deployment' to distribute military units and educational institutions across large areas inside and outside of the country. As Sudan and Libya represented the nearest Arab countries, the command thought it advisable to deploy some units there, out of operational range of Israeli aircraft—especially the Phantoms. With the approval of both countries, the military college was moved to Jabal al-Awliya near Khartoum in Sudan. The naval college was moved to Tubruq and the air college to Gamal 'Abd al-Nasir (al-Azm) airport, both in Libya. The naval units not needed in Egyptian ports were sent to the ports of Benghazi and Sert in Libya and to Port Sudan. Red Sea ports and berths in Safaga, al-Qusayr, and Ras Banas were also used. Some units were sent to Upper Egypt. The reserve officers' college was moved from the canal area to Esna in Qena governorate.

The intensive air war started by Israel in January 1970 was aimed at undermining Egyptian military capability, now reasserting itself after the 1967 losses. There is no question that the United States played a major role in encouraging Israel to launch the air war and in-depth raids by supplying it with offensive weapons and electronic equipment. The United States did not object to Israel's operations within Egypt—Washington even welcomed them. In this connection, Israel's ambassador to Washington, Yitzhak Rabin, reporting to his government on US reactions to the Israeli raids, said,

> When [US Assistant Secretary of State] Sisco invited me to lunch on 13 January he was not in a position to concede that Israel's air operations were equally welcome to the United States. There was no need for him to say it; he knew that I knew. The talks with the Russians had broken down; the United States was not proposing that they be renewed; and the American public's sympathy for Israel was growing stronger every day. I now observed a similar trend within the administration.[2]

Rabin went on to say that "since the raids began there had not been a single American statement—or even unofficial hint—that the Americans were displeased with them."[3]

SOVIET MILITARY SUPPORT

President Nasir flew to Moscow on 22 January 1970 and stayed until 25 January. There he asked for more advanced defense weapons and equipment—missiles, planes, and radars.

The Egyptian–Soviet summit between Presidents Nasir and Brezhnev proved to be critical at the local and the international levels. The main purpose of the visit was to explain the situation on the canal front following the entry of the Israeli air force, and to get a Soviet agreement for an integrated advanced air defense system to face Israeli air superiority effectively and stop its raids inside the country. This required combat aircraft that could intercept and give chase to US-made Israeli planes. It also required a modern network of air defense missiles, sophisticated early warning radar equipment to detect low-flying aircraft, and electronic equipment for obstruction or pursuit.

General Fawzi, who accompanied Nasir on this trip as head of a military delegation, has said that

> it was the most important meeting with Soviet leaders since 1967. Nasir deliberately heightened tension at the talks. He even went so far as to threaten stepping down to be replaced by some man able to reach an understanding with the Americans. He explained that the Egyptian people were passing through a dangerous time with a choice either to surrender to Israel's demands or to continue fighting. The present air defense system could not stop Israel's raids deep in the country.
>
> Nasir asked for complete SAM 3 missile units with their Soviet personnel, complete squadrons of modified MiG-21s with their Soviet pilots, and advanced radar warning and pursuit equipment with Soviet crews. He justified his demands by saying that time was not on Egypt's side; training Egyptian pilots and crews on new equipment would take too long.
>
> During the talks held on 25 January, President Brezhnev announced that the Soviet Central Committee and the Supreme Soviet had approved Nasir's request, adding that this would be the first time a Soviet soldier left the Soviet Union for a friendly country since World War II. The provisions of the Soviet announcement, which Brezhnev read out, can be abbreviated as follows:
>
> (1) Egypt would be supplied with a whole division of SAM 3 missiles—along with its men, equipment, and auxiliary weapons—which would reach Egyptian ports within a month and operate

under the orders of the Egyptian command for the purpose of air defense of Egypt's interior.

(2) Egypt would be supplied with three air brigades comprising ninety-five modified MiG-21 planes (with new engines), Soviet commanders, pilots, instructors, technicians and their equipment, warning and directional radars, technical equipment, and vehicles. These were to be put under orders of the Egyptian command and participate in the air defense of Egypt's interior. They were to be delivered within a month. The Soviet Union would also provide Egypt with fifty Sokhoy aircraft, ten MiG-21 training planes, and fifty modified MiG-21 engines for installation in aircraft Egypt already possessed.

(3) Egypt would be supplied with four B-15 radar systems to raise the efficiency of the available air warning system in Egypt's air defense network.

(4) Egypt was to prepare the installations and facilities necessary—on sites and locations preselected by the Egyptian military command—before the arrival of Soviet men and equipment in Egypt.

(5) The presence of Soviet military personnel in Egypt was to be considered temporary until training was completed for Egyptian brigades of the air defense force and the air forces. Training would be undertaken simultaneously at centers in the Soviet Union and in the United Arab Republic. Once complete, personnel would return to their homeland.

Brezhnev then reiterated that the mission of the air defense and air force brigades was for the defense of Egypt's interior.[4]

The Soviet Union's decision to dispatch troops to Egypt was a major decision and a serious development in its policy vis-à-vis the United States in the Middle East. It was an unequivocal military gesture to back up political support of Egypt.

Egypt's decision to demand Soviet weapons with Soviet military personnel to operate them was also a major decision and a serious new development. Egypt now became more dependent on the Soviet Union both militarily and politically. With the arrival of the Soviet troops, which we chose to call 'friendly forces,' the Soviet Union came to have a prominent presence in Egypt. Soviet advisors helped at all levels of military activity, from the Ministry of War to the units. The friendly forces, along with our missiles and air brigades, took part in the air defense of the country. Soviet naval units used naval facilities in our ports, especially in Alexandria and Port Said. Some Soviet aircraft were stationed at a number of Egyptian airports for strategic reconnaissance operations. Others were stationed deep inside Egypt in areas far from the canal front. However, Egypt's own air defense command remained responsible for all air defense.

It is clear that President Nasir's visit to the Soviet Union in January 1970 was a turning point in the conflict between Egypt and Israel. Soviet military support came at a time when Egypt faced a critical military situation as a result of the Israeli air war. Soviet units participated for the first time in creating an air defense system capable of standing up to the Israeli air force, the most powerful deterrent against the Arabs.

Reaching such an agreement was no easy matter. It was not easy for Egypt to accept certain new conditions and circumstances. On the other hand neither was it easy for the Soviet Union to take on such a calculated step, given its implications and consequences.

While the Moscow decisions were being made,

> on 31 January 1970 [Soviet] Premier Kosygin addressed a strongly-worded note to President Nixon demanding that the United States put a stop to the Israeli bombing raids. The Soviet premier placed responsibility for the fighting along the canal and the raids inside Egypt squarely on the shoulders of Israel *and* the United States. He also indicated that if Israel kept up the deep-penetration raids the Soviet Union might provide Egypt with more up-to-date weapons.

Nixon replied harshly, rejecting the Soviet interpretation and holding Nasir responsible for the military escalation after having violated the ceasefire and initiated the War of Attrition. With regard to advanced weapons for Egypt, the US State Department informed Soviet Foreign Minister Gromyko that "the United States was prepared to seek an understanding on a mutual cease-fire and hold talks with the Soviet Union on limiting the arms race in the Middle East. But if the Soviet Union sparked off an escalation by supplying ultra-modern weapons to the Arab countries, the Americans would be forced to reconsider their arms policy toward Israel."[5]

This showed that the United States supported the Israeli air raids into Egyptian territory to coerce Egypt into stopping the War of Attrition. Israeli air attacks ceased in April, but air and land engagements continued until August 1970 when they too were stopped following US Secretary of State Rogers' initiative. Like Israel, the United States interpreted Security Council Resolution 242 to be 'negotiable principles.' President Nixon declared in a statement in January that peace could only come on the basis of an agreement between the parties and that such an agreement was only possible through negotiations between them. With regard to the Israeli air raids, the United States sent a message to Egypt on 22 February 1970 expressing concern and regret for the victims. Its advice was for Egypt to return to the ceasefire as defined by Security Council Resolution 242 of June 1967, but the ceasefire decision must not be linked to an Israeli withdrawal. If the ceasefire was not accepted, however, then Israeli raids into the heartland of Egypt and against largely civilian targets would continue, perhaps on a wider scale to include economic targets. This was an open threat and a perplexing development on the part of the US administration.[6]

A Barrier of Air Defense Missiles

The new air defense system from the Soviet Union needed special installations which had to be constructed under continuous pressure from enemy air raids, day and night. Nevertheless, construction began. All Egyptian building and construction companies cooperated with the Military Corps of Engineers under the command of Major General Gamal Muhammad 'Ali. In a terrible battle of wills, the enemy concentrated all the powers of its air force to prevent us from preparing the reinforcements and positions for the new missiles in the Suez Canal area, while Egyptian air defense mobilized all its available anti-aircraft guns to make it possible for construction to continue.

This operation exacted a tremendous cost in lives, both military and civilian, and was accomplished under the worst imaginable conditions. Israeli planes would attack the structures to destroy them or at least inflict damage. But as soon as an air raid would end, work would start once more and continue night and day under the umbrella of our anti-aircraft guns and MiG planes.

Setting up the installations for the air defense missile positions became a national symbol, a test of will and self-sacrifice. The volume of engineering works completed between Cairo and the canal area and in the rest of Egypt required about 1.6 million cubic meters of reinforced concrete, 1.4 million cubic meters of standard concrete, 12.5 million cubic meters of earthworks, and hundreds of kilometers of roads. Expenditures during the early days reached approximately one million pounds a day. The plan was to erect the missile positions in forty days, but they were actually completed in thirty-nine days thanks to the determination of the many construction workers involved. This was the Egyptian worker at his best.

The friendly forces arrived and took up their assigned positions in the interior of the country. The Egyptian air defense forces occupied positions on the west bank of the canal. The missile ranges were set up in lines approaching the canal consecutively from the west.

Israel continued its heavy attacks on our positions, but on 18 April 1970 Israeli pilots intercepted radio communications between aircraft flying deep inside Egypt and realized that they were manned by Soviet pilots. Israel's deep raids stopped as of that date.

On the morning of 30 June 1970, Israeli planes were surprised by Egyptian air defense missiles now in position. They suffered unexpected losses and their air force command, in what appeared to be a fit of rage, sent a second strike to penetrate and destroy the defense line. The outcome was even more losses, with three Israeli planes downed by the end of the day. On 2 July two more planes were downed and three more on 3 July. These were all Phantoms or Skyhawks. In Israel, this gave rise to worries about the erosion of the air force. Golda Meir is said to have exclaimed in frustration, "The Egyptian missile battalions are like mushrooms. Whenever we destroy one, another shoots up in its place." She added that "the Egyptians have planted missiles over the entire territory west of the canal, and God only knows where else they will find to plant others."[7] In Egypt, morale soared because of the successes scored.

A US Ceasefire Initiative

The escalation of the War of Attrition, developments in the region following the arrival of the friendly forces, and the growing Soviet presence in Egypt created a new set of factors for US policy to consider. Egypt's determination to continue the war and our rejection of the Israeli and US view on the need for direct negotiations were coupled with growing anti-US feelings in the Arab world. The United States now found it useful to try to limit the military escalation by sponsoring an initiative for a ceasefire. In a meeting with Israeli Foreign Minister Abba Eban in May 1970—also attended by Israeli Ambassador Rabin and Assistant Secretary of State Joseph Sisco—President Nixon tried to sound out Israel's position on the Soviet presence in Egypt. He asked Eban whether Israel's stand remained unchanged since Rabin had summed it up as "give us the tools and we'll do the job." When Rabin promptly answered in the affirmative, Nixon commented, "Good. That was all I wanted to know."

Rabin reports that Nixon then said, in reference to the Israeli raids deep into Egypt, that

> if it were just a question of you and the Egyptians and the Syrians, I'd say 'let 'em have it! Let 'em have it! Hit 'em as hard as you can!' Every time I hear of you penetrating into their territory and hitting them hard I get a feeling of satisfaction. I agree with you that the Soviets and the Egyptians are putting us both [the United States and Israel] to the test. But it's not just a problem of Egypt and Syria. The other Arab states in the Middle East are watching us also. I don't have the slightest doubt about that. . . . We have to play it so that we don't lose everything in the Middle East. . . . We want to help you . . . and you have to help us without harming yourselves or us. . . . We will back you militarily, but the military escalation can't be allowed to go on endlessly. We must do something politically.

Rabin says that "this must have been the thinking that lay behind the 'Rogers initiative' of 19 June 1970."[8]

The US presented the 'Rogers initiative' on 19 June 1970, calling for a ceasefire of ninety days between Egypt and Israel and a resumption of the Jarring mission to implement Security Council Resolution 242.

Egypt and Israel agreed to accept the initiative. A ninety-day ceasefire would take effect at 1:00 A.M. Cairo time on 8 August 1970. The agreement stipulated that neither side would change its military positions in an area extending fifty kilometers east and west of the canal. The two parties were not to introduce or set up new positions in this area, and any activity was to be confined to the maintenance of existing positions or to the change and provision of the troops already stationed there.

Egypt hurried to complete positions for the air defense network in the night hours preceding 1:00 A.M. of 8 August. In the morning of the following day, Israel found itself facing a complete network of defense missiles without any breach of the imminent ceasefire. This was an excellent piece of work by our air defense force and Israel had obviously never imagined that it could be accomplished in such a short time. The whole of the canal region now had missile cover; this was the first brick in the structure which led to victory in the October War. And so the War of Attrition ended and preparations for the 1973 October War began.

10

An Evaluation of the War of Attrition

Four wars have taken place between Israel and the Arabs: the Palestine war in 1948, the Tripartite Aggression on Egypt in 1956, the June 1967 war, and the October 1973 war. The War of Attrition is usually ignored or only casually mentioned by analysts. Opinions of it have also differed, some criticizing it either because it did not settle anything, either militarily or politically, or because of the tremendous—and they believe unnecessary—losses which drained Egypt's capabilities rather than Israel's. Others have concluded that this war delayed the October 1973 war by three years.

The War of Attrition was the longest of wars between Egypt and Israel, lasting for almost a year and a half, from March 1969 to August 1970, during which time land, air, naval, and air defense forces were used. Its political objective and its military strategies and operations were of a special nature. Tactically, it was one of several stages in the armed conflict with Israel after the 1967 defeat and in this respect it differed from a comprehensive war.

The strategy for the War of Attrition is recognized in military practice. Under certain political and strategic conditions when one or several factors—either political or military—delay direct military action, then the 'long-term conflict' becomes a suitable alternative. French military expert General André Boufre calls the theory behind a war of attrition the theory of 'denudation and erosion.' He says that this type of conflict should not necessarily aim at achieving spectacular military victories. Its success lies in maintaining the struggle and steadily escalating it in order to increase the burden gradually on the enemy. Its success depends on forcing the enemy to accept extremely hard conditions, using limited means skillfully and flexibly, and persistently increasing pressure. This affects morale and ultimately builds up the elements that define military power.

The War of Attrition was launched against Israel after two other strategic stages: resistance and active defense. It was of vital importance to our armed forces. Objectively and at the strategic and tactical levels, it should not be judged simply in terms of its incidents. Its value lies rather in the far-reaching impact it had as an extension of the experience accumulated in the two previous stages. It significantly influenced the preparation and planning for the October 1973 war and ensured efficient performance of our armed forces during that war.

Though some maintain that the War of Attrition was both harmful and fruitless, I believe that it was of great benefit and was a necessary practical preparation which made possible the decision to launch the October 1973 war. It allowed both the strategist and the fighter to assert themselves under the difficult conditions which prevailed after the June 1967 defeat. It proved that Egypt's determination and commitment to liberating the land were strong enough to restore confidence after defeat had almost crushed it.

There can be no doubt that the War of Attrition was a tremendous burden on both Egypt and Israel, but in the final analysis it was beneficial to Egypt and proved harmful to Israel.

From a political perspective, for Egypt the war ensured that the Middle East problem remained alive and a priority for the superpowers and other powerful nations. It also meant that Israel, despite its great victory in the June 1967 war, could not impose its political will on us and force us into accepting direct negotiations and peace on its own terms. Moreover, this war sent out a forceful message worldwide that Egypt and the frontline states had not abandoned their occupied lands and would liberate the land by military force if political channels failed. Lastly, it meant that despite the bitter June defeat we had not lost the will to fight and that Israel was paying a very high price for its presence in Sinai. In this respect it must be said that the goal of the War of Attrition was not an Israeli withdrawal from Sinai.

Mahmud Riyad, then foreign minister, gives a fair assessment of this war. He says,

> Throughout 1969–70, the entire conflict was characterized by two basic polarities: the War of Attrition and moves to reach a comprehensive settlement to achieve peace.

> With regard to the War of Attrition, Israel's losses were heavy. Military reports and information reaching us from western sources indicated the success of the war in achieving its objective. . . .
>
> Abba Eban, Israel's foreign minister at the time, said that the ceasefire was received in Israel with a feeling of satisfaction. When Mrs. Meir went on television to announce it, the public reacted as though they had reached a peace settlement. News bulletins would no longer start with the announcer reporting the names of young Israelis fallen in battle. Their losses in life and in valuable equipment had made the War of Attrition very costly to them.
>
> Mahmud Riyad goes on to say that
>
> in principle, the war made Israel's continued occupation so costly that Israel was ultimately forced, at the end of the war, to accept what it had rejected at the beginning. Notably, it retreated from its insistence on separate solutions and accepted the principle of a comprehensive settlement. It also retreated from trying to impose direct negotiations on us and accepted indirect negotiations. Regardless of the developments that took place later, this is what Israel accepted when a ceasefire put an end to the War of Attrition.[1]

From the military perspective, our armed forces needed not only the War of Attrition but the combat stages of resistance and active defense. These provided essential practical training in actual fighting conditions with Israel, or an 'inoculation' against the hardships of battle. Our fighting men found a new confidence in themselves, their weapons, and their leadership. The armed forces came out of this war with useful lessons, particularly on points of weakness and strength in the enemy and in themselves.

Combat ability improved noticeably between July 1967 and the August 1970 ceasefire. We had used a variety of fighting methods, offensive and defensive, in the different branches of the armed forces. This had provided concrete experience which helped identify weaknesses and make allowances to correct for them. Israel's reliance on sophisticated weapons, its air force, and the wide-scale electronic techniques it used to halt this persistent and escalating war inadvertently pressured Egypt to improve and expand its air defense network, set up a missile barrier, and allowed it to test and improve it on the battlefield. It must be emphasized that without the three years of engagement (1967–70)—starting with defensive resistance using whatever arms were available, and then moving gradually into positive and active defense which then developed into the defensive–offensive War of Attrition using all types of weapons and involving all branches of the armed forces—our forces would not have been able to make the transition from the total collapse of June 1967 to a massive offensive operation in October 1973, which included crossing a virtually impregnable water barrier, the Suez Canal. Given enemy air superiority, we would not have been able to launch a comprehensive attack before completing our air defense system. This did not take place before August 1970, when we obtained sophisticated weapons from the Soviet Union and, for the first time in Egypt, set up a Department for Electronic Warfare to use electronic equipment and methods in war.

A question which naturally arises is whether there was an alternative to armed conflict following the June 1967 war. Could the problem have been solved through diplomatic and political channels while the armed forces stood passively by? This would have meant Egypt's surrender to Israel's conditions. War is an extension of politics using other means, and diplomatic activity had to be backed up by as much military clout as the capabilities of the armed forces would allow at the time. Foreign Minister Mahmud Riyad has described the positive impact of military action on political action:

> The War of Attrition forced Israel into a military and political corner. It was not capable of settling the war in its favor, despite its military superiority. At the same time, it did not want to withdraw from Sinai. Therefore, in the face of Egypt's determination to fight—despite human and material losses—its only option was to engage against its will and despite the bloodshed and losses in men, which it could ill afford.

At the end of the War of Attrition, Egypt had gained a number of advantages and learned some invaluable lessons. We had become familiar with Israeli combat style. Israel came to realize that it was unable to destroy the air defense network. The Israeli air force no longer had effective freedom of action, which in turn exposed the Israeli army's actual combat capabilities. On the other hand, our forces were able to operate very much more freely under the protection of both the air defense and the air force.

Naturally enough, Egypt also had to bear heavy losses. We saw this as the inevitable price for the October War just as Israel paid dearly for its stay in Sinai until the October War began.

It is my opinion that Egypt's overall military and political situation by the end of the War of Attrition was better than it was at the beginning. Indeed, the cessation of hostilities on 8 August 1970 did not mean that the wheel of war had stopped; it marked the beginning of a new stage in preparation for the October 1973 war.

In Israel, it was admitted that the War of Attrition had inflicted heavy losses and that the Israeli army had lost the upper hand. At a Labor Party meeting on 29 August 1970, Israel's Foreign Minister Abba Eban conceded that "our losses in number of dead and in valuable equipment has made the War of Attrition an expensive war. Had it not been for the ceasefire, Israel would have had to face an escalation in the war with Egypt and consequently an increase in the number of casualties and an erosion of Israeli air superiority."

In September 1971 the Israeli newspaper *Ha'aretz* quoted Brigadier Mati Beled as saying that from a military perspective, the Israeli army had failed in the War of Attrition and that this was its first defeat on the battlefield since the establishment of the state. Israel had grasped the first straw thrown to it, which was the ceasefire.

General Weisman, later to become minister of defense, mentions in his memoirs that when the Egyptians accepted the ceasefire on August 1970, the Israelis interpreted this as an acknowledgment that they (the Egyptians) could no longer put up with the bombardments. He said,

> But without minimizing the losses they sustained due to our air raids, my fear was that the war would claim the lives of our best soldiers, and this came true. The Egyptians came to have freedom of action for three years to prepare for the October War. It is mad to say that we won the War of Attrition because, on the contrary, it is the Egyptians who benefited most, despite their losses.
>
> During the period from 1970 to 1973, our senior commanders repeatedly said we had won the War of Attrition and this affected our thinking. They should have said we failed to destroy the Egyptian air defense network but had to do so because it would play a decisive role in the next battle and, one way or another, it had to be silenced. We lived under an illusion instead of facing facts. We may have succeeded in raising public morale but we paid dearly for this.
>
> As the War of Attrition continued without our army being capable of stopping it, I gradually realized—unlike many others—that it was the first time we had not triumphed. I have repeatedly said that we failed in this war.
>
> The War of Attrition was the first war Israel failed to win. This fact paved the way for the Egyptians to launch the Yom Kippur [October] war in 1973.

PART III

THE OCTOBER 1973 WAR

Our commitments are being put to the test. The problem of liberating the land is central to our life. . . . The battle will be fought using whatever weapons are available. We will plan for this. . . . Our situation will have to change or our cause will end, die, and disintegrate in 1973.

—President Sadat

11

Planning for War

The decree for my nomination as chief of staff of the armed forces operations department came out in the first week of January of 1972. I was conscious of the heavy burden of responsibility which came with the position at this critical moment, even though I was not starting from scratch and could not ignore the efforts of those men who had preceded me.

We were still licking our wounds from the 1967 June war, which we lost as a result of political and military blunders. Our armed forces had engaged in a series of battles moving from a defensive mode to one of active defense, which had escalated into the War of Attrition, followed by a period of 'no war, no peace' and a stalemate as far as reaching any peaceful solutions to the Middle East problem.

It was clear to us in the armed forces general command that, after the June War, Israel had decided on a strategy to force the Arab will to yield to its own so that peace could be imposed under Israeli conditions. This meant that Israel had to maintain military superiority to be able to impose the fait accompli in the occupied territories, and to prevent the Arabs from considering a comprehensive war by instilling in them a feeling of futility, inadequacy, and despair.

The United States since the June War had become an open and reliable ally of Israel, providing political backing and military and economic support. It poured all kinds of weapons into Israel at a rate which would ensure its uninterrupted military superiority over the Arabs as a whole. The Soviet Union, on the other hand, was providing the kind of military support to Egypt and Syria which precluded any advantage over Israel, claiming that it did not want an arms race in the region. In this way, the superpowers promoted their interests in the region within the framework of a mutual 'understanding.'

In addition to commanding military superiority, Israeli forces had in the June War reached the Suez Canal in the south, the Jordan River in the east, and occupied the Syrian Golan Heights in the north, all of which were natural obstructions and barriers. Consequently, these lines had become Israel's most effective strategic positions.

The Egyptian forces were considered a principal threat and Israel therefore concentrated on Sinai, erecting fortifications and defense lines, building airports and roads, and stationing seasoned men backed by armored units to confront any eventual Egyptian attack. The assumption was that it would be difficult, if not impossible, for large numbers of our forces to cross the Suez Canal—a daunting and unique obstruction—and then have to face strong resistance from Israeli forces. If we did take this risk, then, in the estimation of Israeli Chief of Staff General Elazer, the canal would become our graveyard.

Previous experience had taught Israel, as it had taught us, that in a war no military cooperation was likely between Arab countries. Israel could therefore afford to isolate each front and deal with it separately. And as long as Egypt was unable to carry out a comprehensive attack then other Arab countries would not fight. In conclusion, Israel thought it could impose a fait accompli by force to make the Arabs surrender. This state of affairs suited the United States in its regional policy against the Soviet Union.

Despite the years of political and diplomatic activity by Egypt and other Arab countries, by the beginning of 1972 all attempts to reach a peaceful solution had finally stopped. At that time, the presidential elections in the United States dominated all other considerations. President Nixon tried to please Israel, instructed the State Department to freeze any movement or initiative concerning the Middle East, and responded positively to Israel's request to supply it with more planes.

On 2 February 1972, Israel signed an agreement with the United States for forty-two Phantoms and eighty-two Skyhawks. This new delivery of aircraft was made at a time when the Suez front had been totally quiet for nearly eighteen months. Even more dangerous was the memorandum from the United States to Israel pledging that it would not sponsor any new political initiative before having first discussed it with Israel. As a result, US policy became dependent on Israeli policy, the most alarming commitment so far.[1]

In 1972, Egypt's options therefore were either to accept the fait accompli with its political, military, economic, and psychological drawbacks or launch a new war against Israel under difficult political and military conditions. The decision for war was an inevitable and natural response to the political stalemate.

In the Arab world, the major political goal now became to liberate all Arab land occupied by Israel in June 1967. This was referred to as "removing the effects of the aggression."

At summit conferences, through the Arab League, and in bilateral contacts, efforts were made to create a united front which would include the military participation of some Arab countries. An 'eastern front' was created, consisting of Syria, Jordan, and Iraq under an Iraqi commander. This faced a number of difficulties and was subsequently dissolved at a time when we, the Arabs, most needed it to continue to be strengthened and supported. The collapse of this command at such a critical moment, together with memories of experiences since 1948, forced Egypt to plan a military operation to liberate Sinai on its own. Syria did the same by developing its own capabilities to liberate the Golan Heights, as did Jordan in order to regain the West Bank.

The alternatives presenting themselves to our military command were either to resume the War of Attrition or to launch a comprehensive attack to liberate Sinai. A war of attrition had been the only option open to our armed forces in 1969, and came to a stop with the Rogers initiative in 1970. Its resumption would mean a serious escalation into a broader engagement between Egypt and Israel, with heavier shelling and bombardment, deeper air strikes, naval battles in the Mediterranean and Red Seas, and increased land raids as well as other combat operations penetrating into the heartland of both countries. None of this would achieve any strategic purpose, either military or political, towards regaining Sinai. This option was therefore discarded by both the military and the politicians.

The general consensus was for an offensive against the enemy forces in Sinai as an integral part of the national strategy. The principal players would obviously be the armed forces. The aim was to upset the regional political and military balance and lay the groundwork for conditions better suited for exploiting the power struggle in the region. It was important to define the kind of offensive operation needed, as well as its parameters. These were influenced by a number of factors, the most important being the military capabilities of the belligerent parties and the strategic imperatives each faced.

At the beginning, the strategy was for Egypt to carry out one major offensive operation in Sinai. For this, we needed to have the military advantage over Israel, which we did not have at the time, given the requirements in weapons and equipment. These would take a number of years to obtain. The Soviet Union was constrained by the terms of its understanding with the United States and we lacked another arms supply source. Furthermore, the Soviet Union did not encourage a military solution to the problem, while the United States had publicly articulated and implemented a policy promoting Israel's military superiority under the pretext of maintaining the 'balance of power' in the region.

In view of all this, Egypt had to plan for the liberation of Sinai in consecutive stages, with the gradual development of the armed forces' fighting capabilities in mind and using the arms and equipment already available to us. The planning had to be realistic, taking into account the actual capabilities of the armed forces and exploiting available skills to the maximum. Courage and faith in our mission would compensate for our deficiencies. The momentous decision to fight regardless—with whatever weapons we possessed—was made by President Sadat in 1972 and speeded up our race towards war.

A difficult offensive action would be made even more formidable by the Suez Canal, a natural obstruction with unique characteristics. We had to storm it with a large force of men against strong enemy resistance backed by a fortified defensive line. Storming a water barrier is a complicated operation in itself, but to do so against an enemy with the military advantage was an enormous risk. It was a risk we had to take, provided military planning was good enough to ensure a high probability of success.

When President Hafez al-Asad took over the government of Syria in 1970, the Syrian forces were not in a position to liberate the Golan Heights on their own. A gradual political rapprochement developed between Presidents Sadat and Asad to include agreement on joint military action. It took nearly two and a half years for military cooperation to become a reality, and it became an important factor in the war and a major element in its success.

The Egyptian general command now developed an offensive plan in cooperation with the Syrian forces in which Egypt would storm the Suez Canal, defeat the main concentrations of enemy forces in Sinai, reach the mountain passes, and hold this position in preparation for other combat missions. Simultaneously, the Syrian forces would penetrate enemy defenses in the Golan, destroy them, move forward to the lines of the Jordan River and the east coast of Lake Tiberias, and hold these positions.

The general command of the Egyptian armed forces began a long and protracted study to find ways around the complicated and difficult military problems associated with offensive action. We had to produce an accurate analysis of Israel's military strategy, its defensive system on the Suez Canal and in Sinai, predict its reactions to each of our actions, and evaluate its overall capabilities with some precision.

THE ISRAELI MILITARY STRATEGY[2]

The decision by Egypt and Syria to go to war was a natural response to the political dead end and the prevailing condition of 'no peace, no war' in the Middle East despite the diplomatic efforts of the five previous years. The truth is that this situation suited the two superpowers and Israel, but was not advantageous to the Arabs.

The United States considered Israeli military superiority a sufficient deterrent which would perpetuate the status quo until the Arabs became convinced that the Soviet Union was unable to help them liberate their land in spite of all its political, military, and economic aid. Consequently, Soviet influence would disappear from the region and be replaced by US influence. The US position, as expressed by President Nixon, was to find a balance between full Egyptian sovereignty and Israel's security requirements. US Assistant Secretary of State Joseph Sisco declared publicly that he did not believe that Israel should return all the land occupied in the June 1967 war since the UN Security Council resolution did not stipulate this. In spite of the US anti-Arab position, US interests in the Arab region were not affected or threatened, nor were they likely to be.

The Soviet Union stood by the Arabs politically, but its support to Egypt and Syria was set within well-defined limits which did not allow for an arms race, thereby effectively guaranteeing continued Israeli superiority and forcing Egypt's and Syria's continued dependence on it. This policy promoted the long-term goals and interests of the Soviet Union in the region and, it was believed, contributed to the decline of US influence.

As for Israel, conditions of 'no peace, no war' allowed it not only to consolidate the status quo in the occupied territories but to change its territorial landmarks by linking up with the West Bank and the Gaza Strip economically through its new settlements. In this way, it hoped gradually to accustom the Palestinians to life with Israel and to manipulate public opinion into accepting the 'facts' it was creating on the ground.

On the Egyptian and Syrian side, the condition of 'no peace, no war' was a terrible drain on human and economic resources because of the continued mobilization since the June 1967 war. Troop morale and spirit in both countries had been gradually undermined as they found themselves forced to hold positions year after long year not knowing when the situation would end. Rumors and gossip spread, suggesting that a war was not likely and that Egypt and Syria had no real intention of fighting.

The political climate worsened when the two superpowers held a summit meeting in Moscow from 22–30 May 1972 and agreed to impose a military de-escalation once the immediate Middle East problem was defused. For the Arabs this would have meant accepting continued and indefinite Israeli occupation with no military option.

An analysis of Israel's policy since its creation shows that its main policy lines have always been consistent. They are: first, the gradual expansion of its territory at the expense of Arabs; second, establishing and maintaining military superiority over the Arabs; third, developing close ties with a dependable great power which would help it in achieving its goals and purposes; and fourth, the weakening and dispersing of Arab energies.

Israel's military strategy was therefore transparent since it was based on these basic principles. It was as follows.

- To retain and build on its military advantage so as to dissuade Egypt, Syria, or Jordan from any considerations of a comprehensive war, limiting their options at most to another War of Attrition which Israel felt it could deal with and contain.
- To maintain its close ties to the United States—a reliable friend providing political, military, and economic aid—for the continued occupation of Arab land, the imposition of the fait accompli, and, in case of war, to be able to fall back on a strong ally.
- In the unlikely event that the Arabs began a comprehensive war, then Israeli intelligence (known not only for its competence but also for its close collaboration with US intelligence) would be able to read the signals early on and warn the Israeli armed forces far enough in advance for them carry out a preemptive strike, using most probably the long arm of its air force, its major deterrent force.

Israeli troops were at the Suez Canal, at the Jordan River, and on the Golan Heights, giving Israel the strategic advantage on all three fronts.

It judged that the main threat came from the Egyptian forces and, relying on the barrier provided by the Suez Canal, built fortifications and high earthen defensive hills on the eastern bank of the canal as part of an integrated system of defense which it believed was impregnable to any large-scale Egyptian attack.

In line with its concept of 'secure borders,' Israel concentrated on controlling the Sharm al-Shaykh zone to protect its lines of naval communication in the Red Sea. The theory seemed to be that keeping Sharm al-Shaykh without peace with Egypt was better than peace with Egypt without Sharm al-Shaykh.

Experience in previous wars seemed to indicate that cooperation between Egypt, Syria, and Jordan was only a remote possibility. Israel felt confident enough of this to base its strategy on fighting each front separately. As long as Egypt was unable to undertake a comprehensive offensive across the Suez Canal, then neither Syria nor Jordan would be able to attack separately.

Israeli military strategy was based on the principle of deterring Egypt and other Arab countries by instilling in them a feeling of paralysis regarding a political decision for war and a feeling of impotence with regard to their military capacity for a comprehensive war. In this way, the Arabs would be forced to accept Israel's conditions at the outcome of the 1967 defeat.

We had to prove Israel's theories wrong and the principles on which its military strategy was built invalid.

The Egyptian Military Strategy

In this difficult political situation and under these complicated military conditions, a plan was set for a comprehensive 'local' war in which only conventional arms would be used. The strategic aim was to upset the prevailing balance in the region and to challenge Israel's concept of security and the principles behind its military strategy. This would require time to allow for the participation of other Arab nations, the most important factors being the creation of a united Arab stand and exploring the possibility of using oil as a weapon of political pressure to influence the outcome of the war.

The strategy therefore was an offensive military operation to liberate the occupied land in consecutive stages according to the capabilities of the armed forces, and to inflict on Israel the greatest possible number of losses in men and weapons in order to convince it that an indefinite occupation of our lands was too costly to bear. In this way, Israel's concept of 'security,' which was based on psychological, political, and military intimidation, would be seen to be seriously flawed. The so-called 'protective shield' offered no real protection either in the present or for the future.

Egypt's strategy for the October War was painstakingly built on the principles drawn from the bitter post-June 1967 realities, enriched by new technological developments in the military domain, and shaped by the sweat and blood of lessons from previous wars.

The First Principle: Lessons of the June 1967 War

In June 1967, we did not have a higher national strategy to balance and coordinate the political objectives of the state with its military capabilities. The armed forces were often surprised by political decisions of which they had no previous knowledge and were therefore caught unprepared.

When military operations commenced in earnest, they began with a public military demonstration in support of the politicians. Troops in Sinai were without a clear and well-defined strategic plan and consequently were confused before the war even began. Decisions by the military command were made in isolation, dissociated from the political decisions, and were therefore inappropriate. The armed forces became additional victims in the bitter defeat of this war.

However, in the period preceding the 1973 October War the situation was rectified and a higher national strategy was defined in which the armed forces were to play a major role, supported by other powerful state sectors. At this time, the state channeled all its energies into preparing for war and priority was given to any requirements of the armed forces, while the Egyptian people willingly contributed towards this effort.

Perhaps one of the most important characteristics of this strategy was the deliberate creation of the most appropriate Arab and international climate in which a war could begin. Israel was isolated politically, the international community began to sympathize with the Arab cause, and we won over world public opinion. Furthermore, the political leadership had entrusted the armed forces with a military operation that was within its capabilities.

After our armed forces had quietly and patiently prepared for war in coordination with the politicians, the general command was asked to present the political leadership with a choice of three suitable dates, from a military perspective, for an offensive to be carried out during 1973.

The Second Principle: Israel's Concept of Security

The Israeli concept of 'security' depended on psychological, political, and military deterrence as well as on preserving what Israel defined as 'secure borders' on the lines of the Suez Canal. This had to be challenged.

The decision to wage a war regardless of the political and military complications was a powerful challenge to the idea of political deterrence. Similarly, the decision to carry out a comprehensive offensive operation, and not just a war of attrition or a limited tactical battle, meant that the material components and means of Israeli military deterrence would actually be physically destroyed.

As for enemy fortifications and fortified defensive lines on the east bank of the canal, which relied on the barrier of the canal for their full effectiveness and to which the Israelis referred as their guarantee of security—we had to penetrate and destroy these impregnable lines regardless of natural or man-made barriers and whatever the sacrifice or cost. We had to shatter the Israeli belief in psychological deterrence.

Israel had always initiated the numerous wars and aggressions against the Arabs. We had therefore decided to deprive it of the advantages of a first strike and instead take the initiative ourselves.

It was well known that its air force was Israel's principal striking force. Its reputation had been amplified to terrifying proportions after its marked success in the June 1967 war, a success resulting as much from our mistakes as from its actual performance. Egypt therefore worked towards neutralizing the Israeli air force and weakening it through a strong air defense system in which anti-aircraft missiles batteries operated in collaboration with our air force.

This preparatory work took several years of intensive effort and cost many lives and millions of pounds. A major accomplishment was training the Egyptian soldier on the advanced Egyptian air defense network, with its range of weapons and facilities, so that air defense in Egypt became a frightening reality for the Israeli air force in the October War.

The accepted wisdom in Israel was that a military presence in Sharm al-Shaykh provided security for Israeli navigation in the Red Sea. We had to play down the effectiveness of the Israeli presence there through an Egyptian naval presence off the Straits of Bab al-Mandab, south of the Red Sea, to interfere with Israeli naval lines of communication and to prevent Israel from being provided with oil from Iran.

Israeli strategy depended on short wars and separate fronts. Therefore, our plan was for a lengthy war to force Israel into a long general mobilization with heavy losses in men. Manpower was a limited resource and a weak link in Israel's armor, so inflicting the greatest number of casualties was a key goal. To disperse enemy efforts on more than one front at the same time it was important for military collaboration between Egypt and Syria to be successful.

Israel depended on advance information about Arab intentions first to abort any attack, then start general mobilization, reinforce its lines in the occupied territories, and put itself on a war footing. Misinformation and deception were therefore vital to the success of our attack, and so we made a tremendous effort in that area in order to create the element of surprise. This in itself surprised many people.

The Third Principle: Preparing the Nation for War

The plan to prepare the nation for war began after the June 1967 war. It was conceived to suit the difficult political, military, economic, and psychological conditions in the aftermath of the defeat. While the armed forces were being reshaped and re-equipped, the national economy was being mobilized to carry the burden of war, land was being made available for maneuvers and field operations, and the public was being prepared militarily and psychologically for war.

We had within armed forces operations a special bureau to "prepare the nation for war" which worked in collaboration with other state administrations. Each, for example, was asked to draw up its operations plan in coordination with this bureau.

Other major concerns focused our attention. It was essential to maintain oil reserves to meet the needs of the state as well as those of the armed forces. We coordinated on all aspects of the problem with the Ministry of Petroleum, even going so far as to cover fire fighting in the oil fields when war broke out. Protecting the barrages and dams against eventual aggressive action was discussed with the Ministry of Irrigation and a number of other matters were seen to, such as maintaining the supply of electricity and reviewing the means by which EgyptAir (the national commercial airline) would continue to function during the war.

On 13 December 1972 the cabinet of ministers decided to create a committee from the armed forces to help the various ministries define their functions and their emergency plans under conditions of war. The committee was headed by Major General 'Abd al-Fattah 'Abdallah, aide to the minister of war.

The Fourth Principle: The Role of Arab Potential

Egypt's strategy against Israel was also built on the principle of relying on our own resources, in collaboration with Syria. We believed that the battle itself would open up the opportunities for additional support from other Arab countries as they saw fit.

Nevertheless, in a genuine effort at cooperation, Arab countries from the very beginning worked at "removing the effects of the aggression," especially at the international political level and by providing financial support. In the Arab world, we began to distinguish between the 'countries of confrontation' and the 'supportive countries.' The former (Egypt, Syria, and Jordan) were expected to confront Israel militarily while the latter limited their participation to the political arena and to providing financial support.

In my judgment, this division of roles between Arab countries did not serve its defined purpose. Although it was the countries of confrontation which had lost territory in the June 1967 war and which, rightly, were held responsible for regaining it, Arab security as a whole was seriously threatened in this new situation.

Furthermore, the deciding factor now was the comparative strength and ability of the Arab and Israeli sides. It had become clear that the occupied territories could not be regained by political means and that a military solution was the only option left. Israel, along with the United States and the great powers, saw the balance of power in purely military terms—that is, in terms of Israel's comparative advantage over all the Arab countries united and not just over the countries of confrontation.

The call to battle echoed from all corners of Arab world and was indeed an expression of a nationalism which transcended the boundaries of individual countries. Although we tried to translate this feeling into a reality on the battlefield, it remained only a dream. I will go into the reasons for this in more detail later.

The Badr Plan

Egypt's plan of attack was fleshed out in coordination with Syria and in light of our understanding of Israeli military strategy. It was agreed that both the Syrian and Egyptian fronts would be placed under one commander, who was in fact also the commander in chief of the Egyptian forces, and we called the joint plan the 'Badr Plan.'

The intention was that the air forces of both countries would carry out simultaneous air attacks against enemy military targets in Sinai and the Golan Heights. Then, under the cover of an initial artillery barrage on each front, the Egyptian forces would storm the Suez Canal while the Syrian forces would attack the Golan. It was estimated that the Syrian forces could liberate the Golan in four or five days and hold their positions until the Egyptian forces had fulfilled their strategic mission in Sinai.

The idea behind the Egyptian component of the plan was to storm the Suez Canal along the whole line of confrontation (approximately

175 kilometers) using the Second and Third Armies and, supported by the air force, set up bridgeheads with five divisions, along with the forces of the Port Said sector, at a depth of fifteen to twenty kilometers. The attack to the east of this point would continue—with or without a tactical halt—until we reached the line of the mountain passes, and then to capture and keep the passes.

Consequently, the Israeli forces would be in open territory in the middle of Sinai. They would not be able to create defensive lines because of topographical factors and due to their inability to provide enough men for defensive lines. They would also be exposed to Egyptian attacks east of the passes as the situation developed.

According to the Badr Plan, the Egyptian naval forces would ensure the security of our coastline, intercept the lines of Israeli naval communication in the Straits of Bab al-Mandab, and stop navigation to and from Eilat, which would have serious repercussions on Israel's economy and deprive it of its oil supplies from Iran.

To implement such a plan we had to overcome a number of problems facing our armed forces.

12

The Road to War

The momentum towards war accelerated during 1972 and it became necessary for President Sadat to make several important decisions.

1971 had passed without a settlement, even though President Sadat had declared that this was to be the year of decision in the hope that it would help move the international community towards an equitable political solution to the problem. In a 22 June 1971 address to the naval forces, Sadat had announced that "1971 is a decisive year, and we cannot wait forever." A month later, on 23 July, at the National Congress of the Socialist Union, he declared that "we are coming to a decisive stage in the history of the Arab nation, which is the year 1971." At the end of the session, he repeated these words, saying, "I've said this to you and committed myself before the people and made it known to the world that this year will be decisive for the Middle East crisis."[1]

When the situation remained unchanged, Sadat had to rely on the excuse that the Indo–Pakistani war began on 3 December 1971. By January 1972 unrest had broken out in the universities as students in despair demanded action. The fifth anniversary of the June 1967 war contributed to the unrest as people felt that another year would start with nothing done to remove the consequences of the aggression.

Sadat, sensing that his popularity and reputation were at stake, made a series of statements in which he tried to reassure the people that the decision for war was beyond question or discussion. A forthcoming battle was inevitable for our land to be liberated.

Soviet policy at the time was predicated on a rejection of war and this was reflected in their refusal to provide us with offensive weapons. It became increasingly clear that the Soviet Union would neither support us nor encourage us to carry out an attack in 1971.

General Muhammad Sadeq, minister of war, did not conceal his distrust of the Soviet Union from the general command. On 24 January 1972 he addressed a large group of officers in Cairo and strongly criticized the Soviets for not providing us with the weapons we had asked for, effectively preventing us from fighting. Sadeq added that the Soviets were spreading false and poisonous rumors among the younger officers, the soldiers, and the students to the effect that the armed forces did have the weapons to launch a war but that it was the senior officers who did not want to fight.

I did not approve of General Sadeq's decision to raise these matters at this meeting because I was afraid it would affect morale, given that the Soviet Union—our main source of weapons—was frustrating and blocking our desire to fight. In my opinion, it was a political difference between Egypt and the Soviet Union and there was no point in sharing this information with our officers. If the point, from the perspective of the minister of war and the commander in chief, was to raise awareness and to keep the troops informed, then its negative repercussions would be greater than its advantages.

On 18 March 1972, at a meeting of the Supreme Council of the Armed Forces, General Sadeq told us that rumors of a disagreement between himself and Prime Minister Dr. 'Aziz Sidqi were false, as were rumors of a falling-out between himself and the Soviet Union. The disagreement was simply one of principle. The word had got out that naval bases in Marsa Matruh and Alexandria had been put under the control of the Soviets, and this was not true either. Sadeq added that Lieutenant General 'Abd al-Qader Hasan, deputy minister of war, had returned from Moscow with a new weapons agreement including the supply of T 22 planes and T 62 tanks because the Soviet Union had asked for payment in full and in hard currency, without a 50 percent reduction as was the usual practice, and the Egyptian side had refused to sign the agreement under such conditions so the hardware would therefore not become available. The fact is that the role of the Soviets as reluctant arms suppliers had become difficult to swallow, even though they knew very well that they were our sole source of weapons.

A CHANCE MEETING

In early 1972 I met Major General Ahmad Isma'il by chance at the Cairo airport. He was head of general intelligence at the time, and we were both accompanying a foreign official to the airport. As we came out of the building and found ourselves alone, General Isma'il lowered his voice and asked, "When are we going to fight, Gamasy?" I replied, "When they appoint you minister of war and commander of the forces. Then you'll discover for yourself why we haven't fought so far." Isma'il tried to get more out of me. But I didn't add a word to what I had said. I was sure he was aware through his job of the politics of the situation, and that he also followed our progress in the armed forces and knew we had not completed our preparations for war.

The cycle of training was going determinedly ahead to raise fighting capability with repeated practical exercises in storming water barriers. In Syria, they were making similar efforts at an equally intensive pace. I had witnessed this for myself as a result of repeated visits to various branches of the Syrian forces and their command. Since 1970, when General Muhammad Fawzi was minister of war, I had been responsible for the coordination of military operations between the two countries and I carried this responsibility with me whatever my other positions or duties. I continued after my appointment as head of the operations staff of the armed forces. A small number of officers worked with me in complete secrecy.

Our visits to Syrian positions both on the front and across the country gave us the opportunity to acquaint ourselves with the Syrian commanding officers and to evaluate their forces' degree of readiness and their fighting ability. Visits to the Egyptian forces by the Syrians were made for the same reasons. These visits and shared exchanges were undertaken in complete secrecy. This created confidence between the Egyptian and Syrian military leadership and reinforced the conviction that cooperation between the two fronts was essential to liberate the land.

According to the agreement between Egypt and Syria, the Egyptian minister of war was also commander of the forces on both fronts and was responsible for the coordination of joint military action. This task was not easy; our previous experience of military cooperation between the Arab countries had been more in the line of political gestures, without the structure and discipline of any real military activity. Preparations for the October War, however, were very tough and demanded serious and effective military action which could only come from complete cooperation between the two countries. In fact, had it not been for the understanding between the political leadership (Presidents Sadat and Asad), there could not have been any military cooperation nor could this have been translated into a joint plan and a joint decision for war.

The first steps had been taken when General Muhammad Fawzi was minister of war and were acted upon when General Muhammad Sadeq took his place, and after he was appointed to Syria. I had the opportunity to accompany both men on their visits to Syria and to attend discussions either in Damascus or in Cairo. They were all constructive and positive.

Steps towards military cooperation were well thought out. We moved cautiously, slowly, and reasonably until a real commitment grew to the one purpose, the one goal, and the one path to liberation. This was a major accomplishment in 1972 on our way to the October War.

Ending the Soviet Advisory Mission

The second step which brought us closer to war was the ending of the Soviet advisors' mission in Egypt.

On the surface, matters were following their natural course, but the relationship between Egypt and the Soviet Union had been gradually worsening as a result of the position the Soviet Union had taken on the supply of weapons for a war. The first meeting between President Sadat and the Soviet leadership was in March 1971 in Moscow, when the president brought up the differences between the Egyptian and the Soviet positions. Later, at a meeting with the Supreme Council of the Armed Forces, Sadat recounted that he had said, "You've told me that you've put me two steps behind Israel . . . I'm the one who has been aggressed . . . and with that, I don't ask for superiority over Israel, but only equality. . . . Herein lies the disagreement."

In spite of the Soviet Union's promises to come up with an arms deal before the end of 1971, the agreement was not concluded and the arms never arrived. This may have to do with the fact that the Indo–Pakistani war started on 9 December 1971.

President Sadat said he summoned the Soviet ambassador to tell him that the situation was crystallizing—the year 1971 had almost ended—and to tell Moscow he would like to go there to clarify the situation before the end of 1971. He added, "At the end of December I received an answer that the meeting would be for 1 or 2 February 1972 because the Soviet leaders had a full agenda until then."

1972 dawned upon us. It was now evident that Israel would not budge unless it felt threatened by our armed forces. From this point onwards the rift between Egypt and the Soviet Union grew until relations reached their lowest point in July 1972, when President Sadat decided to end the mission of the Soviet advisors in Egypt.

Reasons for this decision were given in a message to President Brezhnev on 31 August 1972. This said:

- The conclusions of our meetings, especially our last meeting of April 1972, was that Israel, backed by the United States, would not move towards a solution to the problem, whether peaceful or non-peaceful, except if it felt that our armed forces were able to challenge its military superiority. Only then would Israel and also the United States find it in their interest to reach a solution.
- In our repeated discussions, I mentioned that we needed deterrent weapons to make the enemy hesitate to strike deeply within our territory (as it has done in the past), knowing that we could, in turn, reach its own heartland. It was obvious then, and still is, that without these weapons we will not be able to act decisively and Israel will therefore find it unnecessary to change its stubborn position with regard to a solution.

After President Sadat had given concrete examples of the needs of the air, naval, and land forces, which now suffered from shortages and outdated arms and technical equipment (although they were still in use in the Soviet Union), he said,

I would like to summarize, dear colleague, my impressions at this time as it is your right as a friend to know the reasons for my decision.

- The crisis has frozen into a stalemate and there are no ways left open for movement.
- The perception is growing that the United States and the United States alone will be able to find a solution, even after the Moscow meeting.
- Israel's provocative behavior is increasing in the region, and there is nothing to stop it.
- Your message of 8 July completely overlooks issues we had agreed upon and ignores measures we believe must be taken to be ready militarily, if need be, after the American elections.
- America gives to Israel without limit and has completely renewed its air force as well as supplied highly-developed weapons.
- Your message makes clear that the partial embargo on weapons of deterrence imposed on us over the past five years has been extended in this critical period to cover essential hardware I had

written to you about in detail but which you have completely ignored.

I was careful in all my meetings with the Soviet leaders to clarify that we needed no one to fight our battles for us other than our own troops. . . . We do not want our battle to develop into a confrontation between the Soviet Union and America as this could lead to a world catastrophe.

I said that we wanted to reinforce the cooperation between us to the greatest extent, defined as the degree to which our friends in the Soviet Union would provide us with what we need to help us solve our first and last problem, the liberation of our land.

For all of these considerations, I made my decision to end the advisors' mission. It is a position that needed to be taken to end a stage that needed to be ended for us to start a new stage based on a new understanding, good judgment, and well-defined positions.[2]

In my opinion, the Egyptian decision came as an unexpected shock to the Soviet Union given its unquestioned role as sole arms supplier. Egypt had now reevaluated its political and military situation in the light of new circumstances.

When we found out about this decision through General Sadeq there was no room for discussion because it had been officially announced to the Soviet Union. As chief of operations staff of the armed forces, I thought hard about the practical effects this would have on our capabilities and our readiness for war—and of possible Soviet attitudes during the war when, in the heat of battle, we would need to ask for weapons, spare parts, and ammunition. I believed nevertheless that the decision to terminate the Soviet mission had been made after serious and comprehensive study by the National Defense Council. I later discovered that the decision had been made by President Sadat, alone.

The first arms deal with the Soviet Union had been made in 1955, when Egypt under Nasir's leadership had broken the West's arms monopoly. Following this, the Soviet Union had provided military aid after the 1956 Tripartite Aggression on Egypt. The Soviets had rearmed us after the June 1967 war. They had backed us militarily during the War of Attrition and sent Soviet military personnel, weapons, planes, anti-aircraft missile batteries, and electronic equipment to Egypt to participate in the air defense of the country starting in 1970.

Military relations between Egypt and the Soviet Union had gradually been strengthened to our mutual benefit, but the Soviets' continued hesitation to provide the arms with which to liberate our land had made us bitter at a time when this problem was central to our being. We felt, in the armed forces as a whole but especially in the general command, that the Soviet Union had discouraged us from war against Israel. The quality and quantity of weapons they sent, and the timing of their delivery, were dependent on a perspective and a policy towards the Middle East problem which was not ours. Frankly, criticism of the Soviets by the general command rose to a new level during 1972 because they were perceived to be actively hindering our desire to fight and this was affecting the troops' morale.

The decision to end the Soviet mission of experts, advisors, and friendly forces had some repercussions on the armed forces. About 850 Soviet advisors had operated in various commands following the 1967 defeat, working closely with commanding officers on tactical and administrative matters. Their absence would not affect efficiency because our own officers were fully capable. As for the hundred or so Soviet experts, they were attached to new and technical equipment until their Egyptian counterparts became fully trained, at which point their services would be terminated. As for the friendly forces, they were Soviet units manning their own equipment and termination of their mission would seriously affect the efficiency of the Egyptian air defense system. These troops operated highly sophisticated aircraft, missile batteries, and electronic equipment (such as radar), and the Soviet Union for reasons of security would not leave them behind even if we offered payment as in former arms contracts. The manner in which these units' mission came to an end also precluded this.

My feeling at the time was that terminating the Soviet mission would have no direct effect. On the contrary, it was better for us to manage on our own, and we were up to it 100 percent. The war should be planned and executed as a completely Egyptian operation. And that is what happened. Under different circumstances, our battle success would have been credited to the Soviet advisors.

The Soviet Union had naval facilities in Alexandria and Port Said. We expected that they would ask to continue to make use of these facilities, along with two Syrian ports. They were important to the Soviet Mediterranean fleet in the face of US Sixth Fleet activity.

Our main problem was filling the gap left by the Soviet units which had returned home along with their weapons and equipment. There was no period of transition because the Egyptian decision had been final and irrevocable. The thoughts that came to me were: What next? Would relations between Egypt and the Soviet Union deteriorate even more? We were on the verge of war and could hardly discount our need for the Soviet Union at a time when the United States, with all its might, stood behind Israel. The hope was that politics and diplomacy would play their part in keeping relations going to the advantage of both Egypt and the Soviet Union.

Three months after the departure of the Soviet missions I listened to President Sadat speak at the Supreme Council of the Armed Forces, of which I was a member. He said,

> The Soviets are extremely careful with regard to our friendship because they know very well that if their position in Egypt collapses, there is no alternative for them either in Syria, Iraq, or elsewhere. . . . From the days of the czars, Russia has never received recognition from America of any rights in the Middle East, but when President Nixon was in Moscow he officially acknowledged that Russia had interests in the region, and they agreed to respect each other's presence here. Hence their care in keeping up relations with Egypt. . . . And they told Prime Minister Dr. 'Aziz Sidqi quite frankly that their policy would not change; they would continue to offer complete support to Egypt—our decision had not changed anything, Egypt still concerned them. And all of this was recorded in writing . . .

It had been natural for the relationship between Egypt and the Soviet Union to become strained, but it was also in their mutual interest to improve relations gradually in spite of the doubts and mistrust that had sprung up between them.

Dr. 'Aziz Sidqi visited the Soviet Union in October 1972. It was a completely successful visit. The Soviet leadership promised to provide Egypt with weapons, some of which had never been available before, to be delivered during 1973. The first positive sign of goodwill was that the agreement on naval facilities was not canceled. The Soviet Union asked if three troops carriers could continue to anchor at Port Said. Egypt agreed. On 5 October 1972 the three carriers entered port, an auspicious sign.

A second positive signal was the arrival of a Soviet military delegation in February 1973 to examine our needs on the ground. In March 1973, the minister of war, General Ahmad Isma'il, traveled to Moscow where he signed an agreement for weapons, the greater part of which were delivered and were used in the October War.

Nevertheless, relations were no longer what they had been. Caution and mutual suspicion were the rule until the outbreak of the October

War, when relations became more strained as the war ran its course, and afterward.

Mahmud Riyad's Opinion

Mahmud Riyad, former foreign minister and advisor to President Sadat on political affairs, has commented in his memoirs on the severing of the Soviet mission and says that

> it came as a surprise to the Soviet Union. It was the United States' intention that they should be expelled from Egypt and was first mentioned by Kissinger in 1970, then by Rogers in Cairo in May 1971. Their departure in this manner was a political loss of face and a victory for the United States.
>
> In my opinion, the factors which helped precipitate the decision to expel the Soviets from Egypt were, on the one hand, their prevarication, and on the other, lavish US promises to Sadat.
>
> The Soviets hesitated and procrastinated on the military option in spite of their conviction that the United States would never move towards a peaceful solution. They were always very careful to avoid a confrontation with the United States in this region.
>
> Then came the negotiations with Nixon in May on an 'understanding' between them. The Middle East became the focus of international bargaining and lost its urgency as an issue requiring a speedy solution. The consensus was that it was highly improbable for Moscow to withdraw its support for the Arabs, yet its reluctance to help them on the issue of the occupied territories after five years of occupation was seen, from Cairo's perspective, as a kind of surrender. Nothing would have changed this assessment short of intensified military aid and a timetable for delivery.
>
> With regard to the United States, there was no official understanding with Egypt over the departure of the Soviets, so the critical step taken by Sadat was ignored. Official statements by the US administration on its readiness for a comprehensive settlement if the Soviets were to leave were forgotten. Instead, the United States turned its back on this risky decision as though it was the least of its concerns.

Riyad adds, "One of my friends mentioned that he had asked Kissinger when he was no longer secretary of state for the reasons for the negative US response to Sadat's decision. Kissinger replied, 'The US position was completely natural under such conditions. Politics know no ethics and it is not within the US brief to pay for anything which is offered freely—with no one asking that it should be paid for.'"

War With the Available Weapons

The decision by President Sadat "to go to war with whatever weapons we had" was the third step taken to accelerate the progress toward war. On 24 October 1972, the Supreme Council of the Armed Forces held a meeting at President Sadat's home in Giza. The meeting started at 9:00 P.M. and continued until midnight. President Sadat began with a lengthy review of the political situation and the development of relations between Egypt and the Soviet Union since 1971. He spoke of his numerous visits to the Soviet Union, the accomplishments and the disappointments, and why 1971 had not been the so-called 'year of decision,' since weapons requested from the Soviet Union had not been delivered. He explained his reasons for ending the Soviet advisors' mission: the existence of foreign advisors and troops on Egyptian territory in times of war was unacceptable. He said,

> We couldn't possibly begin anything with Soviet advisors in our midst . . . in the midst of our troops—never! That is impossible. This was a basic principle I had. Among the things that brought me to this decision—and I am happy to have done so—is that we must conduct the battle ourselves and we must accept whatever lies in wait for us because this is a reality. . . . We are responsible for our failures or success and nobody else. We must fight our own battles.

Later during this long meeting, he said,

> Now let's come to the situation for which I called this meeting. The truth is that last summer when I spoke to [Minister of War] Sadeq my words were that I could not enter the next round in November 1972 while we were in this position, without having moved the military situation, because, simply put, I'd then have had to concede.
>
> I said to Sadeq, 'I can't enter the next round in November without military movement. Frankly, there is no peaceful solution. We are waiting for November for suitable international conditions [the American presidential elections]. If we had been ready, we could have entered the battle at any time. . . . A peaceful solution means surrender. An understanding now exists between both sides. The solution is in America's hands; a Soviet solution is of no value whatsoever. An American solution will be tacitly accepted by the Soviet Union.'
>
> I told Sadeq that resolutions were not enough. The issue had to be moved militarily as far as it was in our power and capacity to do this. . . . For the Soviet Union it was very important that the issue should end peacefully, even if there are concessions on our part, but in my opinion, events have proven that we should not enter the

next stage from a static position. This has become inevitable for the good of the country.

This is not a matter about which I'm taking your advice. The time has passed for that. Today the armed forces are faced with a test. The June 1967 defeat has made both enemy and friend doubt that we would ever fight again. Consequently, all the solutions I am presented with are based on this logic.

Our commitments are being tested. I am not prepared to accept defeatist solutions or surrender. I will not sit at a table with Israel while I am in such a humiliating position, because that means surrender. In the face of our people, our enemies, and our friends, we must prove unemotionally and with careful planning that we are capable of sacrifice and can stand up and fight and change the situation with whatever means are at our disposal.

My words to the Russians during the next stage—and to the Americans, the Arabs, and my own people—will be of no value to any of them while we remain in our present deadlock. The time for words is over and we've reached saturation point.

We have to manage our affairs with whatever we have at hand—we have to follow this plan to change the situation and set fire to the region. Then words will have real meaning and value.

The Arab situation will remain exactly as it is now as long as we ourselves remain immobile. In fact, it will get worse with the Arabs, the Americans, the Russians, and with our people. In my opinion, it can only end in silence and death.

I have often said and continue to say that neither Russia nor America nor anybody else will fight our battles for us, nor give us what we want. The Russians have to be provoked to give and the Americans provoked to solve. We are the movers and we've reached the point where our basic cause is now under threat.

I've made a decision and told General Sadeq about the next round and that we must not get into it from our present static position or our cause will die. If this happens to us on our own front, it will die for the entire Arab nation because there is no military front of consequence except ours. Israel knows that if it guarantees control of our front, our cause is finished. If we don't act, it will be finished anyway by the beginning of 1973. If we remain passive, our cause will disintegrate and die by the beginning of 1973.

I consider this meeting a historic one. The battle could go either way, but with God's will and the will of our people we will not lose. The situation can't get worse than it is now.

After this long exposition, questions were raised and opinions exchanged, as was usual. But this meeting was exceptionally stormy and agitated as President Sadat, with great emotion, rejected remarks by Deputy Minister of War Lieutenant General 'Abd al-Qader Hasan, calling them an interference with matters of state neither in his right nor his competence to discuss. President Sadat's anger rose as the discussion proceeded, and Vice Admiral Mahmud Fahmi, commander of the naval forces, intervened and tried to rephrase and analyze General 'Abd al-Qader's comments. President Sadat angrily rejected this as well.

By the end of the meeting, it was clear that President Sadat was not pleased with what had taken place—not with the reports presented, the opinions expressed, or the forecasts. My attention was particularly held by the president's emotion throughout. I also noticed that Lieutenant General Sadeq had not commented on the reports, nor had he discussed the forecasts or argued for or against anything.

One fact could be clearly drawn from this meeting. This was that President Sadat had made the decision to go to war with the potential available; that is, to use the weapons and equipment available without waiting for new supplies whose delivery dates were not guaranteed. Indeed, there was no guarantee that the Soviet Union would agree to send them in the first place, and even so probably not in the near future. President Sadat had said at the meeting that "in the past I tried to do all I could with the Soviet Union—I was patient and covered up for them," but he was also sure that we had reached a stage when our very cause had become threatened. "If we don't fight, our cause will disintegrate and die by 1973." If this was how matters stood, then the president's decision to fight at all costs was sound.

Another result of the meeting was that President Sadat needed to have another long talk with General Sadeq about the war. They needed to clarify when it should begin, armed forces capabilities during the next stage, problems facing them, and how to begin the war as soon as possible.

In my capacity as chief of operations staff, I was to accompany General Sadeq on a visit to Damascus a couple of days after the 24 October meeting in Giza. On the eve of our departure, General Sadeq telephoned me at home to say that he'd been asked to meet with the president the following day, and that he'd join me in Damascus after the meeting.

I left on my own to Damascus on 26 October 1972. The next morning, I discovered through the Egyptian embassy and the Syrian press that Major General Ahmad Isma'il had replaced Sadeq as minister of war and had been promoted to the rank of general. I immediately returned to Cairo that same day, arriving in the evening. From the airport, and still in civilian clothes, I drove to my office where I learned that Lieutenant General 'Abd al-Qader Hasan had also been relieved of his post and that Vice Admiral Abu Zikri had been appointed commander of the naval forces in the place of Vice Admiral Mahmud Fahmi. The appointment of General Ahmad Isma'il as minister of war and commander in chief of the armed forces was a fourth step towards the war.

THE NEW COMMANDER IN CHIEF

General Ahmad Isma'il has described the circumstances of his appointment in writing.

> That day was one of the most important and decisive days in my whole life, probably the most important. The date was 26 October 1972, (two days after the Giza meeting) 19 Ramadan 1392, the time 3:00 P.M., and the place President Sadat's home in Giza.
>
> We, the president and myself, were walking in the garden. I did not know why I had been summoned, but I suspected that it was for something important. After a short conversation, what I had anticipated occurred: His Excellency informed me of my appointment as minister of war, effective immediately.
>
> The president then asked me to prepare an Egyptian plan for war against the Zionist occupation.
>
> Our meeting was conducted with the utmost amicability and his conversation was very frank. After the meeting, while I was in the car driving across Cairo, a long chain of memories passed through my mind.
>
> Here I was once more going back into military uniform. The last time I had worn a uniform was on 12 September 1969, when the minister of war, General Muhammad Fawzi, had informed me that I had been removed from my position as chief of staff. Although more than five years had passed, I still remember that at that moment I had said to him, 'All I want is to be able to take part when the time comes for a total war against Israel. I hope by then I'll be back in service even as a platoon commander or a common soldier.' But I went back home thinking that I'd never be given the opportunity to return to the armed forces.
>
> At dawn on 14 May 1971, President Sadat appointed me head of general intelligence. I was happy with the appointment. It was

an acknowledgment of my services as a soldier who had given his life to Egypt and an opportunity to take part, in some way, in the service of my country and in its sacred battle.

I started my new duties but these responsibilities did not distance me from the armed forces and my lifelong friends-at-arms. I was also in regular and direct contact with the armed forces, but I did not expect, as mentioned, that the day would come when I would return to serve in its ranks once more.

But the day had come when the supreme commander, President Sadat, had charged me with a mission and, despite the enormous responsibility and the dangers, I was full of optimism and self-confidence.[3]

It was common knowledge that the relationship between General Ahmad Isma'il and Lieutenant General Sa'd al-Din al-Shadhli had not been good for the last couple of years. With Isma'il's appointment as minister of war and commander in chief at a time when al-Shadhli was chief of staff and subordinate to him in rank, some anxiety was felt about the effects this strained relationship would have on work. In fact, the personalities of both men were very different, as were their professional interests and concerns. Lieutenant General al-Shadhli was not on good terms with Ahmad Isma'il. They were two completely different personalities.

When President Sadat summoned Lieutenant General al-Shadhli at noon of 26 October 1972 to notify him that he had decided to appoint a new minister of war in place of General Sadeq, the president said, "I'm thinking of Ahmad Isma'il." Here al-Shadhli recalls that he was surprised by the name and immediately commented, saying, "Your Excellency, there's a long history of differences between us, going back nearly twelve years since we met in the Congo in 1960. Our relationship has been marked by coldness and indifference. I believe that cooperation between us will be difficult." The president replied, "I know the history of these differences and their details. But I assure you that your relationship with him will be much better than your relationship with Sadeq." Nevertheless, al-Shadhli repeated his reservations and fears that this relationship could affect the military situation and preparations for war. But the president repeated his remark and assured him once more that none of his fears were justified.

Despite the differences between the two men, I must admit that their energies remained totally focused on the coming war, just as the armed forces as a whole were concentrated on preparations for war. Nothing, it seemed to me, came to disrupt this.

However, during military operations in the October War, particularly in the final stages, Isma'il and al-Shadhli had opposing views on strategy and their thinking was very different. It became clear that each had lost confidence in the other and this impacted negatively on the military situation in the last days of war.

DISCUSSIONS OF WAR WITH AHMAD ISMA'IL

Immediately after my return from Damascus, General Ahmad Isma'il received me with the same friendliness that had marked our relationship since our days together at Canal Front Command after the June War. He greeted me joyfully, saying, "I've come back to the armed forces as you predicted," alluding to the conversation we had had at the Cairo airport ten months earlier. He continued, "Vice Admiral Fuad Abu Zikri has also returned as commander of the naval forces and he is now installed in his office in Alexandria."

General Isma'il was referring to the fact that he and Vice Admiral Abu Zikri had left the service at the same time in 1969, and now they had returned together in 1972. He believed it was a rehabilitation—the righting of an injustice—and he was greatly satisfied by it.

I should mention that General Isma'il had been relieved from his functions as chief of staff and Vice Admiral Abu Zikri from his position as commander of the naval forces after a land and sea raid in the Za'farana sector on the west coast of the Gulf of Suez on 9 September 1968, during the War of Attrition.

And now they were both back once more, to carry the heavy burden of responsibility under even more difficult conditions. General Ahmad Isma'il had extensive military experience, especially in the field, where he rose from commander of an infantry platoon to commander of an infantry division. He was then appointed commander of the Suez Canal front after the June 1967 war and then became chief of staff. Vice Admiral Abu Zikri also had extensive experience and had devoted his whole life to the navy. He was deeply respected by his men.

The relationship had been close between the three of us as students during 1965 and 1966 at the Higher Military Institute of the Nasir Military Academy. During that time I had come to know them, their personalities, and their military thinking well. This was of great help during the planning period preceding the war and during actual operations. I worked closely with both men and we had very high expectations of each other at the armed forces high command, which itself was a cohesive and well-integrated team with a single goal driving it forward: the defeat of Israel in the coming war. The command included Air Vice Marshal Husni

Mubarak, commander of the air force, and Major General Muhammad 'Ali Fahmi, commander of the air defense forces, and relations were characterized by close collaboration and high professionalism.

During the first meeting with General Ahmad Isma'il, we discussed the military situation at length. I realized that he was extremely well-informed and had a very precise idea of what was going on in the forces because of his previous position as head of general intelligence. Specifically, he wanted to know how much time would be needed to reach full combat readiness, and I sensed that he had all the determination and will needed to achieve this in the shortest possible time.

Ahmad Isma'il believed that because five years had passed with the army tied down on the canal front, the men were now threatened with what used to be called 'trench disease,' which sapped morale and the will to fight. He also believed that politics had "crept in through the back door" and that an unacceptable level of political activity was going on in some quarters of the forces. This had shaken confidence in many of the commanding officers and, as a result, the nation's defense capability had been open to doubt. Technical equipment and training had been allowed to deteriorate and the troops' living conditions neglected so that conditions on the front were substandard.

Although war is an extension of politics or, as some say, politics by the use of force, this does not mean that the two activities should be confused. Politics has its politicians and fighting its fighters. As military men, we have well-defined duties and missions, and our skill lies in improving fighting capacity and efficiency, not in meddling in politics. History is a witness to the fact that when politics infiltrates an army, it inevitably corrupts it.

General Isma'il was convinced that the weapons we had were perfectly good, but that the general decline in standards and confidence had raised doubts about their quality. He said,

> I admit that there are weapons and equipment better than ours in some areas, but who is to say that ours are not effective simply because they are not of the latest type? Whoever says this is deliberately looking for an excuse not to fight.
>
> At any rate, we have to take this into consideration when we plan missions—the missions should match both the weapons and the capacities available. In brief, the best plan must suit the available conditions to achieve our fighting goals.

With regard to the Syrian front, General Isma'il said, "I was shocked by what has been said about Egypt's and Syria's inability to cooperate or coordinate. The two countries are like two sides of a pincer that can come together to crush and paralyze the enemy. They are both Arab countries and share an ancient tradition and a contemporary history. Today, they are joined by common interests and a common goal. The man in Syria is the same as the man in Egypt—capable and ready to give. So why so many fears and doubts?"[4]

I listened to Ahmad Isma'il, discussed his views at length and in depth, and responded to every question that was raised. I talked in detail of the military situation, our state of readiness, our present plans, and cooperation with Syria.

My honest reply to his question on timing and combat readiness was that the facts suggested that we needed a year to accomplish three essential goals. First, the armed forces should come out of their dugouts and trenches, meaning that their defensive posture of many years had to change into an aggressive and offensive attitude, in line with our plans. This required concentrated training in offensive maneuvers for all branches of the armed forces—and close cooperation between them. I was very clear about this; after Isma'il's appointment as commander in chief we were not going to start from scratch once more. The work had already begun and had to be continued and completed. I also made it clear that the soldiers and their commanding officers were doing their best to match training with actual battle conditions and to overcome the difficulties of the past. I said that General Isma'il would get to see this for himself.

As for politics entering the armed forces, I agreed that it should remain separate. If senior officers were to concentrate on raising combat readiness and training standards for their assigned missions, there should be no room for political exchanges between them. And with the usual frankness to which we had become accustomed during our service together at the canal front, I told General Isma'il that Egypt's defense plan was not open to doubt and that he should be reassured on that score. If some equipment had deteriorated, it could be seen to immediately.

The second important item I raised was the matter of working out the details of the plan in the light of the weapons and equipment we now possessed, without depending on the delivery of new weapons. Experience had shown that agreements were one thing, delivery and timing of delivery another thing. If and when weapons did arrive, it would be just an additional advantage. I told him that the plan lacked the element of surprise which would give us the opportunity to storm the canal with the least number of losses, particularly since the enemy was militarily superior and was in a strong strategic position.

The third point I raised was that we had to complete the process of cooperation with the Syrian forces. This was proving to be a sensitive and lengthy procedure and although we had already moved several stages forward, some steps still needed coordination and agreement between the Egyptian and Syrian military commands. Presidents Sadat and Asad also had to make some political decisions. This would need time.

I explained in detail that my experience with the Syrian military command left me with no doubt whatsoever that cooperation would be successful, contrary to reports he had received that such cooperation was improbable if not impossible. I told him that I believed—and he would see for himself—that Egypt and Syria would cooperate successfully as long as the two presidents saw eye to eye, and that the conditions of the agreement were practicable. This would be one of the factors of success in the coming war, but I would have wished for cooperation with Jordan too so that Israel would have to fight on three fronts simultaneously.

We agreed on these three points. However, General Isma'il felt that my estimate of one year to prepare the army was too long and should be reduced as much as possible. He added two further remarks which in his view required serious attention. First, politics would not be discussed at general command in order to discourage junior officers from the subject. Heavy and intensive training was needed and the inevitability of an early war had to be drummed in, with no substitute for this.

Second, during his years of military service Isma'il had developed the conviction that the human element—the quality of the fighter—and not the weapon was what counted in victory. A soldier, whatever his rank or position and whatever his weapons, had to have confidence in his commanding officers, in his arms, and in the justice of his cause. And his faith in the Almighty came first and last. We had to instill confidence in the soldiers, create trust between them and their commanding officers, and give them confidence in their weapons.

We agreed therefore, during this meeting, on the main elements of a policy to expedite the war and to facilitate coordination with Syria, as this needed more time at both political and military levels.

Numerous meetings took place between General Ahmad Isma'il and the troops in all the main branches of the forces, in the various armies, and in the military zones. I was with him on many of these occasions, when he always emphasized the following ideas:

- Peaceful means to solve the Middle East problem had failed. There was no alternative to war to liberate our land.
- The armed forces were committed to fight at their present potential and capacity. Therefore, there was no need to wait for the arrival of new weapons.
- The main concern of the armed forces was military duty and we had to leave politics to the politicians.
- Our faith in God and the justice of our cause were the guarantees of our success in the war.

Frankly, I believe that General Isma'il's assessment of the situation when he took command, the main thrust of his efforts, and his orders to speed up preparations for war were very much in line with President Sadat's position as clearly expressed to the Supreme Council of the Armed Forces at the Giza meeting on 24 October 1972.

As I have mentioned before, because of his prior experience as head of general intelligence, Ahmad Isma'il devoted a great deal of time and attention to changing the prevailing mood in the armed forces and to creating the proper atmosphere. When I later became closer to President Sadat, I learned that he had agreed completely with the general on the need for a change in the military climate. This in fact could well have been originally President Sadat's personal opinion put into practice by General Isma'il.

After a number of field visits I felt confident that we were moving firmly towards war. The troops and their commanding officers were handling their fighting duties well. Morale was improving day by day and all the men were waiting for the final order. Coordination with Syria became smoother and took on broader dimensions.

My duties as chief of operations staff took up all of my time, so I suggested we appoint a full-time senior officer to coordinate with the Syrian front at the next stage. General Isma'il agreed to appoint General Bahi al-Din Naufal to carry out this task.

And the days passed as we waited for the appropriate political conditions which would herald the order for war.

13

Arab Nationalism and the Struggle

Egypt's military strategy was based on confronting Israel using its own resources in cooperation with Syria. We believed that the actual battle would provide an opportunity for other Arab countries to participate as each saw fit.

The idea that the conflict was an Arab national struggle was shared across the Arab world, and some Arab countries worked at putting this belief into practice. The Arab League tried to set up some form of military cooperation between Arab countries. This was a hope which had remained dormant since the defeat of 1967, in spite of successive Arab summit meetings in the aftermath of that war.

It was essential to us at the armed forces general command that military operations take place on three fronts—Egyptian, Syrian, and Jordanian—and for other Arab countries to participate on these fronts with at least part of their strength. At the Joint Defense Council (one of the administrative bodies of the Arab League) on 27–30 January 1973, we took the opportunity to study this matter in the presence of foreign ministers and ministers of defense from the various Arab countries.

Egypt presented a report in which Minister of War General Ahmad Isma'il outlined the Arab strategic position, the principles of the plan to liberate Arab land, and the general concept behind the planning. The report ended with precise recommendations for joint military action and clear guidelines for specific Arab commitments in military personnel and units.[1]

The report began:

Since the end of the third round with Israel in June 1967, Israel's strategy has been to integrate and absorb its gains and impose a fait accompli in some areas. This requires a response in the Arab national interest to avert the dangers inherent in such a strategy as well as the devastating consequences it can have on the Arab cause. What Israel is now doing in occupied Arab territories and its fortifications and fortresses on the Arab lines of confrontation all provide a clear picture of the nature of its strategy in our region, which aims to dominate the Arab people and force them to surrender. Therefore, to perpetuate the situation which now exists among ourselves will neither help nor promote a solution for the liberation of occupied Arab land.

Based on this understanding, and on the fact that no individual Arab country alone can impose our collective will or enforce an Arab solution, it has become necessary for all Arab political and military efforts to come together to create an integrated political and economic position with regard to our relationships with friendly countries. In this way, victory can be achieved against our Zionist enemy.

The time has come for the Arab nation to give all it has to this battle for self-determination. We all agree that the conflict is a struggle for survival in the face of an expansionist, racist, and colonial power which can only be destroyed by complete and total resistance and a united effort to commit all our potential. Israel's political goal is to impose a legal presence in Palestine and to consolidate this presence by adding new Arab territories and by removing anything obstructing its own growth and development as a first step towards its next stage of expansion, which would realize Israel's dream of creating a Jewish state from the Nile to the Euphrates.

As for Israel's military goal, it is to prevent the Arab countries and the Palestinian resistance from regaining their land either by force of arms or by threatening Israel's national security. In this way, the Arabs will eventually be compelled to give in to Israel's political goals.

The main elements of Israel's strategy are to preserve air superiority and the air force as its main force of attack, but to keep the peace on the ceasefire lines until a solution is imposed to its advantage. This strategy also includes disrupting any unified Arab military action, consolidating the status quo in the occupied territories, and distorting the facts on the Palestinian issue.

After General Ahmad Isma'il's report had covered the strengths and capabilities of the enemy, estimated distribution of enemy troops on the Arab fronts, potential areas of confrontation, and enemy factors of strength and weakness, it became apparent that a united Arab offensive would have to consider the following tactics:

1. Force the enemy to fight on all fronts at the same time and prevent its strategy of fighting on one front at a time.
2. Use both the Syrian and Jordanian fronts to expose the enemy heartland, especially through the air force.
3. Disperse the enemy's mobilized and strategic reserves.
4. Block enemy naval lines of communication in the Mediterranean and Red Seas.
5. Use the *fedayeen* (Palestinian guerrillas) extensively within Israel itself.
6. Start offensive action as soon as possible. (If the average growth of military potential was to continue at the same pace and in the same proportions as today this will be to the advantage of the enemy and will become increasingly difficult to manage as time goes by).

From an Arab perspective, a political goal had been agreed upon at the Kuwait conference of 15 November 1972. This was "to remove the effects of the June 1967 aggression without prejudicing the Palestinian cause and the national rights of the Palestinian people." As for a military strategy, it was "within a general Arab framework to destroy the Israeli armed forces and liberate Arab land occupied after 5 June 1967."

If we look at the major points of strength of the three Arab confrontation states—Egypt, Syria, and Jordan—we find that the Arabs did have the ability to fight on more than one front simultaneously and to force the enemy to disperse its forces. Our land and naval forces were superior and could limit the effectiveness of the enemy air force if the air potential of supporting Arab states was also used. The *fedayeen* could also threaten internal security in the occupied land to our battle advantage.

As for the major weak points of the three confrontation states, these were:

1. A strategic opening created by the absence of Jordanian participation in the military operations, which could affect the military situation.
2. An obvious deficiency in planes and effective air defense systems in the countries of confrontation.

3. The lack of an adequate general reserve on each of the three fronts as well as the lack of a general strategic reserve for the northern and eastern fronts (Syria and Jordan).
4. Lack of one command for the three fronts while the Israeli forces were under one command coordinating action on all fronts.
5. An obvious deficiency in electronic equipment and material.
6. The enemy's ease of movement and maneuverability from one front to another. This was lacking on the Arab side since we were each defending our own lines.

Comparative tables at the time showed that the situation was as follows:

1. Land Forces
- The enemy would be unable to defend itself effectively on three fronts if they were united.
- It would be possible for the enemy to attack any one of the fronts in case there was no counteroffensive from Arab countries supporting the confrontation states.
- The enemy would be unable to attack any one of the Arab fronts in case the other two fronts launched an attack on Israel.

2. The Air Force
- The air forces of the three confrontation states could carry out 1181 sorties a day and drop 1316 tons of bombs.
- If the confrontation states were reinforced by sixteen air squadrons (which had been approved during the previous conferences), then the potential would rise to 1793 sorties a day with 2265 tons of bombs.
- A previous report put enemy air potential at 1360 sorties a day and 2880 tons of bombs, making it clear that in spite of the Arab support that has been approved, the enemy air force would remain superior by a small margin.
- From this we can conclude that in order to carry out an acceptable challenge to the enemy, the minimum air support needed is what the report suggested.

3. The Air Defense
- Air defense in Egypt was good.
- Air defense in Syria was still at a formative stage and Syria still needed about twenty anti-aircraft missile battalions.
- Jordan's skies were open to Israeli planes and air defense reinforcements were needed; that is, seven anti-aircraft missile battalions and one radar battalion.

4. The Naval Forces
   - The naval forces of Egypt and Syria were superior to the Israeli naval forces, but Israeli air superiority limited their freedom of action.
5. Guerrilla Activity
   - This had to be increased and play a bigger role as an integral part of the overall plan. Guerrilla activity had to come from all fronts (Lebanon, Syria, Jordan, and Egypt) to disperse enemy energies and could be used to remove any obstructions in the way of the Arab armies.

The conclusion drawn from the military study and the comparative tables was that there was a "need for a rapid joint-operations plan for the confrontation states which would divide tasks according to individual capabilities and resources." This plan would:

- Take into consideration the need for increased efficiency on the eastern front. This would be achieved by reinforcing Jordan's land, air, and air defense systems so that joint Arab military action could take place at the same time on three fronts.
- Reinforce the confrontation states with additional aircraft to raise their capabilities in air combat and against the Israeli air defense network.
- Provide both Jordan and Syria with a more developed air defense network using the heights in those countries.
- Equip the confrontation states with more developed electronic hardware.
- Keep in mind the factor of speed. Time was of the essence; delay and procrastination would not benefit the Arabs.

After the Egyptian minister of war, General Isma'il, had presented his comprehensive report, the following recommendations were made.

1. The field of operations should be divided into the following three fronts.
   (a) North, which would include the Syrian forces and any Arab force placed under this command.
   (b) East, which would include the Jordanian forces and any Arab force placed under this command.
   (c) West, which would include the Egyptian forces and any Arab force placed under this command.
2. Guerrilla activity was to be initiated from various fronts of the confrontation states and coordinated by front commands in line with a plan approved by the commander of the Arab forces.

3. Fronts would be under the command of the Egyptian commander in chief in his capacity as the Arab forces commander in chief, and assisted by an operations team from countries participating in the battle.
4. The commander of the Syrian air force would be in charge of the air force on the northern and eastern fronts (Syria and Jordan) and the commander of the Egyptian air force would be in complete command of the three fronts.
5. On the basis of previous agreements at the Joint Defense Council on 30 November 1971, and according to the Committee of Foreign Defense Ministers' military subcommittee recommendations, the support countries would provide support to the confrontation states. In brief, this would consist of sixteen squadrons, one armored division, one infantry division, an armored brigade, and two independent infantry brigades, divided among seven Arab countries: Iraq, Saudi Arabia, Kuwait, Libya, Algeria, Morocco, and Sudan. This support was considered adequate for resistance and deterrence. Additional support for offensive operations was also itemized, and support countries were committed to provide it through existing active units, equipment, or financial aid, according to a budget previously agreed on by chiefs of staff.
6. Support troops for deterrence and resistance were to be ready by March 1973 to move to their operations positions following instructions from the Arab forces commander in chief. The additional support units for offensive operations had to be ready as soon as possible, according to the agreement.

I was happy to have collaborated on the minister of war's report and to have attended the meetings of the Joint Defense Council, which were objective and positive. I would have wished to see an implementation of the decisions, however, which were an entirely new development in Arab strategy and could have become a major factor in the success of the expected war. Unfortunately this was not to be, and the council's resolutions did not see the light of day. The Arabs lost a unique opportunity to unite and to cooperate militarily to liberate their land and regain the rights of the Palestinian people.

There must have been powerful political reasons for the lack of implementation. The burden placed on the support countries was not great, was well within their means, and did not affect their national security. To the contrary, it would have ensured collective Arab security and consequently their own national security. The reality of the Arab situation was that it was only bilateral relations which worked successfully to reinforce the Egyptian and Syrian fronts with troops from some other Arab countries after the war had started. However, these forces didn't arrive on the battlefield at the appropriate time. They could have been much more effective if they had positioned themselves on the front before the war, integrated with the forces already there, and made themselves familiar with the terrain.

I must mention here that the October War started without opening the Jordanian front, despite its obvious importance. This did not prevent Jordan from participating with part of its forces on the Syrian front during the action.

We can imagine the results of a war waged on three Arab fronts simultaneously against Israel, with one coordinated plan and under the command of one man, as had been decided by the Joint Defense Council.

This brings into question the Arab League's purpose and charter and raises the hope that it might become sufficiently reformed to accomplish the ends for which it was created.

Plan L

Since the Arab countries were not able to implement the recommendations of the Joint Defense Council, which would have turned the battle into an Arab common cause, cooperation between Egypt and Syria continued on its solitary but positive course.

After the Egyptian–Syrian joint plan had been completed and the troops prepared and trained, with only the timing of the attack and the actual declaration of war remaining, an Arab head of state put forward a new plan of war against Israel. General Ahmad Isma'il called me to his office to look at the plan and give my comments. What I saw in front of me was one more of the many revolutionary ideas brought forward at various times by this leader and applied in his own country, whether through a green book or a book of any other color. He had not given the plan a coded name, so I called it Plan L, and in my opinion it was a sweet fantasy and wishful thinking.

In summary, the strategy behind Plan L was that the Egyptian attack and the crossing of the Suez Canal would not be considered the decisive assault despite the great losses the Egyptian army would sustain, especially as a result of the enemy's air superiority. The alternative suggested was the following.

1. The main air and land attack should come from Syria's direction and the greatest number of Egyptian aircraft should be used to provide air cover under which the Syrian forces could move. Land

forces in Syria could be increased by forces from Egypt, Libya, and other countries.

2. A crippling assault should be launched against Israel from southern Lebanon and northern Jordan, using the *fedayeen*, to widen the area of attack. The enemy, for the first time, would lose the initiative as a result of the air attack from the Syrian front and suffer damage to its own installations and equipment.
3. The Egyptian forces should be kept as a strategic reserve to use after the situation on the Syrian front became clearer. Their role should be limited to naval attacks and landings. In Gaza and the north coastline, a naval attack would be launched against Eilat and Sharm al-Shaykh using scattered paratroop landings to confuse the enemy and disperse its forces. Heavy artillery shelling of the east bank of the canal would mislead the enemy into thinking it was an attack from the canal side, and ease pressure on the Syrian front.
4. The military goal would be to destroy Israel's power, both material and psychological.
5. The political goal would be to impose the United Nations Partition Resolution of 1947.
6. This republic considered the plan mandatory for its participation in the war. Otherwise, it would officially announce its non-participation in a disaster that may bring about the end of the Arab nation.

The Theory and Its Practice

In Egypt we were unambiguous. The plan was not appropriate for the strategic needs of the region. It was unrealistic, impractical, and impossible to implement for a number of reasons. First, the size, condition, and strategic position of the enemy forces and their combat capabilities confirmed the need to attack from two separate fronts at once to scatter and dilute their superior air power (the major threat), to disperse their land forces over more than one front, and to inflict the greatest number of casualties—losses which were a principal point of their weakness—in major battles on more than one front on land, sea, or air. To use the Syrian front for the main thrust of the war might seem theoretically correct because of its proximity to Israel and because of the existence of some Israeli targets within range of our planes. But from the practical perspective, a concentration of Syrian and Egyptian aircraft in Syria was unfeasible because of a lack of sufficient airports to service these planes. Moreover, as it stood, Syrian air defense would be unable to protect such a large number of planes, and we would have to shift additional Egyptian air defense to Syria. This would mean weakening the air cover over Egyptian territory and exposing the armed forces, which could have dangerous consequences. The range of our respective aircraft when taking off from Syria covered only north and part of central Israel; airports in central and south Israel, as well as those in Sinai, would remain outside their range. Consequently, aircraft would be able to regroup in these zones and continue to function efficiently given their long-range capacity. The outcome of the Israeli air attack of 5 June 1967 would not be allowed to be repeated.

Second, a major land offensive from Syria's direction and extending the battle terrain using Jordan and Lebanon faced unresolvable political difficulties, as experience had taught us.

Third, the battle was a battle of honor for Egypt. We had to go through with it both to liberate our land and to erase the shame of the 1967 defeat. That our forces would be exposed to heavy losses was a fact we had to accept. Our land could not be liberated and our pride restored without sacrifice and the acceptance of calculated losses.

Fourth, limiting the role of the Egyptian forces in Plan L to a secondary and diversionary action, with naval landings in Gaza and the north coast and parachute landings in various places, was unacceptable from a military standpoint since these forces could neither be joined nor supported by land forces within the specific time limit. If the Egyptian forces were to carry out decoy or secondary action, then the naval and air landings were doomed to remain just that and the men participating would be killed without having achieved anything more substantial. Political, strategic, and technical targets would not have been achieved either.

Fifth, keeping the Egyptian forces as a strategic reserve to be used only after feedback from the Syrian front, as suggested by Plan L, was wrong both practically and theoretically. A strategic reserve should be used to influence developments on either of the fronts, or in a major thrust, or in changing conditions at the opportune moment. It would be impossible to implement by air because of lack of sufficient air transport facilities, not to mention enemy air superiority. By sea it would be equally impractical because of lack of sufficient naval transport and the time factor. Therefore, if the Egyptian forces were to become a strategic reserve as Plan L proposed, the question became: a reserve for whom?

Finally, if the plan's political goal was to impose the Partition Resolution of 1947, did a comparison of Arab and Israeli forces suggest that Israel could be destroyed militarily? And where had Arab military superiority come from at a time when we were suffering from Israel's military superiority? Politically, would it have been possible to impose a partition, assuming that we could do this militarily?

Our answer to Plan L then was for its author to return to reality. We hoped the day would come when the Arabs would speak with one voice and would use their united military, economic, and political resources to liberate the Golan Heights, the West Bank, and the Gaza Strip from Israeli occupation and to create a Palestinian nation after an Israeli occupation that had lasted twenty-two years, after the Palestinian resistance and the Palestine Liberation Organization had done all they could during those long years. The opportunity presented itself in 1973 to put the philosophy behind the 'Arab struggle' into practice.

Egypt turned down Plan L and concluded that the best strategy for war against Israel was a simultaneous offensive operation by the joint Egyptian and Syrian forces and coordinated action under one strategy with one commander for the forces of both fronts.

14

A Dead End

From the moment the UN Security Council ceasefire resolution was issued on 8 June 1967, Egypt and the Arab countries had worked hard for a peaceful solution to the crisis. They had accepted UN Security Council Resolution 242 of 22 November 1967 in an international atmosphere hostile to the Arabs because of the closure of the Straits of Tiran, which was seen as a direct cause of the June War. In this climate, and while the fighting was still going on, the Security Council had decided on a ceasefire without stipulating the return to pre-June lines. This meant that the international community had accepted the continued occupation of Arab territory until a comprehensive settlement of the Arab–Israeli conflict was worked out in a manner which would satisfy all the parties' demands. The resolution was therefore interpreted as providing a 'balanced' settlement. Egypt, Syria, and Jordan accepted the resolution under the pressure of the collapse of the military front and until the time came when world opinion would be more responsive to their position.

Egypt's acceptance of UN Resolution 242 saw the beginning of a political and diplomatic effort to change the international climate to favor the Arabs, to isolate Israel, to demonstrate that Israel was the belligerent party refusing a peaceful solution, and because of this to prepare international opinion to accept the inevitable military sequel.

Objectively, the resolution itself rejected the principal of the occupation of territory by force and was aligned with the Arab position. It also confirmed the principles of sovereignty, territorial integrity, and political autonomy. All these were basic requirements of the Arab side and could only be premised on the withdrawal of Israel from Arab territory.

The resolution did not accept the Israeli demand for direct negotiations between the Arabs and Israel but created a special body headed by Ambassador Gunnar Jarring, representing the Secretary-General, and to whom it would report directly on the implementation of the resolution by the parties concerned.

International efforts to implement Resolution 242 began with Ambassador Jarring's mission. After intensive efforts to communicate with the various sides, Jarring presented a set of questions to Egypt and to Israel on 8 February 1971. The government of Israel was asked if it was ready to withdraw to the international boundaries between Egypt and Palestine during the mandate period. Egypt was asked if it was ready to enter into a peace agreement with Israel.

Egypt replied that it was ready to implement Resolution 242 fully if Israel carried out all its obligations (the withdrawal to international boundaries from all land occupied on 5 June 1967 and respect for the sovereignty and territorial integrity of the countries of the region). This led to wide support for the Arab position and a more sympathetic understanding of the issues.

Israel's answer was that it would not withdraw to the pre-June 1967 lines, thereby exposing itself to the charge that its intentions were expansionist and consequently losing part of the international support it had relied on for so long. It also insisted that any settlement be negotiated directly by all parties concerned.

The four great powers (the United States, the Soviet Union, France, and Britain) tried to break the deadlock with a proposal made by France in January 1969, but the good offices of these four countries had failed by August 1971 as a result of US obstacles and Israeli insistence on direct negotiations with the Arabs.

During this period, separate bilateral talks between the United States and the Soviet Union also failed to reach any solution to the crisis, and negotiations ground to a halt. At that time US Assistant Secretary of State Joseph Sisco declared that he did not believe Israel had to return the land occupied in June 1967 since the Security Council resolution did not stipulate this.

The Rogers Initiative

As a result of continued clashes and skirmishes between Egypt and Israel, and the eighteen-month War of Attrition with fighting escalating dangerously, the US Secretary of State, William Rogers, on June 1970 presented an initiative for a ceasefire to last for a period of ninety days when both parties would enter new negotiations through Ambassador Jarring to implement Resolution 242. The two parties accepted the ceasefire on 8 August 1970, but Israel did not follow up on the second part of the initiative and was not pressured to do so by the United States, which led to the failure of the Rogers plan.

On 4 February 1971, President Sadat announced that Egypt refused to extend the ceasefire further, because a new 'status quo' was in the making to perpetuate a 'no peace, no war' situation which Israel could exploit to validate its occupation.

President Sadat's Initiative

On 5 February 1971, President Sadat announced his own peace initiative and spelled it out in a speech he gave in May of that same year. It stipulated a partial withdrawal of the Israeli forces as a first step towards complete withdrawal, during which time Egypt would begin to dredge the Suez Canal and open it up to international navigation. Following this, Egypt would accept an extension of the ceasefire for a limited period during which Ambassador Jarring would draw up a timetable for the implementation of the Security Council resolution.

Egyptian forces would cross the Suez Canal to the east bank while arrangements were taking place for the separation of the two armies during the ceasefire period. If at the end of this period no concrete progress had been made, then Egypt would be entitled to resort to force to regain its land. Egypt would refuse to discuss disarming in Sinai but was ready to accept 'zones of disarmament' on both sides of the border in accordance with the Security Council resolution. Any form of Israeli presence in Sharm al-Shaykh was rejected.

Israel's response betrayed its true intentions when it announced that the Sadat initiative offered nothing new and that it would not withdraw from the east bank of the canal. At a press conference, Israeli Minister of Defense Dayan declared that "Israel has no intention ever to withdraw from the last line it has seized." In this way Israel persisted in maintaining the deadlock.

The Council of African Heads of State

At the African summit conference of June 1971, a committee was formed of ten African heads of states for the application of Resolution 242, with a subcommittee of four appointed to contact the parties concerned in the Middle East problem. Their efforts fell through because of Israel's refusal to make a commitment that it would not annex Arab territory.

The African states now had firsthand experience which showed that Israel's intentions were expansionist and that Israel did not act in the interests of peace. International opinion slowly began to shift toward accepting that the Arabs were entitled to use force to regain their lands.

Military Entente and *Laissez-Aller*

In 1972, all indicators pointed to a growing policy of entente as part of the long-term strategy of the United States and the Soviet Union (targeted for a period lasting at least twenty or thirty years, in Brezhnev's estimate). This understanding aimed at ending the cold war and heralding a period of peaceful coexistence between East and West. The danger of such a policy to the Middle East became clear when it was realized that there would be no confrontation between the United States and the Soviets, even under provocation by less powerful nations.

During the Moscow meeting, the two superpowers decided that there would be an easing of military tension in the Middle East region once the crisis there was solved. This meant no force was to be used to solve the problem. The net result in practical terms was that the Arabs would have to succumb to the fait accompli and consequently Israel would be able to impose its own terms for a solution.

These decisions were followed by a powerful psychological campaign whose purpose was to sow the seeds of despair in our hearts, using the June 1967 defeat, the continued Israeli occupation, and the deadlock to pressure the Arabs into submitting to the status quo and accepting what was being offered, which was to the enemy's complete advantage.

The United States Vetoes a UN Resolution

At the beginning of 1973, Egypt launched a concentrated diplomatic offensive by contacting the five permanent members of the UN Security Council.

Support from the Soviet Union was unambiguous. The British position reflected the Conservative government's demand for Israel's withdrawal to the international borders of Egypt. The French understood our position and were sympathetic. The Chinese were backing us in principle. The US position, however, was negative.

The United States believed that we should make concessions for the situation to move, claiming that it couldn't or didn't have the power to pressure Israel. President Nixon declared that the problem was now one of reconciling Egyptian sovereignty over its territory with the requirements of Israeli security.

Egypt asked for a meeting of the Security Council and a report from the UN secretary-general on the Jarring mission. On 26 July 1973, a resolution presented by the group of nonaligned nations was put to the vote and the extent of the growing support for the Arab position became obvious. Fourteen council votes were for the resolution, which condemned the continued Israeli occupation of Arab land, but the resolution was vetoed by the United States.

The diplomatic offensive ended with Israel's isolation. The nations of the world stood on one side of the divide and Israel and the United States on the other. The international mood had become, we felt, more prepared to accept the kind of military action which Egypt and Syria were planning.

Although Israel had become isolated internationally and continued to depend totally on the United States, the Israeli political parties in their elections campaigns for October 1973 competed in their intransigence not only over returning to the pre-June 1967 borders but over the settlements in occupied territories which, they provocatively asserted, would increase and multiply, with Jerusalem remaining Israel's eternal capital.

Slowly and insidiously, feelings of doubt and despair in the ability of Egypt and Syria to fight began to overtake the Arab world, and wild rumors started to spread. The international community began to lose confidence in Arab claims and statements, suggesting that Arabs talked better than they could act. Egypt and Syria, in the meantime, patiently and silently continued to prepare for war.

By the middle of 1973, the international community (other than the United States and Israel) had to face up to its failure to broker a peaceful solution, but sympathy and support for the Arab position was now widespread. The condition of 'no peace, no war' was to the obvious advantage of the two superpowers and Israel. The only options open to Egypt and Syria were either to accept the fait accompli, with all its drawbacks and destructive potential, or to enter a new war. Increasingly, war was seen as a patriotic necessity, both nationally and at the Arab level, in the face of the continued deadlock despite all Arab political and diplomatic efforts. War was in fact inevitable.

15

The Necessity of War

Events in 1973 were leading inexorably to war. It became essential to add the factor of time as a key element after a silence which had lasted two and a half years since the Rogers initiative in August 1970. We had to study the timing of the attack to coordinate political and military efforts and harness the energies of state institutions as discreetly as possible. General Ahmad Isma'il asked the operations staff to look into the matter to be ready to discuss it with the political leadership.

In operations headquarters our judgment was that Egypt had exhausted all the political and diplomatic avenues to break out of the state of 'no peace, no war' or to find an equitable solution to the Middle East problem. It became clear that the entente between the United States and the Soviet Union would not create conditions suitable for a settlement in favor of the Arabs. On the contrary, the present deadlock was advantageous both to them and to Israel.

We felt that any extension of the stalemate would lead to a weakened sense of urgency amongst the Arab states and a loss of confidence in Egypt and Syria's commitment to war. First signs of this had already appeared with the collapse of the eastern front (Syria, Jordan, and Iraq), with Jordan distancing itself from Syria and other Arabs.

Moreover, pressures on Egyptian–Soviet relations were increasing and doubts rose as to their value, despite Soviet support of the Arab cause and the Soviet Union's continued role as our sole supplier of weapons. The unease had naturally increased after the termination of the Soviet advisors' mission in Egypt, which seemed to signal that our fighting ability would decline, particularly with regard to air defense, and this reinforced doubts about our decision to go to war.

In our opinion, time would give Israel the opportunity to limit and restrict *fedayeen* activity, confirm the status quo in the occupied territories, continue to create settlements and try to absorb territory (thereby confusing national boundaries and linking the West Bank and Gaza sector to the Israeli economy), accustom Palestinians to life with Israel, and manipulate international public opinion into accepting the fait accompli. Moreover, despite the US administration's position, US interests in the Arab world were not threatened and were not likely to be in the near future. Militarily, we estimated that further delay would allow Israel to build up its armed forces, especially the air force, and improve its defenses on both the Egyptian and Syrian fronts.

As for Arab support, it was not expected that this would visibly change in the near future, or significantly alter the military situation. On the other hand, a prolonged waiting period could influence morale on the Egyptian–Syrian side and increase the military conscription period in Egypt, which had already been extended to five or six years.

The Egyptian fighter had changed radically after the June 1967 war. Young men with a middle and higher education were drafted and now made up a large proportion of the combat units in technical and professional fields, serving as regular soldiers or reserve officers.

With a general mobilization in place since 1967, the number of soldiers had increased yearly and reached more than half a million. The longer time passed, the greater was the desire for a definitive war to regain our land and to end this suspended state of 'no peace, no war' which was sapping Egypt's economic and human resources and creating increasing internal pressure with every day that passed. For all these reasons, waiting was more costly in the balance. This made it imperative to reduce the time-frame for war to an absolute minimum needed to make final preparations and complete coordination with Syria.

This was our recommendation at operations headquarters. General Ahmad Isma'il did not object when I informed him of this and we agreed that a date for the war was now essential, but that this was partly a political decision to come from Presidents Sadat and Asad.

In Egypt the main topic of conversation became the war. President Sadat announced on several different occasions that he had made the decision to go to war and that the armed forces must be ready. His speech to the Supreme Council of the Armed Forces on 24 October 1972 in Giza had made this clear. However, none of these statements took an official form.

In the meantime, Muhammad Hafez Isma'il, our national security advisor, met Dr. Henry Kissinger twice during the first half of 1973, once in Paris in February 1973 and a second time in April.[1]

President Sadat recorded part of what was discussed between Kissinger and Isma'il at these meetings. Kissinger had said,

> My advice to Sadat is to be realistic. We live in a world of facts and we can't build on hopes and fantasy. The fact is that you have been defeated so don't ask for a victor's spoils. There have to be concessions on your part so that America can help you. . . . How is it possible, in your defeat, to impose conditions on the other party? Either you can change the facts and consequently our perceptions will naturally change with regard to a solution, or you can't change the facts, in which case solutions other than the ones you are offering will have to be found to suit your circumstances.
>
> I hope that what I am saying is clear. I'm certainly not asking Sadat to change the military situation. If he tries that, Israel will win once again and more so than in 1967. In such a situation, it would be very difficult for us to do anything. . . . This loss will be terrible for Egypt and for Sadat personally. He is a man I would like to deal with some day.

Sadat continued, saying,

> Those were Kissinger's words in February and April 1973. So I told myself there's no hope from the Americans. Israel has taken the Americans over and the policies of [President] Johnson still put Israel's interests above America's interests.
>
> As the Egyptian man in the street says, Israel is the guardian of America's interest in the Middle East. Israel has created this role for herself—or else America has created it for Israel. In either case, the result is the same. There is no hope for peace through America as long as Israel does not want peace.[2]

President Sadat took it upon himself to reshuffle the cabinet with himself as prime minister in March 1973. The new cabinet met on 5 April and agreed, with almost no reservations, on the need for war.

National security advisor Muhammad Hafez Isma'il has described this cabinet meeting.

The president opened discussions with a personal evaluation of the situation in the Middle East. He said that although the United States could solve the Arab–Israeli conflict, it did not want to do so in order to allow Israel to impose its will in the Arab world. He was in favor of extending the front to all of the Arab countries and linking this to military action so that political negotiations for a settlement would continue through military action.

Therefore he had asked General Isma'il to look into a breaking of the ceasefire while we went to the Security Council to present our issue and intensify our diplomatic campaign.

Hafez Isma'il continues:

General Isma'il then spoke about his visit to the eastern Arab countries. His assessment was that they were reluctant to get into a war because they feared a repeat of the 1967 debacle. He had not felt any readiness for financial participation. Kuwait's disagreements with Iraq inclined it to a peaceful settlement. Iraq was not ready to participate in a war because of its problems with Iran and preferred joint Arab action with regard to the supply of oil. As for Syria, the Soviets were urging it to avoid a military confrontation.

A discussion followed in which a number of important points were raised. These could be considered a framework for the approaching war.

1. The goal was to 'liberate the land' and not to break the deadlock to force Israel into serious negotiations.
2. Planning for an extended battle should be based on excellent intelligence and projections of Israeli reactions.
3. Time was no longer in our favor, but even so it was necessary to avoid responding to any provocation so as to complete the military buildup and preparations on the civilian front.
4. Precautionary measures needed to be taken against a preemptive strike by Israel, either if it feels that peace puts it in a critical position or if it feels threatened by force.
5. There was a need for continued Soviet military support, despite of our doubts about the Soviets.
6. It was important to maintain control over the flow of oil and transfer Arab funds away from Western financial institutions.
7. We would go to the Security Council (within the framework of our diplomatic campaign) to put on record the final international position on a political settlement before resorting to military action.

The president summed up by saying that it was an excellent meeting—a historic meeting without precedent. He thanked those attending, and assured them that he would not get into a war he risked losing only to have to accept an imposed political solution. If he found that it was not within our capabilities to fight, he would say so, without hesitation.[3]

16

The Timing of the War: El-Gamasy's Notebook

After the Giza meeting of 24 October 1972 I had become even more sure that we were nearing the war. What caught my attention at the meeting was President Sadat saying,

> Today the armed forces are faced with a test. The June 1967 defeat has made both enemy and friend doubt that we would ever fight again. Consequently, all the solutions I am presented with are based on this logic. . . . In the face of our people, our enemies, and our friends, we must prove unemotionally and with careful planning that we are capable of sacrifice and can stand up and fight and change the situation with whatever means are at our disposal. . . . We have to manage our affairs with whatever we have at hand—we have to follow this plan to change the situation and set fire to the region. Then words will have real meaning and value. If we remain passive, our cause will disintegrate and die . . .

By the beginning of 1973, we had concluded that time was running against us. Until an agreement was reached between Sadat and Asad for a date on the war and coordination between Egypt and Syria was completed, it was important for those of us at Armed Forces Operations Headquarters to work out the best timing possible for an offensive operation during 1973 and also give President Sadat some flexibility and choice over the appropriate political climate and to get President's Asad's agreement. In this way, military readiness would mesh smoothly with political choice.

On the initiative of the operations staff, we reviewed the situation on the ground and developed a framework for the planned offensive operation. We studied the technical characteristics of the Suez Canal, the ebb and flow of the tides, the speed of the currents and their direction, hours of darkness and of moonlight, weather conditions, and related conditions in the Mediterranean and Red Seas. We were looking for a time of optimal conditions for us and worst possible conditions for Israel. It was also important to find a time suitable for action on both the Syrian and Egyptian fronts.

We studied the months of the year to select the best months for a crossing in light of all the prevailing natural conditions. We found that the difference between the highest and lowest tide was eighty centimeters in the northern sector of the canal (Port Said to Isma'iliya) while the difference in water level in the southern sector (Isma'iliya to Suez) was two meters. The speed of the currents in the northern sector was eighteen meters per minute, while in the southern sector it was ninety meters per minute. As for the direction of the current, this changed cyclically every six hours from north to south and vice versa. We needed this data to work out how and when best to cross the canal.

We looked for a long night, in the sense that the first half had to be in moonlight and the second in darkness. We intended to assemble the bridges in the moonlight, while the crossing would be effected in darkness. Optimal weather conditions were also essential for air and naval operations in the Mediterranean and Red Seas.

The study also looked into official holidays in Israel other than Saturday, which is their weekly sabbath. These were the times when the enemy was expected to be least ready for war. We found that they had eight religious feasts a year, three of which fell in October 1973. These were Yom Kippur (the Feast of Atonement), the Feast of the Tabernacles, and the Feast of the Torah. Each of these had its specific traditions and rites. What was important to us was to know the effect each holiday had on general mobilization in Israel since their forces depended very largely on reservists for war. The Israeli Army was like an iceberg with the visible part, the active services, and the broader invisible part, the reserve forces. Israel had a number of ways to recall its reserves without making this public, notably by broadcasting code words and sentences through national radio and television. We discovered that Yom Kippur fell on a Saturday and, what was more important, that it was the only day throughout the year in which radio and television stopped broadcasting as part of the religious observance and traditions of that feast. In other words, a speedy recall of the reserve forces using public means could not be made. Consequently, they would have to use other and slower means to mobilize the reserves.

Then we looked at another domestic factor. Elections of the Workers Union (Histadrut) were taking place in September and the Knesset elections on 28 October. The election campaign would certainly be preoccupying the general public, a large part of which was part of the reserve army. October 1973 therefore appeared a good time for war, if all the other factors also proved suitable for an offensive.

On the Syrian front, weather conditions deteriorated after October with the beginning of snowfall and therefore this was a natural cut-off date. We were thus able to identify the most appropriate months in 1973 as May, August, or September–October. The best time was October, as weather conditions were good for a crossing, the nights remaining were long, some nights in darkness for long periods. Furthermore, conditions at sea were suitable for naval operations.

October had three religious feasts and a parliamentary election. The sacred month of Ramadan also fell during October, to the moral and psychological advantage of our own forces. The enemy would not have expected us to carry out an attack during a month of fasting.

From this long and detailed study, we concluded that the day the offensive was to be launched should be an official holiday, that the differences in canal water levels (high and low tide) should be minimal to provide the best conditions for a crossing by boat and for the assembling of our bridges. Moonlight was needed for the first half of the night, with darkness for the crossing during the second half. The timing of the attack was to be scheduled for either May or August or September–October, and a particular day was specified for each.

Saturday 6 October 1973 (10 Ramadan 1393) was the day chosen for the September–October option. Conditions for a crossing were good, it was a feast day in Israel, and the moon on that day, 10 Ramadan, shone from sunset until midnight. Most of the other conditions were there too, and although some people have persisted in believing that 6 October was selected only because it was Yom Kippur in Israel. This is a misconception; a constellation of factors governed the choice of that particular day.

I presented the results of the study—handwritten to ensure secrecy—to General Ahmad Isma'il, who later told me he had discussed it with President Sadat at Burg al-'Arab (west of Alexandria) at the beginning of April 1973. On his return, he handed it back personally and transmitted President Sadat's appreciation. Thanks were also due to the operations command staff as a whole, and later Isma'il's written comment was, "Selecting a day for the attack was an achievement on a high level. This is a job which will go down in the history of war as an example of considerable scientific precision and thorough research."

This was the document to which President Sadat referred as 'El-Gamasy's notebook' in discussions following the war.

I must give full credit to the armed forces operations staff as well as to various specialist bodies in the armed forces who participated with their knowledge and skills in the scientific and technical aspects of the document and without whom it would not have been possible to compile. The document belongs not to myself but to the Armed Forces Operations Staff, which I value greatly and am proud to have headed during a critical period in the history of the armed forces and Egypt.

In his autobiography President Sadat has said that

> in April 1973, President Hafez al-Asad made a secret visit to Egypt. Lieutenant General El-Gamasy was Chief of the Operations Department of the Armed Forces at the time. He brought us a memorandum in which he had listed suitable times for military operations throughout the year from a scientific and military perspective. The notes were handwritten and highly secret. There were three groups of appropriate dates: in May 1973, in August and September 1973, and thirdly in October 1973. [Author's note: actually they were May, August, and September–October 1973.]
>
> The best date was October, particularly since the Syrian front was inoperational from November until spring because of winter conditions there.
>
> During this meeting between Hafez al-Asad and myself at Burg al-'Arab, west of Alexandria, I told him: 'I've decided on a battle this year and have given my instructions to General Ahmad Isma'il. What is your opinion? Asad replied, 'I am with you and will come into the war, and we are preparing for this.'
>
> I agreed with Hafez al-Asad not to start the battle before setting up a joint higher committee for the Syrian–Egyptian forces. This was accomplished and the committee met in Alexandria in August 1973 to make the final arrangements for the battle.[1]

THE ALEXANDRIA CONFERENCE, 22–23 AUGUST 1973

While the city of Alexandria was filled with holiday-makers on the beaches relaxing and enjoying themselves, senior Syrian officers arrived in complete secrecy to finalize matters with their Egyptian counterparts and returned to Syria without anybody having felt their presence.

The Syrians were headed by Major General Mustafa Tlass, minister of defense, and with him were the chief of staff, the chief of operations, the head of military intelligence, the commander of the air force and air defense, and the commander of the naval forces. The Egyptians were headed by General Ahmad Isma'il, minister of war. With him were the chief of staff, chief of operations, head of military intelligence, the commander of the air force, the commander of air defense, and the commander of the naval forces. We were thirteen commanding officers to make up the Egyptian–Syrian joint committee. This meeting was also attended by Major General Bahi al-Din Naufal from the Joint Defense Council.

We met at the office of Vice Admiral Fuad Abu Zikri (commander of the naval forces) to make the final decisions on a number of joint concerns, the most important of which was a final agreement on a date to launch war.

May had passed without a political decision on a date for war. Our meeting took place in the last week in August, so all we had left of the year was September and October. If a decision was not forthcoming for either month, it would mean a postponement till 1974, which went against our evaluation of the military and political situation.

It was decided that the war would take place in October 1973 and the decision was noted down by hand for security purposes. It required confirmation from the political leadership, so President Sadat left for consultations with Saudi Arabia, Qatar, and finally Syria, where he met with President Asad in Damascus on 28 and 29 of August and when they agreed that 6 October 1973 would be the day on which the war would begin.

The Alexandria conference was the last step in the process of military cooperation between Egypt and Syria. This had taken a lot of time but the effort was crowned with success.

There is no doubt that the meeting of the Syrian–Egyptian Armed Forces Higher Committee to decide on war against Israel in a joint and coordinated effort was historic. Military cooperation such as this between two Arab countries, against Israel, had never happened since Israel's creation. The meeting was a powerful indicator, a sign of latent possibilities and the energies behind a war that—in the eyes of Israel and the world—erupted suddenly and unexpectedly.

Among the many paradoxes of those days was the fact that at a time when Egypt and Syria had decided on war, Israel during that same month of August had concluded that peace with the Arabs was not necessary. The fait accompli had been imposed by force.

Nahum Goldman, who at the time headed the American Jewish Congress, was on a visit to Israel that August, researching a book. His main concern was the question of what was better for Israel: holding on to occupied land or a political settlement? Dayan's reply to this (which reflected official opinion) was that the peace which Israel needed had been accomplished since 1967. He said, "We are working towards an 'informal' peace between us and the Arabs; we do not need a formal peace. To try to achieve a formal peace would perhaps be detrimental to the situation we are trying to preserve, which is to consolidate the status quo resulting from the war and to transform it into an unofficial peace."

Goldman said, "My question is precise and I want the answer to be precise. That is, do you believe that Israel's interest lies in the land or the settlements?"

Dayan replied, "I cannot accept anything but a peace based on strength which will give Israel safe borders because they change according to the nature of the growth and expansion of Israel. If we are trying, ourselves, to become a proxy for the great powers in the Middle East, then we have to have teeth and these are military, economic, and geographic. The first—military power—will help accomplish the others."[2]

At this point, we must not forget that the 1973 war demonstrated without equivocation that Israel in reality had not been able to impose a peace by force and that it had been equally unable to impose the so-called 'status quo' following the June 1967 war. The arrogance which had marked Israel's behavior since 1967 led their political and military leaders to believe that the June 1967 war was 'the war to end all wars.'

17

The Decision for War

Preparations for war went on uninterrupted until a few days before the countdown and outbreak. On 30 September 1973, the National Defense Council was unexpectedly asked to meet at the request of President Sadat and a full political and military review was conducted. Council meetings are usually not attended by members of the armed forces, except for the minister of war. At the meeting, General Ahmad Isma'il outlined the concepts behind the battle strategy, clarifying some points and responding to questions. He said:

1. Egypt would carry out the operation jointly with Syria and was confident that the outcome would pressure Israel into accepting the conditions for a peaceful solution.
2. The battle was well within our capabilities. However, reinforcements and supplies from the Soviet Union were limited and would not allow us to liberate all of Sinai.
3. The Egyptian–Syrian forces would strike hard. This would not be a repeat of the War of Attrition; it would be a long war and we expected heavy losses, but the Israeli forces would suffer even greater losses.
4. Time was not to our advantage, either psychologically or materially. Therefore we could not put off a military operation.
5. Israel might start the war to take the initiative if it realized that we were preparing to attack. The element of surprise was therefore a vital factor for success.

6. Our forces lacked air superiority as well as the facilities for strategic mobilization reconnaissance. But Israel would not win this war.

At the end of the meeting, President Sadat summarized matters by emphasizing the following points.

1. War was inevitable—we had to move from a defensive to an offensive mode so long as Israel continued to behave as though it were unconquerable and could therefore force its conditions on us.
2. We had now entered a 'danger zone' where the persistence of the present situation would become a death sentence. The Americans had estimated it would take two years for Egypt to give up hope and capitulate to the situation. Therefore, without a battle Egypt would collapse.
3. We were now going through the most difficult period. There could be no decision more serious than the decision now in hand and we had to take up this challenge.
4. We would not sever communications with America despite having broken the ceasefire.[1]

President Sadat refrained from giving the National Defense Council any date for the war.

President Sadat's own words about the meeting are:

> On 30 September 1973, I convened the National Defense Council and asked members to give their opinions on the situation, and we discussed them at length. Some wanted war and others hesitated. The minister of supply said that existing supplies were not sufficient for a long battle.
>
> After everybody had discussed this and domestic conditions in Egypt, and new developments, I told them, 'Each of you has had his say. Fine, I now want to tell you that our economy today is at zero and we have commitments till the end of the year which we will not be able to fulfill with the banks. When 1974 arrives in two months time, we won't have a loaf of bread for our people. And I can't ask any Arab for a single dollar because the Arabs tell us that they are paying compensation for [lost] Suez Canal revenues and that's enough. If there's no war, there's nothing.
>
> That is how I broke the news and ended the meeting.[2]

On the first day of October 1973, the day after the meeting of the National Defense Council, training maneuvers began, and under their cover the last touches were added to the attack on the Suez front.

The Operations Center moved to its designated location and work began there. At general headquarters we monitored every move made by Israel in response to the decoy plan now being set in motion. There is no doubt that Israel was also concentrating on every Egyptian and Syrian move on both fronts. The following six days until 6 October were extremely critical and sensitive and we could not afford any mistake, misjudgment of the situation, or faulty implementation in light of the many activities taking place in total secrecy. Military intelligence played a major role at this crucial time.

On the evening of 1 October, (5 Ramadan, 1393), the Supreme Council of the Armed Forces met at the Ministry of War. President Sadat listened to reports from commanding officers and then spoke of his own responsibilities with regard to the war. He asked for their total commitment to the plan of operations and urged them to act freely, independently, and calmly. He said, "Each one of you must carry out his duty. I am behind you and I will bear all of the responsibility—historically, materially, and morally. But I can honestly tell you that I have full confidence in you. And on that basis, act fearlessly and boldly."

General Ahmad Isma'il replied, saying, "In the name of all the officers and of the armed forces we pledge to do our utmost to bring victory to our country. Every officer is full of optimism and trusts that it is within his power to accomplish his mission. We all take part in sharing the responsibility with Your Excellency and we all are responsible for our country, along with you."

We read the fatiha together, lifting our hearts to God to grant us success and victory. The meeting was held one evening during the holy month of Ramadan.

The situation was more perilous than can be imagined. We were at a momentous juncture, when the futures of Egypt, Syria, and the Arab world would be played out for long years to come. If victorious, then we would have emerged from a catastrophe we had been living with for years. But if we lost the war, God forbid, then the Egyptian people would be unforgiving of a situation they would find impossible to bear.

On that day, President Sadat issued the order for war under the heading "Directives to the Commander of the Armed Forces and Minister of War, General Ahmad Isma'il 'Ali, 5 Ramadan 1393, 1 October 1973." In this he gave a precise evaluation of the overall situation, the enemy's strategy, and Egypt's strategy (at this stage), stating that the time was now propitious, from a political perspective, to go ahead.

It is important here to provide the text of the directive so that the reader may follow the chain of events of the war in the light of both this and another strategic directive issued on 9 Ramadan (5 October) 1973.[3]

FIRST: ON THE GENERAL SITUATION

1. More than six years have passed since the Israeli enemy occupied parts of our Arab land.
2. Israel enjoys American backing, particularly with regard to the supply of arms. . . . It has tried and continues to try to impose its will on us and to end the Middle East crisis in such a way as to ensure almost complete domination of the Arab region, its security, and its fate.
3. Since the UN Security Council resolution for a ceasefire on 8 June 1967, Egypt has tried in every way to find a solution to the crisis. To this end it has explored various alternatives, from accepting the Security Council resolution of 26 November 1967, the efforts of Ambassador Jarring, the efforts of all the great powers, followed by those of the two superpowers, the initiative presented by the US Secretary of State William Rogers, and the direct offer of an initiative for a solution in which the opening of the Suez Canal would be the beginning of a phased total withdrawal in implementation of the Security Council resolution. All these efforts failed to reach a solution. They were either blocked or frustrated by our enemies.
4. Egypt has initiated limited military operations in 1968, 1969, and 1970. It has also provided powerful support for the activities of Palestinian resistance on the borders or in the occupied territories. . . . None of these operations, although effective to some extent, has produced the desired pressure on the enemy.
5. Egypt has been aware throughout this period that the time would come when it would have to take its responsibilities in hand and that the most important task was to be ready for that day . . . when it was in our power to defend our land and honor.
6. The Egyptian people have endured beyond what can be imagined by friend or foe alike, both materially and psychologically—an oppressive burden which no people could have borne except those believing in freedom and willing to sacrifice for it.
7. Significant improvements have occurred in the Arab political situation in general, and this increases the chances of effective action . . . With a growing energy crisis and international financial problems, under the appropriate conditions Arab pressure could become a valuable factor. . . .

10. The international situation is in continuous flux. . . . We might find ourselves facing long-term situations which would limit our freedom of action and our right to choose the options most suitable to us.

SECOND: ON THE STRATEGY OF THE ENEMY

As we see, the Israeli enemy has decided on a policy based on intimidation, claiming rights it believes the Arabs cannot challenge. . . . This is the basis of the Israeli theory of 'security' which is predicated on repressing the Arabs psychologically, politically, and militarily.

The principal component to the idea of 'security' is to persuade Egypt and the Arab nation that defying Israel is futile and consequently that they have no choice except to bend to Israel's conditions, even if this means making concessions which would affect their national sovereignty.

THIRD: ON EGYPT'S STRATEGY DURING THIS PERIOD

The strategic goal for which I am politically responsible and which I have delegated to the Egyptian Armed Forces, in the confidence of all the reports reaching me on our armed capabilities, can be summarized as follows:

To challenge the Israeli theory of 'security' with military action according to the capabilities of our armed forces, with the purpose of inflicting the greatest losses possible, to persuade the enemy that a continued occupation of our land would be more costly than it can afford . . . and to demonstrate that a security based on psychological, political, and military intimidation is precarious and will not provide protection either now or in the future.

If we can successfully challenge this notion, it will lead to certain results in the near and distant future. In the near future undermining this belief in 'security' could eventually lead to an honorable solution to the Middle East crisis. In the more distant future, this might initiate cumulative changes which would fundamentally transform enemy perceptions, thereby limiting its aggressive tendencies.

FOURTH: ON TIMING

From a political perspective, the time is right for the kind of action foreseen in the third part of this directive.

The internal front, the Arab front (including our cooperation with the northern front), and international conditions now provide us with an opportunity to initiate action. And with Israel's isolation by the international community—and its present domestic climate of party squabbling and in-fighting over the elections—then opportunities will increase.

On that same day, 1 October 1973, a meeting also took place in Israel. Israeli chiefs of staff met to study the situation after signs of increased activity in Egypt and Syria and Arab press reports suggesting that Israel was concentrating its forces on the borders and intended to carry out a military operation against them.

General Eliahu Za'ira, head of military intelligence, presented a detailed report on conditions on the Egyptian and Syrian fronts. This confirmed the existence of a state of high readiness on both fronts. But Za'ira told the chiefs of staff that "this phenomenon occurred in June and nothing happened. However, the possibility exists that Egypt and Syria might carry out a military operation as a palliative to distract attention away from poor domestic political conditions in both countries or as a spectacle for local public consumption."

WEDNESDAY, 3 OCTOBER 1973

Training maneuvers continued in Egypt and final preparations for war were taking place under their cover. General Ahmad Isma'il left secretly for Damascus to determine Syrian readiness for an attack on 6 October. During this short visit, he met with President Hafez al-Asad who assured him that preparations were on schedule and going according to plan.

General Isma'il had already notified his colleague Major General Mustafa Tlass, Syrian minister of war, of the time for the Syrian forces to be ready. I myself wrote by hand the warning order that went to the Syrians. An officer delivered it to Damascus in a sealed envelope, in complete secrecy, without knowing its contents.

Israeli Prime Minister Meir was on a visit to Austria and we were happy that she was abroad at the time because any political decision concerning mobilization or war had to be made by the prime minister and the cabinet.

Immediately upon her return from Austria, a meeting was held on 3 October in response to a request by Minister of Defense Dayan. It was attended by General Elazer, the chief of staff, the commander of the air force, and a deputy to the head of military intelligence. As Dayan mentions in his memoirs, Israel had received information on weapons reinforcements on the Syrian front and possibly on the Egyptian front, and there was news of preparations for war.

Israeli intelligence dismissed the activities on the Egyptian front merely as military maneuvers. There were no signs, it said, that Syria intended to wage war.

FRIDAY, 5 OCTOBER 1973

Our armed forces were at their highest state of alert. At the Operations Center we were closely following enemy activity. This was vital as there were only twenty-four hours left before the war was to start.

On that day President Sadat issued a strategic directive to General Ahmad Isma'il dated 9 Ramadan, or 5 October 1973, the text of which follows.[4]

1. Based on the political and military directive of 1 October 1973 and on the conditions of the present political and strategic situation, I have decided to entrust the armed forces with the following strategic mission to:
   a) put an end to the present military inertia by breaking the ceasefire as of 6 October 1973;
   b) inflict the highest losses possible on the enemy in men, arms, and equipment;
   c) liberate the occupied territory in progressive stages according to developments and the abilities and potential of the armed forces.
2. These missions are to be implemented by the Egyptian Armed Forces on their own or in coordination with the Syrian Armed Forces.

When General Isma'il showed me this strategic directive, I asked him why President Sadat had issued such a document since we already had the directive of 1 October 1973 in which the strategic target was defined and the operations plan clearly stated, as well as the date of attack, which was 6 October.

General Isma'il replied that he had asked for this second directive as a record for history. The new document was a clearly-worded order to break the ceasefire on 6 October. This date had not previously been mentioned. Although political rather than military, the intention had to be openly stated. Moreover, the new directive clearly defined the action required to liberate the land; that is, in progressive stages according to developments and the abilities and potential of the armed forces, so that it could not be interpreted in the future to mean that the liberation of the whole of Sinai had been required. It confirmed, for the record, the strategies set by the political leadership for the armed forces.

18

We Surprised Them Before They Could Outwit Us

Our forces went to war under difficult and complicated conditions in October 1973. The goal was to shatter the Israeli notion of security, which it used as a cover to expand and to impose the status quo on the Arabs.

We had not forgotten what Dayan had said nearly a month and a half before the war, namely that the peace Israel desired it had already achieved in 1967, that a formal peace with the Arabs would be counterproductive for its intentions to consolidate the status quo, and that Israel's borders changed automatically in line with its expanding territory.

We had to go to war, no matter the difficulties or sacrifices, to regain our land. But in this war the following points had to be kept in mind.

- The enemy enjoyed military superiority, and the natural condition is for the attacker to be stronger than the defender. We had to incapacitate the enemy at the initial stage of the war with the assault across the Suez Canal.
- The enemy was behind an entrenched line on the east bank of the canal and had experienced troops on the Sinai front line backed by armored columns. We had no alternative but to succeed in the initial attack, storm the fortifications, and destroy them. And in this way, Israel's idea of security would be challenged and invalidated.
- The planned crossing of the Suez Canal was with two armies, which included five divisions and the forces of the Port Said zone

(nearly one hundred thousand fighters). This could be considered one of the most difficult military operations since the Suez Canal, like the Panama Canal, is one of the two most daunting water barriers in the world.

- A successful crossing required bridges, ferries, and the opening up of passages in the massive embankments on the eastern bank of the canal. Each passage meant moving 1,500 cubic meters of sand and would take several hours. The bridges would have to be ready and in place within eight hours for the tanks and heavy weapons. If we surprised the Israelis and made the crossing, then we would have gained time and prevented a quick response that would have obstructed the work on the passages and on the bridges.
- The enemy's intelligence apparatus had a reputation for being very competent and was known for its collaboration with the US intelligence services. If these services discovered our intention to attack, then Israel would launch a preemptive strike which would make our mission even more complicated and difficult. Israel would also mobilize its reserves and send them to the Egyptian and Syrian fronts within two days.

For all these reasons, we had to make sure we had the element of surprise so that the initiative would be ours for the first time in a war against Israel. We wanted to prevent an early Israeli mobilization and a possible preemptive strike. We also wanted to ensure that the crossing—as well as the assault on the Golan—would be made with the least possible losses because we were already estimating our losses on the canal front in the thousands of dead and wounded.

Our forces in the canal zone were in visual contact with the enemy since there was only the width of the canal (about 200 meters) between us. Troop concentrations on the Syrian front were also under constant observation by the enemy in the occupied Golan Heights and Gabal al-Shaykh, which overlooked the lower plains areas. Thus both fronts were exposed and it was not difficult for the enemy to detect any major changes in numbers of troops or an increased battle readiness. This illustrates how difficult it was to create the element of surprise under these conditions.

Another difficulty was to implement a deception strategy so that it would appear genuine not only to the enemy but also to our own troops, as well to any foreign intelligence agents involved. To this end, a very small number of officers from the operations staff were included in planning the deception or decoy plan, which was written out by hand, just like the operations plan. It consisted of a package of different measures and operations designed to give the enemy the impression that Egypt and Syria had no offensive intentions but were instead working to reinforce their defenses in preparation for a possible Israeli attack.

A TRAINING MANEUVER

The first step in the plan was to start training maneuvers for all of the branches of the armed forces, the armies, and the military zones. Under this cover, the final preparations for the attack would take place so that the maneuvers could turn into an actual assault according to the plan of operations. Instructions were issued for maneuvers to take place during the period 1–7 October 1973.

No special orders were issued to the troops so that it would seem like a normal exercise. It was essential that Israel should find out that we were carrying out these maneuvers, which was what actually happened. Our forces had already conducted maneuvers on a wide scale during the first half of 1973, at which time Israel had been forced to make a partial mobilization and to put its forces on high alert, and this had cost it millions of dollars. We were very pleased about this at the time because we were getting Israel used to 'maneuvers' which would later metamorphose into a real war, but which would seem normal from its point of view. Later, it was demonstrated that Israeli intelligence had indeed qualified our activities in the first week of October 1973 as normal training exercises.

It was necessary to mobilize reserve forces in Egypt before the outbreak of war, even though the enemy would inevitably know about this, as would the families and colleagues of the thousands of conscripts and reserve officers called up. For the mobilization to appear as a repetition of previous maneuvers, thousands of men were made to return to their villages and their workplaces a few days before the war began. Those we required for active service were kept back. The public was taken in, and the news spread that the mobilization was for regular maneuvers and not for war. It was expected that Israeli intelligence would follow these events, which would confirm the deception.

The movement of the troops to the canal front line was gradually undertaken in phases, in secret and under cover of darkness. This was done with no problems and with total discipline. We needed to move a brigade from Alexandria to the canal zone by rail, using several trains to transport men, weapons, tanks, and vehicles. We knew that this would be difficult to hide and would provoke gossip in Alexandria, whose citizens are famously tight-knit and cohesive. Instructions were therefore issued saying that the brigade was on maneuvers in the canal zone until 7 October. Trains were reserved for its return to Alexandria after this date.

Destroyers at Bab al-Mandab

Our destroyers had to reach their zones of operations before noon of 6 October to block the Israeli naval lines of communication in the Straits of Bab al-Mandab. With this in mind, we contacted a friendly Asian country in the early days of 1973 to receive the vessels for repair in their shipyards. After this was done, we then asked Sudan and South Yemen for approval for a friendly visit to Port Sudan and Aden. The schedule was such that the destroyers would in the Straits of Bab al-Mandab on the morning of 6 October.

To keep the purpose of the visits secret, naval command made sure that the destroyers were fully equipped and combat-ready. When the time came, commanding officers were ordered to open a secret envelope with combat orders to obstruct the Israeli lines of naval communication in the straits. This was successfully accomplished.

The mission came as an unpleasant surprise to Israel. It was forced to concede that holding on to Sharm al-Shaykh to safeguard naval navigation in the Straits of Tiran was of no practical value and the case for this was dropped.

'Umra Pilgrimage to Mecca

Each year before the month of Ramadan, thousands of Muslims prepare themselves to go on the 'umra, a minor pilgrimage to the holy city of Mecca in the Kingdom of Saudi Arabia. In this context, the Ministry of War made a public announcement through newspapers and in the armed forces that registration was open for military personnel to take part in the pilgrimage. Instructions were issued to the various branches of the forces to accept requests in the usual manner. News of this published in the Egyptian press was an open letter to Israel and to foreign embassies in Egypt that an attack was not at the top of our priorities.

Within the operations staff, a good friend and colleague, Major General Faruq Fahmi (may he rest in peace) signed up for the pilgrimage. He was known for his strict observance of Islam and went on a pilgrimage whenever the opportunity presented itself. I would not clear his request for several days and he came to my office more than once to try to change my mind. My excuse was that it was his duty to give others an opportunity to go on the pilgrimage. Finally, I accepted his request knowing that he would not be able to travel. That is what happened and he took part in the war alongside us. We pledged that we would carry out the hajj (pilgrimage) together after the war, and we did, thanks be to God.

Unexpectedly, circumstances took a turn in that the Romanian minister of defense asked to visit Egypt. A date was set for 8 October, as is normal procedure, and it was useful to announce this visit, notify the relevant authorities, and organize a complete program for his visit. We knew that war was imminent and that the visit would be canceled. This was not an integral part of the plan but a natural event which we made use of.

A BLANKET OF SECRECY

These were some of the measures taken to mislead the enemy. I will not expand on other operations—and there were many—because to do so would touch on various confidential military and political matters and implicate the media. I've satisfied myself by giving just a few examples.

The second factor needed to ensure the element of surprise was to impose total secrecy within the armed forces so that each commanding officer would be given the orders to fight at a defined hour, according to his command level, in enough time to guarantee preparation for combat. In this way, every level was informed of the time of attack according to a timetable set by the general command and all of the armed forces would be ready by 6 October 1973.

The choice of the hour of attack, 14:05 (2:05 P.M.), was a surprise to everybody. The traditional time for an attack is at first light or last light of day. We didn't follow tradition for many technical and operational reasons. This issue was of importance to the Egyptian and Syrian general commands and was subjected to a long and meticulous analysis until we agreed that the timing should be the same for both fronts.

Transporting the bridges to the Suez Canal was an obvious signal to the enemy that a canal crossing was imminent. Accordingly, transport vehicles and trucks carried the equipment at night, covered with canvas, in detached pieces to be placed in specially-dug pits along the front.

THREE TROUBLESOME EVENTS

During the last three days before the war, three incidents almost exposed us and could have lost us the advantage of surprise.

The first occurred on 4 October when we discovered that the Soviet Union had decided to evacuate Soviet families from Egypt on the evenings of 4 and 5 October. This could neither be covered up, camouflaged, canceled, nor its timing changed. At general command, we were sure that Israel and the United States would hear of this and it would be correctly interpreted as a powerful signal of an imminent and major military operation. Later it was shown to have been treated as such by Israel, along with other information from various sources, which suggested that something was brewing in the region—and which was why Soviet families were being evacuated.

The second incident I learned of when I went into General Ahmad Isma'il's office during a telephone conversation on 5 October. General Isma'il was asking the minister of civil aviation, Engineer Ahmad Nuh, to cancel instructions just issued to protect the civil air fleet (EgyptAir), which included dispatching a number of aircraft out of Cairo International Airport and changing the schedule of some flights. These precautionary measures would have immediately been picked up internationally and Israel would have quickly heard about it. We were able to deal with the situation at the appropriate time so that civil aviation traffic remained normal.

The third incident occurred on the morning of 6 October when someone from the Ministry of Industry telephoned to inform me that a US vessel was carrying out a survey of the northern coastline of Egypt and that the naval forces command had refused to allow the ship to leave the port of Alexandria because of maneuvers by the Egyptian navy. The ministry official requested clearance for the vessel to resume its activities. My immediate answer was that the naval forces were indeed carrying out maneuvers but this did not prevent the ship from going out to sea for its normal duties in any direction east towards Port Said or west towards Marsa Matruh. The ship set sail following confirmation from Vice Admiral Fuad Abu Zikri, commander of the naval forces. The ship had sailed only a few miles when the war broke out, but it was neither exposed to danger nor did it interfere with naval operations.

Deception on the Syrian Front

The Syrian command planned and successfully implemented a decoy plan that accomplished its purpose. We had been troubled in Egypt by an air battle which had taken place between the Syrians and the Israelis on 13 September 1973. As a result, tension was high between the two countries. This event brought to mind the air battle between them on 7 April 1967, which had escalated to the military situation preceding the June 1967 war.

Syria's reaction to the September incident was sound. The political and military leadership chose not to retaliate given that there were only three weeks left until the October War, at which time revenge would be on a greater scale. Neither did they provide the enemy with any opportunity to escalate the situation, which would have led to a state of increased military readiness by Israel.

On the other hand, the tension helped make it easier to increase the concentration of Syrian forces on the front, because Israeli intelligence interpreted this as a defensive response in preparation for a future revenge operation.

The Black Belt

While we were planning to liberate our territories, Israel was planning to occupy more Arab land. In his posthumously published memoirs,[1] General Elazer provides a description of the plan.

At the beginning of 1973 Israeli Minister of Defense Dayan produced a military plan, the map for which he drew himself. He presented it to Chief of Staff General Elazer, calling it 'The Black Belt.' For the plan to be executed, Israel needed first to annex all of southern Lebanon; second, to annex other parts of Syria; third, to create a fortified line similar to the Bar-Lev line in the Ghur Valley of Jordan in order to protect its settlements; and fourth, it foresaw transforming Sinai into a nuclear testing site.

Dayan's intention, which showed up clearly on the military map, was the creation of a 'military belt' around Israel, which, from his point of view, would achieve two major goals for Israel. One, it would protect Israel forever from any Arab military threat. Two, it would give the military initiative to Israel in case it wanted to annex further Arab territories.

In Elazer's words, "Dayan dreamt of an act by which history would remember him—exactly as Bar-Lev did with the line of defense bearing his name on the Suez Canal. This meant that after his 'black belt' was accomplished, its name would be changed to 'Dayan's belt.' Dayan behaved as though the Arabs did not exist or had been finished off forever; as he always told us, 'A dead body doesn't need to be taken into account.'"

On 5 October 1973, an emergency meeting of the Israeli chiefs of staff took place. It was attended by Mrs. Golda Meir and Dayan explained his plan, its timing, and its purpose.

The plan provided for a powerful attack against southern Lebanon and another one against Syria. A heavy attack would be directed against Egypt before it could intervene, hitting its air defense missile batteries in the canal zone and all its airports. Dayan proposed that this operation be carried out between 22–25 October following the two feasts (of Atonement and of the Tabernacles), and before the Knesset elections on 28 October.

Following the discussion and the comments raised by the chiefs of staff, and in the light of the information available to them, Meir asked Dayan for a revised opinion. He was silent for a while and then said, "I would make my strike very soon, on the morning of 8 October." Mrs. Meir agreed to implement the plan on 8 October 1973. In preparation, Israel decided to contact the United States immediately and through the United States to inform the Soviet Union that if Egyptian and Syrian troop concentrations were there for fear of an Israeli attack, the fear was unfounded and there was no need for the present state of tension which the Arabs were creating.

Foreign Minister Abba Eban, who was in New York at the time, relayed the message to Kissinger. Eban's comment was that he understood the message to be a 'bait' with two purposes: first, to underline Israel's good intentions and blame the Arabs for the tension; and second, to appease the Egyptians and Syrians at least until 8 October, the date set by Dayan for the strike against them.

Following this disclosure, is any further proof needed of Israel's intention to deceive us until the time came for it to attack Egypt, Syria, and Lebanon and occupy more Arab land? But we caught them by surprise on 6 October, intent on liberating our land, before they could deceive us on 8 October to seize more Arab land.

The Critical Days Before the War

• Thursday 4 October (8 Ramadan)

Operations centers in the general command, the armies, the sectors, and in the air, naval, and air defense forces were buzzing with activity against a background of completely normal behavior. Not only this, but some commanding officers, on their own initiative, added chores to their regular duties which would trick the enemy on the east bank of the canal into thinking that the military situation was normal.

• Friday 5 October (9 Ramadan)

Our armed forces were on maximum alert and at the Operations Center we followed enemy activities step by step. Only twenty-four hours remained before war.

Chief of Staff Lieutenant General Sa'd al-Din al-Shadhli toured the front that morning, first seeing Major General 'Abd al-Mun'im Wasef, commander of the Third Army, then Major General Sa'd al-Din Ma'mun, commander of the Second Army. He returned to the Operations Center in the evening, reassured that matters were proceeding normally and according to plan.

In Israel, Mrs. Meir called for a restricted cabinet meeting, attended by a few ministers, the chief of staff, and the chief of military intelligence. The subject was the situation on the front. Dayan has summarized the reports presented.

> The Syrians and Egyptians were on a state of alert that could be used either defensively or offensively. In the opinion of General Eli Za'ira, chief of intelligence (and this opinion was shared by the chief of staff), there was no possibility of an attack. If a war was really about to break out, there would be more indications and other intelligence reports. Only when other signs appear will it become necessary to mobilize the reserves and undertake other measures. The chief of intelligence believed it was extremely improbable that the Egyptians would cross the canal with large numbers of troops, but they might open fire and try to carry out raids. US intelligence judged that neither Egypt nor Syria intended to fight a war in the near future.[2]

Nevertheless, the Israeli military command put the army on maximum alert, and did likewise for the air force. It canceled all leave and issued initial instructions for a possible mobilization.

• Saturday 6 October (10 Ramadan)

At the Operations Center, all activity by the enemy was closely monitored and military intelligence left nothing to chance. The situation had to be evaluated more than once during the same day. My personal attention was focused on enemy air activity, which I followed on our radar screens. In the event of a discovery, the Israeli air force would have immediately been in evidence.

On that morning, the iron gates of the Operation Center were locked behind us and the maps for maneuvers were replaced by those of the operations plan. The hour of war was fast approaching. From our intelligence we concluded that the enemy was until now not aware that anything was amiss. The remaining few hours would be critical and the enemy could still use its air force against us. Around noon of that day, General Ahmad Isma'il asked about the status of the enemy. This was the third time he'd asked during that morning. I remember that I replied, "The sword has taken the defenseless unawares, as far as Israel is concerned. It has become too late for them to initiate any effective military action."

Time passed slowly—very slowly. The last hour before our planes took off on a first concentrated air attack was endless. Endless.

Dayan, in his memoirs, reveals that Israel had received information from a reliable source at 4:00 A.M. on that day, 6 October, confirming that Egypt and Syria would attack before sunset that same day. This and other intelligence reports, especially those on the evacuation of Soviet families from Egypt and Syria, were, it seemed, credible and genuine. Israel had to act on the supposition that Egypt and Syria intended to start a war.

Prime Minister Meir held a meeting at 8:00 that morning and four principle measures were taken. The first was the mobilization of one hundred to one hundred and twenty thousand men from the reserves, in addition to the regular army. The air force was already completely mobilized. The emergency plan was known and had been tested during maneuvers. Even though the warning had not provided enough time for a full preparation, it had not come too late. The second was to evacuate women and children from the Golan settlements. The third was a suggestion by Chief of Staff Elazer was for a limited preemptive air strike against Syria. The minister of defense opposed this idea on the grounds that it would only be against Syria, not against all the fronts, and did not target the air defense systems but only air bases inside Syria. Not only that, but it could not start before noon. In Dayan's opinion, this preemptive strike would have no significant effect on the development of the war. The suggestion was therefore rejected. The fourth measure was to warn both Egypt and Syria, through the United States, against war. Mrs. Meir called the US Ambassador in Tel Aviv, who conveyed an urgent message to the White House that Israel had finally concluded that Egypt and Syria were planning an attack at 6:00 that day.

At the same time, Mrs. Meir called Foreign Minister Abba Eban in New York to urge Kissinger immediately, through President Nixon, to notify Brezhnev that Israel had received indications that Egypt intended to carry out an attack on the canal front. If this was a reaction to media information on the Israeli mobilization, then Nixon could confirm that Israel had no intention to attack and ask Brezhnev to report this to President Sadat.

On 6 October at 1:45 P.M. Cairo time, Kissinger got in touch with Dr. Muhammad Hasan al-Zayyat, Egypt's foreign minister, who was in New York. He urged that Egypt not undertake any military adventure. By the time Dr. Zayyat was able to reach Muhammad Hafez Isma'il at the Presidency, the war had already been in progress for over quarter of an hour.

Thus the unexpected had happened. We now had the initiative for the first time in successive wars against Israel. The enemy had been deprived of an early mobilization of its reserves and of a preemptive strike against us. This in itself was a major positive factor in storming the canal and launching the assault in the Golan under more favorable conditions, and reduced our losses significantly.

Israel's deceptive attempts at appeasement were nothing more than an attempt to catch the Arabs off-guard on 8 October 1973 with a war which would have prepared the terrain for the planned 'black belt.' Its strategy failed. On 6 October 1973, we had successfully put the Badr Plan into action to liberate our land.

Israeli Minister of Defense Dayan has commented that

> in spite of our self-confidence we were deeply worried. The reason was not only that we were not used to a campaign in which the initiative was in enemy hands, but also the whole situation didn't suit our nature nor our army's structure, which depended largely on the reserve forces and their orderly mobilization. It is not at all easy to shift in twenty-four hours from working in offices or on tractors, or in front of a lathe, to a field of battle. . . . The Egyptian and Syrian attack on Yom Kippur came as a shock to us even though it was expected . . . and we have to add that the enemy forces attacked with much greater competence than we had estimated when we set out our plans.[3]

Israeli Chief of Staff Elazer, in his memoirs, has also recorded his impressions.

> The October War was completely different from other wars we'd entered against the Arabs. The initiative was always in our hands and mobility for us was easy as we were the attackers. This time they were the ones who attacked. This meant that the timing was theirs, the attack was theirs, but the surprise was ours. And now we had to be on the defensive, which was a bitter pill to swallow.

Dr. William B. Quandt, at the time a member of the US National Security Council staff, has said that the October War "caught most of the world, including the United States and Israel, by surprise."[4]

19

6 October: The Crossing

The first days of the month of Ramadan went by. This is a month of special religious observance. Some prepared for the pilgrimage ('umra), including members of the armed forces who had requested and obtained permission to participate.

The general public believed that the armed forces were carrying out training maneuvers, with fathers, sons, officers, and soldiers away from home and work. They thought, as did the foreign embassies in Cairo, that this had prompted the call-up of the reserves. When thousands of reservists were allowed to return to their normal lives, everyone was sure that maneuvers were over for some and would soon be over for the others.

In the Suez Canal sector, life followed its normal course and civilians went about their normal business, including those companies working for the army immediately behind the front line.

Arab ports on the Red Sea received the friendly visits of our destroyers on their way to an Asian country. The destroyers were in the port of Aden on 5 October.

In the United States, President Nixon was out of Washington on holiday while Secretary of State and National Security Advisor Dr. Henry Kissinger was in New York at the United Nations.

"The Canal Cannot be Crossed"

In Israel, the leadership met and discussed the situation on 5 October. Prime Minister Meir was troubled and asked Chief of Staff Elazer to her home that same evening to re-evaluate the situation. She wanted his assurance that the Egyptian forces would not be able to cross the canal. After listening to his exposition of different opinions and points of view, Mrs. Meir asked him, "Do you think that it is within the capabilities of the Egyptians to cross the canal? This is the crucial issue. I ask you this in your capacity as a military man. I need your confirmation especially after General Bar-Lev assured me a short while ago that an Egyptian crossing of the canal is impossible because he has installed oil tanks connected to pipes which in seconds can transform every inch of the canal confrontation line into a murderous mass of fire."

Elazer replied,

> It is well known that the most difficult waterways in the world are . . . the Suez Canal and the Panama Canal, and this is because of their depth and width and the nature of the water. Add to this the fortified defenses on the Bar-Lev line, the ignitable oil weapon, and the thickness and width of the sand embankment. All of this demonstrates, without a second thought, how impossible it would be for the Egyptians to cross the Suez Canal.
>
> I would agree with General Dayan that any Egyptian military move will not go beyond an air strike against our airports on the fronts, or our command and communications center, which is something we can handle very well and have taken precautions against. It is also common knowledge that the Egyptians and the Syrians are religious nations by nature, so how can they fight during Ramadan while fasting?
>
> Our reports also show that the situation on the two banks of the canal remains very calm.

On the morning of 6 October, Israel began its festivities for the Feast of Atonement. General Dayan, with a few senior officers, was at the Bar-Lev line on the east bank of the canal to inspect conditions there and to wish the troops a good feast. From an observation tower he saw for himself that all was well on the west side of the canal. Egyptian soldiers lay on the shore, some of them playing ball and others swimming in the waters of the canal. Everything seemed calm and normal. Dayan returned to Tel Aviv feeling relieved.

At around 1:00 P.M., President Sadat arrived at the Operations Center in military uniform. With him was General Ahmad Isma'il. Each took up his position, waiting for the time to mark the beginning of the war at 2:05 P.M.

And then, the war exploded into action.

The Explosion

At 2:05, the Egyptian and Syrian fronts burst into action simultaneously against the Israeli enemy. A flame was lit to burn out the oppression and the aggression Israel had inflicted on the region since its creation in consecutive wars and repeated aggressions, the last of which was the June 1967 war.

President Sadat qualified Operation Badr as the spark which ignited the region. Some have thought that 'spark' was the code word for this operation and have used it incorrectly as such. However, the overall plan for the war was code-named 'Badr.' Both the Egyptian plan for Sinai and the Syrian plan for the Golan had their own code names, even though they were totally coordinated. Some reports in Egypt have made reference to a 'Plan 200' of 1970 to liberate Sinai in twelve days. Plan 200 was in fact a defensive plan for the Suez Canal sector following the 1967 war, and I had a part in it as chief of staff of the Suez Canal front. The documents are with the Ministry of Defense. In his memoirs, Lieutenant General Sa'd al-Din al-Shadhli confirms this, saying, "Until mid-May 1971, we had no plan for the liberation of Sinai. . . . When I was chief of staff in May 1971 there was no offensive plan, but we had a defensive plan called Plan 200."

President Sadat, in his memoirs, has also said, "The defensive Plan 200, which I inherited from 'Abd al-Nasir, had collapsed. . . . One month before his death, we went together to general headquarters, where he called a meeting of senior Egyptian officers, Soviet advisors, and Muhammad Fawzi, then minister of war. The defensive strategy of Plan 200 was reviewed and then accepted by all present after seven hours of discussion. These were the military conditions I inherited from 'Abd al-Nasir—a 100 percent sound defensive plan, but no offensive plan. This did not exist."

In this first day of war, our air force struck at Israeli targets in Sinai and the Syrian air force hit enemy targets in the Golan. A heavy barrage of artillery fire from both fronts rained down on specific enemy positions. Our troops stormed across the Suez Canal to engage the enemy while Syrian troops cut through enemy defenses on the Golan.

Events followed each other in quick succession. Unexpected strategic and tactical situations developed, as well as unanticipated technical and engineering problems, and battle action was often unorthodox. Both positive and negative outcomes characterized the process of war in its opening stages.

The political impact of the assault, even in its preliminary stages, was profound and had powerful repercussions on the Arab and international levels. It gave a devastating jolt to Israel, which realized that for the first time that it was at war on two fronts at the same time and that this war was intrinsically different. The savage fighting was to continue for twenty-three days until 28 October 1973.

THE FIRST AIR STRIKE

Communiqués from Sinai and the Golan began to pour into military command in Tel Aviv. These spoke of formations of an estimated two hundred or more Egyptian aircraft attacking positions in Sinai and nearly a hundred Syrian aircraft hitting positions in the Golan and Gabal al-Shaykh. It became clear to the Israeli command that this heavy concentration of aircraft was unprecedented. The attacks were completely coordinated and simultaneous.

The first strike took place at 2:05 P.M. At 2:00 P.M. on 6 October, the Egyptian air force had crossed the Suez front line in the direction of several well-defined targets in Sinai. The large numbers of planes flying at very low altitudes across the canal had galvanized our land forces, injecting them with enormous confidence and filling the enemy with fear and panic.

Our planes struck three bases and airports, ten Hawk anti-aircraft missile battery positions, three command centers, and several radar stations and long-range artillery positions. These were hit simultaneously after our aircraft had taken off from different airports and airbases, flying at very low altitudes along pre-determined flight paths to reach their targets at a precise time.

At the Operations Center our hearts were with our pilots and we waited impatiently for feedback on their first air strike and their safe return, hoping for a limited number of casualties. We expected that a major strike in such large numbers against key enemy positions, which would be under the protection of the air defense system, would produce heavy losses in pilots and planes, and they would be very hard to replace.

As it turned out, our pilots, under the command of Air Vice Marshal Muhammad Husni Mubarak, were highly successful in their mission and losses were minimal, with only five planes downed—a lower number than expected. This reflected the magnitude of the effort taken to prepare and plan in the period before the war. With this air strike and with other successful air battles and combat missions, our air force regained the pride and confidence it had lost six years earlier in 1967.

THE INFANTRY AND THE COMMANDOS CROSS OVER

While our air force was pounding targets deep inside Sinai, artillery fire from more than two thousand guns of various calibers supported by surface-to-surface missiles opened fire against the fortifications on the Bar-Lev line and artillery positions behind that line. The bombardment lasted fifty-three minutes, and shelling was so heavy that in the first minute 10,500 rounds were fired at an average rate of 175 per second.

This blanket of artillery fire inflicted heavy enemy losses in men and equipment. It also helped prevent enemy tanks from getting over the high protective sand barriers to the firing platforms which had been prepared in the event of a crossing.

The air attacks, together with the missile strikes and bombardments against enemy command centers and the obstacles and barriers in Gabal Umm Khushayb (the passes), disrupted the Israeli command chain and their field command lost its capacity for coordinated action.

Under the cover of the artillery and in the face of firing from the fortified enemy positions on the east bank, the Second Army, under the command of Major General Sa'd al-Din Ma'mun, and the Third Army, under the command of Major General 'Abd al-Mun'im Wasef, crossed the canal in consecutive waves from Port Said in the north to Suez in the south. The troops were shouting "Allahu Akbar, Allahu Akbar," which was a deep invocation from the heart.

Troops from the infantry and the commandos scrambled forward to climb the protective sand embankments on the east bank, using ingeniously-made rope ladders, in an assault against the fortified positions and the areas around them. The commandos went ahead of the first attacking waves to take the platforms and the positions behind the Bar-Lev line to prevent enemy tanks from getting to them or enemy troops from reinforcing the garrisons manning the Bar-Lev fortifications. Platforms the enemy might eventually reach were mined.

The Israelis, fighting fiercely under the cover of their strongpoints with their tanks in reserve nearby, rushed forward to face our attacking infantry and commando forces. Troops from our artillery armed with anti-tank guided missiles—one of the surprises of the war—moved forward, alongside the infantry troops, hitting at enemy tanks. This was the critical stage and it lasted for several hours until our tanks, artillery, and heavy weapons had completed the crossing. Fighting was fierce. The Israelis who held on to their positions were killed, some were able to escape from the forts by night, others were taken captive, and some of our fighters were martyred.

Our forces continued to move east across the canal in successive waves using dinghies. In the first minutes, around 8,000 fighters had landed on the east side of the canal. One and a half hours later, they had become 14,000. Five hours later, at 7:30 P.M., approximately 33,000 men had crossed over. And so it went. About 750 boats were used for this operation, and around 1,500 rope ladders for climbing the sand embankments on the east side.

During infantry assaults across the canal, some amphibian tanks and pontoons crossed the Bitter Lakes in the Third Army sector and others crossed Lake Timsah in the Second Army sector. Even though they were few in number, they were highly effective.

One of the outstanding characteristics of the battle that day—indeed, throughout the war—was the example set by the commanding officers, always at the head of their men, fighting alongside them on the frontlines, and dying with them. Suffice to say that officers commanding the platoons and companies had crossed during the first minutes of fighting, battalion commanders had crossed within fifteen minutes, brigade commanders were on the east side within the first forty-five minutes, and division commanders within an hour and a half. Consequently, casualties among officers was higher than average, but duty and the determination to succeed in the mission demanded this of them. Victory and the liberation of their land made the sacrifice of life worthwhile.

Egypt's soldiers raised the flag of Egypt on Sinai over the ruins of the Israeli forts on the Bar-Lev line. These had symbolized Israel's power and had been a sign of Egypt's humiliation. We can imagine the strength of the feelings driving our men forward in their combat mission, their willingness to sacrifice their lives, and then their euphoria when they were able once more to raise their flag on Egypt's sacred soil, after six years of occupation.

We followed the assault throughout, moment by moment, at the Operations Center. Our joy was immense when the news came in that the first Egyptian flag had been raised on the east bank of the canal. Communiqués from both armies flooded in reporting success after success. When President Sadat was certain that the assault had succeeded, he ordered, while still at the Operations Center, the release of the first military communiqué. This was broadcast at 2:10 P.M. and the text read: "At half past one today several formations of enemy aircraft attacked our forces in al-Za'farana and al-Sukhna in the Gulf of Suez, while naval vessels approached the west coastline of the gulf. Our forces are now repelling the raiding forces."

Military communiqués continued to be issued, clarifying the situation, until a fifth communiqué was released at 4:00 P.M. It read: "Our forces have succeeded in overrunning the Suez Canal in several different sectors and have seized the major enemy strongpoints there. The Egyptian flag has been raised on the east bank of the canal. The Syrian Armed Forces have also attacked the enemy positions facing them, and have achieved a similar success in various sectors."

In Israel, the military command was following the situation from the central operations room. They were receiving communiqués from their forces in Sinai reporting that hundreds of boats were carrying Egyptian troops across to the east bank. They learned that their forts on the Bar-Lev line had either fallen or were besieged and that the Egyptian flag was flying high in Sinai. They were led to believe that fighting had extended to include all of the canal front and estimated that our forces there (the infantry and the commandos) could not remain for long without the support of heavy weapons, armored vehicles, and mechanical units. They decided on a counterattack to destroy the Egyptian forces before they could consolidate their positions. By that time (5:30 P.M.) we had reached a depth of three to four kilometers east of the canal with forty-five infantry battalions (around thirty-three thousand men), which would be able to repel any enemy counterattack.

Missiles Against Tanks

Fighting continued along several kilometers. The job was to besiege the Israeli forts, weaken them, and destroy those strongholds which were holding on to their positions. At the same time, our forces were having to repulse enemy tank attacks.

This was one of the most difficult situations the men had to face. It was a critical point during which they had to hold their ground against enemy tanks for six to eight hours, using whatever tanks and heavy weapons were with them, until they were joined by reinforcements of heavy weapons and additional tanks which had to cross the canal on bridges or by ferries. Some crossings were delayed or took time to become operational, and this extended the holding operation even longer.

Infantry combat against tanks is not traditional and requires skill and great courage. That afternoon, our infantry troops faced nearly three hundred Israeli tanks along the front line. Some of them were fighting in tank company groups and others were in the reserves. At general command, we had predicted that the enemy would carry out a counterattack such as this, which is why the infantry troops carried anti-tank guided missiles, as well as other anti-tank weapons. With the commandos, the infantry troops managed to destroy about a hundred tanks, or one third of the enemy tanks present on the front line, with some help from an artillery barrage from the west bank of the canal. The enemy counterattack was repelled in the various sectors. The action provided cover for the engineers who were at work opening up passages in the sand embankments to be able to set up the pontoons and bridges.

Fire Over Water

Israel had equipped every strongpoint on the Bar-Lev line with underground storage tanks filled with fuel and other flammable materials. These were connected to the canal by pipes through which the liquid would flow and be ignited electrically from within the strongpoint so that a film of powerful flames would cover the surface of the water and incinerate the men and the assault vessels during a crossing.

This would have been a very effective way to slow down our forces in some sectors or stop them completely in others, not to mention the heavy losses the assault forces would have suffered. We looked at various ways to overcome the problem, but none were satisfactory. We decided to turn to the Corps of Engineers for a solution. On the evening of 5–6 October a group of engineers swam across underwater to carry out a sabotage mission. We all breathed a sigh of relief when they successfully accomplished their purpose without the enemy getting wind of anything. To be extra certain, units of engineers infiltrated the east bank on 6 October under cover of artillery fire to double-check that the pipes carrying the fuel to the water, which had been blocked the previous evening, had remained blocked.

The Israelis found the system inoperational when they tried to ignite it during the crossing. Engineers who had recently been dispatched to the front to check on the system were taken captive almost immediately after their arrival when war broke out.

We should note that Israeli reports, books, and memoirs on the war have completely ignored this episode. It seems that their failure to implement the device encouraged them to keep it under silence. To be sure, if this weapon had succeeded, its inventor would have become a 'genius' around which legends would have been built.

For the record and for posterity, first-class work from military intelligence led to the discovery of this lethal weapon in enough time before the war for us to be able to respond.

Commandos in the Heart of Sinai

Before the last light of 6 October, while the battle was raging on the east bank, commando units were dropped by helicopter into the heart of

Sinai to harass enemy rear positions and to block movements of its reserves towards the canal. The courage and daring for which the commando units were famous played a major role in confusing and slowing down the reserves' progress towards the principal axes and inflicted losses in equipment and men. The commandos carried out bold and suicidal operations to accomplish their mission. We lost a few helicopters. These were spotted by Israeli fighter planes which destroyed them on the ground after they had discharged their load of men and before they were able to take off.

Probably one of the most important commando operations was one unit holding the Sidr Pass for a period of sixteen days. During this time, the unit prevented enemy reserves from going through the pass, despite the exceptional difficulties of fighting in the middle of enemy forces. These men, with perseverance and with God's help, returned safely to join the Third Army east of the canal after we had lost hope of their return. They were a shining example of the will to fight and stubborn tenacity in the line of duty, whatever the cost.

The commandos were under the command of Brigadier General Nabil Shukri and from the first moment of war undertook countless special missions with both the Second and Third Armies. On the second day of combat, 7 October, the Israeli military spokesman's communiqué mentioned that Israeli forces on the canal frontline had found themselves also engaged in battles with Egyptian commandos who had been dropped behind Israeli lines.

THE ENGINEERS AT WORK

While the battle continued at a depth of some kilometers into Sinai, the Israelis on the east bank watched and observed Egyptian engineers perform the most precise and amazing feats of engineering.

A great many engineers had crossed over in the first assault, carrying not only their weapons but their technical equipment with them. The most vital were water hoses fed by pumps, which produced a powerful jet of water to bore through the sand embankments and create passages through the ramparts.

The engineers worked under the constant threat of enemy fire. Their faces and bodies were covered with mud and whenever a man fell or was wounded, another one immediately took his place and the work went on with the hoses (known as water cannons) splitting, cracking, and opening up the sand shield. Three hundred and fifty devices were used and the operation took place in advance of the two armies, in preparation for the installation of the bridges and the pullied ferries.

More than thirty passages were opened up within several hours of the beginning of combat, each dislodging 1,500 cubic meters of sand. The men remained at their work until sixty passages were opened, and when this number had been reached the engineers had ripped away 90,000 cubic meters of sand.

In his memoirs, General Elazer says that

> the most threatening messages reaching us then were those mentioning that the Egyptians, under cover of heavy artillery and infantry fire, had opened up passages in the sand ramparts by using water pressure from special pumps. They had started lowering ferries and equipment into the water at a number of bridgeheads. These dispatches were very disturbing because they meant that a realistic evaluation of the military operation by Egypt and Syria had come too late.
>
> At that moment we went mad and ordered our air force to intensify their attacks in an effort to prevent the opening of more passages through the sand shield and to stop the ferries and bridges from getting to the water. But the Egyptian air defense, using SAM 6 missiles, brought down five of our planes—two Phantoms and three Skyhawks—within 4 minutes.

BRIDGE CONSTRUCTION

Engineers began assembling the bridges at selected sites on the canal. It was necessary to coordinate action to operate the ferries and start installing the bridges while the breaches were being blasted open on the east bank. Input from the engineers was therefore critical to the success of the assault.

We expected the enemy to go to any lengths to stop the bridges from being installed and to destroy those which were already in place using air strikes and artillery, so as to cut off our forces on the east bank and prevent the flow across the canal of tanks, artillery, and heavy weapons. In this way, the enemy would be gaining time for its tanks to demolish our infantry there. However, they saw to their dismay that our engineers persevered with their task despite technical difficulties and under constant enemy fire. The bridges became a reality within eight hours.

A few passages were delayed and consequently the installation of two of the bridges in the Third Army's southern sector were also delayed. They were also coming up against technical difficulties created by the clay and were under heavy enemy fire, which hampered progress. General Ahmad Isma'il asked Major General Gamal Muhammad 'Ali, chief of the Corps of Engineers, to go in person to the troubled sector to supervise completion of the task. Work was completed after a delay in schedule. The Third Army command also changed the original plan for the crossing and used bridges already available to ensure the continued flow of troops to the east until the two problem bridges were fully installed.

Work was not limited to building 'heavy' bridges. An equal number of 'light' bridges were installed for light vehicles and to attract enemy artillery fire, air strikes, and missiles away from the heavy bridges. The bridge areas were covered by thick smoke screens, which rendered Israeli fire imprecise. This did not stop the enemy from trying to halt the bridge-laying. Indeed, they believed at one point that they had succeeded, but although some bridges were hit, overall the operation was extraordinarily successful.

The Corps of Engineers suffered heavy losses but had set an example through its determination and self-sacrifice. Several prominent senior officers died in the battle, among them Brigadier Ahmad Hamdi. A tunnel under the Suez Canal was named after him following the war.

I was very sorry at the news of his death because I had gotten to know him well after the June 1967 war, when I was chief of staff on the canal front and Ahmad Hamdi was with the Army Corps of Engineers there. He was a calm-natured and determined man and a very competent engineer, totally committed to his calling and profession. During our service together, I can't recall often seeing him at front command headquarters because of the late hours he kept on assignments at the front lines.

While the bridges were being put down, combat was raging east of the canal as enemy counterattacks were strongly repulsed by our infantry and commando forces and enemy tanks destroyed trying to reach the canal line to help their besieged soldiers or to hit the bridges. We were closely following the situation from the Operations Center and were greatly distressed every time we learned of a bridge destroyed because there was a limited number of bridges available.

The first heavy bridge was in place at about 8:30 P.M., nearly six hours after the beginning of the assault. By about 10:30 P.M., eight hours after the beginning of the attack, the engineers had completed eight heavy bridges, four light ones, and had constructed and operated thirty ferries. Our men began to stream over to the east while the engineering units continued to work at maximum speed until we had ten heavy and ten light bridges. It was a great achievement.

By 10:30 P.M. (eight hours into the war), the Corps of Engineers had opened sixty passages in the sand shield, dislodging ninety thousand cubic meters of sand in the process. They had also completed the construction of eight heavy bridges, four light bridges, and constructed and operated thirty ferries.

Tanks, heavy guns, and other weapons were dispatched on the bridges and ferries as soon as these became operational, and all of them were ready to function at maximum capacity by 10:30 P.M. It was great military achievement and a major factor in the success of the assault across the Suez Canal, accomplished under constant and heavy enemy fire.

DISPATCH NO. 22 TO THE ISRAELI COMMAND

The Israeli reaction, as recorded by Israeli Chief of Staff General Elazer in his memoirs, was as follows.

> Dispatches kept pouring in at an alarming rate. We tried as much as we could to remain calm and think rationally. But following the arrival of dispatch No. 22, which announced that the Egyptians had been able to construct ten heavy and ten light (infantry) bridges, and that tanks, armored trucks, and heavy equipment had begun crossing over to the east bank of the canal, we were not able to keep our sense of balance or to think clearly and were overcome with alarm and despair.
>
> The daylight hours of 6 October were practically over without us having achieved an effective counterattack to stop the flow of heavy equipment across the bridges to the east bank where our positions were. This meant that night and darkness would soon come and the effectiveness of our air force would end at a time when the Egyptian forces would be able to consolidate and secure these bridges.
>
> The reality became clearer, bit by bit. Dispatches confirmed that more than thirty thousand Egyptian soldiers were now fighting on the east bank and heavy equipment still continued to cross over. Combat at close quarters meant that our air force could not be used, and twenty-five of our planes had been shot down by 10:10 P.M.
>
> The battle had become violent and savage. All the signs indicated that we faced a meticulous and well-thought-out plan, and we did not know its range or extent, now that we were facing two completely new realities in the history of the Arab–Israeli conflict—contrary to all our military calculations and the principles on which we had built our strategy. The first was that there no longer existed a barrier of water to stop the flow of Egyptians towards our positions on the east bank of the canal. The second was

that the impregnable Bar-Lev line was no longer effective. It was no longer a reliable defensive line after most of the strongpoints had fallen. . . . Now a real face-to-face struggle between the Egyptians and the Israelis had truly begun.

What was actually happening was a real disaster.

Missiles Against Planes[1]

Silence had at first reigned over the air defense positions whose men were on the alert with eyes riveted to the radar screens.

They did not have to wait for long. Enemy aircraft appeared on the horizon at the very time predicted by Major General Muhammad 'Ali Fahmi, commander of air defense. At 2:40 P.M., radar stations and observation points signaled the approach of enemy planes. The anti-aircraft missile batteries went into action and the enemy planes fell one after the other. This was the beginning of the end of the myth of Israeli air superiority, in the early hours of the war. The enemy continued to thrust here and there, to strike at our forces on the east side, to obstruct the work on the passages, and to hit at the bridges, but their attacks were routed.

At about 5:00 P.M., after two hours of continuous air attacks, the Egyptian special services picked up an open radio signal from General Benjamin Berid, commander of the Israeli Air Force, ordering his pilots not to approach the canal any closer than fifteen kilometers to the east.

The air defense figured prominently in the October War. We had worked hard over several years to turn it into an effective deterrent and at the critical moment it had risen to its challenge to defend our borders and protect bridges, ferries, and the assault. It had come into its own.

Red Sea and Mediterranean Naval Forces

Some time before the beginning of the war, it was necessary for our naval forces in both the Red Sea and the Mediterranean to be prepared and ready for operation in complete secrecy.

On 6 October our naval forces, under the command of Vice Admiral Fuad Abu Zikri, came into the war on a wide front. The Mediterranean fleet shelled sectors east of Port Fuad (east of Port Said) and Rumana on the east coast of Sinai. In the Red Sea Sharm al-Shaykh was bombed and in the Gulf of Suez the navy attacked defined targets. Around fifty naval units participated in the first day of operations.

Probably the most significant operation took place in the Straits of Bab al-Mandab with a naval blockade of commercial tankers on their way to Eilat. This lasted throughout the war. Eighteen million tons of petrol were transported yearly from Iran through Bab al-Mandab to

Eilat. Part of this was used locally, but the greater part re-exported to Europe. The petrol was transported in twenty-four large commercial tankers but, as a result of our blockade, not a single ship or tanker was able to gain access to the Gulf of 'Aqaba.

The second noteworthy naval action was to lay mines in the Gulf of Suez. This was done at the very beginning of operations. The enemy was caught unawares. A forty-six-thousand-ton oil tanker went down as well as a rescue vessel, and a two-thousand-ton tanker also hit a concealed mine in the area. The use of mines in the Gulf of Suez was a new weapon in the war against Israel. Mines are dangerous to handle and require skill and precision, considering the high concentration of explosives. However, Israeli shipping, which normally would transport over six million tons from the Gulf of Suez to Eilat, decreased visibly.

The naval operations proved to both friend and foe alike the lack of substance to the Israeli claim that an occupation of the Sharm al-Shaykh sector (since June 1967) would guarantee security and freedom of navigation through the Straits of Tiran at the mouth of the Gulf of 'Aqaba. The blockade also had a significant effect on the Israeli economy and its oil supplies. A major demand by Israel (through Henry Kissinger) in negotiations with President Sadat following the ceasefire was that Egypt stop naval activities in the Red Sea so that navigation could resume to Eilat as before.

A SUCCESSFUL ATTACK WITH THE CANAL ASSAULT

The first day of the war, 6 October 1973, was in short a tough and intense time, with communiqués and reports flowing continuously into the Armed Forces Operations Center. Reports on fighting east of the Suez Canal were good. By the end of the day, we felt that the battle had been to Egypt's advantage. We continued to follow developments throughout the night, when an enemy counterattack was repulsed. A few tanks were able to come very close to the water line and threaten the bridges and boats, but they were knocked out by missiles and small, light, anti-tank guns called RPGs. By the following morning, there were no enemy forces near the canal to hinder the crossing.

What pleased us most at the time was the high morale and spirit of the men and their obvious commitment to complete their mission well. Faith in God was a major psychological element expressed by the troops in their battle cry: "Allahu Akbar."

By the morning of the following day, 7 October, our forces had successfully crossed a complicated water barrier, had within eighteen hours destroyed a fortified defensive line, and had constructed five bridgeheads in Sinai with five infantry divisions and units from the Port Said sector. These had penetrated up to a depth of six to eight kilometers, after five battles, and the Egyptian flag was now flying over Sinai.

The losses were minimal: five planes (2.3 percent), twenty tanks (2 percent) and two hundred and eighty dead (3 percent of manpower).

The enemy had not only lost twenty-five planes, a hundred and twenty tanks, and several hundred dead, but the battle as well. The impregnable Bar-Lev line, which was supposed to secure and defend Israel, fell to us and the invincible Israeli army was beaten.

American military historian Trevor N. Dupuy, known to be close to the US Pentagon and a friend of Israel, has said:

> The skillful planning, characterized by meticulous precision and complete secrecy which accomplished total surprise, as well as efficient execution of carefully laid plans, all contributed to the success of a water barrier crossing that will be remembered in history.
>
> With regard to the plan, no other army would have been able to set it better. With regard to implementation, the Egyptians reported losses of less than two hundred dead on the first day of battle, which is less than what they themselves had expected.[2]

General Dayan was enraged when he learned that a fort on the Bar-Lev line had fallen and that its commanding officer and seven soldiers had surrendered, the first prisoners of war to fall into our hands.

Dayan is reported to have shouted explosively at Eliahu Za'ira, chief of military intelligence, "I hold you responsible for what is happening." In the same explosive tone, Za'ira answered, "I had warned you, but you had always told us that it was impossible for the Egyptians to enter into a war with us or to be able to cross the Suez Canal. You are a minister of defense with experience. Why didn't you sense or feel that a terrible catastrophe was about to happen?"

As the hours crept forward the number of Egyptian troops increased, moving inexorably across the canal to penetrate further and further into Sinai. Israeli losses increased. When Dayan learned that large numbers of Egyptian tanks and heavy weapons were uninterruptedly crossing to engage with the Israeli forces, he shouted, "If I wasn't sure that there was not one Soviet expert left in Egypt, I would have said that we were fighting Russia itself!"[3]

It pleased me to read an article by Ahmad Bahgat in the daily newspaper *al-Ahram* under the title "6 October." Bahgat wrote:

This war came as a surprise as much to the Egyptians as to the enemy. Large sectors of the Egyptian public felt deeply that the June [1967] defeat was worse than had been admitted.

The prevailing feeling was that no one would react and that defeat was our inevitable fate with no escape in sight. Despair increased day by day. . . . But when it appeared inevitable that we were moving towards the abyss, the army reacted suddenly with the canal crossing.

The October battle began, and the amazement felt by the Egyptian people was equal to that felt by enemy intelligence. It fell like lightening. . . . And the Egyptian Army rehabilitated its reputation, stained with defeat. The people of Egypt regained their honor and pride.

Surprise was the principal element of success. The effort exerted by army officers, commanders, strategists, and soldiers was unusual, and done in complete silence. Thus effort was joined to silence to produce a crossing.

But the principal psychological element of success was the army's faith in God and the battle cry of "Allahu Akbar."

These feelings showed that God was greater than fear, death, and life . . . [4]

20

6–7 October: Dayan and the Withdrawal

Dr. Henry Kissinger was awakened at 6:15 A.M. on 6 October 1973. He was in New York, at the Waldorf Astoria Hotel, to attend the UN General Assembly. An urgent message had come through from Kenneth Keating, US ambassador to Tel Aviv, giving details of a meeting with Golda Meir two hours earlier, at her request, on the Saturday of Yom Kippur. Mrs. Meir had said:

> Egyptian and Syrian troop movements, which both Israel and the United States had believed to be maneuvers, are taking on an alarming aspect . . . Israel is sure that a joint attack by the Egyptians and Syrians will take place the same afternoon. . . . Since the Arabs believe they are the weaker party, then the crisis must arise from a misunderstanding of Israel's intentions. Could the United States notify them quickly that Israel has no intention to attack either of them and that the proof of Israel's good intentions is that she will not call up her reserves or call for a general mobilization.

Kissinger says:

> When Sisco woke me up, there were only ninety minutes left for peace in the Middle East. Both Egypt and Syria had managed with unexpected skill to hide their military preparations, but Israel was sure they would not attack for four hours. I was certain at this point that if the Arab attack had been calculated, then diplomacy would not only fail but would be useless. However, my overall assessment of the

> situation remained faulty as it was based on reports coming in from Israel and on our own information, which led me to believe that an attack was probably impossible.[1]

Dr. Kissinger immediately contacted Dr. Muhammad Hasan al-Zayyat, our foreign minister, who was in New York, informing him of Israel's position as he had received it from Tel Aviv. Half an hour later (1:45 P.M. Cairo time) he called again to repeat Israel's commitment and to confirm that the United States would guarantee this, but by the time Dr. Zayyat got through to Cairo with the message the war had already begun.

Dr. Kissinger then requested that Dr. Zayyat ask for hostilities to cease and for both parties to go back to their original lines. Dr. Zayyat rejected this unless it meant a return to the lines of June 1967. After Dr. Kissinger had failed, first to prevent the war then to stop it after it had begun, he flew to Saudi Arabia and Jordan to try to limit military operations and prevent them from spreading. According to Hafez Isma'il, he asked Saudi Arabia's King Faysal to intercede with Egypt and Syria, arguing that Israel could repulse the Egyptian attack in just a few days once it had mobilized its reserves.[2] King Faysal declined to intervene without an Israeli withdrawal and an acknowledgment of the rights of the Palestinian people, and he sent a message to President Sadat assuring him that "we will stand by you in every way possible and pray for God to defend the Egyptian army."

These were some of the diplomatic activities on 6 October, played out against a background of battles on the Syrian and Egyptian fronts, in the Suez Canal region, and on the Golan Heights.

There is no doubt that Israel had concentrated its efforts on making a crossing of the canal virtually impossible. Holding the Bar-Lev line meant the continued occupation of Sinai. An Egyptian military success here could have dangerous political consequences and for this reason Israel had committed a large number of experienced troops to the defense of the canal and Sinai, strongly backed by its air force.

Its defense strategy relied on three major elements: the fortifications on the Bar-Lev line, positioned immediately behind a water barrier which was difficult to cross; successive and echeloned troop concentrations starting at the line of the canal and extending back into the depths of Sinai; and an air force which was superior in number, kind, and weaponry, operating from five bases in Sinai (al-Maliz, Tamada, Ras al-Naqab, Ras Nusrani, and al-'Arish) and from six bases and major airports in Israel (Ramat David, Akir, Hatoor, Hatsrim, Lod, and Tel Aviv).

On the afternoon of Saturday 6 October, 'Operations Group 252' was in northern Sinai under the command of General Mindler. It consisted of three tank brigades with about three hundred and fifty tanks, a mechanical brigade, and an infantry brigade. Southern Sinai had a tank brigade and a parachute brigade. The canal sector had been divided into three parts covering the entrances into Sinai. These were the Qantara–al-'Arish axis, the Isma'iliya–Abu 'Uwigla axis, and the Suez–Mitla and Giddi Passes axis. Two regular units, with reserve forces, were considered sufficient to defend the Bar-Lev fortifications and to repel a crossing. A squadron of tank reserves positioned nearby could reinforce the fortifications and very quickly occupy firing positions on the sand shield. Further back, a second line of tank reserves was available for a counterattack in the case of a successful crossing and would be supported by air and artillery action.

The years of occupation in Sinai had given the Israeli forces an opportunity to train on the terrain and to become highly skilled in defensive action. They were confident of their abilities to stop us from crossing, relying on their fortifications, tanks, and air force.

The Two Plans: Burg al-Hammam and al-Tabashir

For the continued occupation of Sinai and the Golan Heights and to prepare for any contingency, detailed orders had since May 1973 been issued to the Southern Military Command (Sinai) and the Northern Military Command (the Golan) on the reinforcement of the canal line using active units (Operation Burg al-Hammam) and the Golan line using reserve units, (Operation al-Tabashir). The plans envisaged placing the forces on high alert and the mobilization of all the reserves.

We expected Israel to have picked up through its intelligence service some indication of the unusual military activity on the Egyptian and Syrian fronts and anticipated that it would mobilize its reserves to put both operations into action. From our point of view, the most vital concern was to prevent Israeli intelligence from discovering our intentions for an offensive.

It appears that Israel did not see the forest for the trees. On all previous occasions it had discovered that we were conducting training exercises but had not concluded that they were in preparation for war. We had gone through the motions of repeated maneuvers which in some cases were accompanied by open declarations of intent to give the impression that we were preparing for war, or were on the point of war. At the beginning, Israel's response had been to raise the alert level and declare a partial mobilization. This affected the economy and disrupted normal life. With the frequent repetition of these exercises, Israel toned down its response, raising only the levels of readiness of its forces in Sinai and taking its time to declare a state of full mobilization and to prepare for general troop concentrations.

It was relatively easy for Israel to find out that we had called in our reserves before the October War. When it was confirmed that some of the reserves had been discharged back to their daily life and occupations a few days before 6 October, Israeli intelligence concluded that this was another routine training exercise.There is no doubt also that the movements of our warships were monitored when they set sail to Port Sudan and Aden on their way to Asia. It seems that it did not occur to Israeli intelligence that our destroyers could take up positions in Bab al-Mandab to block the Israeli naval lines of communication.

The success of the surprise plan was aided by the arrogance and conceit of the Israeli military command, which was sure we would not be able to carry out an effective offensive across the canal. It did not, however, discard the possibility of limited land or air raids or artillery engagements in the style of the War of Attrition.

Another contributing factor was Israeli intelligence's stubborn insistence that Egypt would consider war only if it obtained long-range aircraft able to strike deep inside Israel, especially at major air bases to paralyze the Israeli air force. As a result, Israeli intelligence believed that under any likely scenario there would always be a warning period of at least forty-eight hours, considered sufficient time for a general mobilization of the reserves.

In a long discussion on the surprise element of the October War, Kissinger says that the Arab surprise was

> the product of a misinterpretation of facts available to everybody. These were not hidden under a mass of conflicting information. Sadat was generous and brave in informing us of his intentions, but we did not believe him. He flooded us with information but our conclusions were wrong. The sixth of October proved the failure of our political analysis.

Kissinger continues:

> Every Israeli or American analysis before October 1973 reinforced our belief that Egypt and Syria did not have the necessary military potential or capability to regain their territories by force of arms. The Arab armies were thus doomed to fail, which led us to think that they would not go on the offensive. Our first assessment was correct but the conclusions we drew from this were mistaken.[3]

In spite of this, the Burg al-Hammam and al-Tabashir operations were put into effect and on 5 October Israel reinforced its forces on both the canal and the Golan fronts and increased the forces available on the canal, the fortifications, and the Bar-Lev line, while the artillery took up firing positions. Egyptian military intelligence also observed the arrival of reserves, and at the emergency depots in Sinai confirmed that tanks were being towed to Sinai that same day.

This explains why the confrontation was so violent from the very beginning of the war. The Israeli forces on the Bar-Lev line fought hard and some of the strongpoints put up a powerful and lengthy resistance.

Bar-Lev and the Line

The Israeli forces were therefore combat-ready and fought fiercely on the canal line, buoyed by the reinforcements which had reached them. Dayan notes in his memoirs that

> the Egyptian and Syrian attack on Yom Kippur, 6 October, came as a surprise, even though it had been expected. On Yom Kippur the Israeli reserve forces were not yet fully mobilized or in position, but this did not mean that they were not ready for war. We must add that the enemy forces (the Arabs) launched their attack very much more effectively than we had anticipated for in our plans.

Here I have to mention that some publications sympathetic to Israel tried afterwards to minimize the military importance of the Bar-Lev line in order to diminish the Egyptian achievement, in one case describing it as "a thin line of forward fortifications for observation purposes, and to provide a base for maneuvers by the light armored forces . . . "

We might recollect the unanimous opinion that the collapse of the Bar-Lev line brought to an end what had been considered an impregnable defensive fortification. With the passage of time it had become a symbol of Israel's power to prevent Egypt from undertaking an assault on the canal, and it had given Israel, its leaders, and its military men a feeling of confidence and security.

The Israeli military presence on the east bank of the canal was a concrete manifestation of the theory of 'secure boundaries' since the canal was a powerful natural barrier on the border with Egypt. As such, it necessitated a military presence which would preclude any possibility whatsoever of a successful Egyptian action either in a crossing or in gaining a foothold in Sinai. The Bar-Lev line was based on a vital strategic premise that a collapse in the line would also imply a collapse in the theory of 'secure boundaries.'

In Israel, there was a general consensus on the strategic importance of a military presence on the canal line even through there was disagreement as to what this was to be. Some rejected the idea of fortifications in favor of the more mobile power of tanks. Others felt it was important to construct strong defenses able to withstand and return artillery fire and capable of stopping a crossing. Israeli Chief of Staff Bar-Lev's opinion prevailed and his ideas were put into effect. The Bar-Lev line, which was essentially a military project, also took on major symbolic significance as a sign of Israel's power to impose a fait accompli on the Arabs.

The construction of the line went through several stages, transforming the fortifications into massive engineered structures supplied with complete combat equipment and living facilities, located all along the relevant confrontation line on the canal, which was 110 kilometers long. There were twenty-two defensive positions which included thirty-six fortified strongpoints controlling the front, the sides, and the rear of the line. Three hundred firing positions for tanks were fixed in the intervals between the fortifications. The locations of the fortified positions enabled them to cover all directions from which a canal crossing or advance into Sinai could take place. Each structure consisted of several floors, starting underground and reaching the top of the sand barrier, and was built with reinforced concrete supported by concrete blocks, rail tracks, or with sand and earth so as to provide complete protection against any direct hit from artillery fire and aerial bombs of more than a thousand pounds.

All the fortified points were equipped with fuel tanks and inflammable material connected by pipes to the surface of the water. When ignited, the canal would be transformed into a huge surface of fire, which (it was established by experiment) would reach 700°C. Each fortified point was stocked with provisions that made it self-sufficient for fifteen days. The inventory of combat material could repel a force evaluated as equivalent to a battalion for a week. In light of this fact, the Bar-Lev line and its thirty-six fortified points were capable of repelling thirty-six battalions. In addition, hundreds of tanks were ready to take up positions on the sand barrier and armored reserves were to be found in the rear.

At any one of the major strongpoints there were twenty-six bunkers with medium and heavy machine guns, twenty-four shelters for the troops, four bunkers for anti-aircraft weapons, three tank positions, six mortar positions, and fifteen circles of barbed wire with mine fields and booby traps between them.

This describes what was found at the first line only. Yet the Bar-Lev line was not simply a peripheral line but rather an integrated and highly sophisticated technical defense system that began with the line of the canal and spread eastward to a depth of around thirty kilometers and included a chain of lines and other barriers such as tank positions, combat areas for armored vehicles, and bases for counterattacks in the direction of the canal line. In addition to this, there was a second line of fortifications at a distance of five to eight kilometers which consisted of eleven fortified positions, underground command centers, sector command headquarters, anti-aircraft missile bases, and long-range artillery positions. Assigned to this defense area were the armored reserves, the mechanized infantry and artillery units, and some air defense units, all of which were highly trained.

I have gone into this lengthy description to record the facts which must be taken into consideration when evaluating the Bar-Lev line. Military experts and specialists have unanimously agreed that the line was entirely fortified, making the Suez Canal a unique case in military history. A crossing and an offensive to regain the Suez Canal would be an example of exceptional military technique to overcome both a water barrier and a fortified line.

American historian Dupuy has remarked, "Suffice it to say that the professional competence in the planning and the implementation of the crossing could not have been accomplished better by any other army in the world. The effect of this meticulous operation on the part of the military staff, and especially the element of surprise that was achieved, was a notable success in the crossing of the canal on a broad front. The Egyptian crossing was the greatest accomplishment of the war."

It was fated that General Bar-Lev should leave military service as chief of staff to be placed in charge of the Ministry of Commerce and Industry after having given his name to this fortified defense line. During the October War, he was recalled to military service to participate in saving the line which carried his name. Time was then running short; the line fell but the man remained.

The first day of war ended with a great military achievement for our armed forces. The Syrians were similarly successful in the Golan and the Israeli forces found themselves in a new and difficult situation. Morale was high and a feeling of euphoria spread across Egypt, Syria, and the Arab world, but at general command we knew that we were still at the beginning of the road. We had followed the battles throughout the night and monitored the flow of our troops eastward as the Israelis tried hard to push them back.

The Second and Third Armies had succeeded in breaching the canal and nearly fifty thousand fighters crossed over to the east bank on the night of 6–7 October, from Port Said in the north to Suez in the south, with about three hundred tanks, anti-tank weapons, and anti-aircraft missiles. These were carried by the men under the cover of a barrage of heavy artillery from 1800 field cannons. Our forces had to complete their initial success by broadening the bridgeheads and destroying the enemy forces facing them. The Israeli forces were fighting hard to stop our troops from digging in. As time went by, more weapons and tanks made the crossing. It was a physical and mental struggle against time.

We were worried because two of the bridges for the Third Army had not been completely installed, and this hindered the movement eastward in that sector. Major General 'Abd al-Mun'im issued orders to transfer traffic to those bridges already in place to keep up the pace of the crossing. This was done despite the added pressure on those bridges already in place, which were now carrying approximately twice their anticipated load of traffic, and the task was accomplished thanks to the determination, flexibility, and discipline of the troops under enemy fire.

The enemy had depended on three principal elements to prevent our forces from either crossing or getting a hold on the east bank. These were their fortifications, their tanks, and their air force.

On the night of 6–7 October, fifteen strongpoints fell; that is, nearly half the total number on the Bar-Lev line. The remaining fortifications were surrounded. The enemy was being given no choices other than to surrender, escape, or die. A practice of the Israeli army was to try to rescue those men who were in difficulty and to retrieve the bodies of their dead, because according to Jewish belief the absence of a body creates problems for the community. Accordingly, a few small tank units cut a path through to the fortifications to try to free the men there, but were stopped. Some individual soldiers were able to escape under cover of darkness, but others failed.

Our land forces pushed forward to surround the strongpoints and stop their fire while at the same time repelling several enemy counterattacks by the nearby reserves, supported by a reinforced tank company. Eight such counterattacks failed. In our estimation (as well in that of the Israeli command), the Bar-Lev line had lost any military value after half the number of its fortifications had fallen and about a hundred tanks (one third of their tanks on the front line) were destroyed.

As for the Israeli air force, it was noticeably active against the bridges which had we continued to install throughout the night, but our air defense effectively prevented them from providing any support to the land forces. The Israeli army had always been almost totally dependent on the air force, and this new situation exposed their real fighting capabilities.

Operations Group 252 under the command of General Mindler, commander of the Israeli armored forces in Sinai, which had been stationed in the heart of Sinai, had now arrived at the confrontation line. Our two armies now on the east bank had to face Mindler's tanks the following day, 7 October, and our air force and air defense force had to prepare for an onslaught from an energized Israeli air force that was waiting to join the battle.

At general command, we had foreseen enemy reactions to a successful crossing and were ready to face them.

In Israel, the cabinet of ministers held a meeting on 6 October at 10:00 P.M. where Chief of Staff Elazer and Minister of Defense Dayan presented reports on the day's events and on operations to be undertaken in the following days.

Dayan argued that Israel had to deal with three factors. First, the size of the Egyptian and Syrian forces, plus the fact that there were no longer the armies he had known in June 1967. They were now very good and fighting with determination. Second, the enemy air defense network, which presented a problem for the Israeli air force. Third, the time needed until the reserves could reach the fronts.

In his memoirs, Dayan says,

> I mentioned my doubts about whether it was within our capability to disrupt seriously the crossing of the canal for the next twenty-four to thirty-six hours. This meant that the Egyptians would have two nights to construct more bridges and more forces would cross into Sinai.
>
> I made clear that the canal area was a dangerous battlefield and that our air force would face a tough challenge when the fight started the following day. We would need a lot of luck for this to end to our advantage.
>
> Following that, on Monday and Tuesday (8 and 9 October) we would have all of the armored forces, according to plan, and would be able to engage in a tank war. It wouldn't be easy, but the possibilities of success were good.
>
> Therefore, I found it necessary to withdraw from the south (the canal front) to a second line and to fight the Egyptians at a range of twelve miles from the canal. As for the north (the Golan), I expected that we would be able to stop the Syrians at the borders.
>
> I candidly expressed my thoughts and point of view. At the end of the meeting, neither I nor the others present felt any relief. I was

strained and tired and sensed a gap between myself and my fellow ministers; they did not like what I had said about the Egyptians being successful, nor my suggestion for a withdrawal to a second line. They wanted the army to drive the enemy back across the canal immediately.

There was no meeting point in our thinking. They were under the influence of the optimism evident in the chief of staff's presentation to them. Above all, their hopes were built on wishful thinking.

Dayan's advice to the Israeli Cabinet was not taken into consideration because Israel was following the advice of the United States, and the United States had a different opinion.

21

7 October: Three Battles on Land and in the Air

While military operations continued to our advantage on the canal front and in the Golan Heights, communications were taking place between Egypt, Syria, and the Soviet Union.

President Sadat records that on Wednesday 3 October 1973, according to a previous agreement (in August 1973) with Syrian President Hafez al-Asad, he summoned the Soviet ambassador in Cairo to inform him officially of Egypt and Syria's decision to begin military operations against Israel.[1] Sadat did not provide any dates for this as he had agreed with Asad that the Syrian president would himself notify the Soviet ambassador in Damascus on 4 October of the commencement of war on 6 October.

On 6 October, at 7:40 P.M., President Sadat met again with the Soviet ambassador at the ambassador's request, six hours after war had begun. The ambassador told him that "President Hafez Asad has informed our ambassador in Syria that war would begin on 6 October . . . " President Sadat adds: "During the meeting, Asad had asked the Soviet Union to work towards a ceasefire forty-eight hours at the most from the beginning of operations. Consequently, the Soviet ambassador had come to inform me officially of this on behalf of the Soviet leadership, and to ask me to agree to it."

Sadat replied to the ambassador, "I doubt that President Asad asked for this before the battle."

The ambassador answered, "I am notifying you of this in an official message from the Soviet leadership. If you have any doubts, you can get in touch with President Asad."

Sadat said, "I will send a message to Asad about this, but I ask you to inform the Soviet leadership that even if this is actually Syria's request, I will not agree to a ceasefire until the political goals of the war have been achieved."

President Sadat reports that he then sent a coded wire to President Asad in which he gave him the text of the message from the Soviet ambassador and his reply to it. Asad's reply arrived on 7 October, twenty-four hours later, despite the critical nature of the subject. It said, "What the Soviet Union claims has not happened." The Soviet ambassador requested another meeting on the evening of that same day, during which the president showed him the answer he had just received from Syria. The ambassador's reply was that he had been asked to relay another message from the Soviet government based on Syria's request (for the second time) for a ceasefire.

Sadat said, "Please drop the subject and consider it closed at this point. You have known since yesterday that I will not accept a ceasefire until I have achieved my battle goals."

In my judgment there was no reason whatsoever for Egypt to accept a ceasefire at such an early stage in the war. The military positions of both Egypt and Syria were holding strong and a ceasefire would have been to Israel's advantage. The political decision to continue military operations until the strategic target had been achieved was right and proper.

Nevertheless, this incident which took place in the first and second days of battle gives the impression that uncertainty and doubt had characterized the political relationship between Egypt, Syria, and the Soviet Union since the beginning of the war.

THE US STRATEGY FOR THE CRISIS

When the war broke out, there was an immediate reaction in the United States and it came as no surprise that the United States should take Israel's side. Israel needed the United States' continued political and military support; in this way the United States could achieve its policies in the Middle East and Israel its goals.

A special task force was created to meet the crisis. It was headed by Secretary of State Henry Kissinger. In a meeting on the evening of 6 October, Kissinger told the task force that he had been in touch with President Nixon (who was out of Washington), the Soviet ambassador, and Israel's foreign minister. Nixon had ordered the US Sixth Fleet to the eastern Mediterranean to anchor near the island of Crete. US military movements were being undertaken carefully and cautiously so that there should be no misinterpretation. Both the US and the Soviet fleets were now in the vicinity of Crete.

In his memoirs Kissinger says,

> The war broke out and we had to face several commitments which seemed conflicting. We had to ensure the continued existence of Israel and preserve its security. At the same time, we had to maintain our relations with the moderate Arab countries, such as Jordan and the Kingdom of Saudi Arabia.
>
> We knew in advance that Europe and Japan would become apprehensive if the crisis period extended too long and would take a different route from ours in the event of a failure.
>
> As for the Soviets, they were behaving wisely and astutely and we could not expect them to lend a helping hand to get us out of our predicament. To the contrary, they might have escalated the crisis.
>
> From the beginning I believed that we were still in a position to control events and that our ally Israel had to win. Our friends the moderate Arabs, in spite of their rejection of the idea of war, would welcome a victory for their Arab brethren. Europe's impulse to abandon us could be dealt with if it perceived that we were in control of the situation. We could also influence the Soviets through the use of reason to put an end to the adventure. We could resort to other means available if diplomacy failed . . .
>
> Now that the war had started, we had to pull our diplomacy out of the corner it was in, and that was not easy. If Israel had a decisive victory then we would have to keep it from becoming a rallying point for Arab grievances. We would also have to prevent the Soviet Union from appearing to be the savior of the Arab world.
>
> If the unexpected happened and Israel was endangered, then we would have to try to save it. We could not allow the dependents of the Soviet Union to destroy our traditional friend . . . [2]

When the war broke out, the United States estimated that the fighting would quickly go to Israel's advantage once its counterattack had pushed Egypt and Syria back to the lines held on the morning of 6 October. US analysts were sure that the war would not last more than seventy-two hours. Then the United States, in coordination with the Soviet Union, would draft a UN Security Council resolution for a ceasefire on those lines. The United States thought this would be to the advantage of Israel, which would keep intact its borders of 6 October, and that the Arabs would be forced to accept this after their failure on the battlefield.

Accordingly, the US policy was to deal with the crisis from a position of strength, to pressure the Soviet Union into compliance by guaranteeing military and political support for Israel, and at the same time avoid a confrontation with the Arabs. In line with this approach, the US administration refrained from calling the Arabs the aggressors or accusing them of provoking the war, a position substantially different from that taken in June 1967. President Johnson blamed that war on President 'Abd al-Nasir, knowing very well that it was Israel which had initiated it and violated neighboring borders to occupy Arab land.

In his memoirs, General Elazer, Israeli chief of staff at the time, says,

> Communications were continuous between the Israeli command and the American State Department for consultation and counsel on the military situation as it developed. On 6 October Israel asked America to give an immediate evaluation on events and for the Pentagon to provide an effective plan to face this situation. America's reply was that Israel should wait until American military experts reviewed the position after the canal crossing by the Egyptians, and the fall of the Bar-Lev line.
>
> The advice, when it came, was for Israel to try to destroy the Egyptian bridgeheads in the early hours of 7 October and to strike hard at the SAM 6 missile network, but to avoid direct combat.

This is exactly what Israel did on 7 October, the second day of operations, following American 'advice.' The word 'advice' here is used by Elazer to avoid the more correct term, which would have been the US 'plan.' In reality, it was in fact a US plan, with two military objectives which were (1) an Israeli counterattack to destroy the Egyptian bridgeheads, and (2) an Israeli air strike to paralyze the Egyptian air defense system.

It should be noted that the proposed plan matched US political considerations in this phase of the war, which were based on the understanding that the battle would soon go to the advantage of Israel. In Kissinger's words: "Our specific strategy was to wait for Israel to regain its military status."

The land and air battles began in the early morning of Sunday 7 October, as we had foreseen in the armed forces general command war plan. On that morning, our forces fought a series of battles. The Second and Third Armies repelled the Israeli counterattacks and the battle of al-Qantara East began, to liberate the city. Air battles were at their fiercest. Commandos set the oil wells alight on the eastern bank of the Gulf of Suez.

The Israeli Counterattack

The Israeli forces started their counterattack on the troops which had crossed to the east using three armored brigades with about three hundred and fifty tanks, together with frontline forces of about a hundred tanks which had taken part in combat on the previous day.

The Israeli tank battalions moved forward in several directions to break through the Egyptian front positions. Their armored forces under the command of General Mindler believed that they would be able to wipe out the Egyptian infantry, and it came as a great surprise to find that the infantry divisions facing them were equipped with anti-tank weapons, missiles in particular. The longer the attack continued, the greater were their losses.

An Israeli tank battalion tried to attack in the direction of al-Qantara East and failed. Another tank battalion launched an attack in the direction of al-Firdan with no success. A third battalion tried to move in the direction of Isma'iliya and failed. A fourth battalion of tanks attacked in the direction of al-Shatt and failed.

After nearly five hours of battle it became clear to both the Second and Third Armies, as well as to the Israeli forces, that the Israeli counterattack had failed after the armored division under Mindler's command had lost about 170 tanks.[3]

The forces of the Second and Third Armies still had to complete the destruction of the fortifications on the Bar-Lev line and advance in-depth eastward, and towards al-Qantara East to liberate the city.

Air and Air Defense Battles

While the Israeli counterattack was being pushed back, Israel (in line with the US plan) moved to destroy our air defense system. In the early morning of 7 October, a vast number of aircraft (up to 160 planes) flew at low altitude over the Mediterranean towards Egyptian airports in the north and center of the Delta, and over the Red Sea towards our airports in the eastern desert.

Israel was still under the illusion that its air force was capable of decisive action against our airports and air defense system, believing it could evade the Egyptian radar network for a surprise attack.

When the Israeli pilots approached their targets, they realized that our air force and air defense had been fundamentally transformed. They found Egyptian fighters waiting to intercept and engage with them, and those planes which were able to slip through at low altitudes in the direction of their targets found themselves within firing range of our anti-aircraft guns and shoulder-fired missiles. Those trying to escape the barrage by flying to higher altitudes became targets for the SAM missiles. The Israelis dumped their loads wherever they could and those lucky enough to survive fled.

After this initial failure to knock out Egyptian airports in the early hours of 7 October, Israeli aircraft switched to the bridges and crossing points in an attempt to sever the arteries feeding our forces into Sinai. Repeated air strikes hammered down, but the air defense came once more into action inflicting more losses on the Israeli air force.

Major and violent air battles took place between large numbers of Egyptian and Israeli planes and lasted far longer than expected. But our air force did not limit itself to providing air cover for the land forces and attacked enemy positions in the central and northern sectors of Sinai, hitting enemy artillery batteries, their air defense system, and their command posts. By the end of the day, the air force and air defense had downed a total of seventy-five enemy planes, twenty-seven of which had been brought down on the first day, 6 October. We lost twenty-five fighters, fifteen of which had been shot down on the first day. Combat performance throughout 6 and 7 October had been outstanding.

The Battle of al-Qantara East

Fighting continued throughout the day along the front from the northern coast of Sinai (east of Port Said) to the eastern coast of the Gulf of Suez. On the northern coast, our naval forces directed a heavy bombardment against Israeli fortifications east of Port Fuad. This was the only strongpoint which did not fall.

In the northern sector on the canal front, the Second Army worked steadily to push the bridgeheads deeper into Sinai for the divisions. At general command, we followed activities in the Qantara East sector with some concern. Al-Qantara was the second town in Sinai, after al-'Arish, and had not only political but strategic importance. It would open up the coastal road for our troops in the direction of Rumana and al-'Arish, which is why we were determined to recapture it and the Israeli forces determined to hold on to it.

The enemy fortifications in al-Qantara East were among the strongest on the Bar-Lev line and consisted of seven strongpoints. Fighting within the town itself differed considerably from desert warfare, which is why it was heavy during that day and continued throughout the night of 7–8 October, when bayonets and knives were used man-to-man to mop up remaining pockets of Israeli soldiers. Troops from the Eighteenth Division under the command of Brigadier Fuad 'Aziz Ghali had managed by the end of the day (7 October) to take control of the town in preparation for its liberation the following day.

In the southern sector of the front, some troops from the Third Army made a limited advance in the direction of the mountain passes, reaching the Israeli southern sector command center near the Mitla Pass and engaging it by fire. By the end of the day (7 October) our armed forces had succeeded in repulsing the enemy counterattacks and completed tasks begun the previous day, the day of the crossing.

The bridgeheads of the five infantry divisions had penetrated deeply and solidly enough to allow for the next missions. Our aircraft had bombed enemy targets in the northern and central sectors in the depths of Sinai after having pushed back (with the air defense forces) enemy raids against our airports. At the same time our naval forces had carried out several combat missions and secured our coastline on the Mediterranean and Red Sea. Our land forces had captured tanks and armored vehicles after the enemy had abandoned them and fled, and a number of Israeli officers, soldiers, and armored units had surrendered with their weapons.

Our losses were limited to a few armored vehicles; we also lost some men, but many fewer than the Israelis.[4]

In the Golan, the Syrians had begun their attack in coordination with the Egyptian assault on the canal front, beginning at 2:05 P.M. on 6 October after an artillery barrage which had lasted for an hour. Syrian air strikes against various targets were launched simultaneously with the Egyptian air attacks. A Syrian commando unit carried out a daring helicopter raid and occupied enemy positions on the heights of Gabal al-Shaykh, despite the fact that this strategic position was protected by the natural rock formations of the mountain itself.

A Briefing in Israel

On the evening of 7 October at 11:00 P.M., the Israeli military command was given a full picture of the situation by the chief of staff, General Elazer. As described in his memoirs, his report said:

- The Egyptians appeared to be following a precise and detailed plan. They had reinforced their positions east of the canal with tanks, armored vehicles, and heavy weapons. They had also began to penetrate into Sinai with bridgeheads.
- The Israeli counterattack had taken place using three additional armored brigades east of the canal. Formations from the air force—

a total of 160 planes—had hit Egyptian troop concentrations at daybreak of 7 October and nine Israeli planes had been lost.

- Egyptian tank units had been able to reach the Israeli command centers at the Mitla Pass and encircle it, attacking from all directions. This was at a time when violent battles were raging in the town of al-Qantara East.
- The Egyptians had captured the seven strongpoints on the fortifications at al-Qantara East. They were showing no mercy in battle. They were blowing themselves up in front of and on top of Israeli tanks. They were kissing the ground in Sinai. More than anything else, this pointed to the previous and mistaken evaluation of the Egyptian soldier, his fighting capability, and the qualitative difference between him and the Israeli soldier.
- The Syrian heights had been transformed into burning fields of flames. The fighting was fiercer than they could have ever imagined. News of the collapse of Israeli positions and the continued advance of the Syrian forces towards the Jordan valley was very alarming.
- Internally, Israel was living through moments of great anxiety after foreign broadcasts had provided details on the war. The civilian population was beginning to sense the catastrophe. Ambulances were now returning from both fronts filled with the wounded. It was becoming obvious that the size of Israeli casualties was very high considering the short duration of the fighting.

Chief of Staff Elazer ended his report with the following words:

With bitterness I must say that starting in the afternoon of 7 October, we lost the control of our forces in the eastern sector. The Arab advance in both the northern Golan and on the southern Sinai fronts is continuing forward at the same pace. We are facing a precise plan on two wide fronts, implemented as though they were one front.

Elazer continues:

As for Dayan, he was not as short-tempered nor as agitated as usual, but devastated and shattered, not knowing what to do or say. We were all in the same mood.

No writer—regardless of his skill—can describe the defeat pictured on the face of a general who has experienced a failure of judgment and is accountable to history. This is how Dayan was.

EGYPTIAN AND US CONTACTS BEGIN

Our forces were marking success after success on two fronts when the first direct contact between Egypt and the United States took place on

7 October. Muhammad Hafez Isma'il, Egypt's national security advisor, has commented extensively on this as follows.

> Beginning 7 October, the president decided to open up direct contact between Cairo and Washington in response to the quickening tempo of diplomatic and political activity, briefing Foreign Minister Zayyat (in New York) on Egypt's position.
>
> In a first message to Dr. Kissinger I mentioned the communications between him and Dr. Zayyat and recorded the following observations in particular.
>
> 1. Israeli provocations had not ceased and the present engagements came as no surprise to those who had followed these provocations, to which we have already drawn attention elsewhere.
> 2. Egypt had been obliged to take the necessary precautions to face with firmness any further Israeli operation since the engagements with Syria on 13 September.
> 3. The present engagements confirmed Egypt's determination not to bow to conditions dictated by Israel, using the occupied lands as a pawn.
> 4. A new situation had arisen in the region and Egypt's position needed to be clarified. Egypt's goal remained constant: a comprehensive peace in the Middle East, not a partial solution. Egypt had no intention of intensifying the engagements or widening the confrontation.
> 5. Egypt's position could be summarized as follows: it wanted an Israeli pullout from all occupied territory. Egypt would then be willing to participate in a peace conference at the United Nations, under appropriate supervision. With regard to freedom of navigation in the Straits of Tiran, Egypt would support this and would accept an international presence as a guarantee for a limited period.
> 6. We hoped we would not be misunderstood, as had happened once before with Rogers in 1971, and that this position would be perceived as a basis for Egypt's negotiating position.
>
> My message on 7 October was a new link in the chain of communications that had taken place for almost a year between Washington and Cairo, which had stopped in July and were resumed by Dr. Kissinger on the morning of 6 October when he got in direct contact with our foreign minister, Dr. Zayyat, in New York.
>
> From an objective perspective, our message of 7 October did not offer anything new, if we exclude the commitment not 'to intensify

the engagements or widen the confrontation.' We wanted to define the principles behind our policy regarding a political settlement to the Arab–Israeli conflict—by ending the occupation of the territories and ensuring the rights of the Palestinian people. . . .

The essence of our message represented a starting point with which to go beyond the ceasefire. We hoped that through the war we could reach the suitable political formula we had been unable to reach in the six previous years. We were nevertheless committed to carrying out military operations within the occupied territories to liberate these territories only and not to go beyond this. To achieve this, we set our goals at two levels.

First, with regard to the battle on the Israeli borders—where we had committed ourselves not to deepen the engagements in order not to involve civilians in population centers, or to harm economic targets—our aim was to safeguard our dense population centers and our vital economic interests.

Second, with regard to the Middle East as a whole, we had committed ourselves not to widen the confrontation and not to implicate Western interests in the region to avoid harming the economies of Japan and Western Europe. The reason for this was to ensure support from the Western nations and to make public opinion sympathetic to our cause.[5]

In his memoirs under the heading "The Beginning of Communications with Sadat," Kissinger writes:

Following a brief period, we managed to get our first direct communication with Cairo (and, in this regard, I remember that I never got in direct touch with Syria throughout the war). The tone was friendly, and the contact was sensible and not 'political.' Hafez Isma'il, President Sadat's national security advisor, sent me a memorandum through the secret services notifying me of the conditions Egypt had set to stop its acts of aggression. They were similar to conditions set the previous May—that Israel should pull out from all the occupied territories, after which peace negotiations could take place as well as a review of the stalled issues, such as navigation in the Straits of Tiran, or a guarantee of the presence of international forces in Sharm al-Shaykh for a limited period. Naturally the memorandum clearly rejected any partial or temporary agreement . . .

Anyone looking at these conditions would see that they only represented a starting point for negotiations. Sadat knew from our

> previous conversations and communications that he had ideas which could not be implemented. I had no doubts that he was not concerned, at the moment, with an agreement but was working towards setting up negotiations. Under the present conditions, communicating with us was itself risky to Sadat and he could not allow this to come to a head as it might imply that he was abandoning Syria or distancing himself from the Soviet Union, whose support was indispensable for continuing the war.
>
> Kissinger continues, saying that
>
> what was important to note was the arrival of the memorandum and not its contents. Sadat was inviting us to participate in the peace project, if not charging us with that responsibility, at a time when at the United Nations we were asking him to give up the lands he had occupied.
>
> I must mention that the memorandum clearly indicated that Sadat understood the limits to what he could achieve: 'It is not our intention to go deep into the territories of others nor to widen the front.' This sentence in the memorandum signals that Egypt did not want to continue its military operations against Israel after the territories it had gained. Nor did it want to hold America completely responsible for the events as Nasir had done in 1967.
>
> Isma'il's memorandum was proof of the possibility of negotiations with countries which had attacked our ally (Israel) and which might not be able to achieve victory because of American weapons. Not one day passed throughout the period of the war when we did not receive a message from Cairo or send one to it.[6]

It is important to discuss the contents of Hafez Isma'il's memorandum and Kissinger's interpretation of it, since Hafez Isma'il explains it differently.

Egypt expressed its military intentions (that it did not intend to deepen the military engagements), and this revealed our intentions to the Israeli enemy through its faithful ally, the United States. It was natural that the United States (politically) and Israel (militarily) should respond to Egypt's intention not deepen or to develop the attack in Sinai and make do with the lines it had reached on 7 October, the second day of combat.

Egypt believed that the commitment in the memorandum would prevent civilian and economic targets from becoming involved in the war. Israel did not respect this and started aerial bombings of the city of Port Said the day after the message was delivered, 8 October, and on all subsequent days. It also began hitting population centers and economic targets in Syria starting 9 October, including an aerial bombardment of the capital, Damascus.

Egypt respected the commitment expressed in its message (not to widen the confrontation line) to avoid endangering Western interests in our region and the economies of Japan and Western Europe. It seemed unnecessary for us to reassure the United States regarding its interests at a time when it stood openly against Egypt and Syria and supported Israel entirely at every level.

Kissinger said,

> When we created the airbridge and sent the required weapons to Israel, and the war was going against Egypt's interest—despite this, we did not sense any hard feelings towards the United States. This was a clever move on [Sadat's] part so that we would not lean towards Israel in the subsequent diplomatic stages. . . . It can be described as an excellent grasp of matters from 'Abd al-Nasir's successor following twenty years of enmity.[7]

There is no question that a nation's political activity has to move in parallel with military operations. However, I believe that political action in this case did not help the military operations when the Egyptian message spelled out that Egypt did not have intentions of deepening its military engagement or widening the confrontation.

22

8 October: Israel in Danger

Monday 8 October arrived. The Second and Third Armies had reinforced their positions in Sinai following successful combat operations the previous two days. The forces of the Second Army were now fighting at a depth of nine to twelve kilometers east of the canal. The Eighteenth Infantry Division, under the command of Brigadier Fuad 'Aziz Ghali, was able to liberate the town of al-Qantara East after having encircled and then penetrated it, fighting in the streets and in buildings until enemy troops gave way. The division captured a quantity of enemy weapons and equipment, including tanks, and thirty Israeli soldiers and officers who had remained in the town. At 9:30 P.M. on the evening of 8 October, the news was broadcast on Cairo radio.

In the Third Army sector fighting was at a depth of eight to eleven kilometers east of the canal. The most noticeable event that day was the success scored by the Nineteenth Infantry Division under the command of Brigadier Yusuf 'Afifi who occupied 'Uyun Musa. The same division also took fortified positions on the east bank where six 155-mm cannons were positioned. These had been used by the enemy to shell the town of Suez during the War of Attrition. At the time, we had not been able to silence them (although we had used all calibers of artillery) because of resistance from the fortifications. Now the Israeli forces had fled under pressure from the Nineteenth Division, leaving their cannons intact in their positions.

On the morning of 8 October Chief of Staff Lieutenant General Sa'd al-Din al-Shadhli visited the front to review the situation firsthand. He began with the command of the Second Army, after which he went to the Second Infantry Division, where he met Brigadier General Hasan Abu Sa'da in the al-Firdan sector, east of the canal. Al-Shadhli then went on to the command of the Third Army and then to Seventh Infantry Division, which was under the command of Brigadier General Ahmad Badawi in the sector south of the lakes, east of the canal. He then returned to the Armed Forces Operations Center in the evening of that same day, after having seen for himself the condition of the forces, and the high morale.

We were following the mobilization in Israel of the reserve forces, on which Israel depended in times of war, along with the existing armored division already present on the front since the beginning of the war, under the command of General Mindler. Two armored divisions had moved to Sinai by 7 October. One was under the command of General Abraham Adan (known as Bern) on the northern axis in the direction of al-Qantara. The other, under the command of General Sharon, was in the central axis in the direction of Isma'iliya. Israel now had about 950 tanks on the front in three armored divisions under the command of three outstanding generals.

On its way to al-'Arish–al-Qantara, Adan's division met with one of the Egyptian commando units, which opened fire on the column of moving Israeli tanks, using its anti-tank weapons to destroy some and damaging others. This slowed down the division for several hours because of the fear of ambush along its route towards the canal. The commando unit acted in broad daylight and suffered casualties because of its courage, perseverance, and the self-sacrifice of its men.

Sharon's division did not meet with the commandos on route to the central axis, but progress was cautious after it was learned that the Egyptian commandos had been operating in the heart of Sinai since noon of the first day of battle. An Israeli military communiqué was issued on 7 October which said that Israeli forces fighting on the canal front were also engaged in other battles with Egyptian commandos parachuted down behind Israeli lines in the depths of Sinai.

At the Operations Center, we had predicted that the Israeli enemy would try to strike a heavy counterblow, using the rescue forces which had reached Sinai to destroy our forces and to reach the canal line. We were certain that both the Second and Third Armies were prepared for this and that Monday 8 October would be a decisive day for the progress of operations. The Israeli command had to be shown convincingly that we would continue to impose our will on them for the success of the coming battle.

On 7 October, while the reservists were still being deployed, Dayan flew to the southern front command in Sinai where he reviewed the situation with the commander there, General Gonin. There is no doubt that Dayan was fully aware of the disintegration of his troops on the front, the huge losses incurred by Mindler's armored division, the collapse of the Bar-Lev line, and the failure to save the men besieged there.

Following an evaluation of the situation, Dayan recorded his opinion in his memoirs.

> During my flight back to Tel Aviv from Sinai, I could not remember any moment in the past when I had felt such alarm as I did at that moment. If I had suffered bodily harm or had personally been facing great danger, it would have been easier. But now, another feeling overcame me—Israel was in danger.
>
> The consequences would be devastating—unless we understood the new situation and redressed it at the appropriate time—if we failed to adapt our fighting to the new requirements.
>
> On reaching Tel Aviv, I said this to Golda Meir in the presence of two other ministers and the chief of staff, Elazer. I urged that we leave the canal line, reorganize ourselves immediately along new lines, holding on to them at all costs, and conduct the war from there.
>
> We were facing a danger which was making us lose our impetus. . . . We had to make a major effort to acquire planes and tanks from America in the shortest time possible. We should perhaps try to get tanks from Europe . . .
>
> The prime minister and both of the other ministers were astounded. I believe that this was to a great extent because I said, in addition, that I did not believe that it was in our capacity at this moment to push the Egyptians back to the other side of the canal . . .
>
> Following my realistic assessment it was obvious from their critical questions that they believed that the weakness lay not in the military situation but in me—that I had lost my nerve, that my evaluation was wrong, and I had been overcome by the pressure.
>
> The chief of staff, who did not agree with my evaluation, agreed to set up a second line instead of the canal line but decided on a counterattack against the Egyptians on the east bank of the canal, to be carried out by Sharon and Adan. The ministers breathed a sigh of relief. They had never considered for a second that we lacked the

strength to push the enemy back at any chosen moment to its positions of thirty hours earlier.

The Israeli Counterattack

The Israeli counterattack began on the morning of 8 October against the forces of the Second Army in the area between al-Qantara East and Isma'iliya. Major General Sa'd al-Din Ma'mun, commander of the Second Army, was faced with two armored divisions, one under Adan in the zone east of al-Qantara and the other under Sharon on the central axis in the direction of Isma'iliya.

Operations staff believed that Adan's armored division would engage the forces of the Second Army while Mindler's division would face the Third Army. Sharon's armored division was the reserve of the Israeli southern front, there to reinforce an eventual success of either of the divisions facing our Second or Third Armies.

Adan's division consisted of three armored brigades (300 tanks). They began their attack in the Qantara sector with an armored brigade against the Eighteenth Division under the command of Fuad 'Aziz.

An attack was launched against the Second Division, under the command of Hasan Abu Sa'da, in the Firdan sector, using a second armored brigade, with the aim of breaking through Egyptian positions and reaching the canal. The forces of the Second Army managed to repel the attack in both sectors. The enemy was forced to withdraw to the east after losses in both men and equipment.

The Battle of al-Firdan

The enemy regrouped with two armored brigades and Adan tried once more to attack Hasan Abu Sa'da. A third brigade was used against the Sixteenth Division, under the command of Brigadier 'Abd Rabb al-Nabi, in the sector east of Isma'iliya while the battle of al-Firdan raged on between the forces of Abu Sa'da and Adan.

The Israeli tanks pressed forward to penetrate Abu Sa'da's positions in the direction of the Firdan bridge and get through to the canal lines. The attacking men suddenly found themselves within a 'killing ground' with Egyptian guns opening fire simultaneously from three directions. The greater surprise was that their tanks were being rapidly destroyed by Egyptian anti-tank missiles and artillery fire. The advance tanks had been coming forward with great momentum. They consisted of thirty-five tanks led by Colonel Issak Yagouri and were one of the forward units of the attack. Yagouri panicked when he saw that thirty of his tanks had been hit or destroyed during a battle which lasted half an hour. He had no other choice but to jump from the command tank and take shelter, along with his crew, in a ditch. They were captured several minutes later by men from the Second Division. His tank was left on the battlefield as a reminder for all to see after the war.

Because of the heavy losses, Adan had to halt the attack and withdraw eastward under pressure of fire from the Second Army.

I felt relieved when news reached me at the Operations Center of the success of the Second Division at al-Firdan under the command of Hasan Abu Sa'da.[1] I got in touch with him by telephone to congratulate him and we had a short exchange in which he spoke highly of the overall strategy and I of his implementation of it. I was happy to learn of the division's continuing high morale and determination.

In the Operations Center, as in the Second Army Command, we were following the land battles closely. An enemy success in al-Qantara East, in al-Firdan, or in Isma'iliya East would have meant that Israeli forces had reached the canal line, which would have affected the military balance for the land forces and was unacceptable.

After his return from captivity following the war, Issak Yagouri did not forget what had happened to him and to his unit. In a 2 July 1975 article in the Israeli newspaper *Ma'arev*, he described 8 October as a "Black Monday" for Israel. He said, "Why did they leave us unprotected on the al-Firdan front on 8 October? The despair I felt at the time was shared by most of the soldiers, and all of us who lived through it will not forget its bitterness . . . When I returned from captivity, I was dismayed by the losses suffered in our tanks. 8 October has become a day of blood, despair, and great pain."

Our attention was directed towards Sharon's division as, in our judgment, it would be drawn into the battle to help Adan. But this did not happen.

At noon on 8 October, Sharon's division moved southward in a direction east of Suez towards Mindler's division, which was trying to break through the positions of the Third Army. It became obvious that Sharon would help Mindler in the hope that a counterattack would be successful in that sector, after having failed against the Second Army.

While Sharon's men were moving toward Suez, Adan's division was entangled in a battle with the Second Army and suffering heavy losses in men and equipment. It had to withdraw eastward after its brigades had been scattered across a wide front forcing it to take up new defensive positions. This was not promising, and the commander of the southern zone requested that Sharon's division turn back to help Adan.

By the end of the day, Adan's division had been defeated by the Second Army and Mindler's division had been unable to break through

Third Army lines. Sharon helped neither of them. This was a day of defeat for the Israeli army, with a failed counterattack—despite the input from its mobilized reserves—and Israeli commanders blamed each other.

The eighth of October also saw increased and effective air activity with concentrated sorties against enemy airports in al-Maliz and Bir Tamada (in central Sinai), against anti-aircraft batteries and Hawk missile sites, and against enemy radar and command centers in both the northern and central sectors. Maliz and Tamada airports were put out of action and a number of helicopters were destroyed on the ground in Tamada. Only the one airport at al-'Arish remained operational, and the command and orientation centers in Umm Khushayb and Umm Margam were also hit.

To accomplish its multiple missions, our air force engaged in a number of air battles over Sinai to shield attacking bombers as well as protect the land forces and the bridge crossings, with some help from our air defense. About 400 sorties were made, a major effort which impacted strongly on the positive outcome of the battles. By the end of the day we had brought down twenty-four enemy aircraft of the Phantom and Skyhawk types, while our losses were ten planes. Israeli prisoners of war later said that as a result of the air losses and the fierce fighting put up by our Egyptian pilots on the Egyptian and Syrian fronts, morale had fallen sharply among their pilots.

In both the Mediterranean and Red Seas, our naval forces continued to bombard enemy coastline positions. On the eastern coast of the Gulf of Suez, commando units raided oil installations in Bela'im, setting fire to them after having engaged with an enemy unit. After their safe return, the flames could still be seen rising high in the sky.

When fighting stopped at around 8:00 in the evening, our armed forces had seen another day of victory. The Second and Third Armies had accomplished their missions successfully. The bridgeheads of the five divisions were now at a suitable depth in Sinai and had the fighting capability for further action, notably to develop army bridgeheads according to plan on the following day, 9 October. This was a decisive day, setting the groundwork for the next stage of operations to the advantage of our forces.

Dayan has recorded his evaluation of the war on that day from Israel's point of view. He says in his memoirs that

> if all the factors had gone well, then our counterattack on 8 October would have been a turning point in the war because its purpose was to annihilate the Egyptian forces which had crossed the canal and which had taken positions on the eastern bank. Israel sent hundreds

of tanks to take part in the counterattack. We thought that 8 October would be the 'day of the tank battle' . . . Israeli tanks did engage, in fact, and a bitter struggle ensued. Our men fought bravely but that day was one of total failure.

That night after a meeting of the Israeli cabinet, Dayan held a separate meeting with the chief of staff and the commanding officers in which he gave his evaluation of the general situation. He said,

> After war had come upon us unawares as it did, and by the end of the first day on the southern front—Sinai—without the timely appearance of our troops (reserves) in their assigned positions, and after the failed evacuation of the fortifications (and there was time for an evacuation), now, at this point in time, with the appropriate forces available there in Sinai—three armored divisions and a large number of planes which have fought throughout 8 October—these also have failed. And everything has come to nothing. The day has passed leaving in its wake a great despair, major losses, and a retreat.

The US Plan for Israel

In Egypt throughout the war we did not know, nor did we find out for some time afterwards, that a US military specialist had arrived in Israel at dawn of 8 October, the third day of the war, to take part in the planning needed to face a deteriorating military situation on both the Egyptian and Syrian fronts.

In his memoirs General Elazer reveals that a US military plan was transmitted to Israel by this official on 8 October. This was the day of the Israeli counterattack which used the strategic tactical reserves against our forces in Sinai in an attempt to return the situation to its pre-6 October status.

The United States had evaluated the military situation on 6 October and advised Israel that same day. The advice was in fact put into effect on 7 October. The arrival of the senior military officer with a US plan may be considered a second step, and the more important one in US military aid to Israel, whose purpose was to prevent Egypt and Syria from finalizing their victory.

It was close to 3:00 A.M. on 8 October when the official arrived at general headquarters. He was from the Pentagon, responsible for the Middle East region, and arrived at Ben-Gurion airport in a military aircraft carrying with him a large dossier of special reports and satellite photographs of all the battles and troop positions.

The situation was reviewed and it was agreed that if the fighting continued for more than six days it would be to the advantage of the Arabs, especially if the Egyptian forces developed their attack eastward in the direction of the passes. This was not considered far-fetched. Also, if fighting continued simultaneously on both the Syrian and Egyptian fronts, as was happening at the moment, this was not to Israel's advantage. The US official concluded that "the only solution is to isolate one of the fronts from the other or, to be clearer, to direct a concentrated strike against one of the fronts to paralyze it—either the Syrian or the Egyptian—until it becomes practicable for Israel to fight on just one front."[2]

The official realized that the Egyptian bridgeheads were now up to eight kilometers inside Sinai and a great quantity of weapons and equipment had crossed over—with over fifty thousand men—to the east side of the canal. He concluded that "it was impossible to think of striking at the bridgeheads." The alternative strategy was essentially to paralyze the Egyptian armored divisions and tank columns on the east bank of the canal, then break through and isolate the bridgeheads, and to draw the Egyptian air force away from the battlefield and back into the Egyptian heartland in the direction of the population centers of al-Manzala and al-Mansura. This would limit the effectiveness of the SAM 6 missiles. The important thing was for Israel to exhaust one of the fronts, isolate the other, and concentrate the attack there. According to Elazer, despite the obvious and visible signs of the disaster, the US expert was still confident that they could limit the damage to the fourth day of battle (9 October).

Fierce battles had raged on both the Egyptian and Syrian fronts throughout the US official's presence in Israel. Throughout that day ("the day of total failure," according to Dayan), alarming news continued to come through to the Israeli command.

The Second and Third Armies were repelling the Israeli counterstrike. The town of al-Qantara East had been retaken. Commando forces were destroying Israeli targets on the east coast of the Gulf of Suez. The Egyptian air force continued its attacks and had put the airports of al-Maliz and Tamada out of action, leaving only al-'Arish operational. The navy had shelled Israeli targets and Egyptian air defense was stopping Israeli aircraft.

In the Golan, the Israelis were putting up a stubborn resistance to the Syrians, and were trying to take the initiative.

The first Israeli airstrike against an Egyptian town began on 8 October at Port Said.

The Air Battle for Port Said[3]

Engagements between the Israeli air force and the Egyptian air defense forces were intense along the combat front throughout 6 and 7 October. In Port Said, however, action had been completely different and was characterized by scattered and sporadic sorties with activities limited to operations of diversion.

Suddenly, starting 8 October, Port Said became the arena for the violent battles between Egyptian air defense and the Israeli air force, and the city came under almost constant savage air attacks, sometimes of more than fifty planes at a time. A captured Israeli pilot explained that Port Said was specifically targeted because it was believed that Egypt had installed strategic ground-to-ground missiles which could hit the principal Israeli cities and towns. (Port Said was the closest Egyptian point to those cities.)

The Israeli command thought a quick victory was possible in this sector since tactically the target—the air defense—was considered detached from the main missile network. However, despite heavy enemy air attacks, the air defense put up a strong resistance, inflicting losses in every attack, dispersing the aircraft, and preventing them from hitting their targets.

Some missile batteries were put out of operation in the air battle, which continued for several days, so Lieutenant General Muhammad 'Ali Fahmi ordered a halt to the firing to make the enemy think that it had succeeded in silencing them. Engagements were limited to anti-aircraft artillery fire and shoulder-carried missiles while repair teams from air defense command moved in and, under heavy and constant bombardment, repaired the faults within forty-eight hours. When Israeli planes flew confidently in once more over Port Said at altitudes beyond the range of the anti-aircraft guns, they were suddenly surprised by tens of missiles bursting upwards from the positions they thought had been definitively silenced. Their planes fell from the sky in clusters, to the relief of the inhabitants of the town. And the battles continued in this manner.

I recall telephone conversations with Major General 'Abd al-Tawwab Hudayb, governor of Port Said, asking for air defense missile action during the temporary lull. Hudayb spoke of the high morale of the population of Port Said but wanted assurances that the missile defense of the town would continue.

I remembered Port Said during the Tripartite Aggression against Egypt in 1956. And again, I recalled the 1967 war when both Hudayb and the citizens of the towns in the Suez zone had taken the same patriotic stand during the battles in the region. For part of this time I had been chief of staff of the canal front and I had seen the people of Port Said fighting alongside the army. Not one single person had hesitated to carry out a commission asked of him towards the war effort, whatever the cost. The people of Port Said were once more in October 1973 demonstrating their willingness to sacrifice.

Efforts to Silence Egyptian Air Defense

I return once more to the US official who had arrived in Israel at dawn on 8 October. He had lived close to the fighting on 8 and 9 October and was no doubt aware of the gravity of the situation for the Israelis. Just before leaving Israel, he held a meeting with military command in which he focused on how to paralyze Egyptian air defense and destroy the air defense network for the air force to have control of the air in the field of operations and to give the Israeli army freedom of action.

After this, the Israeli air force tried every tactic conceivable using electronic devices and special equipment, but with no success. Anti-radar guided missiles and missile launchers known as Shrikes—the United States' most recently developed weapons—went wide of their targets. This was not due to a lack of skill but rather to the preparedness of the Egyptian air defense. On the other hand, the powerful electronic shield did not prevent air defense from engaging effectively and enemy electronic diversions failed to direct fire away from their real targets. This is not to say that the picture was always rosy. We had daily losses in men and equipment, but the air defense network remained effective.

As Elazer writes in his memoirs, the final meeting between the US official and the Israelis ended with the following suggestion from Elazer:

> We must concentrate on the various sectors individually and begin by hitting the northern sector from Port Said to al-Qantara. The same operation will be repeated southward. This means that we will sacrifice a number of planes in a risky undertaking, which is unavoidable.
>
> Following the fall of our first line of defense and the cracks in our second line of defense, we have no choice but to withdraw and reposition defensively along the line of the passes. If Egyptian missile units are able to cross over to the east bank, and if we are encircled there, it will be terrible. It will become very dangerous, as our third defense line in the passes would then be open to Egyptian air cover which will interfere with our air capability.

23

9 October: The 'Specific Mission' is Accomplished

We were now into the fourth day of battle, Tuesday 9 October.

On the Sinai front, we felt completely confident about the military situation. Our forces had accomplished their 'specific mission,' the Second and Third Armies had made bridgeheads in Sinai at a depth of twelve to fifteen kilometers with tanks, artillery, and other weapons—a solid wall against which all the enemy counterattacks had foundered. The most dangerous of these was the enemy attack on 8 October, which failed and was later referred to as the "day of total failure."

Morale was high and getting higher because of the successive achievements on the battlefield since the 6 October offensive. The Bar-Lev fortifications had been entirely destroyed, with the exception of two strongpoints—one was at the most northern point in the region east of Port Fuad on the Port Said–al-'Arish coastal road. It was backed by the sea on the one side and salt marshes on the other. The coastal road from Rumana allowed for reinforcements and the evacuation of the wounded. The truth is that to destroy or to besiege a fortification such as this would have required unorthodox means and some inventiveness. This was the only fortress which did not fall.

The second fortress was on the tip of Port Tewfik at the entrance to the Gulf of Suez. Its garrison of thirty-seven men eventually surrendered, after a long siege, in the presence of representatives from the Red

Cross. It was a historic moment when the Israeli commander lowered the flag of his aggressor country and the Egyptian commanding officer proudly raised the Egyptian flag once more on his own territory.

The battles continued in Sinai where both First and Second Armies tried to inflict losses on the enemy and the Israelis tried to delay the movement of our forces eastward. In general, the military situation on the Sinai front was strong by the end of 9 October. Our armed forces had completed their specific mission in preparation for other missions.

On the Golan front, the Israeli forces were able to push back the Syrians and after several counterattacks they took the initiative. The Syrian forces were forced to withdraw from the positions they had reached.

The situation deteriorated seriously when Israel on 9 October launched air attacks against Syrian economic targets and bombed Damascus the following day. Israeli planes had since 8 October been hitting Port Said, but the Israeli air force had not penetrated deeply to strike at civilian and economic centers inside Egypt and Syria. This was now happening in spite of the fact that Egypt had committed itself in a message to Kissinger on 7 October not to deepen its attacks. It was natural that this message should have reached Israel via the United States.

Minister of Defense Dayan discussed the military situation on both the Egyptian and Syrian fronts in an Israeli press conference on the evening of 9 October.[1] Because of the sensitive nature of this information (it could have affected public morale and that of the army in particular), the prime minister forbade its publication and it remained unavailable until the middle of 1974.

Dayan said,

> We intend to concentrate all our efforts on neutralizing Syria. I don't even know if it is within our power to force Syria to ask for a ceasefire. But I believe and hope we will be able to silence their guns and to contain their strength as much as possible. The Syrians are fighting back and we have to take that into consideration, but we are on the point of limiting their fighting. I cannot divulge the number of Syrian tanks still within our territory [meaning the Syrian territory of the Golan] . . . We want to neutralize the Syrian front because this from my point of view is a first priority as it borders immediately on our land.
>
> It is Syria we have to be careful of. Today we are attacking economic and military targets, electricity, petrol, military barracks,

and airports. Tomorrow, if necessary, we will attack general staff headquarters and the Ministry of Defense. But we can't do this kind of thing daily, not because of military difficulties but for political reasons. . . . To continue bombing Damascus is very problematic . . . but we will do our utmost to neutralize Syria.

In this same conference, Dayan spoke about the situation on the Egyptian front:

The southern front does not give us the same picture. I have to be perfectly frank and clear: we do not have the capability at the moment to push the Egyptians back beyond the canal. The attack on the northern and southern fronts simultaneously has seriously weakened us.

Egypt has enormous quantities and a wide range of Soviet material . . . which is very effective and of excellent quality, especially the individual anti-tank weapons. The actual number of Egyptian tanks east of the canal exceeds ours. Furthermore, they have artillery and missiles . . . The only thing in which we are superior is the air force, except that the missiles pose a problem here.

The whole world now realizes that we are not stronger than the Egyptians and that the mystique which surrounded us [that if the Arabs attacked, Israel would destroy them] has shattered. We have to tell the people the truth and I will do so this evening on Israeli television. I can't guarantee what is likely to happen. It is very possible that we might consider withdrawing to safer and less dispersed lines with natural barriers which would help us organize a better defense plan. . . . This is my view on the situation.

Dayan continued:

We are paying daily the price in equipment, troops, pilots, planes, and tanks. Hundreds of our tanks were destroyed in the battle. We lost fifty planes in three days . . .

Volunteers are rushing forward to enlist and the kind of spirit they have is beyond description. . . . We cannot enter a battle and put up a fight without tanks and planes. Our central concern is the future of the State of Israel . . . the Bitter Lakes or any other such place can go to the devil. . . . We are in need of tanks and planes to protect our country. . . . In spite of all our efforts, our forces are being worn down.

I hope the Americans will send us some planes. They have agreed to sent their new Phantoms. I also hope that they will provide us with tanks . . .

I am not sure the Americans know everything about the course of events, but our policy is based on notifying them of the smallest details.

This then was the situation on the Sinai front, on the Golan, and with the enemy forces on the evening of 9 October.

The Egyptians remained strong but the Syrians had been seriously pressured by the enemy counterattacks, and this had developed to Israel's advantage when the Syrians were forced to pull back. As for the Israelis on the Sinai front, they were unable to complete an effective offensive operation and took up defensive positions to block the progress of our forces eastward.

Israel, according to Dayan, might be forced to withdraw to other lines to organize a better defense. We can infer that Dayan meant the line of the mountain passes, which would have been in agreement with Elazer's suggestion when he said, "Our first line of defense has fallen. Our second line of defense has been shaken. What is left is to withdraw and to reposition at the passes."

During that day (9 October), a naval battle took place in the Mediterranean between an enemy formation supported by helicopters and a convoy of Egyptian launches north of the Sinai coast. The Egyptian launches were able to sink five Israeli vessels and three of our boats were hit. A military communiqué (No. 21), issued from general command at 12:45 P.M., reported on this event.

As for the land battles, our forces completed their hold on the east bank of the Suez Canal and our units advanced all along the confrontation line, reached a depth of fifteen kilometers inside Sinai, and inflicted heavy losses in men and equipment on the enemy. Pockets of Israeli soldiers fled their positions, leaving weapons and ammunition behind. Many of them were taken prisoner. This was the essence of the general command military communiqué issued on 9 October on the situation.

ISRAEL REQUESTS US WEAPONS

On the morning of 9 October Dr. Kissinger learned that Israel was urgently asking for arms and equipment to replace heavy losses, especially in tanks and aircraft. From the US perspective this was a fundamental shift. At 1:40 A.M. that day, Kissinger had been awakened by a phone call from Israeli Ambassador Dinitz asking what the United States could do for Israel in arms and equipment.

The question was perplexing. According to a brief from the US ambassador a few hours earlier, the war ought to have shifted decisively to Israel's advantage. What was the problem? And why the urgency?

Israel's requirements so far were mostly limited to specific types of ammunition and electronic equipment. These had been supplied to Israel, along with Sidewinder missiles, but the United States could not immediately provide a few items such as the new Phantom 4 aircraft (an order was already on its way to Israel).

Kissinger asked the Israeli ambassador to call back early the next morning, but he was awakened by the ambassador once more at 3:00 A.M. with the same message and was given the same reply. In Kissinger's words, "The ambassador would not have done this if he hadn't received notice from his government that he could wake me up when he wanted to."

By 8:20 A.M., Kissinger was with Dinitz in the map room in the basement of the White House. The Israeli ambassador was accompanied by General Mordechai Gur, military attaché at the embassy.

Kissinger says that

> both Dinitz and Gur were talking at once. Israel's losses so far were unexpected and very alarming . . . forty-nine planes were damaged and fourteen of them had been completely destroyed. The number was high but it was not surprising if one were to take into consideration that both Syria and Egypt had large quantities of Soviet ground-to-air missiles. I was greatly shocked to learn that Israel had lost 500 tanks, 400 of them on the Egyptian front alone.
>
> Dinitz asked for this information to be kept secret from all but the president, because the Arab countries which had so far taken a position of cautious reserve might join in if they learned of the Israeli losses.

Kissinger records further details of that meeting:

> The information provided by Dinitz forced us to review the basis of our strategy. All our diplomacy and our policy to rearm Israel depended on a quick Israeli victory. We had gone beyond Israel's claims of being in control and something totally unexpected had occurred.
>
> It would be difficult to transport the tanks Israel needed fast enough. Gur suggested we take them from our equipment in Europe. Even this would have meant a delay of several weeks.
>
> We agreed that El Al would begin to transport spare parts and electronic equipment, but the fleet did not exceed seven planes and could not carry heavy equipment. As for the items which required further consultation, I promised to hold a meeting with the special task force and notify Dinitz before the end of the day.

Kissinger continues:

> I had no doubt whatsoever that Israel's defeat as a result of Soviet arms would be a geopolitical catastrophe for the United States. For this reason, I spurred Israel on for a victory on one of the fronts before the United Nations could take Arab gains as an established right in their forthcoming meetings.
>
> So we began to concentrate efforts on a victory over the Syrians; and as for the Egyptians, the matter would be a lengthy one, as Dinitz said.[2]

A VISIT TO WASHINGTON?

At the end of this meeting, the Israeli ambassador took Kissinger aside to deliver a verbal message from Prime Minister Golda Meir: "Meir is ready to come personally to the United States, even for an hour, to present her case to Nixon to obtain urgent military aid. The visit will be secret."

Kissinger immediately turned the suggestion down because

> nobody would make such a suggestion except in a state of hysteria. This journey would take Meir away from Israel for thirty-six hours at least. Leaving her country at a time of fierce fighting would make it evident that Israel is in a state of panic and despair, and this would encourage the rest of the Arabs, now waiting, to join in the war.

He added, "Because we could not keep a visit by Golda Meir secret, we would have had to announce massive military aid to Israel. . . . The Arab world would have exploded against us and Soviet Union would have found the way open for it." Kissinger had also discovered to his dismay that Dayan had ordered a deep retreat in Sinai.

What could be done to help Israel out militarily?

Kissinger, Israel's key man in the US administration, took it upon himself to call a meeting of the special task force, which presented a number of options to President Nixon ranging from a continuation of the present system (transport of aid using Israeli aircraft) to setting up a direct US airbridge.

At exactly 6:10 P.M. on Tuesday 9 October, Kissinger conveyed Nixon's decision to the Israeli ambassador.

> It has been decided that all the required spare parts and the equipment listed will be delivered. This means both electronic and other equipment (except for laser-guided bombs). All Israeli losses in planes and tanks will be replaced, and a number of tanks and M-60 armored vehicles [the most recent] will be sent. Israel will also receive the most recently developed aircraft. As for the remaining

items, a timetable will be drawn up for delivery. . . . All Israeli losses will be replaced. If it was pressed for tanks, these would be sent, even if this meant using US aircraft.

On that same day, the US ambassador in Amman notified the State Department that the Soviet chargé d'affaires in Amman was pressing King Husayn to join the war, promising the Soviet Union's diplomatic backing. Before the day was over, the same appeal was made to the Algerian President Houari Boumediene.

Kissinger writes,

> Up until that hour, King Husayn had refused to enter the war. He had also refused King Faysal's request for a Saudi division stationed in Jordan to enter the war. Therefore I sent a memorandum to King Husayn in which I entreated him to stay out of the war, promising him I would exert the utmost effort to establish a peace once war had ended. His reply was that he fully backed his Arab brethren with regard to their objectives and criticized Israel for refusing peace since 1967, saying he would refrain from interfering as much as possible on the condition that a ceasefire could be arranged very quickly. Otherwise, he would take part.[3]

The Soviet Union Suggests a Ceasefire

The Soviet Union pursued its contacts with Egypt.[4] On 8 October, the Soviet ambassador to Egypt delivered a message from Brezhnev to President Sadat in which he asked whether "the right conditions now exist to consolidate the military successes and transform these into a solid foundation for the continued political struggle" and about "the possibilities of a ceasefire on present lines." But President Sadat refused to consider a ceasefire before an Israeli withdrawal.

In a meeting with Fawzi, the ambassador expressed his country's esteem for the achievements of the Arab armies, but also spoke of the Soviet Union's concern about the Syrian situation as well as about the concentration of the larger part of the Egyptian forces in a limited area east of the canal.

The ambassador added that as long as it was a limited war (meaning that the goal was not the total defeat of Israel), then the time had come to consider a reasonable political solution. Dr. Fawzi was worried about a negative reaction from our armed forces if they were asked to stop at a time when they were inflicting heavy losses on the Israelis and while their advance eastward continued unimpeded.

The Soviet leadership was not convinced.[5] On 9 October, Vinogradof, the Soviet ambassador, came back with a second message which expressed more clearly the need for a ceasefire. It said that (1) the time had come to consolidate the gains achieved through a ceasefire and to shift the struggle to the political arena for a solution; (2) deteriorating conditions on the Syrian front had encouraged President Asad to ask for matters to move towards a ceasefire; (3) the Syrian army's failure would allow Israel to concentrate its forces on the Sinai front, which would complicate the situation for the Egyptians there; (4) it was therefore necessary to come to a decision that would be to the advantage of both fronts, given that (a) the Security Council, at the request of the United States, has started discussing the crisis and would soon propose a ceasefire resolution, (b) the Soviet Union could not object to the resolution and would abstain from voting, (c) if Egypt refused to implement the resolution, this would lead to other and more restrictive resolutions which would force the Soviet Union to object to them, and (d) continued Soviet objections to any ceasefire resolution would make it difficult in the future to achieve such a resolution if developments required a ceasefire to the advantage of the Arabs.

President Sadat would not agree to the Soviet proposal, and informed the Soviet ambassador that Egypt would ask China to object to the Security Council ceasefire resolution. Arguing that according to President Asad himself the situation in Syrian had not deteriorated, he requested continued military aid from the Soviet Union. In this manner, several ceasefire attempts from the United States and the Soviet Union failed during the first days of the war.

On 7 October, the United States had believed that Israel had the ability to repel the Egyptian and Syrian attack, and on 8 October it believed that Israel's counterattack would succeed and that it would return to the pre-October lines. Consequently, Kissinger had ignored our insistence on linking a ceasefire to an Israeli withdrawal from Sinai and had waited for the outcome of the Israeli counterattack. When by 9 October the counterattack had failed and Israel's losses had multiplied to the extent that it had begun to request arms urgently from the United States to replace its losses and increase its fighting capacity, only then had the United States begun to review its policy in the light of this negative situation.

At a time when the United States was collaborating closely with Israel, providing a steady stream of information on the military situation, its efforts were channeled in two complementary directions. One was military and offered appropriate and timely support to Israel, the second was political and maintained contact with Egypt and the Soviet Union so that any political solution would take the enemy position (that of the

Soviet Union and the Arabs) into account, along with that of its friend and ally (Israel) for the outcome to be to the mutual advantage of Israel and the United States. From the US point of view, the policy was successful insofar as it prevented the opening of a Jordanian front, which would have had a major impact on Israel. The US effort also gave Israel the help it needed to rebuild its fighting capacity quickly.

The Soviet Union put pressure on the Egyptian political leadership to accept a ceasefire. President Sadat remained adamant however, rejecting this consistently from 6 to 9 October, working hard for Syria to continue, and refusing a ceasefire unless it was linked to Israel's withdrawal to the lines of 5 June 1967. "As long as the Egyptian front remained balanced, solid, and able to face and repel Israel's counter-attack, there was nothing that impelled us to accept a ceasefire."

This was President Sadat's opinion, stated clearly to National Security Advisor Hafez Isma'il. And, from my perspective, it was a wise and correct choice since there was no reason to accept a ceasefire when our armed forces were piling on success after success. They had accomplished their specific mission in line with the operations plan. The Second and Third Armies had put down bridgeheads into Sinai at a depth of fifteen kilometers in preparation for the next stage of offensive operations.

The offensive had to continue.

24

10–13 October: The Long Wait— A Tactical Halt

The four days from 10 to 13 October witnessed important developments, first on the Syrian front and then on the Egyptian front, with new political developments at the Arab level and continued contacts between the Soviet Union, the United States, and the warring parties which had a direct influence on military operations in the subsequent stages.

On the Egyptian front, the Second and Third Armies were consolidating the bridgeheads and reorganizing. Fighting continued, while starting on 10 October the Israelis tried to delay any advance eastward with repeated counterattacks using intensified air strikes. Information reached us that military supplies had arrived in Israel and had been unloaded directly at the al-'Arish airport starting 10 October.

Starting on 10 October the Syrian front began to worry us. The Israeli forces had retaken the Golan by the end of that day after a successful counterattack and had moved beyond the pre-war lines by the following day, 11 October. The Israeli air force had already attacked Syrian economic targets on 9 October and bombed Damascus on 10 October.

On 11 October, the Syrian command sent a representative to Cairo to ask for an intensification of operations on the Sinai front to lessen Israeli pressure on the Golan. President Sadat decided to develop the attack in Sinai starting on 13 October, after the Syrian situation had begun to create political pressures on both himself and on General Ahmad Isma'il, commander in chief of the Syrian and Egyptian forces.

On 10 October, Iraq decided to join the war and sent its Third Armored Division to Syria. Jordan, in the meantime, had declared a mobilization and had picked an armored brigade to take part in the fighting on the Syrian front. The following day, 11 October, Saudi Arabia sent an infantry brigade to Jordan in support of the Jordanians.

With the arrival of the Iraqi Third Armored Division on the Syrian front on 12 October and its participation in combat alongside the Syrians, and the Jordanian brigade moving in the direction of the front, the Israeli advance—now beyond the pre-war line—was halted and the attacks stopped.

On the morning of 10 October, President Sadat sent a deputy, Sayyed Mar'i, to Saudi Arabia and to the Gulf countries to urge them to reinforce, in whatever way they saw fit, the Syrian and Egyptian war effort. Egypt's National Security Advisor Hafez Isma'il says that "President Sadat decided to open up a new front to apply further pressure on the West and on the United States. This came in response to American help to Israel and the continued bombardment of Port Said and Syrian civilian targets. . . . In this way, Egypt started to use the economic weapon."

Within the framework of the continued political contacts with the two superpowers, Hafez Isma'il, in the afternoon of 10 October, sent a message to Kissinger and a copy of it to the Soviet ambassador in Cairo. This defined Egypt's position more clearly in the following points.

1. A ceasefire and the withdrawal of Israeli forces within a defined period to the lines of 5 June 1967, under the supervision of the United Nations.
2. Guaranteed freedom of navigation in the Straits of Tiran, using UN troops for a limited period of time in Sharm al-Shaykh.
3. Following a complete withdrawal of Israeli forces, the war would be considered ended.
4. Following an Israeli withdrawal, the Gaza sector would be placed under the supervision of the United Nations until its population was able to exercise self-determination.
5. A peace conference would be held a specified period of time after the cessation of hostilities. It would be under the auspices of the United Nations and all parties concerned would take part, including the Palestinians and the great powers. The issues of sovereignty, security and freedom of navigation would be discussed.[1]

From Kissinger's answer on 12 October it became clear, in Hafez Isma'il's words, that "the United States was not prepared to accept a link between the ceasefire and the political conditions of a solution. The United States was still waiting for Egypt to accept an unconditional ceasefire."

On 12 October, in the middle of the night, the Soviet ambassador delivered a message from the Soviet leadership to President Sadat, suggesting—if Egypt agreed—that a non-aligned nation such as Yugoslavia could present a ceasefire plan. The United States and Britain were working together and Britain would surely propose a plan for a ceasefire on the present lines. President Sadat refused to accept this proposition and said that even though the situation in Syria appeared critical, it would improve. Syria would not ask for a ceasefire, nor did Egypt want anyone to suggest that this might happen.

On the other hand, Dobrynin, the Soviet ambassador to the United States, had contacted Kissinger by phone a little after 8:00 A.M. on Wednesday 10 October and told him that "Soviet consultations with Egypt and Syria have been postponed as they seemed unfavorable. . . . Moscow can now assure Nixon that the Soviet Union is ready not to oppose a ceasefire resolution adopted by the Security Council."

Kissinger asked Israeli Ambassador Dinitz to brief him on the general situation that day and Dinitz had read him a message from Golda Meir to Nixon. In it she expressed her gratitude for the decision he had taken to resume the supply of arms to Israel, and said that this decision (which had reached her the night before) was very timely and had had a powerful effect.

Kissinger replied, saying,

> As long as Israel now feels confident again with the resumption of arms supplies, then Israel need no longer depend on the reservists, nor be obliged to carry out complicated maneuvers. The important thing now is to return to the pre-war lines as quickly as possible, or even to go beyond these on one of the fronts because we cannot postpone the ceasefire proposal at the United Nations for long.

Kissinger had learned that

> Sadat was pressuring King Husayn to enter into the war. It had reached Sadat that Husayn was considering sending an armored brigade to Syria, thereby avoiding the more serious decision to open a new front all along the banks of Jordan River. . . . I immediately implored King Husayn to postpone the decision for

forty-eight hours at least and, at the same time, I hinted that I would try my best through secret diplomacy to put a stop to the fighting, but I still needed some time and his help. Husayn was reasonable, so he didn't openly respond but followed my recommendations nevertheless, which shows that he was a statesman.[2]

Following intensive contacts with the United States, Israel decided to accept a ceasefire on the present lines. Golda Meir sent a message to Kissinger on the evening of 12 October delegating him to present a resolution plan to the Security Council, since Kissinger thought this wiser. The message reflected Israel's response to the unfavorable military situation.

At dawn on 13 October, the British ambassador in Cairo asked for an urgent meeting with President Sadat and informed him that Kissinger had asked Britain's Prime Minister Edward Heath to make certain that Sadat would agree to the ceasefire as the Soviets had assured him he would. Kissinger had told Heath that "if anyone in the Security Council suggests a ceasefire on the present lines, the US government will not object," and said he had reason to believe that Israel would also accept.

President Sadat's reply to Heath's message was: "Tell Kissinger that . . . I have never agreed to a ceasefire—neither to the Soviets nor to anyone else. I've already notified Kissinger that he is to get in touch with Cairo, not Moscow, if the matter concerns Egypt. . . . Also, I will not accept a ceasefire unless the conditions mentioned in the plan are implemented."

During this tactical waiting period (10–13 October), fighting had continued in Sinai and the Golan. The Soviet Union had begun to supply Syria and Egypt with arms and equipment, and the United States modified its plans to be able to transport the largest quantity of US weapons to Israel in the shortest time possible.

The order for an US airbridge went out on 13 October, by which time Israel had used up its stock of strategic weapons. General Elazer has recorded that

> if the American weapons had not reached us by 12 October it would have meant that the greatest catastrophe had happened and that our end was near. We had completely gone through our strategic stock of weapons, and Egypt and Syria could now go further than anyone in Israel could imagine.

We in Egypt had to rethink our attack in Sinai to ease the pressure on Syria.

After the Army Bridgeheads

The strategy behind the October War was to destroy major Israeli concentrations in Sinai and to reach strategic lines from which we could achieve political goals.

President Sadat disclosed the military strategy when he said, "We have crossed over and accomplished our first stage by seizing all of the Bar-Lev line. What remains is the second stage, to reach the passes."[3]

On 9 October, the time had come for Egypt to decide when to resume the offensive eastward towards the passes in line with this strategy. We did not expect the Israelis to take up defensive positions until the end of the war. To leave the enemy without continued pressure meant that the initiative would go to them. Israel would try to penetrate one of the frontline sectors for its defense to be 'active,' with some forces perhaps reaching the canal line. We had to prevent the enemy from carrying out such an operation, so we had to keep the initiative in our hands. This could not be done without a continued offensive eastward.

The Israeli forces in Sinai were at a disadvantage; morale was low and fighting capability had suffered in the failures and losses. In the Golan, however, the situation was developing to its tactical advantage. It became evident to the Israeli command that our bridgeheads had penetrated to between twelve and fifteen kilometers into Sinai and that we had a vast number of tanks, artillery, and other weapons to fall back on, forcing them to take up defensive positions on a wide front nearly a hundred kilometers long, from al-Qantara in the north to Suez in the south.

It was my opinion that we had to use this situation to develop the attack eastward, without waiting long, to deprive the enemy of any opportunity to consolidate its position. A resumption of the offensive would be under the best conditions for us and the worst for them.

I discussed this with General Ahmad Isma'il on 9 October in two meetings held at the Operations Center. I found him very wary of a rapid advance eastward. He wanted to inflict maximum losses from our positions in the bridgeheads before resuming an attack. General Isma'il also thought that our land forces would become unnecessarily exposed to the Israeli air force and that air defense, fighters, and missiles were still unable to provide adequate protection.

In our discussion, I explained that a resumed offensive would mean close combat with enemy forces which would limit the effectiveness of the Israeli air force. To reduce this even further we should use our air force; it had already proved its worth against enemy planes during the four days from 6 to 9 October. Moreover, even though our air defense ground-to-air missiles were few, they were easily transportable. We could also move some air defense missile battalions forward in successive stages.

I said that keeping the initiative in our hands by remaining on the offensive and building on our successes would create an opportunity, despite acceptable losses. Waiting, on the other hand, gave the Israelis a better opportunity to consolidate their positions by the time we resumed our attack.

The discussions were conducted objectively. I knew from previous service with him that Isma'il was a very cautious man. I found that in spite of his convictions, the issue of "projected losses from enemy planes" dominated his thinking—he would repeatedly say that "we have to keep our armed forces intact." Despite our long discussion, he decided that a tactical halt was necessary. After this, there would be a renewed attack in light of further developments. It was a decision he would not change.

Following these two lengthy meetings with General Ahmad Isma'il, a man who I respected and esteemed, I told him, "I beg you to remember that after our first successes and the canal crossing, the war plan requires that we should proceed to take the passes, with or without a tactical halt." In other words, the principal of proceeding eastward to the passes was predetermined and there was no disagreement over this. The only question now to be raised was when the offensive would be resumed.

Development of the Offensive

The timing of the resumption of the offensive was among the most important factors for its success. It was clear that the longer the delay—the tactical halt—after 9 October, the greater Israel's opportunity to reinforce and to consolidate its position. In other words, the shorter the delay the better for us. Setting a precise time was extremely difficult because of the many complex factors and variables which governed this decision.

The situation on the Golan front showed signs of a tactical success for Israel and it was not encouraging to receive communiqués from the Syrian command claiming they were in control. Frankly, by 10 October Israel had the advantage in the situation. Israel had sent its air force against economic targets in Syria on 9 October, bombed the capital, Damascus, on 10 October, and bombed military targets on 11 October. At this point, a representative from the Syrian command had arrived in Cairo to ask for intensified operations on the Sinai front to ease pressure on the Golan.

The military situation on the Syrian front put political pressure on President Sadat and military pressure on General Ahmad Isma'il, who commanded the two fronts. Therefore, in the early hours of 12 October President Sadat ordered General Isma'il to resume the offensive eastward on the Egyptian front to ease the pressure on the Syrians.

On the morning of 12 October General Isma'il issued orders to resume the offensive at 6:30 A.M. the following morning, 13 October, but at the same time, to hold fast to the bridgeheads. Following requests by Major General Sa'd Ma'mun, commander of the Third Army, and after he was recalled to meet the commander in chief at the Armed Forces Operations Center on the evening of 12 October, the offensive was delayed until 6:30 A.M. of 14 October.

AL-SHADHLI'S OPINION

Chief of Staff Lieutenant General Sa'd al-Shadhli opposed the idea of continuing the offensive for reasons he gave personally to General Ahmad Isma'il. In his memoirs, al-Shadhli, under the heading "The Mistaken Political Decision," says that on his return from the front on 11 October, Ahmad Isma'il had broached the subject of resuming the attack towards the passes. Al-Shadhli opposed the idea because the Israeli air force was strong and posed a dangerous threat to land forces moving in open terrain without air cover.

Ahmad Isma'il resumed the conversation the following morning. He argued that the purpose of an offensive was to ease pressure on the Syrian front. Al-Shadhli disagreed once more on the basis that the offensive would not be successful and neither would it ease the pressure on the Syrians, for the reasons he had given before. At around noon, Isma'il brought up the subject once more, for the third time in twenty-four hours. He said, "A political decision forces us to take up an offensive towards the passes, and this must begin tomorrow morning, 13 October." He emphasized that this was a political decision, and that we had to respect it. All that could be done was to postpone the attack to dawn of 14 October, twenty-four hours later.

WHY THE LONG WAIT?

The following question must be raised: Why did the Egyptian military command not seize the opportunity provided by its successes up till 9 October—and after it had accomplished its specific mission—to resume the offensive towards the passes?

Analysts and commentators have provided different answers. Some have concluded that Egypt's plan for the October War aimed at an offensive operation with a limited objective which was to cross the canal and to seize the Bar-Lev line only. Others have concluded that the plan aimed at an offensive operation to cross the canal, destroy the Bar-Lev line, and seize the passes as the final goal. Here, opinions differ. Some attribute the idea of building on the successive advances and relying on speed to al-Shadhli, while others attribute the idea of a tactical halt before reaching the passes to General Ahmad Isma'il.

I must confirm that the strategy for the 1973 October War was never limited to seizing the Bar-Lev line. The plan had a broader military goal which was to reach the line of the passes and seize this as a final target.

The plan naturally included the crossing of the canal, the destruction of the Bar-Lev line, repelling enemy counterattacks, and a renewed offensive towards the final goal (the passes) whether after a tactical halt or not, depending on the immediate circumstances. In other words, an offensive eastward in the direction of the passes had been decided on under all conditions.

As for the attribution to Lieutenant General al-Shadhli the idea that the successful first advances should be used to speed up the offensive, this idea was refuted by al-Shadhli himself in his memoirs, where he says,

> Much has been said of the reasons which prevented the Egyptians from developing their offensive eastward immediately following their successful canal crossing. Many rumors have spread, claiming that I was for a quick rush eastward, whether on 14 October or much earlier than this. The armed forces have refused to comment either way on this matter, either through the media or academically.[4] Because of this, the international press has confirmed these rumors. I have been described as a daring and fearless paratrooper, aggressive, bold, etc. But I would not like people to link these wonderful characteristics with the decision to extend the war eastward. I was always against the idea, whether at the planning stage or at the operational stage, for many reasons mentioned elsewhere.[5]

I must mention, discreetly and with respect, that the war plan for October 1973 had been set after the staff of the Operations Department of the Armed Forces had worked on it for a period of some time, after the main branches—air, naval, and air defense—of the forces, as well as the various services and commands, had contributed to it with their input, and after Chief of Staff Lieutenant General al-Shadhli had agreed to it. The commander in chief had ratified the documents with signatures from all of us, mine included, a long time before the war.

Since the plan had been set to achieve a strategic target (to reach the passes), it is unacceptable for the chief of staff to say that he was against this strategy at the planning stage.

With regard to the directing of actual operations, circumstances or situations might change or new factors might appear during the plan's implementation requiring a readjustment to suit the new conditions. In this case, the capabilities of the commander in chief come into evidence, as well as his leadership in managing change to achieve strategic goals.

How did Commander in Chief General Ahmad Isma'il justify the long wait—the tactical halt—which was to be following by a resumption of the offensive towards the passes?

AHMAD ISMA'IL'S POINT OF VIEW

Now that General Ahmad Isma'il is no longer with us, I have found it best to refer to an interview with him by Muhammad Hasanayn Haykal, editor in chief of *al-Ahram*, on 18 November 1973, following the war.[6] Most people both in and outside of Egypt were astonished when our forces did not push eastward beyond the lines of the bridgeheads in Sinai, particularly as the Egyptian military communiqués (and these were true) gave the impression that this happened despite the fact that the fighting had not stopped.

Haykal: "May I ask (and allow me to be frank) why the total offensive was not carried out with the necessary speed? . . . Some military experts have said that the great success of the crossing was not exploited soon enough. There are many questions about this. Did our planning focus on the crossing alone? Were we not able to recognize the opportunity which presented itself? Were we slower than we should have been? Or what really happened?

Ahmad Isma'il: All these questions must be asked, and in my opinion there is no harm to this. I will take the points you raise, one by one.

Did we plan for a crossing only? Naturally not. We had much more ambitious plans because war is a give-and-take between alternative plans—a debate between alternative kinds of firepower and alternative kinds of mobility. It would not be reasonable to take one step and then delay and not know how to proceed with the options in planning, firepower, and mobility. Of course, the crossing took a great deal of our attention, because it was a stepping stone whose detail we had studied at length since we knew it was the starting point and also would give us the advantage of taking the initiative.

What could come next? There were various possibilities. We studied them all in the smallest detail. But, in the end, the matter rested on how the enemy would respond. The plan for the canal crossing was a complete one and what followed was also covered by the plan. Selecting an option, however, depended on the enemy's reaction.

Were we not able to recognize an opportunity? To me, the question was not one of opportunities but rather one of calculations. No matter what opportunity appeared possible, I could not engage in an adventure. We began operations under the protection of the well-known missile net, and I obviously had to advance beyond this. It was imperative, whether other people saw opportunities or whether even I saw them myself, to wait—to make sure that my men were sufficiently protected in the rear.

I had to give my armored vehicles the chance to enter the battle, and I had to give my mobile anti-aircraft missiles the chance to come in. Our air force did a heroic job, but if I had pushed my forces into the 'opportunity' people talk about while my defenses against the enemy's air superiority were not in place, it would have meant that I had put the entire load on the aviation and handed it a burden it could not carry when I knew that the critical hours were yet to come.

Were we slower than we should have been? I don't know. What I do know is that I kept to the plan. The plan, I mean the original plan, required a tactical halt after completing the crossing and after the bridgeheads were secured—a halt during which I would evaluate the situation in light of the enemy's reaction, get ready for the next step, take sufficient precautions, and advance. The tactical halt was not a period of inaction, but a time where we absorbed enemy counterattacks and destroyed them . . .

With all of this, and I don't think that I'm broadcasting a secret the enemy doesn't know; we were forced to carry out a broad offensive sooner than was appropriate. Our aim was to reduce the pressure on Syria. Major armored battles took place[7] and they were out of missile range. When I felt that we had pushed the enemy to withdraw part of its forces from the Syrian front and had shifted part of its aviation away from there, moving its reserves hastily to our side, I preferred to return to the bridgeheads to continue consolidating these, to turn them into a rock on which an enemy attack would founder.

Haykal: I will ask once more, and please accept my perseverance: Were we more conservative than necessary?

Ahmad Isma'il: Was the planning and implementation of the crossing—which you yourself have seen and heard praised by international experts—was that conservative? Those who have heard me speaking to the forces know that what I tried most to avoid was this. At the same time, I didn't want us to be rash. . . . War is more than just an adventure.

MY POINT OF VIEW

There is no question, militarily or politically, that the plan was set to reach the passes as a final goal of the war.

The plan did not call for a tactical halt after storming the canal and setting up the bridgeheads but required the development of an offensive eastward to seize the passes, whether with a tactical halt or without one, depending on the situation.

The timing of the offensive, in order to exploit previous successes, was one of the most important factors in its success. The shorter the waiting period after completing the specific mission of 9 October, the better it would have been for us. Commander in Chief Ahmad Isma'il was slower and more cautious than necessary. This made him delay in a "tactical halt" from 10–14 October. He believed, as he himself has said, that he "could not be reckless."

He should have taken the risk—after we had lost the opportunity to exploit our successes speedily —to achieve our final strategic goal of reaching the passes.

The burden of directing operations to implement a plan falls on the shoulders of the military command without interference from the political leadership. This is proper procedure. I tried during the war to find out the reasons for the delay, and whether there was any political arm-twisting that caused the commander in chief to behave in this manner. If this was so then he did not tell me.

When President Sadat gave directives in the early hours of 12 October to resume the offensive after the deterioration of the Syrian front, General Isma'il immediately issued orders that same day for it to begin on the following morning, 13 October. It was then postponed to 14 October for military reasons. It was clear from his behavior that the tactical halt of 10–13 October occurred with the agreement and approval of President Sadat. The decision to resume the offensive following the halt was a political decision.

Regarding this, Mahmud Riyad, director general of the Arab League at the time, said that Hafez al-Asad had invited him on 12 November 1973 (nearly two weeks after the war) to Damascus to discuss the situation. In a conversation that lasted from midnight till 2:00 A.M. President Asad spoke of the Golan experience. He said, "The agreement between myself and President Sadat was that Egypt should occupy the passes, but the Egyptian forces stopped ten kilometers east of the canal." He added, "Maybe the Egyptian command tried to rectify its mistake on 14 October when it put its reserves into Sinai. But the opportunity had been lost after eight days had elapsed since the successful crossing, and after the factor of surprise had lost its impact on Israel." President Asad also mentioned that there had not been enough coordination with the Egyptian command, despite the fact that General Ahmad Isma'il was the commander in chief of both fronts.

The tactical halt was taken as an opportunity by Israel to consolidate on the Egyptian front and become more effective on the Syrian front. It also allowed the United States to continue its hasty provision of weapons and equipment to Israel to compensate for losses and to build up its fighting capability until 12 October.

The United States carried out air reconnaissance of the Sinai front and the Sinai interior on October 13 in which it discovered that the Twenty-first Armored Division had moved from the west to the east of the canal in preparation for action the following day.

The direct outcome of the tactical halt was that Israel successfully concentrated its attention on the Syrian forces in the Golan. At the same time, the United States was playing a clever political game, directly supporting Israel militarily while also gaining time through its diplomatic contacts with the Soviet Union and Egypt. Therefore, the tactical halt had a direct and significant impact on the development of operations in the next stage, and this was not to our advantage.

With regard to the political context as it influenced military operations, I was not aware, in my capacity as chief of staff of the Operations Department of the Armed Forces, of any political moves by the leadership which either supported military actions or exploited their results. Following the publication of the memoirs of various political leaders after the war, two items on the tactical halt and on the delayed offensive against the passes caught my attention.

First, Hafez Isma'il, national security advisor, sent a message to Dr. Kissinger on 7 October expressing President Sadat's point of view. It mentioned that Egypt did not intend to intensify the engagements or broaden the confrontation. Kissinger interpreted this to mean that it implied that Egypt was not willing to continue military operations against Israel after the territories it had gained. The question which poses itself is whether President Sadat's idea not to intensify the engagements was connected to the tactical halt and his decision to delay the offensive against the passes.

The political management of the war should have emerged from military action on the battlefield. On 7 October our forces on the canal front had accomplished an amazing feat, the Syrian forces were advancing successfully in the Golan, the enemy had not recovered from the surprise attack, and the reserve forces had not been mobilized. On that same day, Dayan suggested to the Israeli cabinet a withdrawal from the canal line. Under these circumstances, the political moves appeared out of step with the military achievements and, what was more dangerous, the political leadership had divulged its military intentions. This made Kissinger (and consequently Israel) assume that Egypt was not willing to continue military operations beyond the land it had liberated.

Second, the other matter which shook and upset me was a mention in Hafez Isma'il's memoirs under the heading "The Tactical Halt." It said:

> Our forces had, in the preceding period, accomplished their specific mission. Through my conversations with General Ahmad Isma'il before the war began, I knew that he did not intend to advance to the mountain passes. The instructions from the general command that the goal was the occupation of the passes . . . all this was meant to motivate the lower-ranking officers during the bridgeheads stage to continue to work towards a well-defined target.[8]

I wish General Ahmad Isma'il were alive to explain what has been ascribed to him—that "he did not intend to advance to the mountain passes." I was not convinced by the reasons provided, namely "to motivate the lower-ranking officers . . . to work towards a well-defined target."

There are certain military conventions about which there is no disagreement. At the tactical level each unit on the offensive has an immediate mission, then a subsequent mission and a direction for the next advance. On the mobilization strategic level, the field army has an immediate mission and a subsequent mission. In other words there is always an immediate mission and a final mission.

I believe that we entered the October War with a unified understanding in the general command of the armed forces. I cannot imagine that General Ahmad Isma'il intended for our forces to destroy the Bar-Lev line after crossing the canal and then stop there at that line. Since we had achieved this by the end of 9 October, why did President Sadat not accept the ceasefire proposal at that time, or even on any of the following days to October 12? It was completely clear to President Sadat that the final goal of the war plan was to reach the passes. He himself has asked in his memoirs whether it was possible that the commander of the armed forces thought differently from the head of state.

THE US AIRBRIDGE TO ISRAEL

While the fighting continued in Sinai and on the Golan from 10–13 October, efforts continued for a ceasefire. It had become clear to the United States since 9 October that the situation was critical for Israel as a result of heavy losses in weapons and equipment, a matter the Israeli ambassador had made clear in his meeting with Dr. Kissinger that same morning in the White House. The prime minister, Mrs. Meir, had suggested traveling to Washington to make the request for weapons personally. Kissinger had not encouraged this and took on the task himself as US Secretary of State, National Security Advisor, and head of the special task force set up for the crisis.

In the evening of 9 October, Kissinger conveyed to the Israeli ambassador the US president's decision to send to Israel all the spare parts and equipment it had listed, and this included all the electronic equipment it requested (except laser-guided bombs), replacing all of Israel's losses in planes and tanks. The United States would also send a number of M-60 tanks, which were its most recently developed models. Israel would also receive the newest type of aircraft. As for the rest of the items on Israel's list, a schedule was to be drawn up for their delivery. The United States guaranteed the replacement of all of Israel's losses. If it needed tanks they would be sent, even if US transport was necessary.

A new development emerged on the political scene when President Sadat at dawn on 13 October turned down a ceasefire proposal at a meeting with the British ambassador in Cairo, who was there at Kissinger's suggestion. On that same day, 13 October President Nixon issued a directive for an airbridge for the transport of military equipment to Israel. By this time Israel had exhausted its strategic supplies of weapons.

Kissinger says in his memoirs,

> I had not doubt whatsoever that Israel's defeat as a result of Soviet arms would be a geopolitical catastrophe for the United States. For this reason, I spurred Israel on for a victory on one of the fronts before the United Nations could take Arab gains as an established right in their forthcoming meetings.

Israel found that the seven El Al jumbo jets were not enough for its transportation needs, so it attempted to rent US civilian transport aircraft to speed up the operation. Aviation companies approached refused to collaborate however, fearing an Arab boycott.

The United States considered using its own military transport aircraft to the Azore Islands in the Atlantic. From there, El Al or other civilian aircraft could transport the material to Israel. In this way, Israel would have the advantage of the shorter distance and be able to increase the number of flights. However, this system provided neither the speed nor the volume of transport needed. A special task force recommendation was taken up by President Nixon to create a US airbridge using US military transport to carry weapons and equipment directly to Israel from US depots. The United States' positive response was a life-giving artery to Israel.

Kissinger made a huge effort to create the airbridge, as he himself makes clear in his memoirs, starting from time of Golda Meir's urgent appeal on the morning of Tuesday 9 October. That same evening Israel was given a promise to replace all its losses. Based on this commitment, Israel stopped counting and measuring the material in its arsenal; it could now use it freely without consideration. Kissinger has remarked that "if I have been more insistent than my colleagues about the matter of a speedy delivery of Israel's needs, it is because I wanted to balance our support for Israel by reducing the period of hostility with the Soviets."

In the airbridge[9] the United States used 228 transport aircraft including 51 C-5 and 17 C-141 transport planes. The aircraft carried out 569 missions, including 147 missions for the C-5s with nearly 11,000 tons of equipment and 422 missions for the C-141s with 11,500 tons.

The number of aircraft allowed to land in Israel each day was set by the US secretary of defense (six C-5s and seventeen C-141s) for political reasons. The airbridge continued for thirty-three days, from 13 October to 14 November 1973, during which time nearly 24 percent of the planes used belonged to the US air transport command. The airbridge was able to carry 22, 497 tons of weapons, equipment, and ammunition to Israel, approximately 39 percent of which was delivered from 13 to 24 October 1973. In addition, eight Israeli civilian aircraft of the 747 and 707 variety delivered 5,500 tons of equipment in the same period.

The United States also created a naval bridge assigned to transport large-size equipment. The first vessel arrived in Israel on 2 November with a cargo of 33, 210 tons of tanks, cannons, and vehicles. The total delivered through the naval bridge represented 74 percent of the total requirements of the military aid package.

The airbridge and the subsequent naval bridge were fed from depots and warehouses in the United States. It is worth mentioning that some

European countries—Britain, Spain, Italy, Greece, and Turkey—refused to provide services such as landing rights, refueling, and airspace rights to US transport aircraft during their flights, which forced the Americans to take long and complicated flight routes to reach Israel.

A wide array of weapons, equipment, and ammunition reached Israel through the airbridge, notably engines and wings for Phantom aircraft, air-to-ground missiles, components for Skyhawk, Falcon, and Chaparral aircraft, air defense system equipment, air-to-ground missiles, technical material for the maintenance of aircraft engines, etc.

The land forces received tanks, TOW anti-tank missiles, various types of artillery weapons, cannon pieces, tank and artillery ammunition, signals equipment, etc. It should be noted that the US airbridge started on 13 October, the day before the resumed Egyptian offensive against the passes, and Israel was able to push back that attack.

It should also be noted that those days which witnessed the most intensive airbridge activity were 15, 16, 17, and 21 October, when the breach was made in the Deversoir region (north of the Bitter Lakes), giving Israel the initiative on the Egyptian front which it kept until the ceasefire of 22 October 1973. With the airbridge, the United States had raised the combat efficiency of the Israeli forces in the last phase of the October War, shifting the balance of military power to Israel's advantage and in the process exposing its unqualified support for Israel.

My evaluation is that the airbridge and US air reconnaissance over the canal front on 13 and 15 October were major factors behind the successful penetration of our lines (the battle of the Deversoir). Without the direct and flagrant assistance from the United States, Israel would not have been able to mark the successes of the last phase of the war.

25

14 October: The Development of the Offensive

On 13 October at 1:00 P.M., a US SR-71 aircraft crossed into our air space from the direction of the Mediterranean at Port Said, at an altitude of well over twenty-five kilometers and at over three times the speed of sound. It proceeded to cross the whole of the canal zone and from there the Red Sea, reconnoitering the ports of Hurghada and Safaga and our airports and air defense system in the region. It then turned westward and moved south over the town of Qena, then northwards towards the Delta, flying over the airports and air defense system there. After it had completed the reconnaissance, it returned to the Mediterranean and to its base in Europe.

We got in touch with air defense command to find out why it had not been intercepted. The reply was that it was flying out of missile range and that our fighters could not catch up with it. We repressed our anger and frustration, expressing our feelings out loud.

This incident clearly meant that the United States was reconnoitering for Israel's benefit. The position and size of our forces both on the front and in the interior of the country was now no longer secret. This was the first direct and open military action by the United States for Israel.

Development of the Offensive

As previously mentioned, it had been decided that our forces would develop the offensive eastward toward the passes on the morning of 13 October but this had been postponed to 14 October.

The main force to change position was the Twenty-first Armored Division (in the Second Army sector), which moved from west of the canal to the east in the region of the Deversoir along the middle Sinai axis in readiness for an attack in the sector of the offensive. Some air defense missile battalions also moved east of the canal to extend the defense's range and depth. The US air reconnaissance of 13 October had picked up these new positions, specifically that of the Twenty-first Armored Division, as well as the conditions of the other forces in Sinai.

Our forces began the offensive at 6:30 A.M. after softening the terrain against major Israeli targets and after an extensive artillery barrage lasting over fifteen minutes. There were four axes, two in the Second Army sector and two in the Third Army sector.

The attack relied principally on the armored forces with the Twenty-first Armored Division spearheading the main thrust along the middle axis in the direction of al-Tasa. An armored and an infantry brigade moved towards the Mitla and Giddi Passes on the southern axis, and an armored brigade towards Rumana along the northern axis from al-Qantara.

We were using the Twenty-first Armored Division from the Second Army reserves; a mechanized division of the reserves remained west of the canal. We also used an armored brigade of the Fourth Armored Division from the Third Army reserves. This division remained west of the canal.

The goal of the offensive was to reach lines west of the passes to restrict the Israelis' freedom of movement in the face of the army bridgeheads from al-Qantara in the north to Suez in the south. We also wanted to force Israel into shifting part of its land and air capability to Sinai to reduce pressure on the Syrian front so that the situation there could stabilize.

Our forces advanced against heavy resistance and a thick blanket of smoke and fire from enemy tanks and anti-tank guided missiles. Intensive air strikes slowed down the advance. A few hours into that day, 14 October, the biggest and most deadly tank battle of the war took place, in which around 1500 tanks from both sides took part, reinforced by artillery and anti-tank missiles and under the cover of continuous air activity on both sides. Our losses that day were heavier than those of our enemy and our attack came to a halt after we had lost 250 tanks.

Enemy defenses and resistance were so conspicuously strong that it was evident that they had been expecting the confrontation. The immediate thought was that details from the US air reconnaissance of the previous day had reached Israel, allowing it to take steps to block our advance.

It is worth mentioning that in a conversation I had with Dr. Kissinger during one of his visits to Egypt after the war, he told me that the United States had identified the Twenty-first Armored Division crossing to the east bank of the canal. The United States had concluded that we would resume the offensive soon. I told him that Israel had confirmed the crossing and drawn the obvious conclusions on our intentions. I meant that the United States had provided them with the reconnaissance information of 13 October. He neither replied nor commented, but the expression on his face gave him away.

The air force opened the way for the attack. It hit enemy targets in Sinai, repelled enemy air attacks, and engaged in several battles downing fifteen Israeli Phantoms against nine of our MiGs. The total number of sorties came close to 500. In spite of this, the size and concentration of aircraft was clear and obvious, suggesting that their major efforts had shifted from Syria to the Sinai front.

Lieutenant General Muhammad 'Ali Fahmi, commander of the air defense forces, has commented on this:

> From these events we can deduce that the Egyptian forces were now facing the United States of America and not Israel on its own. A sudden surge in the size and density of enemy air attacks was noticeable starting 14 October, as well as a change in the activities of the anti-radar electronic jamming stations and the missile launching sites.[1]

General Elazer recorded in his memoirs that

> America agreed to our request to send advanced types of 'smart' missiles and mortars, and electronic jamming devices, and began shipping them to us. We found that the United States had prepared them for immediate use and had sent American experts along with them to train our men quickly in very advanced techniques for weapons America itself had not used yet. A few hours before noon of 11 October, we had received another new consignment of Phantoms and Skyhawks adding up to seventy planes, aside from the advanced equipment.

Returning to the Operations Center in the early morning of 14 October, I stood in front of one of the wall charts to follow the progress of the offensive which had begun that morning. At 8:30 A.M., President Sadat arrived without warning and stood beside me. He immediately questioned me on the situation. I said that our forces were obviously facing powerful resistance from the enemy and the advance had slowed down substantially, despite our proven fighting capability and the competence of some of our most outstanding officers. I added that we had to wait until a clearer picture emerged on the Twenty-first Armored Division now leading the principal attack on the central axis. The Second Army command had informed us that its commander, Major General Sa'd al-Din Ma'mun, had been under medical supervision for nearly an hour now and that his command had been taken over by the chief of staff, Major General Taysir al-'Aqqad. This news did not comfort us.

President Sadat stood in front of the map, listening to my description of the offensive and the situations of the Second and Third Armies at the bridgeheads. I remember telling him that the information gathered by the previous day's US reconnaissance seemed to have reached Israel, which had prepared vigorously for our attack. The president left the Operations Center for the Presidency after requesting a report on the outcome of the present battles when this became clearer. He had listened calmly to my exposé, showing neither alarm nor satisfaction. No doubt he sensed my anxiety about developments on the battlefield.

That day, 14 October, ended in bitter fighting after the offensive had been delayed then stopped. Fighting continued through 15 October when the battle of the Deversoir (subsequently known in Egypt and the Arab world as 'The Breach') began.

An Analysis of Offensive Operations

An honest assessment of this operation is that it was not a success and its goal was not achieved. We lost an enormous number of tanks. These, however, when added to previous losses, were still less than total enemy losses by the end of 14 October.

Its lack of success encouraged analysts and observers to focus on this operation. In reality some mistakes were genuine but others were not. Some commentators have said that we used the reserves in the renewed offensive, thereby depleting them. Others suggest that we used up all of our reserves in the operation; that is, other armored divisions than the Twenty-first Armored Division. This is completely false. The Second Army used the Twenty-first Armored Division to spearhead the attack and kept the Twenty-third Mechanized Division, a brigade of parachutists, and a commando unit back in reserve on the west side of the canal. As for the Third Army, it used one armored brigade from the Fourth Armored Division in the initial attack. The rest of the Fourth Armored Division remained in reserve on the west bank of the canal.

At the five bridgeheads on the east bank we had four armored tank brigades distributed so that one brigade was approximately at the bridgehead of each division. The order was to develop the offensive to west of the passes and at the same time keep the bridgeheads intact, so we could not use these armored brigades in the operation and leave the two armored divisions (the Twenty-first and the Fourth) in reserve, as they had been since the beginning of the war.

26

15–20 October: The Breach

The violent fighting continued from the previous day until 15 October. Our inability to develop the offensive gave the Israelis the opportunity to launch a strong counterattack in the Second Army sector. On that same day, a US reconnaissance plane flew over the canal zone for a second time since 13 October. Naturally, any information it gathered reached Israel. The Israeli land forces made limited sorties against the Second Army for scouting and reconnaissance purposes, concentrating on its right flank in the Deversoir region east of the canal, and the battle soon began.

The Tale of the Breach

I choose to call this the "Tale of the Breach" because the Israeli and foreign media focused on the crossing of a few Israeli forces west of the canal in the Deversoir region, south of Isma'iliya, to highlight Israel's success in this battle so that it became a tale and seemingly the only battle of the war.

Each tale must have its hero. General Sharon was the hero of this story, in line with Israel's habit of creating a hero for every war against the Arabs.

General Dayan had been the hero of June 1967, although he had only become minister of defense three days prior to the commencement of this war, finding the plan already set and his men ready to implement it. Nevertheless, after the war he indulged in political remarks and comments, which pleased the Israeli public, humiliated the Arabs, and made the Israeli army legendary. In 1973 Dayan himself became the symbol of Israel's defeat.

They had created a hero out of General Bar-Lev because he was responsible for the fortified defenses on the east bank of the canal which became, in the eyes of Israel and the world, an impenetrable line and a security shield. But in October 1973, the line fell to the Egyptian forces.

General Sharon's turn came in the October War to supply the media with provocative political statements, turning him into a hero for the Israeli public. After a chain of defeats, the battle of the Deversoir provided an opportunity for the media to exaggerate its reports.

Many people in Egypt and the Arab countries have asked why the breach happened. It is their right to raise this question, given the successes of our armed forces which, in one day, had included the creation of five bridgeheads by five infantry divisions in five battles, as well as air and naval battles, and the effectiveness of the air defense system. They had hoped, as we did, that Israel would not be able to create a breach in our lines.

Citizens in Egypt and in other Arab countries were made increasingly vulnerable after hearing foreign broadcasts and reading foreign press reports based on Israeli sources. A media blackout on the battlefield was in force here, in contrast to the exaggerated reporting in the media elsewhere.

It should have been our duty in Egypt to treat the breach clearly and objectively through the Egyptian media during combat and immediately after the war. We did not and this stimulated people's curiosity, leading them to think that there was some secret there.

Instead, President Sadat made statements which gave the impression that Lieutenant General Sa'd al-Din al-Shadhli had not taken the appropriate measures while on the canal front during the time of the breach. This generated even more interest from the public.

Why the Breach?

We had fought at a depth of twelve to fifteen kilometers in Sinai after the historic crossing. The 'infallible' Bar-Lev line had fallen and the Israelis had failed in all their attempts to repel or destroy our forces, the war went on for days without hope of its coming to an end, and Israel's military strategy had been built on the idea of a short lightening war. Casualties were increasing daily. All of this put the Israeli military establishment in a humiliating position after having been models for their people since the June 1967 war.

The president of Israel expressed the feeling at a meeting with the military command in the Operations Room: "You will have to pay the price of your arrogance and I do not know how you will face the people of Israel after what has happened." Golda Meir described the situation in a phone call to President Nixon, asking for weapons and equipment. She said to him, "I do not know how I will face the families of the many dead of this war." Consequently, the military leadership desperately needed a military operation which would restore the army's self-confidence and the Israeli people's confidence in it, after they had once sung its praises.

The Israeli political leadership had lost its equilibrium when its political theories and its military strategy had collapsed. The Arab territory occupied in June 1967 did not provide the expected security and its military superiority over the Arab countries did not impose the status quo. Therefore, before fighting stopped, it had to recuperate the image it had created of itself, through a military adventure and the backing of the two great powers.

From a US policy perspective, it was important that Israel should have at least one battle success before a ceasefire because a total defeat on the canal front meant a political defeat for the United States in the Middle East if Soviet weaponry was the decisive factor in this war. Israel's success in a battle before the fighting stopped also gave the United States a political bargaining card in the negotiations that would follow the war. What encouraged Israel to undertake the military adventure of the battle of the Deversoir was US military aid, which was based on an evaluation by the Pentagon of the military situation on 6 October, US participation in military planning on 8 October, the rapid transfer of weapons through El Al up until 12 October, US air reconnaissance on Israel's behalf on October 13 and 15, and the US airbridge supplying Israel with its needs in tanks, planes, weapons, and technical equipment, which started on 14 October and continued to the end of the war. For all of these reasons, Israel had to demonstrate its ability to undertake some positive military action in order not to risk forfeiting its role in the service of US policy in the Middle East.

How the Breach Occurred

There was intense fighting on the canal front in the Second Army sector on 15 October. In light of information received from US air reconnaissance, the enemy targeted its major assault at the right flank of the Second Army using armored forces, heavy and concentrated axial bombardment and artillery fire, and anti-tank missiles. This was in the

Deversoir region, east of the canal. The aim was for the right flank to fold back from the south to the north and for some of the armored forces to open a passage reaching the east bank of the canal.

The enemy had two armored divisions operating in the main battlefield east of the Deversoir and other forces operating along the rest of the lines of confrontation with the Second and Third Armies. The two Israeli armored divisions were under the commands of Generals Sharon and Adan. Each division consisted of three tank brigades (about 350 tanks per division), a paratroop brigade transported on tractored vehicles or a mechanized infantry brigade, and support weapons.

The two divisions, the enemy's principal attacking power, faced our Sixteenth Infantry Division supported by an armored brigade under the command of Brigadier General 'Abd Rabb al-Nabi on the right flank and the Twenty-first Armored Division under the command of Brigadier General Ibrahim al-'Urabi. This was a division which had been involved in the previous days' tank battles and remained in combat up until 15 October after it suffered heavy losses in tanks.

Sharon's division attacked the right flank of the Second Army. In his memoirs, Dayan mentions that

> this division was assigned to create a bridgehead in the Deversoir region. To do this, it had to guarantee a desert passage 2.5 miles wide south of the Deversoir and north of the Bitter Lakes, east of the canal. It also had to seize a piece of land east of the canal known as the 'Chinese farm' to establish a base and create a passage and a bridgehead through which Adan's division would cross to the west bank.

A First Attempt at a Crossing

Sharon's attack was met by a stubborn and violent response from 'Abd Rabb al-Nabi's division, which slowed down and restricted the enemy advance in spite of the fact that it had penetrated through the positions on the right flank of the division. Under the cover of heavy and sustained fighting, men from the Israeli paratroop brigade worked a passage to the east shore of the canal during the night of October 15–16 and in light boats crossed over to the region of the Deversoir on the west bank. A company of tanks (seven to ten) joined them and the paratroops and tanks disappeared into a tall and dense wood of trees to set up a crossing, according to plan.

A battalion of tanks with equipment intended to use the same desert passage to the east bank for a third crossing. But fighting on the right flank never abated enough that night, and the passage was blocked by the continued battle, supported by the artillery, until the morning of 16 October. Consequently, the Israeli equipment was not able to reach the east shore of the canal.

It has to be mentioned that the interim commander of the Second Army, Brigadier Taysir al-'Aqqad, had estimated the number of tanks which had crossed that night to be smaller than the number which had actually infiltrated to the west bank. This became clear to us at the Operations Center when we received the first communiqué on the morning of 16 October. This mentioned seven to ten tanks. But the actual number which took part in combat on the morning of 16 October was closer to thirty tanks (a company). Consequently, the communiqué issued from Cairo about the infiltration was based on an erroneous estimate from Second Army command, and there was no intention whatsoever to deliberately play down the figures. The error was due to incorrect information. We can see from this the importance of precise information and analysis during combat, particularly given its impact on military operations in the first place and on the politicians and the media in the second place.

As a result of the fierce response put up by the Second Army, which stopped the Israeli equipment from getting to the canal shore, the Israeli detachments that had already crossed over to the Deversoir on the west bank became isolated. A battle for the crossing did not take place and was aborted. In his memoirs, Dayan has described this critical situation, saying,

> At 6:15 A.M. on 16 October, I phoned the prime minister and gave her the bad news: we were not able to put up the bridges across the canal. The way have been blocked by Egyptian units occupying the northern sector of the eastern bank. They have now moved southward, reached the road, and have driven a wedge in our bridgehead. We hope to push them back and move our bridges into the water and set them up during the day.

Dayan adds that "the prime minister was extremely worried that the Egyptians would cut off the advance troops and a major discussion took place in the cabinet about that possibility."

Thus, Sharon's first attempt at setting up a crossing failed on the night of 15–16 October, thanks to the strong resistance of the men of the Sixteenth Infantry Division, who were not only battling against Sharon but were also involved in the fighting at the Chinese farm.

The Battle of the Chinese Farm

The night of October 15–16 passed slowly. For me it was one of the toughest nights of the war because of the losses suffered by the

Sixteenth Infantry Division. My respect and esteem for them was boundless. They were conducting themselves with great courage and determination in the face of the enemy.

From early morning on 16 October fighting escalated and intensified on the main battlefield east of the Deversoir in Sinai and at the Chinese farm, an experimental farm built many years earlier by the Ministry of Agriculture northeast of the Deversoir.

The Israeli command was forced to pull in a new armored division—Adan's division—to open up a route north of the Bitter Lakes at the rear of Sharon's division. This was to transport the equipment for the crossing to the east bank after Sharon had failed to do so himself.

Our division under 'Abd Rabb al-Nabi engaged in one of the bloodiest battles of this period at the Chinese farm, during which both sides suffered heavy losses in men and equipment. 'Abd Rabb al-Nabi's division was able to stop Adan's men from advancing to the canal and opening up a route. The Israeli command was obliged to fly a paratroop brigade in from south Sinai to end the fighting to their advantage. Casualties were terrible and Israeli tanks had to come in to extricate the paratroops.

Dayan described this battle as follows.

> Adan's division went into battle at the Chinese farm. The Egyptian units stood very firm, firing heavily and with precision against our tanks and any armored vehicle which tried to approach them. The number of tanks hit kept increasing, and by the early evening the commanding officers of the two brigades informed General Adan that their men were not able to move the Egyptians an inch or to drive them back. They said they would not be able to open up the passage to the canal.
>
> It was decided after this to attack the Chinese farm by night, using infantry troops. A paratroop brigade would be airlifted from south Sinai for this. . . . I heard through the southern command that the paratroopers had suffered terrible losses under a most bloody and difficult operation during the night.

Dayan continues with a description of the battlefield following the battle.

> I couldn't hide my feelings when I saw it. Hundreds of military vehicles were shattered and burnt to a shell. Israeli and Egyptian tanks with hardly a yard or two between them. I had never seen such a sight, either in reality or in paintings or in the worst war films. . . . Tanks, armored transport vehicles, broken trucks which had

turned over and burnt—all this was a terrifying witness to the dreadful battle that had taken place.

The battle occupied most of the attention of the Second Army Command, while a second battle was raging in the sector of the Sixteenth Infantry Division on the army's right flank. During this time, General Adan managed to move floating pontoons forward to the water line, where a bridge was set up on 17 October.

FIGHTING WEST OF THE CANAL

On the morning of 16 October, General Ahmad Isma'il accompanied President Sadat to the People's Assembly where Sadat announced Egypt's perspective on solving the Middle East problem.

Chief of Staff Lieutenant General Sa'd al-Din al-Shadhli and I were at the Operations Center when the first communiqué reached us about the 7 Israeli tanks in the Deversoir region, west of the canal. The news was alarming. How did it happen? When?

We quickly got in touch with Brigadier Taysir al-'Aqqad, acting commander of the Second Army. Al-'Aqqad judged that this negligible number of tanks had infiltrated west under cover of the fighting on the army's right flank east of the canal. He thought that they would be taken care of rapidly. It later became clear that about thirty tanks were in the Deversoir area on the west bank at that time, and about a brigade of paratroopers had also crossed into the zone during the night. From this point on there were errors in judgment due to incorrect information about the size of the enemy force.

The decision was not easily made at general headquarters, but because of the dangerous implications, the Twenty-third Armored Brigade (at the time stationed east of Cairo as part of the general command reserves) was placed on high alert and ordered to the front, in the Second Army sector, to help deal with the infiltrated Israeli forces.

General Ahmad Isma'il came back from the People's Assembly to find the situation under control. Agreeing with the measures taken, he nevertheless decided to appoint Major General 'Abd al-Mun'im Khalil, from Cairo, commander of the Second Army and to return Major General Taysir al-'Aqqad to his duties as chief of staff. Khalil was chosen because he had once been in command of the Second Army before the war.

In continuous contacts between general command and Second Army command we tried to get a clear and precise picture of the evolving situation both east and west of the Deversoir. The enemy had been able to push the right flank two or three kilometers north, and some of its forces had obviously reached west of the canal. I summoned Major General 'Abd al-Mun'im Khalil to the Operations Center and gave him a brief on the situation in the presence of the deputy head of operations. I told him that the enemy had been able to penetrate our positions in the army's right flank and some tanks had infiltrated west on the night of 15–16 October—about seven tanks or more were in the Deversoir area. We considered the situation critical in this zone. I explained that one of the mechanized infantry brigades from the Twenty-third Mechanized Division, stationed west of the canal with the army reserves, had been asked to engage with the enemy west of the Deversoir and had indeed engaged with the enemy this noon. The situation was not clear in the penetrated sector.

During the day, we began to receive reports that a number of air defense missile battalions had been attacked by enemy tanks. Groups of seven to ten tanks (a company) would fire from about a distance of one kilometer on the missile positions, then move rapidly on. Judging from the sequence of attacks, it seemed that the enemy was using nearly a battalion (thirty tanks) on this mission. The situation became unclear as it was difficult for the Second Army command to specify the size of the force or pinpoint its positions. At general command we decided to contain this force within the Deversoir area. The Twenty-third Armored Brigade was moved from east of Cairo to take up position on the Cairo–Isma'iliya desert road close to the area penetrated, in preparation for battle against the enemy tank force.

STOPPING THE BREACH FROM THE EAST

We had to decide on the most effective way to deal with the situation. The breach in the Deversoir was allowing the enemy to pour in westward. One unit was already west of the canal and had engaged with us. On the evening of 16 October, after careful deliberation, the commander in chief decided that the breach on the east of the canal had to be stopped, in order to prevent more of the enemy forces from coming in and to isolate those already operating on the west bank. We had to contain and destroy them.

Implementation started on 17 October. Forces east of the canal were now starting to close the breach. The plan was to send a brigade of the Twenty-first Armored Division (Second Army) south. Simultaneously, the Second Army would send the Twenty-fifth Armored Division forward towards the north and seal the breach from the east, while a brigade from the Twenty-third Mechanized Division would engage the enemy on the west side of the canal.

During its advance from the Third Army sector, east of the lakes, the Twenty-fifth Armored Brigade was heavily bombed from the air and was exposed to an attack on its right flank, incurring heavy losses which forced it to halt the advance. Consequently, the breach was not blocked from the east. To keep the breach open, the enemy used Adan's division against the right flank of the army, pushing them three or four kilometers north. Adan was then able to push forward the unit responsible for the bridges and float a bridge across the canal under continuous shelling from the Second Army. Two tank battalions and two paratroop battalions from Sharon's division crossed to the Deversoir area west of the canal.

Dayan mentions the problems faced by Sharon's division in reaching the east bank to protect the area around the bridge crossing:

> His division fought bravely and suffered the worst losses. His men seized the bridgehead on the east of the canal in a fierce tank battle in which they were exposed to continuous heavy enemy fire . . .
>
> In this battle, more than two hundred men were killed. All the company commanders were killed twice over. First the original commanders were killed, and then those who had replaced them were killed. The present ones are the third in line within just a few days.

18–20 October

Fighting continued both east and west of the canal. But the west bank now took first priority when following the bridge in the Deversoir area; enemy forces poured westward in increasing numbers and took the initiative.

Sharon's forces moved north towards Isma'iliya, intending to enter the town for the political clout this would give them and to be able to threaten the Second Army's rear positions. The Second Army faced the threat with the 150th Paratroop Brigade, two commando battalions, and the Fifth Armored Brigade. They were able to halt Sharon's advance at the Isma'iliya canal, thereby frustrating the political designs as well.

Adan's armored division crossed over on the night of 17–18 October, ready to advance south towards Suez. Some of the Israeli forces then moved west and south to widen the breach on the west bank of the canal, and concentrated on destroying the Egyptian air-defense missile batteries to allow their air force to operate freely west of the canal.

From the evening of that day, and now that the enemy had two divisions west of the canal, it was inevitable that major battles would take place in the area west of the Deversoir. We had in reserve all of the Fourth Armored Division (except for an armored brigade east of the canal in the Third Army sector), the Twenty-third Mechanized Division, the paratroops and commandos, and the Twenty-third Armored Brigade.

It was decided to return the armored brigade from the Third Army sector, east of the canal, to join the Fourth Armored Division and complete it in the west. It was impossible to return the Twenty-first Armored Division (in the Second Army sector) to the west to join the reserves, because it had been fighting in the east since 14 October. Instead, the Fifteenth Armored Brigade was brought back from the Qantara sector to join the Second Army reserves in the west.

During 19 and 20 October, the enemy's armored forces advanced west and south towards Fayed under superior Israeli air cover. Our air force made a major effort during this critical period, along with air defense, to protect the land army. The average number of sorties in the breach zone was 330 sorties per day between 15 and 18 October and 250 sorties per day from 19 to 22 October. The contribution was significant and every kind of plane available was used.

Because of the enemy's land and air superiority west of the canal, and now that they held the initiative, it became necessary to place the Fourth Armored Division—the principal force—under the direct command of general command so that it could be used in the sector of either the Second or the Third Army, west of the canal, depending on developments.

Against this background, President Sadat arrived at the Operations Center and after listening to a report by General Isma'il, it was decided to send Lieutenant General al-Shadhli to the Second Army command to head off a deterioration by identifying the appropriate measures to wipe out the enemy forces west of the canal, as well as try to close the breach east of the canal. Both assignments were in the Second Army sector.

Lieutenant General al-Shadhli was with Second Army command by the afternoon of 18 October. I was in constant touch with him. After he had been made fully aware of the facts, he returned on the evening of 20 October with recommendations on how to deal with the enemy on the west side of the canal. His opinion was to withdraw four armored brigades from the east to the west within twenty-four hours for a decisive battle against the enemy forces. From his point of view, this would not be detrimental to our defense capabilities in the east. Al-Shadhli also believed that the situation was critical and requested that the president of Egypt come to headquarters immediately so that al-Shadhli could transmit his ideas directly to him.

An Operations Meeting on 20–21 October

When President Sadat arrived at the Operations Center at around 10:30 P.M. on 20 October, Lieutenant General al-Shadhli, Major General Muhammad Husni Mubarak, Major General Muhammad 'Ali Fahmi, myself, Major General Fuad Nasir, head of military intelligence, and Major General Sa'id al-Mahi, head of artillery, were already gathered in the conference room. The president met with General Ahmad Isma'il alone for about an hour before the meeting began. Naturally, Isma'il gave the president a report on the situation and his opinion on how to deal with it, which diverged from that of Lieutenant General al-Shadhli. The main point of difference was that al-Shadhli believed that four armored brigades should be shifted from the east to the west; Ahmad Isma'il rejected this. The president, with Ahmad Isma'il and the minister of state for presidential affairs, 'Abd al-Fattah 'Abdallah, came into the conference room. The president asked for the individual opinion of everyone present, one by one.

First the head of military intelligence gave us a general brief, emphasizing that the intention of the enemy was to occupy Isma'iliya or Suez, which would give them political leverage as well as affecting our military situation.

I was the second speaker. I stressed that our forces east of the canal were strong enough to withstand any enemy maneuver. Given the scope of our presence in Sinai, we should not let go of this or expose it to any risk. It was essential to maintain the status quo east of the canal, without the withdrawal of any significant number of troops. My opinion was that a withdrawal of any armored brigades from east to west of the canal would lead to a weakening of the eastern defenses, which was unacceptable. Moreover, the psychological effects of a withdrawal of the armored brigades on the forces in the east would be very negative. I remember having presented figures on the principal weapons—tanks, artillery, and infantry—and particularly on the quantity of ammunition available in the east, making it clear that all of these were sufficient to keep our forces effective there.

As the president listened to the remaining senior commanders, I noticed that Lieutenant General al-Shadhli had not spoken. In any event, the president decided "not to withdraw any of the forces from east of the canal and to contain the enemy in the western sector."

Shadhli has explained his silence during the meeting in his memoirs.

> The president asked for each man present at the meeting to give his opinion, one by one. Each man spoke with total frankness and

> honesty. After having listened to them all, the president did not ask me to add my word, commenting that 'we will not withdraw any soldier from the east'. And I did not comment nor did I say anything. 'Abd al-Fattah 'Abdallah nudged me and whispered 'say something.' But I ignored him. What should I have said after the president had made a decision without wanting to hear me out? I wanted to withdraw four armored brigades from the east and he opposed the withdrawal of one single soldier. He had not come to that decision through lack of information, but with a complete knowledge of the situation. . . . He knew all the facts and this was his decision.

In the complicated conditions now facing our forces, opinions were numerous and points of view differed; however, when a commander in chief or any lower-ranking commander makes a decision, his men are committed to executing it. Al-Shadhli and I lived through the same war together. He visited the front more than once and, on occasion, was with the forces in Sinai, but I must mention that on his return from the front on 20 October, he was not dispirited, as President Sadat has described in his memoirs.[1] I do not say this in defense of al-Shadhli or for any specific reason—nor do I say it against President Sadat for any reason, or even out of self-interest—but this is the truth for the historic record. There was a difference of opinion between the chief of staff and the commander in chief over how to face the military situation. It is the duty and the right of every responsible member of the command structure to present opinions and suggestions on a given situation. But the final decision is that of the commander in chief responsible for the operation, and this has to be obeyed by all.

The general command complied with the decision taken by the commander in chief in line with orders from the supreme commander of the armed forces. I continue to believe that the decision was right and sound for dealing with the situation which faced us.

When the meeting had ended, President Sadat left the Operations Center without any indication that he was considering a ceasefire, having repeatedly turned this down so far.

27

25–31 October: Three Resolutions for a Ceasefire

Following President Sadat's return to his office at Tahra Palace on the night of 20–21 October, he made a decision to agree to a ceasefire and recorded the reasons for this as follows.

I found out that the American satellite was providing Israel with information hour after hour and had notified them [the Israelis] that the Twenty-first Armored Division had moved from the west bank of the canal to the east to ease the pressure on Syria at President Asad's request and insistence. For the record, I must declare that Russia, which claims to support Arab rights, never informed us of anything observed through its satellites, which were also following the battle.

While I was following the war at the Operations Center, I started to sense that events were beginning to take a dangerous turn. The American airbridge to Israel was using al-'Arish airport to land giant American aircraft and offload tanks and the latest weaponry—and al-'Arish lies immediately behind the frontline. I began to notice another danger in the tank battles, the violence of which the Israelis themselves admitted, and in which the Egyptian forces effectively demonstrated their capability. Whenever I had hit ten Israeli tanks, I found others replacing them in even greater numbers. America had come into the war to rescue Israel after heeding the familiar call on the fourth day to 'save Israel.'

America was openly using the Egyptian airport of al-'Arish, visible just behind the front, to transform the Israeli defeat into a victory. At that moment, I recalled America's actions on the German front in the Second World War, then on the Japanese front.

The third dangerous development was that a missile was launched against two Egyptian missile batteries, rendering them totally unusable. I later found out that this was a new American device called the 'television bomb' still being tested in America, which had been sent to Israel's rescue.

America came into the war to help Israel with weapons still at the testing stage, like the 'Maverick' bomb and other weapons. I know my own capacities and limits. . . . I will not fight America.

Therefore, after my return from the Operations Center, at 1:30 A.M. on the morning of 19–20 October[1] I drafted a telegram to my partner in the decision, President Asad, in which I informed him that I had decided to agree to a ceasefire. I recorded my position, which was that I did not fear facing Israel, but refused to face America. . . . I would not allow the Egyptian armed forces to be destroyed once more. . . . I was ready to account for my decision to my people in Egypt and to the Arab nation.[2]

The president added,

On that night, 19-20 October,[3] I made the decision for a ceasefire, as I had been fighting America on my own for ten days, along with its most recently-developed weapons—most of which had not been used before.

The situation was not what the world imagined. For the world believed that the Soviet Union was standing by our side and had created an airbridge to help us. In reality, matters were very different: America and Israel faced me, and the Soviet Union was holding a dagger to my back ready to stab me at any moment when I'd lose 85 or 90 percent of my weapons, as had happened in 1967.

I asked them to summon the Soviet ambassador and I told him, "I have accepted the ceasefire on the present lines" [At that time, Kissinger was on his way to Moscow for a ceasefire.] I told the ambassador, "The two great powers have to guarantee a ceasefire and the immediate implementation of Resolution 242.[4]

In the early hours of 21 October, President Sadat called National Security Advisor Hafez Isma'il and told him that he had decided to ask for a ceasefire in light of developments on the military front. The president added that he had sent for the Soviet ambassador to inform him of this.

Describing the exchange that took place, Hafez Isma'il said,

> We agreed that I should notify Kissinger in Moscow of our acceptance of the proposal in his message dated 16 October, adding the reservations made by the president. . . . I didn't know what had happened exactly to make us move so rapidly towards acceptance of a ceasefire . . . that was not conditional on an Israeli withdrawal.[5]

After the United States and the Soviet Union had agreed to a resolution by the UN Security Council for a ceasefire within twelve hours of its issuance, the Security Council met in the evening of 21 October and at 5:50 A.M. on 22 October issued Resolution 338. This resolution (1) invited all warring parties in the current war to cease their fire and immediately end all military activity at the positions they presently occupy and to do so within twelve hours of the issuance of the resolution, (2) invited all the parties concerned following the ceasefire to implement Security Council Resolution 242 and all its clauses immediately, and (3) required immediate negotiations between the parties concerned, as soon as the ceasefire commenced and under appropriate supervision, with the goal of establishing a just and permanent peace in the Middle East.

When the resolution was passed, both Egypt and Israel agreed to a ceasefire beginning at 6:52 P.M. Cairo time, 22 October. It should be mentioned that Kissinger visited Israel on his way back to Washington. He notified Cairo of this visit, hoping that Cairo would conclude that his purpose was connected with implementing the Security Council resolution without delay and organizing American–Soviet supervision of the subsequent peace moves.

Hafez Isma'il sent a message to Dr. Kissinger saying that "a visit to Cairo might serve the same purpose." Kissinger thanked him, but said the invitation had reached him after he had left the Middle East region. He hoped he would accept the invitation at the soonest opportunity, especially after a ceasefire was established.

On 22 October, with the Security Council resolution, Israel had accomplished neither a political nor a strategic military goal.

After its tactical success in the battle of the Deversoir it now had a limited bridgehead on the west bank of the canal. The Israelis were operating in the southern sector of the Isma'iliya Canal to the north, in Gabal Ganifa to the south, in the Bitter Lakes to the east, and facing the Fourth Armored Division to the west. They were linked to their main forces east of the canal by a passage covering an area of nearly seven kilometers.

On that day, when fighting had officially stopped, the forces of both the Egyptian Second and Third Armies were in their positions east of the canal and, from a tactical perspective, intact. Israel did not have the capability to move them and consequently the outcome of the war until then had been foreseeable. However, west of the canal, our forces were trying to contain the enemy.

President Sadat's evaluation of the situation, as described to his aides, to the deputy prime minister, and to the national security advisor in Tahra Palace, was that we had destroyed 500 Israeli tanks, and our forces had then taken part in the battle of 14 October (the resumed attack towards the passes) two days ahead of schedule to ease the pressure on Syria. As a result, we had lost 220 tanks. This battle presaged the Israeli penetration of the Deversoir region. The president believed that the Israelis had taken the advantage as a result of direct military aid, which increased with every landing of a transport aircraft at al-'Arish. He added that he was not prepared to accept fighting the United States and the inevitable destruction of our forces.

The president spoke of Soviet pledges to guarantee that the superpowers would ensure the implementation of the Security Council resolution, the top priority being an Israeli withdrawal. Yet he qualified his words by saying that matters would not be resolved at once, but gradually.

In the discussion that followed, Sadat said, "We entered the war to show Israel that war did not solve problems. It solved nothing." He added that "we have gained the respect of the world after having suffered its contempt" and that "we cannot achieve the liberation of Sinai militarily."[6]

Israel Breaks the Ceasefire

When Resolution 338 was passed for a ceasefire starting at sunset of 22 October, Israel accepted this officially but had no intention of respecting it. Israel knew that its forces were in a weak military position west of the canal in the Deversoir region if combat resumed. Also, it had not achieved any specific political or military goal because of its failure to push Egypt's forces out of the east and back to west of the canal. It was unable to threaten or to cut off the communication lines to either of our armies to break off their supplies. It had equally failed in its attempts to reach the town of Isma'iliya.

Israel was therefore determined to invest its energies in a massive effort to obtain some political or military advantage before it respected the ceasefire. It brought in fresh troops to the west of the canal on the nights of 22–23 October and 23–24 October to reinforce its presence in the Deversoir region. It continued fighting and its forces were able to advance south to the rear of the Third Army, cut off the Suez–Cairo desert road, and occupy the town of Suez.

As the Israelis were preparing to enter Suez, the general command issued instructions to the governor of Suez to defend the town. General Ahmad Isma'il and Mamduh Salem, the minister of the interior, kept in close touch with the governor and the civilian authorities to organize an effective response from the troops within the town to prevent the enemy from entering and to wipe out those that did. The fact is that Brigadier Yusuf 'Afifi, commander of the Nineteenth Infantry Division, on his own initiative gave all the assistance necessary, distributing weapons to the defenders of the town.

On the political level, Hafez Isma'il got in touch with Kissinger to inform him that Israel was violating the terms of Resolution 338, asking the United States to put a limit to the latest developments and to restore the situation to its previous condition when the resolution was issued on 22 October. Contacts were also taking place between the Soviet Union and the United States, but the United States through these diplomatic exchanges was (according to Hafez Isma'il) trying to gain time to give Israel the opportunity to complete its military purpose west of the canal. President Sadat sent a message to President Nixon in which he asked the United States to act effectively, "even if this requires the use of force," to impose the ceasefire resolution as Israel was using the ceasefire to improve its position on the military front. President Sadat held the United States responsible since it had guaranteed that the Security Council resolution would be implemented.

To make the military situation clear and to correct misleading information broadcast from abroad, the general command issued a communiqué summarizing the military situation on the morning of 24 October. This pointed out the following.

1. Our forces in Sinai occupied the eastern shores of the Suez Canal from Port Fuad northward along 200 kilometers, to a depth of twelve to seventeen kilometers, including the town of al-Qantara East, except for a small breach in the north, seven kilometers long, running alongside the Bitter Lakes. That is, our forces controlled an area of approximately three thousand square kilometers east of the canal.
2. There were no enemy forces on the west of the canal in the northern sector of the Isma'iliya road or in the north.
3. There was no enemy presence in any of the principal towns of the canal (Suez, Isma'iliya, Port Said).

4. A few scattered enemy units had infiltrated some areas west of the canal. On morning of 24 October, the enemy had attempted to cut off roads leading to Suez, but our forces had prevented this.
5. Supplies to our forces east of the canal continued as usual and had never ceased.

Violent engagements continued from 22 October to 24 October in which the air force and the Fourth Armored Division played significant roles. We had put the Fourth Division under the direct command of general command, rather than under the command of one of the armies, because enemy forces west of the canal were in an area which could threaten their rear.

I must acknowledge that during this period the enemy had the initiative. The zone west of the canal was full of reservoirs and depots which, because of their function and setup, were difficult to defend, so we had a high casualty rate and material losses.

President Sadat came to the Operations Center more than once, staying with us for hours and followed developments closely. I was communicating directly with Brigadier 'Abd al-'Aziz Qabil, commander of the Fourth Armored Division, and the message was to continue to pressure the enemy, stop it from expanding its area of operation, and delay its advance towards Suez.

In one of the president's visits to the Operations Center, I explained why the situation was not to our advantage. After sitting through my repeated communications with Qabil, the president felt reassured by the obvious energy and fighting spirit of the Fourth Division. He did not forget the stand taken by Qabil and his division under these very difficult conditions. In our proposals following the war we had suggested decorating Brigadier Qabil according to normal standards of rank, but the president in his own handwriting raised this to the Star of Honor, usually given to officers for acts of bravery in the face of the enemy.

At Egypt's request, the UN Security Council met on the evening of 23 October to pass Resolution 339, confirming the contents of the previous resolution. This also "urged" the parties concerned to return to their previous lines.

Both Egypt and Israel accepted the resolution and committed themselves to applying it, starting at 7:00 A.M. on the morning of 24 October.

The Battle of Suez

In spite of Israel's official commitment to Resolution 339, its army was given maneuvering space in the hope that the town of Suez would be occupied for the political, military, and media advantages of this.

Two of Adan's armored brigades moved to enter Suez from the north and the west after intensive and lengthy shelling and aerial bombing to break the spirit of the town. The battle of Suez began on 24 October inside the town and the people of Suez fought alongside members of the Nineteenth Infantry Division.

It is painful to describe the fighting. On the one side were Israeli tanks and armored vehicles, and on the other was the population of Suez fighting in the streets and in buildings.

Thanks to the valiant and combined efforts of the citizenry, the police force, the civil authorities, and the troops available, enemy forces which had entered the town were routed after heavy losses in dead and wounded. Burnt-out tank hulks littered the principal road leading into the town and were left there as testimony to the failure of the Israelis to occupy Suez. The enemy was forced to withdraw and take position outside of the town. The battle of Suez was the battle of townspeople but also that of all the people of Egypt. The twenty-fifth of October has become a national holiday celebrated yearly by both the people of Suez and the nation, symbolic of the bravery of ordinary people and an example of sacrifice.

Israel continued to flout Resolution 339 and its forces advanced south to the port of al-Adabiya, south of Suez, and occupied it.

On the evening of 25 October, the Security Council passed Resolution 340, based on a proposal by the non-aligned countries for an international force to supervise the ceasefire and for return to the lines of 22 October.

Israel had been able to cut off the Cairo–Suez desert road, which was subsequently used as a bargaining chip by the United States when Kissinger came on the scene immediately after the war. With some US brokering, Egypt and Israel agreed to negotiate on consolidating the ceasefire and on ensuring supplies for the Third Army.

It was decided that I should be Egypt's representative to the negotiations taking place at Kilometer 101 on the Cairo–Suez road under the auspices of the United Nations, to discuss the military aspects of the implementation of Security Council Resolutions 338 and 339 and also to make provisions for the passage of a convoy of non-military supplies to the Third Army.

The Egyptian and Israeli delegations met at 1:30 in the morning of 28 October to begin these negotiations.

In this way, the war came to a stop on 28 October, 1973.

28

28 October: After the Hostilities Had Ceased

On 28 October, the Second and Third Armies in Sinai were securely positioned overall and sufficiently equipped to be able to continue fighting for some time. West of the canal, our forces had encircled the Israelis and were fighting them.

The Israeli forces in Sinai did not face our two armies effectively. On the west side of the canal, attempts to intimidate the town of Isma'iliya or occupy the town of Suez had failed. The Cairo–Suez desert road, however, had been cut off. This was the principal supply route to Suez and to the Third Army in Sinai, on the east bank of the canal.

The troops west of the canal were increasingly becoming a drain on Israel and were unlikely to accomplish any further useful mission—their losses continued and the evacuation of the wounded went on. Supplies were being brought through the seven-kilometer-wide gap in the Deversoir or transported by plane. Defensive positions had to be kept up in anticipation of an Egyptian assault which could occur at any time or place, and from any direction. A battle was expected over control of the Cairo–Suez road. The Israelis could not return to the east of the canal and could not undertake any further military action west of the canal.

Judging from the course of the fighting on the west side of the canal, it became clear that the Israeli command aimed to score not only military but political points. It intended to occupy one of the principal canal towns, namely Isma'iliya, followed by Suez, in that order. This would give it enormous political and psychological clout and would put enormous pressure on Egypt. Neither town was taken.

Strategically Israel's intention was to pressure us to pull out enough of our major fighting force for it to be able to retake positions held on the morning of 6 October, thereby wiping out our military gains. It failed strategically, although it did succeeded tactically in cutting off the Cairo–Suez desert road after violating the Security Council ceasefire resolution and disregarding the 22 October ceasefire lines.

It is worth pointing out that following its failure to achieve any real strategic advantage west of the canal, Israel, used the media to exaggerate its tactical success, transforming it into a psychological victory. It was to be expected that the United States through Dr. Kissinger would use this for political advantage following the war.

Israel and the foreign media made much of the Deversoir breach, which was used as an example of Israel's successes west of the canal. In Egypt, it should have been our responsibility to organize a media campaign to counter this by exposing the facts as we saw them and discussing them frankly and openly. We did not do this, thereby sparking interest in Egypt and abroad. The task should have fallen to general command, but at the time we did not pay the matter enough attention.

In an interview with Muhammad Hasanayn Haykal published in the newspaper *al-Ahram* on 18 November, 1973, General Ahmad Isma'il was quite straightforward about this. He said,

> Our treatment of the 'breach' in our military communiqués was not what I would have hoped for nor what I had been committed to since the first moments of the war. This was to say nothing but the truth. At no time did I mean or say, or allow anybody else to say, anything but the truth concerning the breach.
>
> This means that at most times our communiqués reflected a true picture of what we saw. I confess that our judgment of this [the breach] was blurred for many reasons, but we did try to express what we saw.

I have to emphasize that the tactical success of the Deversoir created for the Israelis a disadvantageous strategic situation, which would certainly have led to a strategic failure if the fighting had been resumed once more and after a regrouping had taken place.

After Israel had succeeded in creating the breach and after Resolution 338 had imposed a ceasefire on the lines of 22 October, it became essential that the Israeli command protect its forces in a limited sector west of the canal by dispersing them over a wider area. Consequently, more troops were sent west of the canal.

The outcome was untenable strategically for several reasons. One, Israel now had a large force (about six or seven brigades) in a limited area of land, surrounded from all sides either by natural or man-made barriers, or by the Egyptian forces. This put it in a weak position. Moreover, there were the difficulties in supplying this force, in evacuating it, in the lengthy communication lines, and in the daily attrition in men and equipment. Two, to protect these troops the Israeli command had to allocate other forces (four to five brigades) to defend the entrances to the breach at the Deversoir. Three, to immobilize the Egyptian bridgeheads in Sinai the Israeli command had to allocate ten brigades to face the Second and Third Army bridgeheads. In addition, it became necessary to keep the strategic reserves at their maximum state of alert.

Thus, Israel was obliged to keep its armed force—and consequently the country—mobilized for a long period, at least until the war came to an end, because the ceasefire did not signal the end of the war. There is no doubt that this was in total conflict with its military theories and its conception of war. Its economy could not survive this type of situation.

In spite of the arrival in the region of the UN emergency forces under the command of General Selasvuo to oversee the ceasefire, a war of attrition began west of the canal in order to prevent the Israeli forces from consolidating their defensive position. We wanted to inflict the greatest amount of damage possible in men and equipment until the time came to attack. Four hundred and fifty-two incidents occurred between the ceasefire and Resolution 340 and the signing of the first disengagement agreement between Egypt and Israel through the offices of Dr. Kissinger.

Toward the end, the Israeli forces on the west bank of the canal changed from being a pressure point for us to becoming hostages which we could use to pressure Israel. They were becoming a burden on Israel's economy in men and equipment. Then came the Egyptian–Israeli agreement to disengage, and the reality of these conditions became evident when Israel requested to evacuate the Deversoir area and withdraw its forces east, away from the canal.

29

The October War in the Strategic Balance

With the ending of the October War of 1973, the fourth round in the Arab–Israeli conflict came to an end. We (the Arabs) probably agree that the roots of this conflict must be studied in depth.

We need to attend more closely to the activities of world Zionism, the great powers, their goals and purposes, and those achievements which allowed them to create the state of Israel in the land of Palestine. We need to attend to what Israel has done and continues to do with the support of world Zionism.

In this context, a series of wars between the Arabs and Israel took place beginning with the 1948 Palestine War, followed by the English, French, and Israeli Tripartite Aggression in 1956, then the June 1967 war. An overall glance at these three wars shows that Israel was able to gain advantages from each war while the Arabs carried the losses.

A critical look suggests that the Arab struggle against Israel in the twenty years since its creation in 1947 to the June 1967 war was governed by constricting political considerations which hampered Arab efforts in the armed conflict. The comparison between the abilities and potential of the Arabs and those of the Israeli enemy is not truly reflected in the painful conclusion of the 1967 war, when Israel was able to expand once more at the expense of Arab land by occupying Sinai, the Golan, the West Bank, and the Gaza Strip.

An intensive study of Israeli policy indicates that Israel has set itself certain fixed priorities: gradual expansion at the expense of Arab land;

maintenance of a superior military force as a means and as a goal; association with a powerful nation or a reliable ally which would help it reach its goals; and the weakening and dispersing of Arab energies.

Israel since its creation has conducted itself in its conflict with the Arabs in such a way as to be able ultimately to gain control over the Arab region. This it has done by pursuing its goals in gradual stages and taking into consideration international, regional, and internal policies.

A military theory emerged from the Zionist mindset, which was the concept of Israeli 'security'—a cover under which a planned expansion could take place, a means by which international public opinion could be manipulated, and a mask behind which the Israelis themselves could hide in order to justify their military adventures. It is obvious that military force is necessarily a cornerstone of this concept.

The Israeli strategy depended on continued military superiority over the Arabs in order gradually to occupy more and more Arab territory and impose this fait accompli by force of arms, while at the same time encouraging, in the face of this, a feeling of paralysis among the Arabs.

Israel's understanding of 'security' differs from that based on the principals of international law. In Israel, 'security' has meant the means by which political goals could be achieved.

Israel has never defined 'secure' borders, and its leaders have since the creation of the state deliberately avoided any mention of the geographic parameters of the country or its boundaries. Israel often calls for 'secure borders' and describes them as boundaries based on defensible natural barriers from which it may also attack. These are invariably in the territories of neighboring Arab countries.

Under the cover of 'security' and 'secure borders,' Israel has grown and expanded by force of arms, gradually appropriating consecutive tracts of Arab land. In 1948, Israel increased its share of the territory addressed by the UN Partition Resolution from 56.5 to 74 percent of the land of Palestine. In 1956, Israel gained the right of navigation in the Straits of Tiran at the entrance of the Gulf of 'Aqaba. Ben-Gurion announced to the Knesset the annexation of the Sinai Peninsula. However, he was forced to withdraw this statement as a result of efforts by the international community. And in 1967, Israel occupied parts of the territories of three neighboring Arab countries and announced that it needed these lands for its 'security.'

The Israeli understanding of 'secure borders' stems from an aggressive, expansionist ideology which stops at nothing and can only be a cause of continuous friction in the region. The Israeli leadership has refused to understand that linking 'security' to land is unacceptable and that a policy of expansion goes against historic precedent.

As a result of the 1967 war, which we lost as a result of a series of political and military errors, Israel was able to occupy Sinai, the Golan, the West Bank, and the Gaza Strip. Israel used its military power to impose 'facts' on the ground in the face of the Arab inability to liberate the land by force of arms, consequently bending to the Israeli political will.

On the necessity of military might as a tool for expansion, Ben-Gurion said, at the end of the June 1967 war, "We must use our military conquests as a foundation for the establishment of settlements and to create 'facts' which would force the Arabs to yield and to accept them." On one occasion Ben-Gurion was asked about Israel's borders, as none had been clearly drawn up since its creation. His reply was that "Israel's borders are where its soldiers stand."

This was Israel's understanding of the situation a short while before the October 1973 war. It believed it could hold onto the land by force. Israel had become intoxicated by its military successes and arrogance had overcome the leadership. The Arabs were held in contempt as Israel tried to take on the role of the most powerful nation in the region.

During six lean years from 1967 to 1973, Egypt went through hard times. The hardships were at all levels—political, military, economic, social, and psychological—as it became increasingly clear after failed international political efforts that our land would not be returned except by force, whatever the cost and sacrifice.

We were faced with a choice: "to be or not to be." Our armed forces had been reorganized from the foundations up after the June 1967 war, and I must repeat that the reforms had affected every aspect of the forces after the weak performance and the unhappy results of that war. Even in peacetime such a thorough reorientation would require many years. There is no question that it was extremely difficult to accomplish in the warlike conditions in which we lived.

It was inevitable that the process would take time and that our armed forces would have to go through consecutive levels of capability, from resistance to active defense and escalating into the War of Attrition, all of which were contracted into a period of three years. We received weapons from the Soviet Union and were trained on some of these on the Suez Canal front during intermittent engagements with the enemy, some of which were brief and others longer.

We had to engage with the enemy, for the forces lacked fighting experience, but also to expose our areas of weakness and those of the enemy. We needed to restore our confidence in ourselves and in our leadership, as well as to wear down the enemy. The skirmishes and engagements were essential preparation for the October War. Politically, they also played their part in keeping the problem from gathering dust on the shelves of the United Nations.

Some people have argued that the War of Attrition was responsible for delaying the October War by several years. I emphatically reject this. It would have been impossible for us to rebuild the armed forces from zero—from a state of near-collapse following the June War and with all the pessimism and unhealthy practices absorbed in the previous ten years—and shift immediately to an offensive mode of operation which would have included the storming of a formidable water barrier against a superior military force.

Some have criticized the War of Attrition by saying that it was actually an attrition against ourselves. It was to be expected that some form of attrition would cost us something, but the most significant consideration was who would gain more from this. There is no question that our forces profited more (militarily) and it was inevitable that we had to pay the price for the experience. Israel too paid a high price for its continued occupation of our land. The alternative for Egypt would have been to decree a passive calm on the canal front, keeping the troops in their trenches subject to an enemy attack at any moment or to the terrible psychology of 'trench-disease.' Then there would have been no better option for Israel than to continue an indefinite occupation of Sinai until it was able to annex it formally. Could there have been a worse alternative for us than this?

Overall, our armed forces went through an extraordinary period between 1967 and 1973, a time during which they were being reorganized and were fighting simultaneously. The reforms required planning, training, the creation of new cadres—in other words, a professionalization of the military to overcome the negativism of the past ten years. The major problem was the need for new weapons.

The main problem we faced in Egypt was the inability to supply our forces in a timely way with the range and variety of weapons and equipment to allow us to carry out a comprehensive offensive operation to liberate Sinai. This was because the Soviet Union, which was the only source of our arms supplies, believed that the Middle East problem should be solved peacefully and rejected the military alternative. It gave us the weapons it deemed appropriate—in quantity and type, and delivered according to its own schedule—which obviously did not create the conditions we needed to become superior to Israel. On the other hand, the United States was inundating Israel with all kinds of weapons to ensure its military superiority over the Arabs.

By the end of 1972, when the time factor had begun to work against us, President Sadat on 24 October 1972 made the momentous decision to fight with the weapons and equipment we had. We needed to replace the deficiency in weapons with good planning and a great deal of courage. This implied, however, that combat capability was not open-ended and that the offensive would need to happen within a certain range and depth.

During the first week of October 1973 President Sadat announced his decision to go to war under the most critical political and military conditions.

He knew that Israel had military superiority over the Arabs. The natural thing is for the attacker to have superiority. We had to overcome this through the application of good military principles so that the advantage would be ours in the opening stages of the war—the most difficult and critical stage. This did happen.

He knew that the Israeli enemy was in the most advantageous strategic positions. The natural barriers on which it relied helped it immeasurably to hold on to the land and defend it.

He knew that Israeli forces had concentrated their energies against us, building fortifications, creating defensive lines, constructing roads and airports, and selecting and designating specially-trained forces (mainly the regulars) to face an attack. It became imperative for an offensive force to cross into Sinai and destroy their fortifications, to challenge the concept of Israeli 'security.' This is what actually happened.

He knew that a storming of the Suez Canal (with its unique features as a barrier) in large numbers—two armies or nearly 100,000 men—would be one of the most difficult operations. This great achievement was accomplished.

He took into consideration our negative experience in previous wars with the lack of military cooperation between Arab countries, Israel, with its superiority, could potentially deal with each front separately. But military cooperation between Egypt and Syria became a major positive feature of this war—and this was not expected by Israel or anyone else.

Sadat also knew that Israeli intelligence was notorious for its proficiency and its information-gathering activities in the Arab world. Cooperation with US intelligence could unveil our intentions and give

Israel the opportunity for a preemptive strike to abort an offensive and provide the time necessary for a mobilization. We were able nevertheless to achieve the element of surprise and to make use of this so that, for the first time, the initiative was ours.

Within these complicated political and military conditions, the decision to go to war was an extremely difficult one for a head of state. When evaluating the outcome of the war strategically and militarily, we must keep these conditions at the front of our minds.

The strategic goal Israel had set itself after June 1967 was to prevent, militarily, the Arab countries from liberating their land and oblige them to bend their will to the Israeli purpose by imposing a fait accompli on which peace would be imposed on Israel's terms.

This meant that Israel needed to maintain military superiority over the combined Arab countries to prevent us from even considering a war against it, as well as to create a feeling of impotence and despair regarding an armed confrontation. Israel did gain superiority with the obvious and open assistance of its reliable ally the United States, which backed it politically and supported it militarily and economically.

The strategic mission of the Israeli forces on the Egyptian front was to prevent our armed forces from crossing the Suez Canal or to be in a position to destroy any such forces which might cross to the east bank. This would inevitably lead to political surrender to Israel's terms. Not one person in Israel doubted the wisdom of this policy and many other countries were in tacit agreement with it.

In Egypt, the strategic goal was defined by President Sadat in his resolution for war dated 5 Ramadan 1393, or 1 October 1973.

> The strategic goal for which I take personal political responsibility on behalf of the Egyptian armed forces, and on the basis of all that I have learned and heard regarding our state of readiness, can be summarized as follows:
>
> To challenge the Israeli concept of security through a military operation using the possibilities available to our armed forces. The aim is to inflict severe losses on the enemy and to persuade it that the continued occupation of our land is too costly to bear. . . . Therefore, its concept of security based on psychological, political, and military terror is not the impregnable shield it believes it to be, either now or in the future.
>
> And if we are able to challenge the Israeli concept of security successfully, it will lead to certain results in the short and in the long term. In the short term, challenging the Israeli concept of security

can lead to certain conditions which will open the way for an honorable solution.

In the long term, challenging this concept could create cumulative changes leading to a basic change in the enemy's conceptions, psychology, and aggressive attitudes.

President Sadat's other directive was dated 9 Ramadan 1393, or 5 October 1973. In it he charged the armed forces with three strategic missions. The first was to break the ceasefire starting 6 October 1973, the second was to inflict the greatest possible losses on the enemy, and the third—the most important—was "to liberate the occupied land in consecutive steps according to the developing capabilities of the armed forces."

The resolution for war was issued on 1 October 1973, five days before the actual war, and was followed by the president's decision on 5 October (one day before the war) to break the ceasefire beginning on 6 October. Our armed forces had several days earlier begun to take the necessary measures needed, including "opening the forces" in preparation for implementing the war plan, according to schedule, at 2:05 P.M. in the afternoon of Saturday 6 October 1973.

President Sadat's written directives were a record and a confirmation of previous spoken decisions. He followed the steps outlined in the plan and worked at setting up some form of cooperation between Egypt and Syria. In this way, a strong tie was established between the political and the military (strategic) goal and with the strategic missions the armed forces were required to undertake.

The strategic goal was to defeat the Israelis west of Sinai, occupy the strategic zone on the Sinai passes line, and reach the Ras Sidr oil fields on the east coast of the Gulf of Suez. The missions were defined according to this goal.

It was natural that the goal of military operations and missions should be governed by the amount of weapons obtainable from the Soviet Union. It is also clear that the quantity of weapons available, given political pressures from the superpowers, would not allow our armed forces to achieve superiority over Israel to liberate Sinai in an offensive operation.

The political leadership made an intensive effort to purchase weapons, whether through the Soviet Union (the main supplier) or through other channels, but was unable to obtain the arms and the equipment needed to achieve superiority.

The only available alternative was to concentrate Arab military power and use some of the Arab forces. The Arab Defense Council of the Arab League defined the proposed participation in a session held in January 1973. For one reason or another this was never implemented, but this did not prevent some Arab countries from taking part in the war and using part of their forces a week after fighting had commenced, that is, in the last days of the war. This meant reduced effectiveness since there had been insufficient preparation and lack of coordination with the other forces.

Subsequently, the Jordanian front was not opened and the Palestinian front remained inactive, despite their importance.

Given all of this, the strategic goal as defined by President Sadat in a written document, the resolution of 1 October, was to "challenge the Israeli concept of 'security' through a military operation, using the possibilities available to the armed forces." The president repeated this more precisely in his 5 October strategic directive when he declared that the third mission of the armed forces was "to liberate the occupied land in consecutive steps according to the developing capabilities of the armed forces."

President Sadat was persuaded some months before the war that this would be the strategic goal and mission of the armed forces, and for this reason did not instruct us to "liberate Sinai by military force."

Looking closely at the strategic goals and missions of both Egypt and Israel in this war, I must immediately conclude that Egypt achieved its strategic goals and Israel did not.

The concept of 'security' to which Israel had clung was shattered and the idea of 'secure boundaries' proved to be false. Israel's policies, based on political intimidation, clearly failed in the face of Arab resolve to wage a total war.

This reliance on military and psychological intimidation collapsed with the offensive by Egypt and Syria—a comprehensive war which in no way could be compared to the War of Attrition—against all odds and against an enemy which was militarily superior.

Secure boundaries were no longer secure after we had crossed the canal and destroyed the Bar-Lev line; Israel had imagined that a water barrier and a fortified line were a safe boundary.

The policies which had relied on a 'superior' military strength to impose a fait accompli were proved patently misguided when, for the first time in its history, Israel was forced to withdraw under the pressure of the Egyptian military forces. The war deeply shook and shocked Israeli society after it lost confidence in its army, itself, and a government which had promoted territorial expansion by brute force—or the forcible imposition of the status quo on the Arabs—and after the invincible Israeli army was reduced to its real stature. A myth which had threatened the Arabs for many long years had disappeared. In October, Israel suffered more losses in men than in the 1956 Tripartite Aggression, the June 1967 war, and the canal skirmishes combined.

To summarize, Israel's concept of 'security' collapsed. As James Schlesinger, US secretary of defense at the time, described it, "The Israeli theory of security failed. . . . The Israelis have come to realize that their security cannot be achieved simply by preserving military superiority. The aura of an invincible state is now open to question."

In fact, following the war, the Israeli leadership admitted that they had been living under the illusion of a strong state since 1967. They had been immoderate in their belief in their superiority and conceited in their bragging. In December 1973, Dayan said, "The October War was like an earthquake for Israel. The events of this war cleared our vision and exposed what we had not seen before."

The October 1973 war was essentially the opposite of the June 1967 war.

We seized the initiative from the enemy after having for the first time achieved a surprise attack and put the enemy on the defensive. June 1967 was the last victory for the Israelis, but October 1973 was the first victory for the Arabs. International public opinion in June 1967 was biased, hostile, and provocative toward the Arabs. But in October 1973 the enemy was almost completely isolated from the world. Politically, June 1973 came to a dead end and a state of 'no peace, no war,' whereas October 1973 put an end to this state of affairs and emphasized the need to find a genuine solution to the Middle East crisis.

It was the first Arab victory in modern times. As the Algerian al-Mujahid commented, "The whole of the Arab nation today feels a sense of deep pride and thankfulness toward the armies of Egypt and Syria, who have achieved the first irrevocable victory for the Arabs. No matter how it ends, it will remain a fact that this ended the 1967 humiliation and restored pride to the Arabs."

The October War contained many surprises which the enemy used as excuses for its defeat. But General Elazer had to concede that the major surprise was the quality of the Arab soldier. He says in his memoirs that

> each war carries with it its surprises. The greatest of the surprises was that the Egyptian as well as the Syrian soldiers demonstrated competence, self-sacrifice, and sufficient motivation which exceeded

by far that shown in the previous war. The Israeli army was caught completely by surprise by the training and competence of the Arab soldier.

The October War proved that the Arabs' use of oil as a weapon was a highly effective complement to military action.

Without going into the vast and complex domain of economic studies, figures, and statistics, one can nevertheless say that the Arab oil-producing countries managed the oil war intelligently, wisely, and flexibly. They decreased production, prioritized and classified their enemies, and set their prices to achieve the desired effect. First a decision was made to reduce oil production by between 5 and 10 percent below the levels of September before the war, to be decreased by 5 percent for each of the following months. Spontaneously, the average decrease rose by a higher percentage than was set by the oil-producing nations. When the effects of the price increases became apparent and everyone began to feel the strain—and in order to avoid a rupture in relations with Western Europe—the Arabs decided to limit the decrease to 15 percent beginning January 1974, on the basis that this was a suitable limit without major negative repercussions.

Depriving consumers of their supplies was not applied haphazardly. The Arabs differentiated between consumers according to their stand on the Arab issue and Israel. It was natural that a decrease in the production of Arab oil should be linked to an increase in prices. This was to restore the balance of trade between raw materials and manufactured goods on the world market and also to compensate for any decrease in oil revenues.

In all events history will record that the use of oil in the October War was highly successful. It became an important weapon, along with war as a military option, in the quest for a political solution. The oil weapon reversed the political balance in the same way that the war reversed the military and strategic balance. History will also record that as a result of the October War, Arab oil-producing countries entered an era of economic liberalization, with greatly increased oil revenues, after they claimed the right to set the prices for themselves.

The oil war was an effective weapon that supported military operations. Its immediate outcome was a reevaluation by Europe and Japan of their relationship with the Arab countries and with Israel, and the Arabs got the advantage.

The October War changed the military, economic, and political realities in the Middle East. It confirmed the fact that peace, security, and stability will never be achieved in this region unless Israel gives up its aggressive intentions and its expansionist goals.

It is commonly accepted that war is an extension of politics by force of arms. Therefore the political management of a war, both during operations and once they have ceased, must also be evaluated so that the military and political performance can be assessed in the final analysis.

This is not, however, the appropriate place to discuss Egyptian and Arab political action during the war. I was the third most senior officer in the armed forces, chief of staff of the Operations Department of the Armed Forces, and consequently was not able to be completely in touch with political activities relating to military action during and immediately following the war.

Nevertheless, I would have preferred for the National Defense Council or the cabinet, or both, to remain in permanent session throughout the period so that President Sadat would not have had to shoulder the full burden of responsibility for the political administration of the war. Important and major developments took place during this time—developments which required consultation and an exposure to different points of view for the most appropriate decisions to be made.

Formulas for a ceasefire came up more than once. The nature of the political cooperation between Egypt and Syria also came up. Political relations with the Soviet Union were cautious and restrained, limiting any mutual understanding, while contacts between the United States and President Sadat remained ongoing, despite the United States' support for Israel and its hostility to Egypt and to the Arabs. There was also the matter of the US airbridge which used the Egyptian airport of al-'Arish to land supplies for Israel, as well as the US reconnaissance flights over combat zones for Israel's benefit. There were the Israeli air bombings of Port Said and attacks on economic targets in Syria, and the bombing of Damascus. The scheduling of an appropriate date for a ceasefire was also an important issue.

When the military situation shifted to Israel's advantage between October 22–25,

> the president was alone. . . . He had chosen to face the situation on his own. He had taken several fateful decisions before . . . perhaps he did not find it necessary, with an escalation of the crisis, to seek his colleagues' advice or that of his aides, preferring to go through it alone. He wanted to be the author of the victory when we became victorious, and now he refused to be anything other than the person responsible for the shift in fortune on the battle front.[1]

While I believed that these critical hours provided the perfect conditions for which he had created the National Defense Council and under which it should be convened to carry its responsibilities in taking these fateful decisions, the situation required a 'new mandate.'

Some years after the war, a passage in Dr. Kissinger's memoirs caught my attention. It concerned his activities during the war in providing Israel with military and political support, his administration of US policy in the context of the information made available to him, exchanges with the enemy (Egypt and the Arabs), the continuous flow of information received from his friend and ally Israel, and contacts with the other superpower, the Soviet Union. In other words, all the myriad facts of the situation were before Kissinger and were assessed by him and the US special task force. Therefore, the political process regarding the Middle East was highly informed, to both Israel and the United States' advantage.

We, the Arabs, went into this war under complicated military and political conditions. A war involves many strategic considerations, each of which translates into a multiplicity of tactical battles. This is what happened throughout the October War, but any war is evaluated in the final analysis according to the political, military, and strategic goals achieved.

In June 1967, Israel believed that the 1967 war would end all wars and that the Arabs must concede total defeat. Dayan made his well-known comment in this context, saying, "It is the war that ended all wars; nothing remains for the Arabs except to ask for an audience to present their respects, particularly as they know the phone number. The address is 31 Kaplan Street, Jerusalem."

Israel's delusions of grandeur were a result of the successive wars since 1948 that encouraged this self-deception: it had never been defeated—on the contrary, its victories grew from one war to the next until 1967, when it took fewer days to achieve more.

Then came 6 October 1973, and with the erosion of its foundations Israel's self-constructed edifice collapsed. It tasted military defeat.

Objectively, the October War was a real victory for Egypt and the Arabs. We made mistakes, but these do not diminish the value of our achievements—particularly since our forces accomplished missions many had imagined were not possible.

I must add at once that the October War created a dividing line between two eras in the history of our conflict with Israel. It marks a decisive turning point in the development of that conflict, and this was to the Arabs' advantage.

We must not simply boast of victories in this war. Rather, we must extract its lessons at all levels. Israel was victorious in three wars. The Arabs were the victors for the first time in the fourth war, and this was the beginning of the end of the idea of Israeli superiority in any future wars. Let us hope that Israel now acknowledges this. The concept of Israel's 'security' has been shattered. In 1967 it was victorious from lines it did not at the time consider secure, and in 1973 it was defeated from lines it did consider secure.

Hopefully Israel will also realize that our generation, which had been defeated in the June 1967 war, was the same generation which claimed victory in October 1973, six years later. It cannot be claimed that one generation replaced the other for victory to become a reality.

Four wars have taken place in this region in over a quarter of a century. From 1948 to 1973 Israel deliberately provoked three of them with the purpose of forcibly appropriating Palestine and expanding into Arab territories. We, the Arabs, began the fourth war—a war of liberation—to reclaim our land and our rights. I am absolutely certain that the repossession of Sinai was a result of the October 1973 war. We would not have been able to accomplish this through political channels. We still have ahead of us the task of liberating other Arab land. This is our right. We must emphasize that we are working to regain the rights of the Palestinian people. It is a question of justice. Truth and justice are the only paths to peace in this region.

Until we regain our full Arab rights, the goal of peace will remain a distant dream and the road to peace will be very long. There is some hope that the international peace negotiations held in the United States will lead to positive results and peace in our area. But we must ask ourselves a serious question: Does Israel's behavior since the October War, with the passing of twenty years until 1993, indicate that Israel is working towards peace? Or is it still trying to impose a status quo on the Arabs?

The true military confrontation between the Arabs and Israel began with the October 1973 war. Before this, in the opinion of many people, war was a hopeless option. Following the 1973 war it became a real possibility and the beginning of the end of the Arab–Israeli conflict. Dayan had said that the June 1967 war was "the war to end all wars." President Sadat called for the October War to be the last. The fact is that the June 1967 war was not the war which ended all wars, and there is no indication from Israel that the October 1973 war will be the last, as Sadat had wished. The fourth war in October 1973 was inevitable because there was no alternative. A fifth war will again become inevitable if there is no alternative.

Part IV

The Kilometer 101 Talks

As President of the United States, as an American, and as Richard Nixon, I respect those who fight and who put their lives on the line. You fought well . . . and we respect this. . . . I mean fighting, good fighting, the spirit itself. In my three capacities I must admit that you did all of this very well.

—Richard Nixon

30

First Meetings at Kilometer 101

As fighting on the canal front was drawing to an end at noon on 28 October, I predicted that it would resume because Israel had already violated UN Security Council Resolution 338 of 22 October and Resolution 339 of the following day, and had not ceased military operations with the resolution of 25 October either.

Political contacts continued between Cairo and Washington on 25 and 26 October with the aim of dispatching medical material to the Egyptian Third Army.[1] President Sadat had warned that the continuation of the current situation would affect Kissinger's visit to Cairo, "which involves proposals we hope will be a turning point towards a final peace." He also warned that he might be forced to adopt other measures to open a supply line to the Third Army.

On the evening of 26 October, Kissinger sent a message to President Sadat, on behalf of the US president, relating to two suggestions proposed to Israel. The first invited international observers to occupy positions between the Egyptian army and the Israeli army immediately, to supervise the implementation of the ceasefire, and the second allowed the passage of army convoys with food, water, and medicine to Suez and to the Third Army.

At Egypt's request, Foreign Minister Dr. Muhammad Hasan al-Zayyat had initiated contacts at the UN headquarters with the aim of calling a Security Council meeting. He was instructed to confirm that the Third

Army would not surrender, that Egypt would be forced to embark on unilateral action, and that it now stood at a crossroads.

After the UN Security Council meeting had begun, a message from Dr. Kissinger reached Hafez Isma'il at 3:30 A.M. on 27 October. This noted Israel's acceptance of the proposal to hold direct talks with Egypt on means to solve the problem (the ceasefire and the supplies), and asked Egypt to define the place and time for a meeting and to state the rank of its representative to the talks.

At the Tahra Palace, the president decided to accept the talks and appointed Lieutenant Mohamed Abdel Ghani El-Gamasy as the representative of Egypt. In a message to Washington through Hafez Isma'il he proposed a meeting at 3:00 P.M. on 27 October at Kilometer 101 on the Cairo–Suez desert road. The talks, under UN supervision, would discuss military considerations for the implementation of Security Council Resolutions 338 and 339 and for the passage of one non-military supply convoy to the Third Army, also under United Nations supervision.

On the afternoon on 27 October Dr. Kissinger informed Hafez Isma'il of Israel's approval of the Egyptian proposal.

At around six o'clock on the morning of 28 October, as I was sleeping at the Operations Center, an officer woke me up to say that General Isma'il wished to see me immediately in his office (which also served as a lounge). My spontaneous reaction was to ask, "Where has the fighting broken out? When?" The officer replied that there was no fighting; the situation had not changed.

When I walked into General Isma'il's room I found him lying on a small metal bed, looking completely exhausted. He sat up to say,

> There is an American initiative, which has been accepted by both Egypt and Israel, to hold a meeting between representatives from the Egyptian forces and the Israeli army in the area of Kilometer 101 on the Cairo–Suez desert road. The point is to discuss military problems resulting from the ceasefire and the overlapping of the armies. They must be separated by placing international emergency forces between them. The second topic of discussion is the provision of the city of Suez and the Third Army east of the canal with non-military supplies through one convoy of lorries. Israel, at America's request, has agreed.

General Isma'il said that the meeting had been set for 5:00 P.M. of that same day, 28 October, under the supervision of the United Nations

Emergency Forces (UNEF). It had also been decided to appoint me to head the Egyptian military delegation.

I objected because I neither wanted this job nor had any desire to see it through. I had spent all of my life fighting Israel, and furthermore the October War had not ended—the ceasefire was just temporary. Also, there appeared to be no need to discuss military matters with them. I apologized and requested a replacement for the task.

General Isma'il replied that a meeting had been held that night with President Sadat, which had only ended in the early hours of this morning, during which it had been decided to give me the task because as head of operations I was fully acquainted with the frontline positions of our forces and the enemy and with the combat lines of 22 October.

I explained to General Isma'il that the task I was being required to perform was to define a 'buffer zone' to separate our forces and the enemy that the United Nations Emergency Force (which had now started to arrive in the Suez area) could use to enforce the ceasefire. This was a job for UNEF, and we were required to cooperate with them only in the performance of their duty. Therefore there was no need to discuss the matter at a meeting between Egypt and Israel. As for the question of supplies for the city of Suez and for the Third Army, Israel had complied with US directives on the passage of a convoy of non-military provisions. If this had been achieved through political channels, then no doubt the United States could instruct Israel regarding further supplies and Israel could not object. It would be in the interest of the United States to continue in this role. We as the Egyptian Armed Forces should prepare ourselves for military action to open the Cairo–Suez road by force if the supply operation was delayed or halted in spite of US efforts.

General Isma'il turned my argument down. He asked me to carry out the job as had been decided. I had to do so. After contacts with UNEF, General Ensio Silasvuo was also appointed as UN representative to attend the Egyptian–Israeli military meetings.

I asked for a representative from the Foreign Ministry to join our delegation so that the ministry could be kept fully informed on any subject relating to political action. This person would also be an advisor to the delegation on political or legal matters. Counselor 'Umar Sirri of the Foreign Ministry was appointed in the capacity of advisor to the delegation, rather than as representative of the Foreign Ministry, so as to preserve the purely military nature of the talks.

Thus a three-man team was created with myself as head and Brigadier Fuad Huwaydi and Counselor 'Umar Sirri as members. At a later stage, the delegation included, apart from myself, Major General Taha al-Magdub, Brigadier Fuad Huwaydi, and a representative from the Foreign Ministry as advisor.

We headed towards the area fixed for the meeting—Kilometer 101—in a jeep, escorted by another military vehicle carrying armed shock troops. A third vehicle belonging to the UN Emergency Force, flying the UN flag, carried officers from this organization in their distinctive uniforms.

When we had almost reached Kilometer 95 on the Cairo–Suez road, we met UNEF Commander General Silasvuo returning from the Israeli-held sector, heading for Cairo. General Silasvuo said that no officers in the Israeli sector had been appointed to start the talks. He suggested that there might have been some delay in delivering the messages on the meeting. So I decided to return to Cairo.

I went back to the Operations Center. After contacts through diplomatic channels, General Ahmad Isma'il confirmed that there had been such a delay, explaining that there was a difference of several hours between New York and Cairo. A new time was set for 1:00 A.M. on 28 October at the previously-arranged place.

So the Egyptian delegation returned once more to Kilometer 101 to find an Israeli officer waiting in front of a radio-equipped vehicle at the forward line. He was our guide to the appointed location for the meeting, an Israeli-held position about four kilometers into the desert. The meeting started at 1:30 A.M. on 28 October and lasted for three hours, ending at 4:30 A.M.

Before Kilometer 101

A tent for the negotiations had not yet been set up in the area of Kilometer 101 when the first scheduled meeting took place in implementation of the agreement between the United States, Egypt, and Israel and under UN supervision. A piece of tarpaulin had been strung up between a tank and an armored car, under which was a wooden table with a number of wooden chairs around it. The place was lit by field lights.

When we got there, a line of Israeli officers led by Assistant Chief of Staff Aharon Yariv gave the military salute, to which we answered similarly. We then sat around the negotiating table, with the UNEF representative at the head of the rectangular table and the delegations on either side. We conducted the talks in English. The press was not present, which is why nothing was published about this first meeting.

I explained that the aim of these military talks was the implementation of UN Security Council Resolutions 338 and 339. This required separating the forces of the two sides to enable UNEF to work towards consolidating the ceasefire. I added that the matter of non-military supplies to the city of Suez and the Third Army had been settled at the political level by the United States, Egypt, and Israel. The agreement provided for the passage of a convoy of lorries carrying the supplies. I said that we expected the Israeli side to respect the agreement and not to obstruct the passage of the supplies.

General Yariv spoke about the importance of peace between the Arabs and Israel and expounded at great length on the politics of peace and on relations between the Arabs and Israel. He then moved to the general military situation resulting from the October 1973 war without specifying any practical measure to separate the forces for UNEF to perform its task.

I knew—from documents from the Egyptian intelligence service—that General Yariv had been head of Israeli military intelligence for many years before the June 1967 war and that he had been very competent. A short time following the end of his military service he had been recalled to take up the post of Assistant Chief of Staff for Special Tasks during the October War. He was in close touch with Prime Minister Golda Meir and was fully acquainted with the politics of the Arab–Israeli situation, which is why his contribution to the first military meeting was of a general political nature.

I requested that we confine our talks to those military matters we were meeting to discuss and to put aside the question of peace because it was neither the objective nor within our brief. I had been listening to General Yariv talk about peace and my mind had gone back to the successive wars which had erupted in the region since the state of Israel had come into being—wars whose purpose was to expand territorially at the expense of the Arabs and to impose a fait accompli on them. I could not forget that Israel itself had been created by force of arms, had imposed itself on the Arab homeland by force, expanded by force, and believed in force as a way of life.

The talks moved on to the military situation and what could be done to make the ceasefire hold and ease tension on the front. There were numerous items to be discussed and these would need successive sessions for any agreement on measures of implementation, especially as each side was using this first meeting to explore the other side's intentions. We gave first priority to the return of the Israeli forces to the 22 October lines and to the guarantee of supplies to the city of Suez and the Third Army on the east bank of the canal. The Israeli side gave priority to the exchange of prisoners of war and to keeping their forces on the Cairo–Suez road.

As for the passage of the supply lorries, there was no difficulty here because it had already been settled at the political level. Accordingly, the convoy was sent out with the supplies the following day.

It is worth noting that we did not agree on implementation procedures for any of the items under discussion. All the matters raised at this first meeting were discussed again in the course of lengthy talks and subsequent meetings.

This first meeting—held before the Kilometer 101 negotiations had been set up—was dramatic. It was a first meeting between Egyptian and Israeli officers who had fought one another for long years and were officially still fighting because the October War had not ended. The journey to and from the meeting place was disturbing. We went through our forward lines and our soldiers stopped us—as was their right and duty—pushing their weapons into our faces and demanding to know who we were and why we were proceeding in the direction of the enemy. The journey back was even more difficult. We came back at dawn after the meeting had ended. When our soldiers stopped us at gunpoint to check who we were, I would say to every guard at every post "the password is night" and give him the number of his unit and the name of his commanding officer for further assurance.

We held several meetings at this initial location and discussed the components of a stable ceasefire, the 22 October lines, prisoners of war, supplies to the city of Suez and to our forces on the east bank in the Suez area, and the United Nations Emergency Force.

Egyptian–US Talks in Washington

While military talks between Egypt and Israel were beginning, political and diplomatic efforts took a new turn. On 28 October, President Sadat decided to send a personal envoy, Acting Foreign Minister Isma'il Fahmi, to Washington. The decision was made at the Tahra Palace at a meeting which included Vice President Husayn al-Shaf'i, Minister of War General Ahmad Isma'il, National Security Advisor Hafez Isma'il, Minister of State for Presidency Affairs 'Abd al-Fattah 'Abdallah, and Isma'il Fahmi. After the president had expressed his views on the ceasefire and on adopting specific measures for separating the Egyptian and Israeli forces, it was agreed that Isma'il Fahmi would leave for Washington that same day on a special plane to meet with President Nixon. His appointment as foreign minister was later announced during his presence in the United States.

Isma'il Fahmi himself has described the purpose of the visit.

> The general plan for negotiations as we had prepared it at the Foreign Ministry envisaged the following steps: Israel's withdrawal to the 22 October lines and the return of prisoners of war. Then Israel would withdraw to lines inside Sinai, east of the passes, while the Egyptian forces would remain in their positions. The UNEF would be deployed between the Egyptian and the Israeli forces. After the Israeli withdrawal to the 'disengagement' line, Egypt would lift the blockade of the Bab al-Mandab straits. With the disengagement, Egypt would start clearing the Suez Canal. During a period to be agreed upon, Israel would withdraw to the international borders. At this point the state of war would be considered ended.[2]

After Isma'il Fahmi and Kissinger had held several preliminary discussions, a meeting was held with President Nixon on 31 October with both Fahmi and Kissinger attending. During this meeting Nixon said,

> As President of the United States, as an American and as Richard Nixon, I respect those who fight and who put their lives on the line. You fought well like the Vietnamese and we respect this. I hope you don't misunderstand me—because the Vietnamese are communists—I simply mean fighting, good fighting, the spirit itself. In my three capacities I must admit that you did all of this very well.[3]

Nixon went on to say that as a result, the picture had changed and so had the US stand and his perceptions as president. He then went straight into the heart of the subject and said that Kissinger had presented him with a troop disengagement plan which he considered "constructive" and that the United States could easily adopt it as a basis for future action. Isma'il Fahmi also mentions a request he made to Kissinger for "US guarantees to Egypt that the Israeli forces on the west bank of the canal would not undertake any military action. Nixon accepted this, and asked Kissinger to provide the guarantee."

Isma'il Fahmi adds, "I left President Nixon with a feeling of real achievement. It was obvious that the October War had radically changed the US attitude towards Egypt. The Americans had learned a lesson on the confrontation states in the Middle East. The United States realized that it was no longer possible to ignore these countries. . . . Washington had come to see a vital role for Egypt to play in the peace process."[4]

The Kilometer 101 Talks

Several days after the first meeting, the military talks between Egypt and Israel moved from their location between tank and armored car to three tents erected in the Kilometer 101 area on the Cairo–Suez desert road. The middle tent, which had the UN flag flying in front of it, was allotted to the United Nations Emergency Force. This is where the talks—subsequently known as the Kilometer 101 talks—took place. The tents on either side were for the Egyptian and the Israeli delegations. The media was given access to the meetings which were conducted under the supervision of the United Nations and its representative and the commander of the United Nations Emergency Force. They lasted for many months and may be divided into three stages.

The First Stage

Seven meetings were held at Kilometer 101 and focused on consolidating the ceasefire, the exchange of prisoners of war, and the non-military supplies to the Third Army. The talks did not have any positive results, either about the disengagement or the separation of the forces, because of the radical differences between the Egyptian and the Israeli sides.

At this point, Kissinger arrived in Cairo for the first time on 6 November 1973. His meetings with President Sadat led to a six-point agreement sponsored by the United States and accepted by both Egypt and Israel.

The Second Stage

Talks were held in Cairo and Geneva within the framework of the peace conference taking place in the Swiss capital. Progress was made on select topics under discussion, but again there was a stalemate over the disengagement despite the fact that by then ten meetings had been held at Kilometer 101, before the Geneva conference. In a second visit to Cairo on 13 December 1973 Kissinger had said that the question of disengagement should be on the agenda of the Geneva conference. A military committee was therefore set up, headed by Major General Taha al-Magdub, to discuss with an Israeli counterpart deadlocked subjects at the Kilometer 101 talks. However, this led nowhere.

The Third Stage

Finally, on 11 January 1974, Kissinger announced in Aswan a US troop disengagement proposal acceptable to both Egypt and Israel.

As Chief of Staff of the Egyptian Armed Forces, I signed the disengagement agreement on 18 January 1974 at Kilometer 101, with Israeli Chief of Staff General Elazer representing Israel. The documents for implementation were exchanged on 24 January 1974 and went into effect as of that date.

It is worth noting that the talks held on the military level faltered or stopped at every stage until the problems were solved by US Secretary of State Henry Kissinger in a practical application of Kissinger's step-by-step diplomacy.

31

The Six-Point Agreement

The first stage of the talks had been held in a tense military atmosphere as exchanges of fire continued between the two sides, and we often had to interfere with front military commands to stop the firing and then proceed with our work at Kilometer 101.

The talks included measures to strengthen the ceasefire, the supply of the city of Suez, removal of the wounded from Suez, non-military provisions to the Third Army east of the canal, and the exchange of prisoners of war.

On the Egyptian side, our target was securing the Israeli forces' return to the 22 October line in implementation of UN Security Council Resolution 339, because this would redress the imbalance created by Israel's violation of Resolution 338. This would mean a withdrawal of the Israeli forces from the Cairo–Suez desert road, thereby solving the problem of supply to the city of Suez and the forces on the east bank of the canal. We understood Israel's concern about the exchange of prisoners and the wounded, so we linked these to an Israeli withdrawal to the 22 October lines.

At this stage, the Israeli side was primarily concerned with the problem of the prisoners and the wounded, and the retrieval of the dead, because of domestic pressure on the government. It was obvious to us that the question of separating the Egyptian and Israeli forces for the emergency force to operate as a buffer was not a priority.

Discussions took place at several meetings with each side sticking to its viewpoint. The Egyptian side insisted on the issue of disengaging, because in our view it would entail moving the Israeli forces away from the Cairo–Suez desert road and this would keep it open for supply. From a UN perspective, this would have enabled the emergency force to perform effectively.

The Israeli side agreed in principle to discuss disengagement measures. It presented an initial proposal calling for the withdrawal of the troops on both sides to ten kilometers east and west of the canal and setting up a buffer zone on both banks of the canal for the emergency force. This would have meant Egypt giving up all the military gains of the October War, and we rejected it immediately.

At a subsequent meeting, the Israeli side proposed the withdrawal of the Third Army to the west bank, and the withdrawal of the Israeli forces from west of the canal to Sinai. The United Nations Emergency Force would operate in the areas vacated by the Egyptians and the Israelis. I explained that our troops on the east bank would not withdraw from recovered Egyptian territory. As for a withdrawal of the Israeli forces from west of the canal, this was a step we accepted. At the end of the discussion we rejected the Israeli proposal.

At a third meeting the Israeli side offered to take a "big step" by withdrawing the forces from the west to Sinai but not to the 22 October line. This would be a provisional step after which an agreement could be reached on withdrawal to the borders, provided this would take place after solutions had been found for "other subsidiary problems."

The Egyptian side expressed readiness to implement this step. I proposed that the distance should not be less than thirty-five kilometers east of the canal while keeping all our forces in position east of the canal. I proposed a buffer zone between the two forces wherein the UNEF would operate. We expressed readiness to discuss the question of prisoners of war and the wounded, linking this to supplies to the city of Suez and the forces east of the canal.

It was obvious that the Israeli side was not serious in its proposals at this early stage of negotiations, which was viewed as a prelude to discussion on other topics. At the fourth and fifth meetings, the Israeli delegation once again concentrated on the problem of pressures on the Israeli government on account of the Israeli dead and the prisoners of war. It expressed readiness to discuss supplies to the city of Suez and the Third Army east of the canal. We agreed in principle on arranging an exchange of prisoners and the wounded, provided this would take place at a special location to be arranged with the Red Cross. I demanded that at the same time the Israeli delegation give a definite reply on the main issue as defined by the Security Council, namely the return of the Israeli forces to the 22 October lines. However, the Israeli side asked for a deferral on this.

By the sixth meeting on 3 November 1973, the Egyptian delegation felt that we were in a vicious circle and that the negotiations would be stalemated. We were still insisting on a return of the Israeli troops to the 22 October lines to solve the problem of supplies to the city of Suez and to the troops east of the canal. However, the Israeli side insisted first on the exchange of the prisoners of war and the postponement of the troop disengagement and the supplies question. The Egyptian side did not accept this. In an attempt to keep the tenuous thread going—before talks broke off—the Israeli side conceded that the questions of disengagement and the return of their forces to the 22 October lines were in fact the central concern, but that these were being studied by the Israeli government as a prelude to later discussion.

It appears that Israel was hoping to draw inspiration for a solution from the United States.

At this point (6 November 1973) Kissinger arrived in Cairo for the first time for talks with President Sadat which took place on 7 November. Agreement was reached on the six points which were also accepted by Israel on 9 November.

During Kissinger's visit to Cairo, Egypt and the United States resumed official diplomatic relations, which had been severed since 1967. A celebration was held at the American embassy garden where the Spanish flag was lowered and the American flag raised in its place. (Spain had been looking after American interests in Egypt.)

Before the end of Kissinger's visit, it was announced that Herman Eilts had been appointed US ambassador to Cairo and Dr. Ashraf Ghurbal Egypt's ambassador to Washington.

On 11 November 1973, talks resumed at Kilometer 101 and the six-point agreement was signed. I signed for Egypt and General Aharon Yariv for Israel while General Silasvuo attended as UN representative. The agreement included the following points.

1. Egypt and Israel agree to observe scrupulously the ceasefire called for by the UN Security Council.
2. Both sides agree for discussions between them to begin immediately to settle the question of the return to the October 22 positions, in the framework of an agreement on the disengagement and separation of forces under the auspices of the United Nations.
3. The town of Suez will receive daily supplies of food, water, and medicine. All the town's wounded civilians will be evacuated.

4. There shall be no impediment to the movement of non-military supplies to the east bank.
5. Israeli checkpoints on the Cairo–Suez road will be replaced by UN checkpoints. At the Suez end of the road, Israeli officers will participate with the United Nations to supervise the non-military nature of any cargo.
6. As soon as the UN checkpoints are established on the Cairo–Suez road, there will be an exchange of all prisoners of war, including the wounded.

Commenting on this agreement, Isma'il Fahmi says,

> These were all the issues I had discussed with Nixon and Kissinger, with the exception of the point about the exchange of POWs, which Sadat approved without consulting me and despite the fact that I had a different opinion on this.
>
> However it is important to say that the six points were the fruit of serious discussions between the Egyptian and the American sides and not a solution proposed by Golda Meir as Eban claimed in his autobiography. . . . The six points announced during Kissinger's first visit to the Middle East were agreed upon in Washington.[1]

Muhammad Hafez Isma'il, National Security Advisor, reports on President Sadat's summary of the outcome of Kissinger's visit at a meeting with his aides.

> It was surprising to hear the president say he had spent most of the time with Kissinger over a 'disengagement' with the United States and not with Israel as we had thought. The president believed that he had turned over a new page with the United States. In his assessment he believed that the United States alone was capable of giving momentum to the situation—without the cooperation of the Soviet Union. Finally, Sadat expressed confidence in 'the man' (Kissinger), saying that he was sincere and carried out what he promised. Thus Dr. Kissinger won his first round in Egypt.
>
> With the passage of time, Kissinger managed to convince President Sadat to accept the 'step by step' settlement strategy instead of direct action to reach a comprehensive settlement. The pursuit of this strategy gave the United States an opportunity to convince Egypt of the uselessness of depending on the Soviet Union. It also gave Israel a chance to establish and normalize relations with Egypt while its forces gradually withdrew behind the international borders over a period of several years.[2]

A series of meetings began on 12 November 1973, the day following the signature of the six-point agreement at Kilometer 101, to discuss measures for the implementation of the agreement and to set a timetable for the arrival of supplies to Suez, the evacuation of the wounded from the city, and the exchange of prisoners. The meetings also aimed at arranging how and when the UNEF would take over the transit points on the Cairo–Suez road, and the regular supply of the Third Army troops in agreement with UNEF. At 8:30 in the morning of 15 November 1973 I stood at Kilometer 101 to follow up on the procedures for a convoy of lorries carrying supplies to Suez and vehicles for the evacuation of the wounded, while a third convoy was being prepared for the Third Army east of the canal. Planes were at that moment carrying our prisoners of war from Israel to Cairo, while others were simultaneously transporting Israeli prisoners of war from Cairo to Israel. Thus all the problems covered by the agreement were solved except point two, which remained under study.

Troop Disengagement and Separation

We started the tenth meeting at Kilometer 101 on 15 November to discuss the implementation of point two of the six-point agreement. This stipulated that "both sides agree that discussions between them will begin immediately to settle the question of the return to the October 22 positions in the framework of an agreement on the disengagement and separation of forces under the auspices of the United Nations."

The Israeli side presented some general principles in order for the process not to appear a defeat for either side: the lines should be parallel and movement would be to temporary but nonetheless strong lines. Israel also asked for measures to be adopted which would contribute to an atmosphere of peace and which would reduce the potential for war by restoring normal life to the canal zone. It also proposed a UNEF buffer zone between the Egyptian and the Israeli forces.

Clearly, these principles were a prelude to returning to Israel's earlier proposal on mutual withdrawal. So the Egyptian side immediately spelled out the basic facts which it could not be allowed to ignore. I said the battleground was on Egyptian territory and that the disengagement lines would be on Egyptian territory. I further noted that the military situation in the canal zone, especially in the Suez sector, was tense and could deteriorate with unfortunate consequences if it did not change quickly.

Given this, the Egyptian side proposed that the disengagement take place with the withdrawal of Israeli forces to the east canal line while a large area would be set up to absorb the UNEF and separate the warring forces. This would take place according to a definite timetable.

Although the Israeli side accepted these basic principles, it again raised proposals rejected earlier—just as we had expected. We turned these down for the same reasons they had been turned down in the first stage of the talks: they ran counter to a basic principle, which was the categorical rejection of any project based on the Egyptian forces relinquishing any of their positions east of the canal in Sinai. I proposed the withdrawal of the Israeli forces to the al-'Arish–Ras Muhammad line provided a withdrawal to the 22 October lines would be the first stage, to be followed by subsequent stages to other lines in Sinai up to the al-'Arish–Ras Muhammad line and later to the Egyptian borders. A buffer zone for the UNEF would be set up between the warring forces at every stage.

The Israeli side rejected this proposal as unbalanced and said that it would put it in a weak position. It also said that withdrawal to the 22 October lines did not safeguard its troops. For these reasons, the Israeli side would agree to withdraw in one stage to a line to be agreed upon east of the canal, provided that they would not have to face difficult or critical situations. Measures would be taken to prevent another surprise, while the blockade on Bab al-Mandab would be lifted and navigation resumed in the Suez Canal.

After several meetings, lasting over many days and many long hours, we saw that the talks were going around in a vicious circle: the Israeli side was presenting contradictory proposals to delay an agreement on the disengagement and separation of forces (point two of the six-point agreement). The Israeli delegation would propose mutual withdrawal, then it would suggest a wide-scale Israeli withdrawal from Sinai. Then once again it would advance proposals we had already rejected. Finally General Yariv came to saying that he had not been authorized by the government to discuss withdrawal to the 22 October lines or the final lines for the disengagement. He apologized, explaining that the Israeli government was not in a position to settle these matters because it was waiting for the results of the Israeli elections scheduled for the end of December 1973 and early January 1974.

At the meeting held on 26 November 1973, it became necessary to ask the Israeli delegation to define its position if it wanted the talks to proceed in the right direction. With this in mind, I clarified several points. First, any line to which Israel would withdraw and which would not safeguard the canal citizens was unacceptable. Second, for the talks to continue in this manner was a waste of time and would lead to no results. Accordingly, Israel had to define its official response clearly. For this definition to be clear, we requested that the Israeli delegation answer the following questions: what was the extent of an Israeli withdrawal east of the canal which the Israeli government would accept? What was the size of the forces that Israel would keep in Sinai? What would be the duration of the Israeli stay on the temporary first line before proceeding to the following line? What was the second line of withdrawal eastward?

The Israeli side promised to answer these questions at the following meeting.

The next meeting on 28 November 1973 was the seventeenth and the last. We had hoped to get concrete replies from the Israeli side, but Yariv started describing the tense situation on the front and talked of the necessity of respecting the ceasefire despite the failure to reach an agreement on disengagement. He explained that the disengagement would be on land, sea, and air, paying special attention to lifting the blockade on Bab al-Mandab, and repeated the Israeli view that the disengagement should apply to both sides and not to a withdrawal on their part only.

At this point, UN representative General Silasvuo intervened and asked Yariv to answer the questions put forward by the Egyptian delegation at the previous meeting. Yariv replied that his government did not accept the basis proposed by Egypt so he could not answer the questions raised at the previous meeting.

Faced with this situation, I said that the Israeli reply had led us to a deadlock over disengagement and we had no alternative but to demand that Israel implement the UN Security Council Resolution on the return of Israeli forces to the 22 October lines.

At that point, I decided to break off the meetings because they were no longer useful and no progress had been made after seven successive meetings. I told the press immediately afterwards that the talks had reached a stalemate.

It had been established that the Israeli government was playing for time by prevaricating and by avoiding a specific decision on the disengagement and separation of the forces at this stage.

After I presented my report to President Sadat, with the minister of war attending—as was customary after every meeting since the beginning of the Kilometer 101 talks—an official spokesman for Egypt made a statement announcing Egypt's decision to suspend the Kilometer 101 talks in view of Israel's continued prevarication in implementing item two of the six-point agreement signed on 11 November 1973. It was also announced that Egypt held Israel responsible for any consequences arising from the non-implementation of the Security Council resolutions.

Within the framework of the peace conference held in Geneva starting 21 December 1973 and attended by representatives from Egypt, Jordan, Israel, the United States, and the Soviet Union (Syria abstained), it was agreed to form a military working group to discuss the question of the disengagement of the Egyptian and Israel forces to reduce tension in the region.

The Egyptian delegation was headed by Major General Taha al-Magdub, the Israeli delegation by General Mordechai Gur, and the UN delegation by General Silasvuo. The group held six sessions at the UN Geneva headquarters from 26 December 1973 to 9 January 1974. As with the Kilometer 101 talks, the Israelis prevaricated in Geneva.

The Israeli delegation argued that it did not have any specific ideas on disengagement because the Israeli government was still considering it and had not reached any decision. At this point, the Egyptian delegation demanded a suspension of the meetings until the Israeli delegation had received instructions from its government. The Israeli side asked for a one-week period of grace. 15 January was set as a date for the following meeting, which in fact was never held.

On 10 January 1974, the United States announced that Dr. Kissinger would leave for Egypt to help solve the problem. With Kissinger's arrival there, instructions were given to the Egyptian military delegation to return to Cairo. Egyptian–American negotiations then started in Aswan.

THE ASWAN NEGOTIATIONS: THE DISENGAGEMENT AGREEMENT

Kissinger arrived in Aswan on 11 January 1974 to negotiate with President Sadat on an agreement for the disengagement and separation of the forces, a matter over which neither the Kilometer 101 nor the Geneva talks had yielded a decisive or specific solution.

It had been clear to us when it came to the implementation of the six-point agreement that the Israeli side had set obstacles to the implementation of point two concerning the settling of the question of the return to the 22 October positions in the framework of agreement on the disengagement and separation of forces under the auspices of the United Nations.

After the tightening of the noose around the Israeli delegation at the Kilometer 101 talks and after several meetings, General Yariv had been forced to state—in the presence of General Silasvuo—that he was not mandated by his government to discuss the withdrawal of Israeli forces to the 22 October lines and that the Israeli government was not in a position to settle these matters pending the outcome of the elections scheduled for December 1973–January 1974. I had never believed that this reason was valid.

The procrastination was repeated at the Geneva talks when Mordechai Gur, head of the Israeli delegation stated, in the presence of Silasvuo, that he did not have definite ideas about disengagement because the Israeli government was still studying the subject and had not yet taken any decision in this respect—after six sessions of military negotiations in Geneva!

I believe that Israel—in agreement with Kissinger—was committed to avoid coming to any positive results until the arrival of Kissinger himself, so that the agreement would be contingent on his presence and consequently the US role would be manifest in his ability to solve the problems between Israel and the Arabs.

Kissinger met with President Sadat and Foreign Minister Isma'il Fahmi in Aswan, and started his shuttle between Aswan and Jerusalem. Some time after this, General Isma'il asked me to travel to Aswan to participate on the military side of the Egyptian–US negotiations.

My real role in Aswan began when I was asked to attend a round of talks between the Egyptian and the US delegation at the New Cataract Hotel. I had not been informed by President Sadat of any prior agreement between him and Kissinger, following their talks, over any military matter which would be included in the agreement. I had believed that such military subjects would be discussed during the exchanges between the Egyptian and the US delegations so that Kissinger could be familiarized with our views and consequently reach an agreement satisfactory to both sides during his shuttles.

The Egyptian delegation comprised Foreign Minister Isma'il Fahmi as head, as well as myself, Mahmud Riyad, Ahmad 'Usman, 'Umar Sirri and others from the Foreign Ministry. The US delegation was headed by Henry Kissinger and included Bunker, Eilts, Saunders, Atherton, Quandt and the legal advisor of the State Department. We held secret talks for about two hours and the subjects were both political and military. Kissinger briefed the attendees on the military items of the agreement he had reached with President Sadat. It came as a surprise both to me and to the participants to hear Kissinger say that President Sadat had agreed to reduce the troops on the eastern bank of the canal to 7,000 men, thirty tanks, and a limited number of artillery pieces.

At that moment, I felt the enormity of the troop reductions—we had two armies with more than ten times that number of men. We had thought we needed to have 300 tanks east of the canal as well as a large number of artillery pieces to support our forces in Sinai. I remember I rejected the proposed troop reduction. I told Kissinger bluntly, "You're giving Israel what would guarantee the security of its forces and denying us everything that would safeguard our forces. I do not approve this and I cannot as Chief of Staff of the Armed Forces justify it to our forces." Kissinger said he was formulating a peace strategy for the future, which was an important goal. To achieve this, an agreement had been reached on the proposed number of Egyptian troops and weapons east of the canal. I told him I was not speaking about peace but about safeguarding our forces. I left the meeting room angry, with tears in my eyes, and I went to the bathroom.

Isma'il Fahmi has said that after I had left the room "everybody started to feel uneasy and the Egyptian delegation was touched by the same feelings El-Gamasy had. One could easily tell from the looks of the US delegation that it could feel the injustice done Egypt. But Kissinger was thinking of nobody but himself. His face grew pale and he kept muttering 'was there anything wrong in what I said?'"

I returned to the meeting room and kept silent up to the end of the meeting. Kissinger showered me with praise saying that Israel's military men appreciated the skills of Lieutenant General El-Gamasy and that Israel feared him more than any other Arab military commander. But I kept silent without commenting because compliments would not wipe out the real problem we were about to face.

I had appreciated the enormous effort and the sacrifices in the war, and there seemed to be no need for this huge concession which might endanger our armed forces. I had expected President Sadat to consult General Ahmad Isma'il, or me, when I arrived in Aswan to sound out our opinions on the military aspects of the agreement, including the size of forces that should be kept in Sinai in order effectively to defend the military gains there. There was no need—politically or militarily—to accept this reduction in troops and weapons.

At the end of the meeting I contacted General Isma'il in Cairo and briefed him on what had happened. I asked him to fly to Aswan (about an hour and half away by plane) to discuss the subject with the president while we were still in the process of negotiations and before the conclusion of an official agreement between Egypt and Israel.

The alternative solution would have been for him to contact the president to explain his viewpoint directly, which agreed with mine. I do not know what happened between General Isma'il and President

Sadat after my phone call, but the following day the president summoned me to his office at his Aswan resthouse. We were alone. The president hastily said that he had heard of my anger at the negotiations session the previous day and my disapproval of the limited size of the troops he had agreed on with Kissinger, but he believed that the number of the troops east of the canal should not become an obstacle in the way of disengagement and consequently an obstacle in the way of Kissinger's political strategy to bring peace to the region in the long run. The president was also thought that the UNEF in a buffer zone between the Egyptian and the Israeli forces would be sufficient to prevent a resumption of hostilities.

I explained to the president that from the military point of view the proposed size for our troops east of the canal would not ensure the defense of the land our forces had liberated in a confrontation line about a hundred kilometers long. I also explained that Israel would not forget the defeat inflicted on it in the October War. For these reasons we should not categorically rule out the possibility of an Israeli attack on our forces, despite the presence of UNEF—which was neither assigned to fight nor could stop a resumption of hostilities from either side. I said that in general command we considered it essential to have two reinforced infantry battalions comprising about 35, 000 men, 300 tanks, and a large number of artillery pieces of varying calibers east of the canal after the deployment of UNEF in the separation zone between the Egyptian and the Israeli forces. Besides, our forces in the east should be under missile air defense protection. We had never even considered the kind of limitation in troops or weapons agreed in principal with Kissinger. I stressed that we still had time to revise this proposal.

In conclusion, I suggested that the president summon General Isma'il to Aswan to discuss the matter and get his opinion. The president replied that he would not call Ahmad Isma'il. The agreement with Kissinger must be honored for the development of the political strategy now being formulated with the United States. Then the president went even further and charged me with the responsibility of drawing up an appropriate plan for defense, east of the canal, using the limited number of troops. He also entrusted me with the task of monitoring the execution of the plan, and stressed that the achievements of armed forces operations in the October War must be reiterated under new conditions.

According to the implementation of the Aswan agreement, the status of the troops in Sinai became as follows.

1. Our forces were operating in the area of land on the east bank of the canal up to the forward lines reached in the October War. This

was the area of "limited troops and weapons." The front line would be referred to as 'Line A–A.'

2. The troops had withdrawn from the west bank of the canal. The Israeli troops would operate in an area of land in Sinai west of the Mitla and Giddi Passes on a line referred to as 'Line G–G.' The front line would be referred to as 'Line B–B.'
3. The UNEF were operating in a buffer zone or the 'separation zone' between the forward line of the Egyptian forces and the forward line of Israeli forces.
4. The air forces on both sides were allowed to operate in their respective front lines without interference from the other.

In an exchange of letters with President Sadat and Prime Minister Golda Meir, President Nixon set restrictions which were binding to both in the 'limited troops and weapons' areas accepted by the two sides. Thus troops operating in these areas were to be 7,000 men in eight battalions, thirty tanks, and a limited number of artillery pieces defined by type and caliber.

There was a provision barring surface-to-air missiles in the area to a distance thirty kilometers west of the Egyptian forward line and east of the Israeli line. It was also agreed that the United States would carry out regular reconnaissance flights to ensure that both sides abided by the provisions of the agreement. Reconnaissance information was to be relayed to both sides.

The military situation on the canal front was therefore stabilized with the implementation of the disengagement agreement, despite the Egyptian concessions and although we could have avoided them. As a result of this agreement, the Egyptian forces held on to the lines they had reached in Sinai during the October 1973 war while the Israeli forces withdrew eastward in Sinai, and this included the Israeli forces which had been on the west bank of the canal. This was a first Israeli withdrawal ever from land it had occupied and it was done under the pressure of Egyptian military strength in the October War.

The disengagement agreement between Egypt and Israel was a military agreement, evidenced by the fact that it was signed by both the Egyptian and Israeli chiefs of staff. Nevertheless, the agreement had a major political impact which cannot be ignored. It marked a turning point in both US and Soviet relations with Egypt. The United States asserted itself through the prominent role it had assumed in finding a political solution to the Middle East problem. Egyptian–Soviet relations receded after their preponderance over many years.

PART V

EGYPTIAN–ISRAELI MILITARY NEGOTIATIONS

The gap between our positions is immense.
—Weisman

We differ on all points.
—El-Gamasy

32

Probing Intentions in Gianaclis

After returning from his short visit to Jerusalem, President Sadat called me to a meeting with him at his Isma'iliya resthouse, which, built by the Suez Canal Authority on Fursan Island, overlooked the canal directly.

When I arrived I found Vice President Muhammad Husni Mubarak and Prime Minister Mamduh Salem with him. The president told me that there was agreement on a meeting in Egypt between Israeli Minster of Defense Ezra Weisman and myself to lay down the basis of peacetime military relations between the two countries.

We did not discuss the strategy for negotiations with Israel nor fix any date for its beginning. The meeting generally centered on the talks and meetings which had already taken place with the Israeli side during the visit to Jerusalem, but no details were given. The president did not speak of any specific agreement between himself and the Israeli leaders on the future of military or political relations between the two countries. He did not tell me either at this time or at any earlier or subsequent meeting that secret meetings had taken place in Morocco under the auspices of King Hasan. Egypt had been represented by Hasan al-Tohami from the Presidency and Israel by Foreign Minster Moshe Dayan.

I was on hand to receive the Israeli delegation at the military wing of Cairo International Airport. The Israeli delegation arrived on board a special US Air Force plane using the international air route.

Since President Sadat's announcement in Isma'iliya of Weisman's arrival for negotiations, I had revised military studies on strategic military relations between Egypt and Israel in a stage of peace. The studies had been undertaken at my request by a military team. We concentrated in particular on military measures to ensure Egypt's security in this strategic direction, which had constituted a constant threat to us. We also concentrated at this early stage of negotiations on discovering Israel's intentions with regard to Sinai because Israeli officials held varying views in this respect, saying it was part of Israel's security and repeating in official declarations since the June 1967 war that Israel would not withdraw from the occupied lands to the pre-June 1967 border.

As for Weisman himself, the information we had on him was that he had been a pilot in the British Air Force in Egypt during the Second World War. He had served in the Israeli Air Force until he assumed command of it and was proud of having developed it. After this he had served in the Israeli high command until he had become the second man there. He had hoped to become chief of staff of the Israeli army but he was unable to obtain the post to which every military commander in Israel aspired. On the political level, he came from a family which played a political role in the establishment of the state of Israel. His uncle on his father's side was Dr. Chaim Weisman, the first Israeli head of state. On leaving the military service, Weisman had joined the Herut movement and orchestrated the election campaign of the Likud party which brought Menachem Begin to power, and Weisman was appointed minister of defense. He was known in Israel as a Zionist and a hawk.

It was natural for Israel to prepare for the negotiations in Egypt in the follow-up to the talks held in Jerusalem during Sadat's visit. I learned later from Weisman's memoirs that before coming to Egypt he had obtained information from US intelligence about me. He said that a few days before he traveled to Egypt, he asked for and actually got my personal file from US army intelligence because he was eager to learn everything about me. After reading the reports and documents he said he realized that I was cultured, talented, introverted, and a nationalist, proud of being Egyptian. He went on to say that in all my photos in the press and on television he never saw me smile. The reports made him think that I was just his opposite and he was worried about the difficulty of communicating with an introvert.

On the morning of 20 December 1977 I was at the Cairo airport with Chief of Operations Major General Hasan al-Geredli, Brigadier Fuad

Huwaydi from military intelligence, and Colonel Kamal al-Tanahi, military secretary. We were waiting for the arrival of the US plane carrying Weisman, along with Hertzel Shabir, commander of the southern zone, the director of military intelligence, Shlomo Gazett, and Military Secretary Colonel Shatilla. They were all in civilian clothes.

My mind went back to the times since my graduation from Military Academy, and I realized that I had lived all of my military life with Arab–Israeli enmity and I remembered the successive wars in the Arab region since the establishment of Israel in 1948. They were all waged to defend the Palestinian people's right to their homeland and to safeguard our own Arab homeland against Israel's expansionist designs. The questions that haunted me were: is Israel persuaded of the importance of peace? If many have cherished this hope after Sadat's visit to Jerusalem, will Israel abandon Arab lands occupied in the June 1967 war? Will it restore the Palestinian people's legitimate rights? How will Egypt's national security be protected in peacetime conditions? Will the October War be the last with Israel?

The plane landed. Weisman appeared on the plane steps leaning on a stick because his leg had been injured in a car accident in Israel; he had been in the hospital on Sadat's visit to Jerusalem. I had paused at this piece of news when it was reported by the Israeli media, thinking that it was just a pretext for not receiving Sadat in Jerusalem or for not attending the Israeli Knesset session which the president was to address. It so happened, however, that later after leaving the hospital he attended the parliamentary session and took part in the talks and meetings with Sadat and his aides. He became one of those Israelis close to Sadat after his visit to Jerusalem and he was to be a major political link between Israel and the president without for a second abandoning the Israeli government's policy following the Jerusalem visit, throughout the later stages of negotiations, in the Camp David agreements, and in the peace treaty between Egypt and Israel.

I received Weisman and the men accompanying him. After introductions and courtesies, I informed him that he and I would head for Isma'iliya to meet President Sadat while the rest of the Israeli delegation would proceed to Gianaclis for the talks and would stay at the presidential resthouse there.

Sadat had requested that Weisman meet him in Isma'iliya immediately after his arrival in Cairo and before the start of the talks. The time was too early for this meeting, which neither Weisman nor I had expected to take place so soon. Weisman and I flew to Isma'iliya by helicopter and we headed directly for the resthouse on Fursan Island. The president was sitting with Vice President Husni Mubarak in the big garden overlooking the canal. He welcomed Weisman and asked him about his flight and his health. The talks took on a social and human aspect as they turned to the past, when Israeli artillery shells had destroyed some houses in Isma'iliya before it was rebuilt in all its beauty after the October War. It was easy to distinguish the east bank of the canal, with the ruins of one of the Bar-Lev fortifications obvious before our eyes.

Weisman recounted that on the opposite side he had faced the heavy bombardment from our forces and had made a narrow escape. In his memoirs he added, "In the interest of truth, I have to admit that I felt my heart wrench as I saw the Bar-Lev line in ruins. From time to time I would sneak a glimpse at it. It is obvious that this meeting could not take place except after the Egyptians had succeeded in crossing the canal in 1973, but the price we have paid was extremely dear."

As for me, I felt satisfied whenever I saw Weisman look at their fortified line destroyed by our forces on 6 October; I hoped that this would be a lesson for the Israelis—to turn to a real peace rather than resort to repeated aggressions against Arab countries. I fleetingly remembered the statements made by their leaders about the impregnability of their line and the impossibility of penetrating it. General Dayan had said in 1969 that "Egyptian military operations—if they happen—will never undermine Israel's tight grip on the Bar-Lev line. . . . It is a powerful, impregnable line and we are strong enough to defend it forever." Meir was more philosophical when she said, "All the fortifications we possess make any thought of the Egyptian forces crossing to the east bank an affront to the intelligence."

The conversation between Sadat and Weisman moved from the past to basics—the present and future. The president said that he (Weisman) would fly with me to Gianaclis for the talks and the exchange of views and that whatever we agreed upon would be as though it had been agreed with him personally. He asked Weisman to speed up the achievement of a real peace.

After speaking about peace, the president, in reply to Weisman's questions, clarified points on the normalization of relations between Egypt and Israel, the operation of a civilian airline between the two countries, and the exchange of ambassadors. The president's answers were all positive, stated in the affirmative, indicating that he meant a full, real peace between the two states and a complete Israeli withdrawal from Sinai. The president asked Weisman to tell Begin to announce his acceptance of the principle of withdrawal from all the occupied land and the settlement of the Palestinian problem so that we could then proceed towards a real peace.

Weisman wanted to go to Sadat's meeting equipped with ideas and ready for any proposal. But when he stood in front of Sadat in the garden of his house, Weisman became convinced of all the assessments which said that we would not compromise on what we considered necessary, namely total Israeli withdrawal. On the other hand, Weisman also sensed the price Sadat was willing to pay in return for withdrawal, namely complete peace, an exchange of ambassadors, opening up civil aviation, and complete normalization of relations between the two peoples. Weisman had not imagined before the meeting that Sadat would be speaking with this determination on complete peace and explaining that he wanted peace as quickly as possible.

IN GIANACLIS

Before we left Isma'iliya on our way to Gianaclis, Sadat asked Weisman if the Israeli people knew of his presence in Cairo. He replied that it was censored by the military and that this meant that it was still a secret there.

In Egypt, there had been no prior announcement of the meeting. The media were not at the airport when the Israeli delegation had arrived, and Weisman's visit was a secret here too.

I quickly ran through the justifications for the secrecy of the Gianaclis meeting, and concluded that the meeting between the Egyptian and the Israeli delegations should be announced and there was no point keeping it secret. The harm this could do to Egypt should be avoided. So as we were bidding farewell to leave the Isma'iliya resthouse I asked Vice President Husni Mubarak—on the side—for an announcement of the meeting because there was no point in imposing secrecy.

In the evening of the same day, as the two delegations were meeting around the negotiations table at the Gianaclis resthouse, the military secretary placed a piece of paper in front of me informing me that Cairo Radio had announced the meeting. I immediately informed Weisman and the two delegations and we resumed our talks. About an hour after this, I received a phone call from Cairo, from the Minister of Information 'Abd al-Mun'im al-Sawi, requesting permission to send the press to Gianaclis. I refused because we were still in the first session and had done nothing worth talking about. I told him that I preferred more discussions to take place before meeting with the media and that what Cairo Radio had announced was sufficient. We agreed on that but al-Sawi, may he rest in peace, was neither persuaded nor satisfied.

My idea in managing the talks was that the Egyptian delegation should concentrate its effort on the topics of vital interest to both Egypt and Israel in order to lay open their real intentions towards peace. Were they really serious about a full withdrawal from Sinai, and when would that take place? What were their intentions with regard to the settlements they had built in Sinai, south of Rafah and on the west bank of the Gulf of 'Aqaba, and when would they evacuate them? What did they think of maritime navigation in the Gulf of 'Aqaba and its relation to Sharm al-Shaykh after Dayan had said before the October War that "Sharm al-Shaykh without peace is better than peace without Sharm al-Shaykh?" What was their view of peacetime military conditions given the many different Israeli political positions before the October War and the excuse of Israeli 'security?'

All these basic subjects could not be discussed in just one or a few sessions. However, they served as guides to disclose their real intentions in reaction to the Jerusalem visit. We wanted to know whether the concepts and military policy they had held before Sadat's initiative to Jerusalem had changed.

ISRAELI WITHDRAWAL FROM SINAI

Before the beginning of the Gianaclis talks neither of the delegations had asked for an agenda and neither had shown any enthusiasm to draw one up. As the military topics to be discussed were linked and complemented one another in many ways, it was hard to divide them up. It seemed even better to have open discussions which would reveal the real attitudes towards the basic items.

At the opening of the negotiations I made a short statement on the importance of peace in the region and proceeded directly to the subject by asking Weisman to spell out Israel's view on the withdrawal of its forces from Sinai and when and how that would take place.

I did not want a narrative on political developments in the region since the establishment of the state of Israel, or on the wars that had raged between us, because I did not want to invite useless discussions and wanted to save time for the talks on the future we were working towards.

Weisman spoke at length on the Israeli position, emphasizing especially the problems of Israeli security. He said they had come to us with an open heart, trusted our intentions, and wanted peace as we did. He praised President Sadat's peace initiative and said he understood the difficulties the president was facing in the Arab world as a result of his visit to Jerusalem. (By this he was referring to adverse reactions in the

Arab world to the visit.) He said that Israeli Prime Minister Begin was also facing difficulties, but did not elaborate on this.

In his exposition, Weisman explained that in the year 2000 there would be 100 million Arabs versus seven million Israelis, so Israel had to ensure the future of its sons. He noted that they were a small nation with a small army and that if they lost a war they lost everything. As an example, he cited our attack in October 1973 before they could call up the reservists. He said that while they had a large air force, they had only five or six airports while Egypt and Syria had about forty.

In the course of his speech, he proposed working to avoid any accidental confrontation between the Egyptian and Israeli forces during the current stage of negotiations. He had thought of a direct telephone link between the commander of the Israeli southern area and the commander of the Egyptian Third Field Army. Having now analyzed the problems of Israeli security, he suggested a change in the Egyptian–Israeli border area, that is, exchanging parts of the land of Sinai for parts of the Negev. He did not go into any details or specify areas.

That Weisman should link the question of Israeli security with a proposed alteration to the Egyptian–Israeli borders at the very time we were discussing their withdrawal from Sinai clearly gave credence to our well-considered understanding of Israel's expansionist policy and military strategy.

A territorial expansion at the expense of Arab land had been one of the objectives of world Zionism since the establishment of Israel. After the June 1967 war Israel promoted the concept of 'secure borders,' using this to fuel and justify its regional ambitions. It tried to give security a military and a geographic definition, linking it to land considered to be of strategic importance. Despite a diversity of ideas and opinions on what constituted secure borders as expressed in statements by the leadership and in party programs, there was agreement on two basic points. The first was no withdrawal to the borders preceding 5 June 1967, and the second was no withdrawal from any occupied territory or part thereof before agreement on Israel's final borders with its Arab neighbors. Then there was Dayan's project which envisaged the annexation of part of Sinai to Israel from a line east of al-'Arish in the north to Sharm al-Shaykh in the south. This satisfied the principle of non-withdrawal to the pre-June borders and guaranteed an expansion which would ensure the continued presence of the Yamit settlement south of Rafah and all the settlements on the west bank of the Gulf of 'Aqaba. The Rafah and Ras al-Naqab airports would remain in place, and Egypt would be deprived of this strategically vital area.

There was also the Weisman proposal which advocated the annexation of a vast area of Sinai to Israel in the form of a triangle with its base on the Egyptian border and its apex in the middle of Sinai directly up to east of the passes. The triangle included the land from east of al-'Arish along the northern axis to al-Gifgafa and al-Maliz on the middle axes down to Nakhl and Ras al-Naqab in southern Sinai. The proposal gave Israel greater political and military advantages than Dayan's plan.

Allon, Rabin, and Meir had other proposals but there is no need to go into them because they are examples of one and the same objective, namely an identical policy goal and military strategy using different means. Weisman's proposal at the negotiations to alter the border aimed at annexing to Israel the area of the Yamit settlement south of Rafah. The Rafah airport in northern Sinai and Ras al-Naqab airport in the south of Sinai are not part of Israeli territory. Both airports were built by Israel on Egyptian territory close to the borders during the period of occupation following the June War. To make the proposal acceptable, Weisman presented it as an exchange of land.

To resolve the matter, I rejected any border alterations as a matter of principle; there was no need for this and it was unacceptable. This meant that the Egyptian side did not accept that the Yamit settlement and the two airports would remain because this ran counter to a total Israeli withdrawal from Sinai.

After the discussions and the justifications, and the sweet and bitter words exchanged, the talks ended with a refusal to make any change to the borders. I told the Israeli delegation, "Let it be clear that we cannot agree to your proposal on changing borders."[1]

Troop Reduction

With his usual political shrewdness, Weisman moved the conversation to the size of the armed forces, saying that Egypt had a large army and asking if we intended to keep it that way or to reduce it after peace. He noted that our army had been stationed near Cairo until 1967 but that now it was concentrated in the canal zone and could cross the canal in just a few hours. Why not have both sides pull back their large troop concentrations to lines in the rear? I replied that since 1967 our forces had lived in a state of constant readiness and that we had about three quarters of a million men. Naturally—if peace was achieved—the size and positions of the troops would be changed according to the new situation.

I seized this opportunity to say that a discussion of the question of troop reductions in the peace process must cover all of the land, air, and naval forces, and that we should start by reducing the air force for both sides. We both knew that Israel's air force was its main striking power. Israel could not agree to cut its size or limit the number or types of planes.

The two sides at the military talks were fully aware as they spoke that the size of any state's armed forces as well as positions and types of weapons, either in times of peace or war, were a basic factor in national security and military strategy. Therefore questions such as these were not subject to discussion either in times of war or peace. The subject itself was not open to objective discussion or to any practical implementation. Consequently we did not reach any results in this respect. I remembered an aside between Weisman and myself. He said, "You have a big army" and I answered, "And you have a big air force."

The real purpose of raising this question was to understand the Egyptian leadership's intentions in the peace process. On our part, we too discussed it to discover what their ulterior objectives were. We had to explore their depth and intentions.

Positions of the Egyptian Forces in Sinai

Since we had spoken about troop reductions it had to be made clear to the Israeli side that the size and position of our forces in the canal zone or in Sinai were not negotiable. So I continued my discussion of the previous subject, saying that the distribution and positioning of our forces in the peace process would differ as we would have troops in al-'Arish and aircraft operating out of Sinai airports.

Then came the surprise.

Weisman said, "I have to remind you that Sadat promised Begin he would not move troops east of the Mitla and Giddi Passes."[2]

My surprise was great and my shock greater still as I heard of this promise. The president had not told me anything about it before the start of the negotiations. I could not refute a statement which I was now being told Sadat had made in Jerusalem. Besides, it was not appropriate to show that I did not know of a promise made by the head of state—in the name of Egypt—on such a major military concession.

As minister of war and general commander of the armed forces, and as the person in charge of state's defense affairs, I sensed a great danger. Naturally, I ought to have been consulted on a subject that would gravely affect Egypt's defense strategy from a direction that was, still is, and will continue to be the main source of threats to Egypt. Only then would the political decision be up to the lawful decision maker.

I decided to discuss the matter further with the Israeli side because Egypt's national security made it imperative to do so. The defense of

Egypt in this vital strategic area (regardless of peacetime or war conditions) required freedom of military action in Sinai. I could not ignore this, whether the report on Sadat's words was true or false, accurate or not. I was confident that if we could reach some positive conclusion with Israel, in Egypt's favor, but which canceled out or invalidated the promise, it would be easy to find the right military justification for this.

I said to Weisman, "President Sadat is not a military man. The problem facing us in this instance is how to defend our country." The discussion between us became heated and I tried to explain Sadat's stand and to distance Egypt from a commitment he was said to have made, on the grounds that the head of state discussed subjects broadly and generally in his capacity as a statesman. However, from a military perspective he did not interfere with the size of the troops stationed in Sinai or the lines on which they operated because this was linked to Egypt's defense plan which was laid out by the military. But Weisman clung to the promise Sadat had made, which said no Egyptian forces east of the Giddi and Mitla Passes line.

Weisman was quite surprised at what I said. He had never imagined that any Egyptian would dare claim the right to break a pledge the Egyptian president himself had made, which is what it seemed to Weisman I had done. We had a heated discussion.

I explained to the Israeli side—in the military style they were definitely familiar with—that keeping the line of the passes obviously required stationing our forces east of this line and that the defense of Sinai and the Suez zone necessarily required the presence of our forces east of Sinai. Naturally, for an effective defense our air force had to operate from Sinai airports east of the passes line. Over and above this, and more important, was the fact that the proposed alternative ran counter to Egypt's sovereignty over its land because it meant disarming the greater part of Sinai.

No doubt all of us in Egypt and Israel knew that the passes line was the last defense line we had to insist on for a defense in this direction. This meant that the defense strips and lines had to be in the area between the passes and Egypt's eastern borders (about 150 kilometers) and that the main airports in Sinai had to be east of the passes (Tamada, al-Maliz, al-Sirr, and al-'Arish) unlike the Sharm al-Shaykh airport in southern Sinai. The experience of earlier wars between Israel and Egypt substantiated this.

Weisman interrupted, saying, "In this way you can reach Beersheba." The discussion became animated. I addressed Shabir, commander of the

Israeli southern zone saying, "Let us assume you're a commander asked to defend the canal zone. How would you organize the defense?" I wanted to get to the bottom of their thinking. In Shabir's view, a small force was enough against an attack from the direction of Sinai.

I did not take what he said from a military angle; more important was his implicit support of the idea to limit the Egyptian forces in Sinai, which followed Weisman's logic that the Egyptian forces should not cross the line of the passes, as per the promise Sadat was reported to have made.

Brigadier Fuad Huwaydi then spoke about the importance of the Sinai airports; our forces should not be deprived of them, for defensive purposes. He asked, "How can we tell an Egyptian pilot he is not allowed to land in al-Maliz or Tamada airports?" Major General al-Geredli explained that we needed security as much or more than they did, and asked if Israel would accept the disarmament of Eilat or Beersheba.

Weisman's response was that President Sadat had called for a breaking of the barriers of distrust between us and that al-Geredli's words were in the spirit of the atmosphere of distrust that had prevailed in the past.

This long and sharp exchange outraged the Egyptian delegation. It exposed Israel's intention for us not go beyond the passes line in Sinai, which would leave the larger part of Sinai without military forces although it covered the main operations axes in mid- and north Sinai. It would also deprive our air force of the use of the airports in Sinai because all of these lay east of the passes line.

Weisman and the accompanying delegation felt our adverse reaction when I clearly opposed thinning our forces in the canal zone in the transition to peace. I also strongly opposed denying our forces freedom of action east of the passes line. I explained that this, in reality, would signify disarming the larger part of Sinai, which was unacceptable. I also stressed that Egypt's sovereignty over its land was inviolable. I further said that the People's Assembly would not accept this, whatever the explanation by the head of state.

I realized that Israel wanted to limit the troops and types of weapons in the canal zone during the peace process and was angered. I said I opposed the thinning of Egyptian troops near the Suez Canal and the disarmament of Sinai, which I believed would have a detrimental effect on Egyptian sovereignty. I added that not even President Sadat could explain this to the People's Assembly, which would turn its back on him and withdraw its confidence in him. I said, "If you speak about disarmament this means that Sinai is not our land and it is lost."

Discussion of this subject ended without any definite result or agreement. Our side had decisively rejected the passes line as a limit for our troops and had insisted on the use of our airports in Sinai by our air force. We also affirmed that Egyptian sovereignty in Sinai was inviolable.

Warning Stations

We moved to a new subject triggered by a proposal from the head of Israeli military intelligence, Shlomo Gazett, that Israel have a presence in the Kharm and Halal Mountains to set up Israeli warning stations in order to monitor our military activity. It seems that the Israelis had learned a lesson from the October 1973 war with all its strategic, tactical, and engineering surprises. While the proposal appeared to be for intelligence purposes, it had a deeper significance. However, I did not discuss that because the whole subject was unacceptable as a matter of principle. Gazett seemed to have forgotten that Israeli Intelligence was famous for knowing what went on in the Arab world in the smallest detail, that it cooperated with the CIA, and that it had reconnaissance and early warning systems in Sinai. Nonetheless we had taken them by surprise in October. Their intelligence services did not provide them with an early warning and their fortifications had not protected them from destruction.

The full picture came into focus after Gazett had made the proposal. Israel's intentions on the future of military relations with Egypt became clear. It wanted to thin out our forces in Sinai and to keep them behind the passes line for the larger part of Sinai to become demilitarized. On top of this, it wanted to have warning stations in east Sinai to detect the military activity of our armed forces.

Did this make sense? Would any Egyptian military or political leader accept it? I knew that negotiations usually started with a maximum number of demands, but a discussion of warning stations—and all the other subjects raised—was unacceptable and we rejected the proposal outright.

Unchanged Concepts

At the end of this long day at Gianaclis—two long sessions suspended only for coffee breaks and meals—I held a meeting with the Egyptian delegation to examine and evaluate what had been done. The main outcome was that we had uncovered Israel's intentions vis-à-vis military relations between the two countries once a political agreement on peace was reached. They too must have understood our intentions. We thought of how to counter their views and proposals and how to safeguard Egypt in this vital strategic direction.

Our demand was a withdrawal of their forces from Sinai. They demanded changing the Egyptian–Israeli borders with a land trade, which we refused.

Their demand was that our troops in Sinai should not go beyond the passes line, implying the disarmament of the greater part of Sinai, which we refused.

Our demand was that our forces should have freedom of action in Sinai without any restrictions, which they refused.

Their demand was to have Israeli warning stations east of Sinai, which we refused.

Consequently, the positive outcome of these talks was almost nil. The picture looked grim, the road to military agreement was full of obstacles, and the road to peace appeared long and thorny.

A question arose: if this was their attitude towards Egypt, whose president had taken the peace initiative and visited Jerusalem, what would their attitude be towards the West Bank and the Golan? I had thought that as a result of the visit to Jerusalem and the discussions there, a military agreement between Egypt and Israel would not face great difficulties, compared to a political agreement which would have to deal with a just and comprehensive settlement to the Arab–Israeli conflict and which inevitably faced complications and difficulties. However, the facts as they appeared to me at this early stage of military negotiations left me with the conviction that Israel's political concepts and military strategy of before the Jerusalem visit remained unchanged after the visit.

THE SECOND SADAT–WEISMAN MEETING

On the following day, 21 December 1977, we (Weisman and I) headed from Gianaclis to Isma'iliya by plane to meet President Sadat before Weisman's return to Israel.

I was not able to reach Sadat by phone on the night of 20–21 December to brief him on the talks before he received Weisman. I thought I would see him in Isma'iliya before the meeting or he would hear a report on the proceedings and on the radical differences between my views and Weisman's, but this did not happen.

President Sadat, accompanied by Vice President Husni Mubarak, received us at one of the houses belonging to the Suez Canal Authority rather than the resthouse on Fursan Island. Sadat started talking to Weisman. He looked extremely angry and tense. He told Weisman that Israel was still pursuing its old ways and that officials in Israel did not understand the importance of his visit to Jerusalem and the risks he had taken. He added that he was ready to sign a peace treaty with Israel, exchange ambassadors, and guarantee freedom of navigation, in return for Israeli withdrawal from Sinai—including all the settlements—but that he did not accept the presence of a single Israeli soldier in Sinai. If Israel wanted Sinai airports to become civilian, the question could be discussed. If Israel needed airports, it could build them on its own land in three or four months; Mubarak had built an airport in Marsa Matruh in three months. I tried to put in a word about the question of turning the airports civilian, in order to settle the matter in Weisman's presence, but Sadat did not allow me to proceed and went on speaking himself. Turning to the peace process, he said, "We—Egypt and Israel—do not need UN forces to be stationed in Sharm al-Shaykh or along our borders," suggesting that joint Egyptian–Israeli, and possibly US, forces could perform the task of observation.

The talks turned to minor issues like the Ras al-Naqab airport, which at that stage did not affect the core of the Egyptian–Israeli talks. Sadat's tone calmed down a little as he spoke about a "comprehensive peace."

The meeting came to an end and I still did not know why Sadat had been angry in contrast to the welcome and the cordiality of the previous day. Obviously he was not ready to listen to what had happened at Gianaclis or to the main topics discussed, which would influence the course of the negotiations and the future of military relations between Egypt and Israel.

I believe—and this is my own deduction—that he was reacting to what he had learned about the attitude of the Israeli government because what he said to Weisman was a strongly-worded message to Begin.

It seems the United States had informed President Sadat of the outcome of Begin's visit to Washington a week earlier. During his visit Begin had presented the Israeli peace plan to President Carter. Begin was supposed to present this same plan to Sadat at a meeting in Isma'iliya in the next few days. It appears that the plan was so unacceptable that Sadat had hastened to signal the message via Weisman before Begin's arrival in Isma'iliya.

Weisman and I returned from Isma'iliya to Cairo by helicopter. We kept silent during the trip. As I thought over the point we had reached, it seemed to me that peace between Egypt and Israel was neither simple nor easy to accomplish rapidly, and that a just and comprehensive peace and a settlement to the Middle East problem as a whole were even more difficult and complicated.

The meeting between the Egyptian and Israeli military delegations in Gianaclis was meant to explore intentions. Israel's intentions were not good and the outcome was not encouraging. I had expected the peace initiative and the visit to Jerusalem to provoke a positive and prompt reaction from the Israeli side. However, the military and political negotiations during the following days and months proved that my expectations were not well-founded.

33

An Unhappy Birthday

A few days after my first meeting with Weisman in Gianaclis I found myself returning to Isma'iliya to take part in the negotiations between the Egyptian delegation, headed by President Sadat, and the Israeli delegation, headed by Prime Minister Begin.

We were three, on 25 December 1977, at Abu Suwayr military airport, Vice President Husni Mubarak, Prime Minister Mamduh Salem, and myself, to receive the Israeli delegation comprising Begin, Foreign Minister Dayan, Defense Minister Weisman, and others.

It was an ordinary reception without any protocol. There were no flags, no musical band, and no welcome signs at the airport. It seems they had not expected an ordinary reception. They had expected us to observe the same protocol in receiving Begin as they had in receiving Sadat in Jerusalem. Weisman made this remark to me on our way to Isma'iliya. He said they had received Sadat in Jerusalem with full honors but that we had received them in Egypt in a very commonplace manner. I did not reply. Ignoring the remark was wiser.

Sadat's visit to Jerusalem was a historic event and took place amidst lavish international media coverage. No one in Egypt or Israel or any other part of the world had predicted that the president of the largest Arab nation would make a peace initiative to the state of Israel, which is why it was in the limelight and the headlines, with expectations that it would bring a just and lasting peace to the Middle East. However, events proved that this was not to be when Israel did not respond with any sincere or positive gesture which might run counter to its policies and objectives in the region. Thus Begin's first visit to Egypt was viewed as a straightforward political activity and was accorded a simple reception without any extraordinary quality.

Begin disembarked from the plane followed by Dayan and Weisman. This was the first time I was to meet Begin and Dayan, although I knew a great deal about them—essentially that both had an intense dislike of the Arabs. The three—Begin, Dayan, and Weisman—were known to be Israel's hawks, sharing views on the Arab–Israeli conflict and actively working towards the realization of Israel's military ambitions. Both the policy and the strategy had endorsed Israeli expansion, military superiority, and imposing 'facts' on the Arabs.

I recalled Begin's killings in Palestine and the 1948 Deir Yasin massacre which was associated with him. I remembered his much-publicized statement to the Israeli Knesset after the June 1967 war in which he had said, "There will be no peace for the people of Israel or in the land of Israel. There will be no peace for the Arabs or in the Arab lands. We will continue to liberate our homeland and all of our land from the yoke of the Arabs. The war between us will continue even if the Arabs sign a conciliation treaty with us."

As for Dayan, he was the commander whose military life ended in the October 1973 war with a failure and defeat he had not expected. Dayan had thought that Israel had guaranteed its security as a result of the June 1967 war, saying at the time, "Who could have dreamt of such security!" He had dreamt this and imagined that matters were settled for Israel in the occupied Arab land until he woke up on Saturday 6 October to find that our armed forces had crossed the canal and that his line of fortifications no longer had any military value. Dayan had been the first to ask for the withdrawal of his troops from the canal line when the Israeli chief of staff reported that it was collapsing and in ruins. The war had done him great personal damage. He turned to politics and became foreign minister after the Israelis had held him responsible for the failure in the war, and the families of the war victims had heaped harsh and humiliating criticism on him.

We arrived at Isma'iliya where President Sadat received the Israeli delegation at the house where he was staying and where the negotiations were to be held. The meeting was cordial and smiles were flashed at the local and foreign media which had converged on Isma'iliya hoping for spectacular results from the second meeting between Sadat and Begin after their first meeting in Jerusalem.

I was happy to find Muhammad Ibrahim Kamil, the newly-appointed foreign minister, at Isma'iliya. He was an enthusiastic nationalist with a record of political struggle since his youth. I was glad that he had assumed this post at a time when we were in need of a firm national stand in the long and complicated struggle ahead of us. He had been Egypt's ambassador to the Federal Republic of Germany before his appointment as foreign minister on 24 December 1977, staying in office until his resignation on 16 September 1978, before the signing of the Camp David agreement on 17 September 1978. He had taken the oath of office in Isma'iliya on 25 December before President Sadat, the day the Israeli delegation arrived. He immediately joined the Egyptian delegation to the negotiations.

We moved to a vast room. The two delegations sat around the negotiating table. Sadat and Begin were meeting separately in an adjacent room. After about half an hour they came out and the Isma'iliya negotiations began.

The Israeli delegation was headed by Begin and included Dayan, Weisman, and others. The Egyptian delegation was headed by Sadat and included Vice President Husni Mubarak, Prime Minister Mamduh Salem, myself as minister of war, as well as Foreign Minister Muhammad Ibrahim Kamil, Ministers of State Butrus Butrus Ghali and 'Ismat 'Abd al-Magid, and Dr. Usama al-Baz from the Foreign Ministry.

When Sadat and Begin entered the negotiating room after their separate meeting, Begin said that he and President Sadat had agreed to form two committees. The first was political, comprising the foreign ministers of both countries, and would meet in Jerusalem. The second was military, comprising the defense ministers of both countries, and would meet in Cairo.

President Sadat opened the session by welcoming the Israeli delegation. He said that the purpose of this meeting, held on the land of Egypt, was to work together to end the suffering of both peoples. He said, "We meet to tell the world that we are working for peace until love replaces the hatred we have lived with for thirty years." To give his statement a human touch, Sadat said the meeting coincided with his birthday.

Begin replied with appropriate words, praising Sadat's determination and expressing his best wishes on his fifty-ninth birthday. He said that the Israelis had received him with their hearts during his visit to Jerusalem, adding that peace had become a joint responsibility and hoping for an end to all wars. He went on to say that he carried with him a plan in two parts, the first concerning withdrawal from Sinai and the second, self-rule for the West Bank (referring to it as Judea/Samaria) and Gaza.

The Israeli Peace Plan

Begin presented his plan with an explanation of the first part, the withdrawal from Sinai. He read in English, which he spoke fluently, from papers in front of him, stressing the words to emphasize their meaning.

The Egyptian understanding at this stage of the negotiations was that the two sides had agreed on "a declaration of principles for the achievement of peace," and that it was within the framework of these principles that details would be discussed. However, Begin delivered a speech he had written himself and knew well. It included details we were not ready to listen to because we had not yet agreed on the principles.

In his plan, Begin proposed that the Israeli settlements in Sinai would remain in place. They were between Rafah and al-'Arish and on the west bank of the Gulf of 'Aqaba between Eilat and Sharm al-Shaykh.

Dismay appeared on the faces of the Egyptian delegation, especially since this proposal had been rejected when Weisman had discussed it with me in Gianaclis. Weisman had discussed it a second time with President Sadat a few days earlier, and he too had turned it down. The president had also turned down the idea of any Israeli airports in Sinai.

At this point Sadat looked at Weisman as if to say he had already rejected this plan, so why was Begin repeating it? But Begin continued to read his galling speech. He said that the civilian settlements would remain under Egyptian administration and that their presence would not violate Egyptian sovereignty, adding that he could not leave the settlements without means of self-defense so Israel would keep some troops to protect them. He expressed hope that President Sadat would understand the human principle involved.

Trying to show that he had made a concession and was departing from the established Israeli canon, Begin said that in his view this new decision was considered a cancellation of the policy adopted by the Israeli government since 1967, which provided for the continued existence of these settlements under Israeli control, noting that he himself had contributed to the adopting of this policy as a minister in Meir's government.

Begin concluded the first part of his peace plan by proposing that the peace treaty with Egypt would remain in force until the year 2001, after which it would be reexamined.

The dejection and dismay we felt turned into impatience, and our eyes expressed it. The atmosphere had become unhealthy as a result of what had just heard and of the cigarettes we consumed as we listened.

Begin's plan meant no Israeli withdrawal to our international borders, which was ludicrous. 'Ismat 'Abd al-Magid intervened, citing UN Security Council Resolution 242 which provided for withdrawal from occupied Arab land. He explained that to Egypt it meant withdrawal to its international borders with Palestine. Begin replied that Egypt had deployed its forces in Sinai in 1967, closed the Straits of Tiran, called for throwing Israel into the sea, and demanded the withdrawal of the UN Emergency Force from Sinai. Having said this he then proceeded to qualify Egypt's behavior at the time as an act of aggression and consequently argued that Israel was in a state of a legitimate defensive war. He concluded that for these reasons Israel was entitled to keep the lands it occupied in self-defense. To substantiate his interpretation, he opened a book with him, saying it was by an authority on international law, and read out a few paragraphs affirming a country's right to retain occupied territories if these were acquired in a defensive war.

Begin had ignored the general consensus that the June 1967 war was a war of aggression on the part of Israel against three Arab states, with the aim of expanding and occupying more Arab lands. There was no discussion following Begin's proposed peace plan, because it was totally unacceptable in form and content. We had reached the end of our tether and breathed a sigh of relief when Begin stopped speaking, but he obviously had not felt the adverse reaction to his speech and proceeded quickly to pull out his remaining punches, moving to the second part of his plan on self-rule in the West Bank and Gaza.

He said that Israel was of the view that it must have sovereignty over the West Bank and Gaza, claiming that it had rights to them. He noted that so long as there were others—meaning the Arabs—who held a different view, he proposed leaving the question of sovereignty open. He went through his plan systematically, article by article, giving Israel all that it needed to ensure direct control—politically, militarily, and economically—and giving the Palestinians a limited administrative role to run their affairs. There was nothing new in the Israeli plan. It was tantamount to a declaration of Israel's intentions to annex the West Bank and Gaza.

The plan barred the establishment of a state of Palestine and denied the Palestinians the right to self-determination. It gave the Palestinians the right to choose Jordanian or Israeli nationality and entitled the Israelis to buy and own land on the occupied territory. According to the plan, Israeli martial law would be lifted and Israel would be responsible for law and order. Thus—in Israel's view—the Palestinians would enjoy administrative self-rule for the first time.

President Sadat said very briefly that Egypt had commitments to the Arab world. The commitments, undertaken at the Rabat summit conference, provided for Israeli withdrawal from the territories occupied in 1967 and for the settlement of the Palestinian question on the basis of the Palestinian people's legitimate rights. The president underlined the urgency of agreeing on a "declaration of the principles of peace." The Egyptian plan totally contradicted the Israeli peace plan but was in perfect accord with international legitimacy and UN resolutions.

No agreement was reached on making "a declaration of the principles for peace" or on a joint communiqué on the Isma'iliya talks. Each side was to make a separate statement in line with its own views.

In the morning of the following day, 26 December 1977, a press conference was held with a huge amount of the press attending. Sadat said, "We have made progress on the subject of withdrawal. As for the Palestinian question, Egypt's position is for Palestinian state to be established on the West Bank and Gaza, but the Israeli attitude is that the Palestinian Arabs on the West Bank enjoy self-rule. We differ in this respect but have agreed to discuss this question at the political committee."

The Isma'iliya conference ended as it had begun, with the creation of a political and a military committee for negotiations. This was the only achievement. It was one of the worst conferences I have ever attended. We were talking at the conference as if Sadat's visit to Jerusalem had not taken place. We spoke as though the October War had not occurred. Begin presented a peace plan and it was unacceptable to us. Sadat raised the question of making a declaration of the principles of peace and it was not acceptable to them. The result was that the conference was a complete failure.

US President Jimmy Carter wrote in his memoirs on 1 January 1978 that Sadat and Begin had met in Isma'iliya right after Christmas, with two totally contradictory reports on their assessment of the meeting. Begin's report said it was a great success and noted that just because no joint communiqué was issued this did not mean it was not positive. But Sadat considered the discussion a total failure and a step back in the peace process. It seemed that Sadat's visit to Jerusalem had not produced anything—in the absence of any real rapprochement between Israel and Egypt—except that it had made the Geneva conference impossible.

President Sadat used to make a televised speech to the nation on his birthday every year. He was always in high spirits on these occasions but that year, 1977, I think he was despondent. We were all unhappy with the results of that gloomy and sterile meeting. We had not reached any agreement on a declaration of principles for a just and lasting peace in the region. We had not agreed on a total Israeli withdrawal from Sinai, which was an integral part of any peace between Egypt and Israel.

We were not able to find an objective basis concerning the West Bank and Gaza, which was part of a settlement to the problem. I returned to Cairo recalling President Sadat's speech to the Knesset in which he explicitly and powerfully defined the basis for ending the Arab–Israeli conflict, through the implementation of the UN resolutions and the principles of international law. He had explained that this was the means by which, ultimately, a comprehensive and just peace in the region would be achieved, to the advantage of all its peoples—including Israel.

But now, after the Isma'iliya meeting, Israel was trying to water down the peace initiative to achieve the very same objectives it had set itself before the initiative. Israel had seized this opportunity to become even more intransigent in its demands. It had capitalized on the hostile Arab reaction to Sadat (both personally and to his initiative), to pressure him to make more concessions for his initiative to be the success he had wanted. The Israeli peace plan which Begin had presented at the Isma'iliya conference demonstrated that Israel intended to swallow up the West Bank and Gaza while scoring maximum political and military points on signing a final agreement with Egypt.

At the time I believed that it was not an auspicious beginning, politically, and that the end would be as bad, both politically and militarily. Consequently, I felt I had to give top priority to military action, as I have always done. It was the certain and dependable guarantee to achieve the objective of liberating our land. No doubt politics play the principal role in any conflict between states but war was an extension of politics by other means and I asked myself if the October War the last one with Israel.

The question that haunted me was: had Sadat expected what had happened?

No doubt he had expected the two sides to agree on the declaration of the principles of a comprehensive and just peace and on the principle of total withdrawal from Sinai as an initial response to his visit to

Jerusalem. After that, details would have been worked out in specialized committees. The distinguished journalist Ahmad Baha' al-Din recorded an interview with President Sadat immediately before the Isma'iliya conference showing the president's own perception of the situation and expectations of the conference. The interview, whose honesty and veracity I trust, shows that President Sadat had expected something totally different from what happened.

I quote parts of Mr. Baha' al-Din's text.[1]

'A Beautiful Dream and a Big Illusion'

I go back to my meeting with President Sadat at the pyramids resthouse in December 1977. All our conversations were serious and focused on the heart of last week's events. But I also asked him a non-political question about his personal impressions of Israel as he saw it and the persons he had met with. I found that this question opened the door to a subject dear to him. He explained in detail the wonderful popular reception he got and the enthusiasm of the Israeli people who were moved by joy at the enormity of the surprise gesture. At last, the leader of the largest Arab nation had gone to them after a long and bitter hostility, and the doors of hope and peace began to open before them.

President Sadat told me, 'Begin is a difficult man with dry emotions. Dayan is the wisest and most candid of them all. The strongest personality I met is Golda Meir.' He told me that he had returned with Ezra Weisman nearest to his heart. He added that although Weisman was not in an official post [defense minister at the time], and that his leg was in plaster so that he walked with a cane, he went immediately to see the president at the King David Hotel where he was staying, and spoke with great optimism about the prospective peace. The president went on to speak at length about Weisman, who seems to have fascinated him. He quoted Weisman as saying that his sole wish in life was the success of peace and spending the rest of his life in a small house he would buy in Alexandria which he adored and from which he treasured the happiest memories as a youth. 'Weisman used to come to me every day and often twice with his heavy plastered leg. He used to ask me if I wanted anything away from official channels. Whenever I asked for anything he would tell me in Arabic in the Egyptian dialect—which he fully commands—'at your service Mr. President."

When the helicopter appeared in view to take him directly to Isma'iliya, Sadat rose to his feet and we headed to the terrace. He bade me farewell and moved towards the aircraft, then made the most important statement, spontaneously, as if he were speaking about platitudes. 'Monday I'll spend in seclusion, rest, and meditation—I have no appointments. Tuesday morning, the official Israeli delegation will arrive in Isma'iliya. We will hold a session in the morning and another after lunch.' He said it as if the talks were a mere formality with a foregone conclusion. 'Wednesday morning, Begin and I will hold a press conference to declare the principles of agreement.'

Before I could show any sign of surprise or obtuseness at the lightning speed and absolute simplicity of it all, Sadat went on to say, as we were walking side by side, 'After the televised interview, Begin and the accompanying delegation will leave for Jerusalem and I will go directly to Cairo and head for my Giza home. I want to go to the People's Assembly on Saturday morning to explain the principles of the agreement and the whole story to stop all those virulent tongues with the results that I will announce.

'If you don't have to travel, I'd like you to write me the speech. It will be the most important speech in my political life.'

We shook hands as he said, 'I'll phone you at your home, which is not far from mine, as soon as I return on Wednesday morning. You'll have the rest of Wednesday and the whole of Thursday to write the speech and we'll go through it together on Friday.'

I took my car to return home. As the sun was setting in the quiet desert of the pyramids I felt the whole world turning. I definitely felt that the president was true to himself in every word he said. He did not need to tell me anything else. But I could not believe that all of his expectations would be fulfilled. Would even 70 percent of what he had said to me be achieved? (I had known Sadat to be optimistic and sometimes groundlessly so. He has a marked tendency to listen to the rosy side of news and events.) Was he the victim of a tremendous deception and did Israel's aim remain to give nothing, and to maneuver and gain time as I had told him? Or had he gone too far in his dreams and was in a cloud, under the glare of the propaganda, the coverage, the international attention and praise, especially from the West? It was the Western world with its more powerful, attractive, conspicuous, and adroit media that influenced public opinion, and which Sadat cared for more than anything else.

Following this, what subsequently happened at the Isma'iliya talks is well known. On Wednesday morning I was alone at home in front of the television set waiting for the press conference and announcement of the principles of agreement. Everyone was astonished and shocked by the press conference, but I can say without exaggeration that I was one of the few who were more shocked than most. . . . I had been one of those who had heard Sadat personally draw a very rosy picture of the outcome. Sadat appeared on television—sitting beside Begin—looking like a mummified body, unable to move. It was clear to me that he was experiencing the hardest moments of his life in front of the whole world. He had to bear the unbearable because he was so committed to the continuity of the peace process. The man beside him had neither wanted peace nor to restore an inch of Sinai.

I became sure that what Sadat had talked to me about a few days earlier was a dream, a huge illusion, and an enormous deception resulting from his absolute confidence in Carter, his capabilities, and his promises. I realized at the same time that Sadat could never break out of this, whatever might happen, and that concessions would follow in succession if he were to realize even a small part of it.

What made matters easier for me was that after the press conference Sadat did not return to Cairo as scheduled. There was no need to write a speech or to go to the People's Assembly to deliver it. There was absolutely nothing to be said. Instead of returning to Cairo, Sadat headed directly for Aswan.[2]

34

THE HIGH DAM BETWEEN THE EGYPTIANS AND ISRAELIS

After the Isma'iliya conference had ended in failure, I went over all that had happened at the Gianaclis meeting that indicated Israel's intentions towards Sinai. They had tried to demilitarize most of Sinai and insisted we implement the promise they said Sadat had made in Jerusalem—that our forces would not cross the line of the passes. They had worked assiduously at keeping the Rafah and Ras al-Naqab airports in place in Sinai. They had defended the continued existence of the Yamit settlement south of Rafah and the settlements from Eilat to Sharm al-Shaykh.

Then Begin had come to the Isma'iliya conference to demand that we give Israel—according to the proposed Israeli peace plan—all the rights that would ensure the virtual annexation of the West Bank, and he had prevaricated on the "declaration of the principles of peace" proposed by Egypt.

The picture fell into place before my eyes. The road to peace was to be long—very long—and full of trials and obstacles. I anticipated that we would reach a blind alley sooner or later.

The Isma'iliya meetings exposed the wide chasm between the Egyptian and the Israeli positions. Reports and news items indicated that Israel was determined to build new settlements in Sinai to create a new status quo. The reports quoted Begin, Dayan, and Sharon as saying that Israel had the right to settle in any place. But the Egyptian press adopted a wonderfully nationalist stand towards the policy of the

Israeli government which had worked to abort the opportunity for peace that had appeared on the horizon after Sadat's visit to Jerusalem.

President Sadat had remained convinced that his peace initiative had to succeed. But at this stage, after the Isma'iliya conference, he learned about the building of new Israeli settlements in Sinai and accordingly announced that he would not allow the presence of any Israeli settlement in Sinai. In various press statements, he declared that his visit to Jerusalem had given Israel more than it had dreamt of since its establishment.

In this unfavorable atmosphere, it was decided to hold a meeting of the military committee in Cairo in the first half of January 1978.

It was obvious to us that the outcome of the military negotiations would affect the political and military situation. Positive results would pave the way for a political agreement not only on the future of Egyptian–Israeli relations but also on the central problem, namely the question of Palestine, and on the means of settling it in a way that would guarantee a just, lasting, and comprehensive peace in the Middle East. This was what the political committee was to discuss.

At this stage, I judged that it was essential to ensure Egypt's defense all along this vital and crucial strategic path. This required a total Israeli withdrawal from Sinai and unrestricted freedom of action in Sinai to defend Sinai, the Suez Canal zone, and the whole country effectively.

Sinai had been a battlefield since ancient times, but its military importance for the defense of Egypt had grown after the establishment of the state of Israel in 1948. It remained of paramount importance and a first priority in the defense of Egypt in war and peace.

In 1956, Israel's part in the Tripartite Aggression on Egypt was to attack our troops in Sinai in coordination with Britain and France, when it seized the opportunity to 'annex' Sinai, and Ben-Gurion officially announced the annexation to the Knesset. This was the first practical proof of Israel's intentions in Sinai.

In the June 1967 war, Israel was able to occupy Sinai for the second time—as a result of our mistakes. The Israeli then said that the Suez Canal line constituted the best secure border, setting up settlements and two airports there. This was the second practical proof of its intentions to annex Sinai.

As a result of the October 1973 war and later of Sadat's initiative to visit Jerusalem, it became clear to the Israelis during the negotiations that followed that we were determined on a total Israeli withdrawal from Sinai. Their new plan became to try and change the international borders and maintain a presence, after withdrawal, under the pretext of security. More important still, they tried to demilitarize Sinai and limit the number of our forces there, to weaken Egypt's ability to defend Sinai and to put themselves in a strong strategic position for the next round with Egypt—once a suitable opportunity had presented itself in the future.

An Israeli military delegation headed by Weisman arrived in Cairo by air. At Sadat's request, I asked Weisman at the airport to continue to Aswan to meet with the president before we proceeded with our work.

An air force Mystere 20 plane was waiting to take us there while the rest of the delegation headed for the Tahra Palace in Cairo, where the negotiations were to take place. During the flight, our conversation was reserved because the general political atmosphere did not allow for anything else. I told Weisman we could no longer understand what they were doing. Obviously I was referring to their recent political maneuvering which had created a state of political tension between the two states. Weisman made no comment.

We could not spend almost an hour and half on the plane without conversing. We spoke about our memories of the last wars. He preferred to speak about the June 1967 war, for political reasons and because of their victory then. He had been head of the Operations Room at the time. For my part, I preferred to talk about the October 1973 war for different political reasons and because of the victory we had scored. I had been head of the Operations Center at the time. No doubt the picture had been reversed in both wars. We spoke to kill the time and without indulging in objective discussion or arguments.

I asked Weisman why Israel had taken part, with Britain and France, in a war against us to deprive us of the Suez Canal, which had been nationalized as a matter of right because the waterway was ours.

I knew how difficult it was for him to answer my question, but I wanted to hear his reply and his interpretation. He could not say that Israel had played a role assigned to it to serve British and French interests in the region. He could not say that the purpose was to expand and to annex Sinai. He could not possibly have said any of that. Weisman replied that this war was, to him, consigned to history. It was a diplomatic reply which saved him from having to go into the subject. We drew nearer to Aswan.

We could see, from the window, the lake and the city which had witnessed so much of Egypt's history. The High Dam had become a symbol of Egypt's determination and will. Egypt had fought energetic political battles against US and British policies to obstruct its construction. The Egyptian response had been to nationalize the Suez Canal company, and this had led to the Tripartite Aggression on Egypt. The political triumph in the building of the High Dam and the nationalization of the Suez Canal company were among the major events in Egypt's modern history.

As the plane was preparing to land at Aswan airport, I remembered with great pride the efforts made by our armed forces in October 1973 to defend Aswan and the High Dam. These were major and vital targets which Israel could not be allowed to touch, but we had not ruled out the possibility of an attempt. Our aircraft had been ready and air defense missiles had been deployed in the desert around Aswan. We had also developed the means with which to stop the enemy from approaching the dam by water.

We headed directly from the airport to President Sadat's resthouse in Aswan. It was a two-story stone building set in a garden on a beautiful site overlooking the Nile. The place was serene and peaceful. President Sadat greeted Weisman and asked about his flight and the panoramic view from the plane. As usual, Weisman took advantage of the occasion of a social exchange to introduce subjects he wanted to speak about. So he replied that the flight had taken about an hour and fifteen minutes to get from one city to another within Egypt. But Israel was a small country, he said; if he had flown from Israel east for an hour and fifteen minutes he would have reached Baghdad, adding that everything was small in Israel so the area around Rafah seemed vast to them though it only constituted about 0.5 percent of Egypt.

Sadat did not let these remarks pass without comment. He said that he knew his people very well and that they would not accept any solution short of a full restoration of Sinai, and without the pressure of Israeli settlements or airports in it.

As the conversation began to flow, Weisman spoke about Israel's security, saying that many Israelis lived near the borders. Beersheba for instance, was only thirty kilometers away from the borders. He was trying to find his way to Sadat's heart by talking at the level of human feeling. He added that the Israeli man on the street admired Sadat in person and perceived him as a man of courage—a shop in Tel Aviv had actually called itself "Sadat Wear," recalling that he himself had earlier likened Sadat's visit to Jerusalem as man's first landing on the moon. If Sadat lost this admiration and goodwill, it would be a terrible loss. Weisman concluded that the situation called for courageous decisions.

Sadat listened intently to Weisman but nevertheless firmly rejected the presence of settlements, emphasizing that he was not ready to approve the presence of settlements and airports which remained in the hands of Israel and that neither would his people accept it.

The talks continued for over an hour on the subject of settlements and airports in Sinai. Weisman tried to wrench out an acceptance of principle, but Sadat was firm.

The subject had already been discussed with me in Gianaclis and was turned down. It had been discussed once more in Isma'iliya at the Sadat–Begin talks and the president had rejected it. Here again it was being brought up for the third time and once more it was rejected.

There was a barrier as high as the high dam between Israel and Egypt in their thinking.

Weisman and I returned to Cairo for the start of negotiations at the Tahra Palace. I opened the working session with the remark that we were meeting to solve our military problems—including the problems of the settlements and the airports in Sinai—in the interests of peace between us. I specified the two questions because both sides had held divergent views on them since the first meeting and they had to be settled. Leaving settlements or airports in Sinai in Israel's hands meant that Egypt's sovereignty over Sinai was not complete and Israel's withdrawal not total. It would be impossible to accept this. Consequently the military talks would break down if Israel failed to make a total and comprehensive withdrawal from Sinai.

Weisman went into Israel's understanding of security to underline its importance. He spoke of Israel's isolation and of the presence of Israeli settlements near its border. He made a point of saying that as military men—all of us—we had an acute awareness of the gravity of war and that we could reach a better understanding than the politicians. He paid tribute to President Sadat for putting the clock forward and expressed hope that the process would not stop.

We listened with total attention and with the tension visible on our faces. I said, "I'm not convinced that the settlements are as important as you wish to demonstrate. The number of settlers is small and can be easily absorbed inside Israel. The presence of these settlements in Sinai means your expansion at our expense, and the people will never accept it." Weisman took the floor to say that the question of the Rafah and Ras al-Naqab airports was also linked to Israeli security, stressing that it was Israel which had built them and that they had cost tens of millions of dollars. According to the Israeli peace plan, Israel would return Sinai to Egyptian sovereignty with only the settlements remaining in its possession and the airports accorded a special status.

At this point I had reached the conclusion that the discussion of the subject should stop, but Lieutenant General Muhammad 'Ali Fahmi intervened and asked Weisman about the importance of those airports.

Weisman replied, "For the defense of Eilat." We asked, "From whom?" and Weisman answered, "From Jordan and Saudi Arabia. I hope we will not have to defend them from Lieutenant General El-Gamasy's forces."

After a long discussion Weisman proposed turning one of the air bases into a civilian airport and keeping the other under Israeli control. He also proposed keeping the rest of the airports under UN supervision until the year 2001. This was not acceptable to us.

Our insistence on Israeli withdrawal from the airports sent a red signal to Weisman's mind. He knew that our attitude was not without reason. Israel's security depends to a great extent on its air force. Weisman feared that the purpose behind the Egyptian demand for the airports was to strike a blow at the Israeli air force, particularly as we were well aware of the importance of these airports in this respect. There were ten airports in Sinai. Some were fully operational while others were kept for emergencies. Sinai was an early warning zone against any air attack on population centers in Israel. It enabled Israel to station aircraft in several airports to prevent a preemptive strike.

We were going around in circles on the question of airports and settlements. Weisman was in fact strictly committed to the 'Israeli peace plan' which Begin had presented at Isma'iliya. I, along with the Egyptian delegation, was strictly committed to Egypt's sovereignty over its land and to the necessity of ending Israel's occupation of Sinai in a complete and comprehensive manner. I said, "Not a single Egyptian accepts the ceding of a single inch of Egypt's land."

I was—and still am—convinced that Israel's concept of security comes principally from its expansionist policy. Its application would have no limit and would only lead to continuous confrontations in the region. It was high time for the Israelis to see that linking security with land was unacceptable and that a geographic expansion could never defeat historic realities.

After that I proposed a demilitarized zone on both sides of the international borders. This meant terminating the two airports under discussion and a cancellation of the Yamit settlement south of Rafah. It was Israel's biggest and most important settlement in Sinai. In my proposal I clearly explained that the demilitarized zone would be inside Israel just as it would be inside Egypt, in the border area. Weisman rejected the proposal saying that the gap between us was wide.

I also observed that we differed on all points.

The talks on this first day at the Tahra Palace ended without any progress.

At the second session on the following day, the main speakers were Israeli Chief of Staff General Gur and Egyptian Chief of Staff Lieutenant General Muhammad 'Ali Fahmi.

Gur described his participation in previous wars between Israel and the Arabs and spoke of Israel's sufferings. From this point he moved on to the importance of "Israeli security," saying that one of Israel's main concerns was what the borders were which prevent Egypt from waging war if hostilities broke out on Israel's eastern and northern borders, especially since problems with the Arab states and the Palestine Liberation Organization remained unsolved. Gur was of the view that both sides had to make concessions for an agreement on peace, explaining why the airports were essential for the defense of Israel, and adding that the distance between Israel and Syria was a four- to six-minute flight and between Israel and Egypt ten to twelve minutes. Israel had six operating military airports and it was risky to deploying large number of planes in a small number of airports.

General Gur appeared to want to underline the importance to Israel of the Rafah and Ras al-Naqab airports. My colleagues and I were struck by Israel's logic, which called for one state to occupy part of a neighboring country because the number of its airports did not accommodate all of its planes. This was what Israel's security was about—the end and the means to every territorial expansion. It was familiar to us in Egypt and in all the Arab countries, and all of us rejected this thinking.

Lieutenant General Muhammad 'Ali Fahmi took the floor to observe that we were spending far too much time talking about the past and ought to concentrate on the future in a way that would enable each side to guarantee its defenses, and to prevent an aggression. He said, "If General Gur is speaking about the importance of early warning, we do not accept that this should be at the expense of our territory. Neither do we have the means of early warning from the direction of the sea," adding that he had heard that Tripoli was within the range of Israel's air force. The Israeli side kept silent and made no comment.

As the negotiations proceeded, someone came in to say that I had an urgent phone call from Vice President Husni Mubarak. Mubarak told me that Israel was building a new settlement in Rafah and asked me to raise the matter with Weisman because "while we are speaking about peace they are building a settlement in Sinai."

I was surprised and angry at what I had heard. I returned to the negotiations room furious, and told Weisman what I had learned. Weisman excused himself to telephone Israel, and the talks were suspended until he could get through to his government using facilities inside the palace. (Direct telephone communications had been set up between Egypt and Israel following an agreement between President Sadat and Israeli Prime Minister Begin, and the communications had been under the supervision of the Ministry of War until they were stopped on the orders of President Sadat in the aftermath of a political crisis between the two countries. He had subsequently decided to set them up again.)

After a short wait, a reply came through from Prime Minister Begin's office denying the establishment of a new settlement on the outskirts of Rafah and asking that President Sadat be informed of this. Having done that, we resumed our discussions.

We moved from the question of airports and settlements to defining the size of the forces on either side of the borders. I said that we had agreed on setting up a demilitarized 'separation zone' on both sides of the borders, as I had understood. Weisman interrupted me saying we had not agreed on a demilitarization on either side but had simply spoken about it as a matter of principle. He stressed that "we have no room for demilitarization. Where? In Beersheba?" •

This round of negotiations ended with no progress on the questions of the settlements and the airports. Israel, as its delegation emphasized, was still insistent on its 'peace plan' which ran counter to Egyptian sovereignty and to total Israeli withdrawal from Sinai. We, the Egyptian delegation, were committed to securing total Israel withdrawal from Sinai, with no settlements and no airports under any pretext.

Unfortunately, and lamentably, Israel had played the tune of 'Israeli security' throughout the negotiations, starting from the beginnings at Gianaclis, then at the Isma'iliya conference, and right through to that day. The concept contradicted the rules of international law and was a reflection of its political ambitions. It had been used to mislead world public opinion and to persuade the Israeli people to accept a number of military adventures. The concept had been supported in many ways, chiefly through the cultivation and use of military power to impose a fait accompli on the Arab states. However, the October 1973 war had called the concept into question and demonstrated decisively that Israel's illegitimate political objectives would never be fulfilled. It also proved that security for Israel would only come within the framework of justice and the realization of legitimate Arab objectives—that is, the liberation of occupied Arab lands and the restoration of the Palestinian people's legitimate rights.

During this stage of negotiations, Israel had insisted on keeping not only its settlements in Sinai but also the Rafah and Ras al-Naqab airports, under the pretext of 'security.' In fact, it had aimed at confirming the idea of expansion for secure borders at the cost of Egypt's security. This was totally unacceptable. Israel had forgotten that before the October War it had achieved victory from borders it now claimed to be insecure and was defeated in the October War from lines it had considered secure.

Weisman rightly said that the result of the palace negotiations was a huge gap between the two positions and that, as I had said, we differed on all points.

In fact, there was a wall—a high dam—between the Egyptian and the Israeli conceptions.

35

The Settlements and the Airports Once More

Attention now focused on the meetings of the political committee in Jerusalem.

The Egyptian delegation, headed by Foreign Minister Muhammad Ibrahim Kamil, left for Jerusalem on 16 January 1978. Kamil has written:

When we arrived at Ben-Gurion Airport, we were received by Foreign Minister Moshe Dayan and a number of ministry officials. He delivered a short speech welcoming the Egyptian delegation and wishing the political committee success in its work. Then he asked me to say a word.

I delivered a speech we had prepared for the occasion. I said that we had come with open hearts and minds and with the real and sincere intention of building a just and lasting peace together. I said that we were looking forward to working jointly for clear and definite results. There were certain basic facts which we had to face with courage and foresight. These were that there could be no peace with the continued occupation of land, or the denial of the Palestinian people's national rights—mainly the right to self-determination. Furthermore, there could be no lasting peace unless the peoples of our region worked to create conditions favorable to living in a secure atmosphere.[1]

The political committee held its first session on the morning of 17 January. Attending were the three delegations: the Egyptian headed by

Muhammad Ibrahim Kamil, the Israeli by Dayan, and the US by Secretary of State Cyrus Vance.

Muhammad Ibrahim Kamil's opening statement stressed that the objective of the meeting was a comprehensive peace, not a separate peace, based on a complete Israeli withdrawal from all Arab territories occupied since June 1967, including Jerusalem, and to insure the Palestinian people's basic rights including the right to self-determination.

Dayan's statement underlined that the aim of the political committee was to reach a peace treaty between Israel and its neighbors, to set out the principles for a just solution to the problem of the Arab Palestinians, and to agree on a peace treaty between Egypt and Israel.

Vance focused on the necessity of a withdrawal from the territories occupied in 1967, an agreement on secure and recognized borders within the framework of normalized relations and peace according to UN Security Council Resolutions 242 and 338, and a solution to the Palestinian problem in all its aspects, emphasizing that such a solution must recognize the legitimate rights of the Palestinian people and their right to self-determination.

Begin precipitated a crisis at the dinner banquet, when before a large number of guests, journalists, and television network correspondents he delivered a discreditable and discrediting speech, saying,

> How can this person from Egypt dare ask us to redivide our capital, Jerusalem, after its unification and demand our withdrawal to the pre-1967 borders? Has he forgotten that we were defending our lives and children from their aggression? Over and above this, he is demanding the right to self-determination for Arab Palestinians. Why? To set up a terrorist state at our doorstep and slaughter our women and children?
>
> The Arabs enjoy the right to self-determination in twenty-one states and now they want to set up another, a new state through self-determination in order to finish us off. I say it loud and clear: no to the division of Jerusalem, no to withdrawal to the 1967 borders, no to the right to self-determination for terrorists.[2]

Muhammad Ibrahim Kamil's reply was discreet but decisive. It was no longer possible for the Egyptian delegation to stay in Israel for continued negotiations. President Sadat called them back to Cairo, and the committee did not resume work in Jerusalem again despite US endeavors.

Carter returned to the United States on 6 January (after a visit to India and the Middle East, and a one-hour meeting with President Sadat at

Aswan Airport) greatly worried about the deteriorating relations between Begin and Sadat. Despite all of Dayan's pledges, the Israelis were doubling their settlements in the occupied lands. It seemed that every time the United States made some progress on the Arab side there came a decision to build a new settlement or a provocative statement by the Israeli government to sweep away the progress. The stand taken by the Jerusalem government was not only humiliating to US efforts, but also a threat to peace prospects. It also put Sadat in an increasingly difficult situation inside Egypt and in the Arab countries.

Cyrus Vance shuttled between Israel and Egypt in an attempt to salvage the negotiations which had started with Sadat's visit, but his mission had practically no hope. Begin's speech in Israel was considered an insult to Egypt and Sadat ordered his representatives back home, threatening to break the negotiations. Carter asked him to revoke his decision but he refused. However, as he held Defense Minister Weisman in high esteem, he allowed an Israeli military delegation to go to Cairo.

IN CAIRO

Some time later and in this murky atmosphere, President Sadat decided to resume the work of the military committee and Weisman arrived in Cairo at the head of a small delegation.

I found that we had nothing new to discuss. It seems that Sadat thought that a meeting of the military committee, following the suspension of political talks, would be seen as a sign of continued contacts and negotiations between the Egyptian and the Israeli sides. On the other hand, perhaps this was meant to satisfy President Carter.

I proposed discussing subjects which had proved intractable and about which we had not reached any conclusions, in order to put a decisive end to them. I meant the questions of the settlements and the airports. I expected Israel to spell out its stand at this session—to indicate whether it still held to its former position or had modified it—for Egypt to be able to respond.

But Weisman repeated Israel's stand based on a return of Sinai to Egyptian sovereignty conditional to Israel's security needs, and settlements remaining in place and airports under Israeli control.

I repeated Egypt's stand: Israel's security needs must not be at the expense of our territory. I proposed an Israeli pullout from Rafah and Ras al-Naqab to take place in the last phase of an Israeli withdrawal. Weisman did not agree but said they would consider the idea of finding a solution based on a phased withdrawal factor, although in this case it would take a longer time. We proceeded to the subject of the settlements on the outskirts of Rafah. The discussions were long and tense. I said, "As I have already explained, keeping the settlements runs counter to our sovereignty. We have principles we can never back away from, namely no infringement on land and sovereignty. The problem of the settlements is Israel's own business and Israel must find a solution to it." Weisman repeated Israel's view that the settlements were one of the components of Israel's security.

I had never been convinced at any stage that settlements would ensure Israel's security. When the state of Israel was established it had depended on border settlements as warning points and areas of concentration for its armed forces. But after the creation of an army which depended mainly on the reserves, it found that it had to evacuate the settlements when their residents were called up. Accordingly, the concept of settlements in the occupied Arab territories had developed and changed to become a means of territorial expansion and a way to impose an Israeli political, economic, and military reality onto new areas which could only survive with the support of an Israeli military presence.

I explained that the settlements in the Gulf of 'Aqaba accommodated a small number of Israelis and that it would be very easy to evacuate them quickly. That would leave the Yamit settlement. I said we were ready to receive any Israeli who wanted to live in Cairo or any place except the Rafah area, and to treat Israeli individuals like other foreigners, according to Egyptian law. I concluded by stressing that "if the Israelis remain in Rafah, this will be the spark which will trigger off the next war." What I said clearly meant that the Yamit settlement could not remain.

Weisman's response was that we should study Israel's problems just as they, the Israelis, were trying to understand our problems and that Israel could not change its position on the question of the settlements. And so, we did not agree.

The third topic after the settlements and the airports was the idea of early warning stations when peace was achieved. Israel had installed early warning systems in Sinai before the October 1973 war. The main station was in Umm Khushayb and had been a prime target for our air force and artillery from the first day of the war because it could detect movements and activities even on the west bank of the Suez Canal. As a result of the second disengagement agreement between Egypt and Israel (endorsed and followed up by the United States in 1975) Israel had placed an early warning station in the passes. Non-military US personnel with advanced equipment were to monitor the implementation of the agreement by the two sides.

The Israeli side suggested—in the words of Military Intelligence Director Shlomo Gazett—that Israel keep three warning stations in Sinai until it became clear that the peace between Egypt and Israel was holding.

I asked, "How long would that take?" Gazett replied, "Fifteen years." I asked, "Who would administer them?" He answered, "The persons administering them at present or Israel civilians, but not US or UN forces." I asked, "And how would they receive supplies?" Gazett replied, "Through a pass leading to the stations."

I was overcome with anger at this proposal: three Israeli warning stations to be operated by the Israelis in Sinai for fifteen years after the conclusion of peace, with a special supply line!

When the Israeli side felt my indignation Gazett said there would be no objection to Egypt having warning stations inside Israel's territories. Weisman supported the proposal as a good idea and in line with the principles of a "quid pro quo."

Practically, this proposal meant that Sinai and southern Israel would become one chaotic patch, traversed by Israeli and Egyptian troops for fifteen years after peace. It also meant that an Israeli force would be stationed in Sinai and an Egyptian one in south Israel throughout this period. It was an entirely new approach with profound ramifications and complications, not to mention the negative political, military, and socioeconomic aspects which made it unacceptable.

I told the Israeli side, "There is no country in the world that sets up warning stations in another country and against that country." And I rejected the proposal.

The last and most serious topic in the discussions was what they called "security arrangements."

A member of the Israeli delegation, General Tamer, explained. He said that the Egyptian and the Israeli armies should be separated by some 150 kilometers. This area was vital to "Israel's security." Weisman immediately added that Prime Minister Begin and President Sadat had agreed in Jerusalem that no Egyptian forces would be stationed east of the Mitla and Giddi Passes and that the area lying east of this line would be demilitarized. My reply was that there was some misunderstanding on the subject because the president had not meant that the area east of this line would be demilitarized but rather that our main forces should not go beyond it. As for the area east of this line up to the international borders—about 150 kilometers—we would keep a force there not exceeding a division or perhaps even less. I said that I disagreed that a written agreement between us should include any restrictions on the movement or stationing of our forces in the area east of the passes.

Weisman asked whether Begin could have misunderstood Sadat to this extent. I replied that they had talked about the main forces but that other troops were to be stationed in the area east of the passes, adding up to a brigade or a battalion.

There was no point in extending the discussion because each side held to to its views.

The question of security was to Israel a policy, a strategy, a means, and an end. Under this pretext Israel could demand anything and in the meanwhile deny it to the other side, thereby insuring itself against it. Since the beginning of the military negotiations, Israel had placed every one of its demands under the cloak of 'security.'

Demanding the demilitarization of the larger part of Sinai was security.

Demanding the persistence of settlements in Sinai was security.

Demanding the retention of two airports in Sinai was security.

Demanding the installation of Israeli warning stations in Sinai was security.

Demanding a limitation on the Egyptian forces in Sinai was security.

Numerous examples spring to mind—from Israel's creation up to the present day—when security was the excuse for repeated Israeli aggressions on the Arab states. Before the end of the negotiations I asked Weisman, "What do you consider important to Israel's security, in your view? Do you want Sinai disarmed or troops and settlements on the outskirts of Rafah and the Ras al-Naqab airport? I want to know the price we have to pay for Israel's security." Weisman replied, "The problem of the Rafah settlements is a separate issue. As for the demilitarization of Sinai, it is vital to both states." I asked him, "Without the settlements and the airports?" He said, "I did not say without settlements."

My questions were meant to probe how far they would go in threatening Egypt's security and how ready they were to move towards peace if they had a real desire for it. All the negotiators were military men and knew the significance of the questions and the answers.

I wound up the discussion by saying, "You want us to pay an extremely high price for Israel's security." This round of negotiations ended without agreement on any subject.

Egypt's National Security

The theory of 'Israeli security' formulated by Israel's leaders since its establishment reflects the political objective Israel has worked to achieve; that is, implanting in the Middle East a racist state with ever-expanding borders to dominate the region politically, economically, and socially, and to have a say in world affairs. Israel based this theory on three pillars: secure borders, possession and use of military power for deterrence, and a strategic alliance with a world power which would guarantee the success of its objectives at every stage. For these reasons Israel's leaders deliberately ignored the demarcation of international borders. Ben-Gurion said that Israel's borders would be where its soldiers stood. The possession of superior military power was the cornerstone of the theory. Israel had come into existence and had expanded through superior power. It had safeguarded its security through deterrence, by preventive war and wars of aggression. As for its strategic alliance with an international power, it had once depended on Britain and later on France. At present it depended totally on the United States.

In the application of its security theory, Israel depends on its military superiority to put a speedy and decisive end to any threat, on holding the initiative, on carrying the war into the enemy's territory, and on making a war as short as possible in order to avoid a long mobilization. A successful application of this theory means depriving the enemy (the Arabs) of their means of security and keeping them constantly in a weaker strategic military position.

Under the pretext of security Israel's demands at the negotiations would have been a strategic threat to Egypt's national security and would have given Israel a significant military advantages in any potential armed conflict with Egypt, a possibility which could not be ruled out in peacetime.

Sensing the Danger

Weisman's statement that there had been an agreement between Sadat and Begin in Jerusalem—and his remarks during the preliminary stages of negotiations at Gianaclis that Sadat had made a commitment to Begin that the area east of the Mitla and Giddi Passes would be demilitarized—had worried me.

Although I had made an objective assessment of this during the negotiations, I still wanted to seek clarifications from President Sadat in person.

I phoned President Sadat and repeated Weisman's words. I also explained the dangers Egypt would be exposed to if such a promise had really been made. I explained how serious it would be to demilitarize the greater part of Sinai (150 kilometers) up to the Egyptian borders in northern Sinai, and I pointed out that placing our troops on the passes line meant their concentration in the last defensive line in Sinai. I explained that this would not provide for the defense of Sinai or the canal area, only fifty-five kilometers away. I further explained that in this manner we would be leaving about 150 kilometers as a strategic vacuum without defense lines, thereby giving Israel an opportunity to cut through and occupy it without resistance in a very short time. The new position would inevitably deprive us of the military airports in Sinai, which were all east of the passes. This was the situation in northern Sinai, not to mention southern Sinai. I summed up the strategic situation: it put our forces in a weaker defensive and offensive position, which was unacceptable from a military perspective. I asked him to intervene to avoid a grave situation.

Sadat only listened. Every so often, he would say, "yes . . . yes . . . yes . . . yes . . . thank you."

After having also briefed him on the final outcome of the military negotiations, I said that we had reached a deadlock and that political intervention was needed at the highest levels in both countries to resolve this.

I did not enjoy a moment's peace after that. I seized the opportunity of President Sadat's Camp David talks at the end of 1978 to propose appointing a military man to the Egyptian delegation because military affairs would be of special importance in determining relations between Egypt and Israel. But the president turned this down.

At the time, I had been thinking of nominating Major General Taha al-Magdub because of his excellent strategic thinking. He had also been head of planning at the Operations Center during the October War and had contributed a great deal to the military negotiations. He was a man I trusted to become the president's most useful aide in the Camp David negotiations, but this was not to be.

The Camp David agreement was—from the military perspective—incomplete because of the lack of military advice at the negotiations.

36

Political Meetings at the Barrage (March 1978)

Under a cloud of general Arab hostility to Egypt and to Sadat in person, and with the suspension of the political negotiations and a deadlock in the military negotiations, President Sadat turned to diplomatic action to break the stalemate, relying mainly on his own efforts.

I was not in close touch with the political activities of the Foreign Ministry except for the feedback I received as a member of the National Defense Council—which met under the chairmanship of the president—or from whatever cooperative activity was taking place between the Foreign Ministry and the Ministry of War. I only began to feel part of the political effort when Sadat invited Weisman to visit him in Cairo. Weisman had asked Sadat to meet him again later the same year in Salzburg, Austria. The invitation was extended through the communications setup installed after the Jerusalem visit.

In an unstable political climate, Arab delegates arrived in Cairo to attend the Arab League meeting on 27 March 1978, but Syria, Libya, Algeria, and South Yemen boycotted the meeting in protest against President Sadat's visit to Jerusalem.

On Sadat's invitation, Weisman arrived in Cairo on 30 March 1978, one day after the close of the Arab League meeting. Cairo announced his arrival, and President Sadat was confident that he was the right person to become a political link between Egypt and Israel, especially after their relationship had become closer. Sadat had not wanted to discuss relations between the two countries with Foreign Minister

Dayan, though both Weisman and Dayan shared identical political views and Weisman abided strictly by his government's policy. This became obvious in the talks held in Cairo—which were not few—when he presented a determined and consistent argument for the implementation of the Israeli peace plan presented by Begin at the Isma'iliya conference in December 1977, and attempted to score bargaining points within the framework of this policy.

On this visit Weisman was accompanied by Aharon Barak, the Israeli government's legal expert. Weisman, Barak, and I proceeded directly to the barrage to meet President Sadat, at his request, at his resthouse overlooking the Nile.

I had expected the meeting to be devoted to settling the differences that had emerged at the military negotiations, but talks began and ended with the Palestinian question.

Weisman spoke of the possibility of reaching an agreement on Sinai, especially since it would be under Egyptian sovereignty, but said Israel could not abandon the West Bank and the Gaza Strip, repeating Begin's earlier statements at Isma'iliya that nobody should have sovereignty over the West Bank and that Israel had not in fact imposed its sovereignty over it. He said that Sadat had earlier told him, and the United States had subsequently announced, that there would be no Palestinian state but a federation with Jordan, which could be negotiable. Weisman concluded that the matter of the West Bank should not obstruct a peace treaty between Egypt and Israel.

Sadat's response was that there would be no peace without a settlement of the Palestinian problem. If we wanted a lasting peace, this problem had to be solved because a lasting peace would not come from a separate agreement between Egypt and Israel.

Weisman then pointed out that the plan proposed by Israel guaranteed self-rule to the Palestinians after which they were free to reach an agreement with Jordan or form a federation with it, and insisted that a separate Egyptian–Israeli agreement would help to realize a peace.

Sadat repeated what he had said, but more clearly. A separate agreement between Egypt and Israel would be detrimental to Egypt because it would be interpreted to mean that Sadat had abandoned the rest of the Arab world and concluded a secret deal with the United States and Israel. Hence the urgency of a solution to the Palestinian problem, because if a solution were found Sadat would then be able to declare that Israel was ready to withdraw from the West Bank.

This was followed by a discussion on the kind of authority which would assume power in the West Bank and the Gaza Strip and the future of the Israeli settlements there. In this respect, Weisman spoke of the necessity of keeping them there as they were. He also spoke about security, ways of maintaining it, and the authority which would enforce it. The discussions then turned to political and legal details.

Sadat's view was that the situation should return to pre-1967 conditions. This meant relinking the West Bank with Jordan and the Gaza Strip with Egypt. As for the question of security, this was open to negotiations. The principal authority in the West Bank would be an elected legislative body and an executive council. The two councils would include representatives from Jordan and Israel. As for the Gaza Strip, representatives would be from Egypt and Jordan. What was important was for Israel to announce its readiness to withdraw from the West Bank and the Gaza Strip.

I believe that the main purpose of the discussions was for Sadat to obtain Israel's agreement that it was ready to withdraw from the West Bank and the Gaza Strip. Weisman did not commit himself, or make promises, but he made it clear that a total withdrawal from the West Bank and Gaza was unacceptable to all Israeli parties.

This meeting was attended by Vice President Husni Mubarak and myself, but neither of us took part in the discussions between Sadat, Weisman, and Barak.

On the following morning, 31 March 1978, President Sadat requested another meeting with Weisman. Once more we found ourselves at the barrage resthouse talking in the shade of the same ancient tree.

President Sadat immediately announced that Palestinian representatives from the Gaza Strip had not accepted the view expressed on the previous day and had insisted on their right to self-determination. He added, "This is their wish and it would be difficult to implement the proposal without the Palestinians supporting it." Accordingly, the proposal which had been presented by Sadat himself the previous day and discussed in detail was shelved and the situation continued unchanged—as it had been before the meeting. What had happened in the interval between the first and the second meetings? Had Sadat reconsidered his assessment of the situation? Were there new reasons for canceling his proposal? Did the Foreign Ministry take a different view which he accepted? I do not know. I did not probe into the matter because it was not within my area of expertise.

When Sadat invited Weisman for a meeting, I had expected it to be for a discussion on military matters as mentioned earlier. But the entire discussion was actually on the Palestinian issue and the future of the West Bank and the Gaza Strip. All of this was the business of the foreign minister but he was not invited to attend, and I surmised that the purpose of the meetings was to convey a message to Begin on the Palestinian issue without making it known publicly; people would be left with the impression that the talks were of a military nature since the Israeli defense minister and I were attending. I think the president's situation was becoming increasingly sensitive. He could not depend on Begin—who was creating obstacles to a comprehensive solution—and he could not depend on the support of the Arab states. The United States was not trying hard enough to bring the Egyptian and Israeli views closer—which it could have been doing by pressuring Israel towards the moderation needed for the just and comprehensive peace which Sadat's initiative sought.

Sadat felt bitter at the intransigent position Begin had adopted since the failure of the Isma'iliya talks. Begin had categorically refused to recognize any Palestinian rights to self-determination, or to put a halt to the settlements in the West Bank, or to implement the UN resolution on the West Bank and the Gaza Strip. This attitude was now threatening Sadat's initiative after he had expected a very much more favorable Israeli response to his visit to Jerusalem. I personally believe that he needed to break the political ice, which would explain why he invited Weisman to Cairo and proposed restoring the West Bank and the Gaza Strip to pre-1967 conditions (after introducing some modifications)—to get an Israeli statement on a willingness to withdraw from them.

Foreign Minister Muhammad Ibrahim Kamil had not been asked to attend the Sadat–Weisman meeting. In his memoirs Kamil says,

> On the following day, 29 March, the Arab ministers started leaving for home in the morning. By the evening, the arrival in Cairo of Israeli Defense Minister Weisman was announced.
>
> Two days later President Sadat called me on the telephone to say that Weisman had not brought anything new. He had asked him to tell Begin that he [Begin] had not yet responded to the peace initiative and that Egypt was not after a separate or partial settlement but a comprehensive peace based on total Israeli withdrawal from all the occupied Arab territories.

An Invitation to Visit the United States (June 1978)

An invitation arrived from US Secretary of Defense Harold Brown for an official visit to the United States, proposing the first week of June 1978 as a suitable time.

I phoned President Sadat to let him know of the invitation, and suggested putting it off because there were no new developments in our military relations with the United States. Besides, the United States had not played as influential a role as expected—after the Jerusalem visit—in moderating Israeli intransigence, despite the fact that the it provided Israel with all its military, economic, and political support and consequently had a powerful influence. Earlier, the United States had agreed to sell us a number of F-5 planes which Saudi Arabia would pay for, but we had not yet received them. The F-5 could not be compared with other types of sophisticated aircraft the United States was supplying Israel, or with the Phantom planes Israel had owned for some time and had used in the October 1973 war.

During the telephone conversation I said, "Israeli Minister of Defense Weisman paid an official visit to Washington two months ago. I think inviting me to visit Washington means—politically—that the United States is trying to give the impression of dealing with Egypt on an equal footing with Israel, which is not true." But President Sadat asked me nevertheless to accept the invitation; he thought it had great political significance.

I started my visit with a meeting with Secretary of Defense Brown. He had received me in front of the Pentagon where, according to protocol, there was a guard of honor. After reviewing and saluting the guard, we had proceeded together to Mr. Brown's office.

I was accompanied by senior army officers and during our week in the United States we had the opportunity to make several visits and attend a number of meetings. The program of the visit was carefully organized, as would befit a superpower like the United States, and on every occasion we were accorded a warm welcome.

My talks with Brown were of a narrow political character touching on the hope for peace between Egypt and Israel. Military relations between Egypt and the United States were limited then and no political groundwork existed to allow for a discussion on rearming our forces. Brown was cool in his conversation and thoughtful. He had had a long experience in the field of armament before assuming this key position in the US administration.

The itinerary included a visit to the Operations Room. Following a US request, I went alone. There I listened to extensive information about the Soviet forces and their deployment in Europe. I was astonished at the mass of information the United States had on the Soviet Union. We moved from the Operations Room to the Communications Room, which was in immediate and direct contact with all US military commanders across the world.

At a meeting with Secretary of State Cyrus Vance at the State Department—which was attended by our ambassador to Washington

Dr. Ashraf Ghurbal—we spoke about the steps taken towards peace between Egypt and Israel and the difficulties facing us. Vance was playing a key role in the peace process. I had not been authorized to introduce or to discuss any specific subject because these were usually dealt with at the level of the Foreign Ministry or by President Sadat himself (he had recently been to the United States in February of that same year), as well through continuous contacts between the two countries.

A third meeting was with Brzezinski, national security advisor at the White House. Egypt's ambassador also attended. I found Brzezinski well-informed on the military points of difference between Egypt and Israel in the negotiations on Israeli withdrawal from Sinai.

However, he chose to discuss only one major point of difference, namely the possibility of changing the Egyptian–Israeli borders in the Rafah region to keep the Yamit settlement inside Israeli territory. I explained Egypt's total rejection of the idea. I said that we had already discussed it with the Israeli side and given the reasons for our stand. I gave him the same reasons I had given Weisman, and concluded by saying, "It's the trigger that will spark off a new war between Egypt and Israel."

I emerged from my meeting with Brzezinski with a very good impression. My admiration for his understanding of international issues and Middle East affairs was later confirmed following a second conversation at an Egyptian embassy dinner given by Dr. Ashraf Ghurbal on the occasion of our visit to the United States, where guests included senior members of the US administration, the secretary of defense, the national security advisor, and other leading figures who had accompanied Kissinger on his trips to Egypt.

At the end of my first meeting with Brzezinski he announced that he would take me to meet with President Carter separately. At the Oval Office, President Carter described very briefly and sequentially the extent of the efforts being made to bring the Egyptian and Israeli views closer together. He asked me to tell President Sadat that the United States was determined to do everything it could to remove the obstacles to peace in the region. The meeting took about twenty minutes, during which time no one but President Carter spoke.

I came out with the impression that the United States would put its weight behind the peacemaking process.

When I returned to Cairo, I phoned President Sadat for an appointment to present my report on the visit and to deliver President Carter's verbal message. The president asked me to accompany him to

Alexandria that same day, and during the flight we talked of nothing else—the visit, my impressions, and President Carter's verbal message.

Sadat was satisfied with Carter's attitude and efforts, which he expected to succeed. He declared the US visit a political success and a useful step towards future military cooperation between the two countries.

IN SALZBURG, AUSTRIA (JULY 1978)

I was at home on the afternoon of 12 July 1978 when President Sadat's secretary called from Salzburg, Austria, where the president was on a visit. The president was asking that Weisman to be invited to join him in Salzburg the following day, 13 July, and wanted me to attend the meeting.

I flew in on the morning of 13 July and was received at the airport by the Egyptian ambassador. We went directly to the hotel, where the president was relaxing. The location was beautiful. It overlooked a wide lake surrounded by green mountains. The city was quiet and flowers decorated all the window sills and the balconies. During the flight from Cairo to Austria I had gone through the morning papers issued in Cairo, and had come across a news item in *al-Ahram* headlined "Gamasy Says No Meeting with Weisman Before Defining the Outcome of the London Conference." The text said, "Lt. General Gamasy has said that there will be no more meetings between military men from Egypt and Israel before the emergence of anything new for discussion." I had always been in the habit of making precise statements to the media in the conviction that military matters should not be open to contradictory statements and that the honest facts should always be made available in due time to the people. The published statement was correct because military negotiations had reached a dead end. My last meeting with Weisman had been at the barrage on 31 March 1978 when President Sadat had asked to meet him on political relations not military negotiations. I did not expect a resumption of the military talks before the political situation had been clarified at the London conference, scheduled to be held in a couple of days, which Muhammad Ibrahim Kamil, Dayan, and Vance would be attending.

I was upset, and deplored a situation in which I was on my way to meet with Weisman in Austria at the very time the Egyptian press was quoting me as saying I would do no such thing. I wished I had had an opportunity to clarify my earlier statement, especially as this meeting had been arranged by the president himself on 12 July for the following day, that is July 13, the very day *al-Ahram* published the statement, but there had been no time to correct it.

When I reached the hotel, I had a short meeting with Muhammad Ibrahim Kamil. Hasan al-Tohami was sitting with a foreigner he introduced as Karl Cahan, an Austrian businessman close to Chancellor Kriesky. Cahan subsequently came to Cairo from time to time, where he met with President Sadat, and their meetings were reported in the press.

Weisman arrived and I escorted him to President Sadat's suite. Sadat welcomed him warmly and told me he wanted to talk with him privately. I left the room and joined our ambassador to Austria, Ahmad 'Usman, and Hasan al-Tohami on the terrace. Neither the foreign minister nor I attended the talks, which lasted for about two hours.

Before leaving the hotel, Weisman invited me over to dinner at his hotel but I excused myself, asking him to stay for dinner at my hotel instead. He too gave his apologies. Then Cahan invited us both to a restaurant in the mountains with a view on the city, where Weisman and I talked about all matter of things except the meeting between him and Sadat. I remember well that I said that I did not expect the London conference to succeed. My reasoning was that the respective political positions had not changed and Israel had not made any positive gesture towards peace. Weisman too expected it to fail.

On the following morning President Sadat joined us for a short while on the terrace. He did not mention the details of the meeting with Weisman, simply saying that it had been a useful way to urge Begin forward before the opportunity initiated by the visit to Jerusalem was wasted, and stressing the urgency for some positive move from them before October 1978 and the end of the UN Emergency Force's presence. The president had met with Shimon Peres before receiving Weisman and this, in his view, was also fruitful for the same reasons.

I later learned that President Sadat had asked Weisman to convey a proposal to his government whereby Israel would declare its readiness to withdraw from al-'Arish and Mount Moses, which would be placed under Egyptian administration before the conclusion of a peace agreement, as a token step by Israel towards peace. The recovery of Mount Moses would have been used to build three places of worship there: a mosque, a church, and a synagogue.

A few days after the Salzburg meeting, the Israeli press published the proposal. Sadat was angry at the leakage of news he considered secret, and asked me to send a cable to Weisman to that effect. Weisman replied and explained that he could not have prevented it under Israel's political system, expressing the hope that these matters would not affect the spirit of mutual trust between them.

A few days later, President Sadat expressed his displeasure by sending the Israeli liaison group back to Israel.

I sent Weisman the message announcing their return. This said that there was no need for the liaison group in our country and that we had made arrangements for their return to Israel on 27 July 1978 on an Egyptian aircraft via Lod airport.

When the decision was announced, US ambassador Herman Eilts phoned me to ask whether it was necessary. I replied that there was no immediate need for the group to remain in Egypt and that the decision would be implemented.

Direct contacts between the Egyptian and Israeli leadership were broken off in this way.

My assessment is that President Sadat had come to believe that Israel was putting obstacles in the way of all the negotiations in a bid to water down his initiative and to gain time to deepen Egypt's alienation from other Arab countries. This would ultimately have helped Israel increase its hold on the West Bank, keep the Palestinian question suspended, and put pressure on Sadat to reach peace in terms most favorable to Israel.

To save his initiative from failure, Sadat had to break the political stalemate through the United States and his own contacts with Israel. His visit to the United States in February 1978 was a bid to bring it into the process as an active partner. Then, through Weisman at the barrage and in Salzburg, he tried to jolt the Israeli government into being more responsive. The Israelis were intransigent and their position remained unchanged. President Sadat found himself in a situation that was becoming more difficult every day. By the end of July 1978 the peace initiative was no longer anticipated to succeed through direct contacts between Egypt and Israel. The United States, with its regional interests at heart, had, as Carter has said in his memoirs, to put pressure on the Israeli prime minister and the Egyptian president to accept comprehensive negotiations wherein Carter would become both the organizer and the arbitrator at one and the same time.

Hence the idea of calling a meeting at Camp David.

37

Summit Meetings in the United States

The United States had made an assessment of the situation in the Middle East and had concluded that Sadat's position was becoming more sensitive every day. He could not count on an flexible option from Israel nor on support from Arab leaders. Some kind of intervention appeared necessary, one way or another, if the peace process was to be salvaged.

President Carter decided to invite Sadat to the United States for talks over a weekend at Camp David. Carter's impression was that Sadat felt that Israel's real intentions were direct negotiations with the Arabs and recognition of its existence and its right to a real peace. The Israelis would never have hoped that Egypt would accept their demands but Sadat had decided to accept them all at once. His visit to Jerusalem had caught them unawares when they had not been ready for peace; nor were they ready for it yet.

Sadat bitterly reviewed Begin's policy since the failure of the Isma'iliya talks. He blamed the Israeli prime minister for ignoring Dayan and Weisman's advice for moderation and giving in to pressure from Minister of Agriculture Aharon, who proposed an extensive program for the establishment of hundreds of Jewish settlements in the occupied territories. Sadat believed that Begin did not have a real desire for peace and told Carter that he intended to announce on Monday at the International Journalists' Club that Egypt would put an end to the negotiations, and that so far they had given the Israelis more than they could have dared dream of a year earlier.

Ultimately, with the help of Brzezinski, Vance, and Mondale, Carter managed to convince Sadat to modify the announcement he had intended to make. Instead, Sadat would announce a readiness to resume talks with Begin if the latter accepted UN Resolution 242 to the letter.

They then moved to other issues that needed to be solved. Sadat accepted a partial disarmament of Sinai but adamantly refused even to consider the possibility of keeping Jewish settlements in the Sinai peninsula after the establishment of peace—even if they were placed under UN supervision. Although he opposed the division of the city of Jerusalem, he believed that control over the holy places should be jointly guaranteed by Arabs and Jews.

The talks seem to have ended on a more conciliatory note. Sadat expressed satisfaction when Carter told him he was waiting for Dayan's visit and intended to extend an invitation to Begin before the end of spring.

MARCH 1978: THE SIX NOS

The Israeli forces were still in Lebanon after a Palestinian commando operation inside Israel on 11 March 1978 when Israeli Prime Minister Begin arrived in Washington on 21 March at the invitation of President Carter. It was similar to the invitation which had been extended to President Sadat a month earlier.

At the beginning of their talks, Begin and Carter had lunch alone. They spoke about the past, then moved to the Oval Office and spoke about the present. After an extensive exchange of views, they gradually got closer to the core issues. Begin told Carter that he was personally hurt when his peace plan was rejected after it had been invited. He went on to say that Sadat's visit to Jerusalem was only a theatrical gesture and that Egypt wanted total Israeli withdrawal and the establishment of an independent Palestinian state. Carter told him that this was not true and that he himself would guarantee it. In reply to a question on what he intended to do for peace, Begin did not offer any new proposals.

Carter made careful preparations for the work session with Begin and Dayan. He prepared the points that he and Sadat had agreed would make peace possible: no total Israeli withdrawal from the West Bank, no independent Palestinian state, a pullout of Israeli troops to positions that guaranteed Israel's security, changes in the borders between Israel and the West Bank, a hand-over by Israel and Jordan to the local authorities, no demand for sovereignty (by any one country) for five years. After this time the Palestinians living in the occupied territories could chose either to join Israel or Jordan or enjoy independence. The points also stipulated that there would be no expansion of the settlements or any increase in their number during the transitional period.

Carter subsequently read out to Begin and his aides a summary of what he thought represented their position.

- No to any Israeli political or military withdrawal from the West Bank.
- No to a stop to the building of settlements.
- No to a withdrawal of the Israeli settlements in Sinai.
- No to putting them under Egyptian or UN protection.
- No to the application of UN Resolution 242 to the West Bank and the Gaza Strip.
- No to any recognition of any Palestinian authority or to the right to self-determination by choosing one of the options mentioned earlier.

Begin then told Carter that his understanding of his position made it totally negative. He did not, of course, discuss any of the points.

38

The End of the Stage of Conflict

By the end of July 1978, Carter was in an uncomfortable position. While convinced that peace in the Middle East was a vital necessity to the United States and that he had to do something, he didn't know what that thing was. He was also annoyed at the Democrats in congress and the party leadership who were pressing him to extricate himself from his commitments and to bridge the gap, as they called it, in Israeli–American relations. Their attitude was exceptionally ridiculous because it came at a time when he was preoccupied with providing Israel with the best guarantees by strengthening relations with Jerusalem.

Begin and Sadat, in different ways, seemed to have exhausted all the possibilities. Even if they agreed to meet they would have no chance of reaching an agreement because of the chasm separating them. To break out of this maze, Carter had to play with both sides and try to make them both win. This was not a comfortable solution, besides being fraught with danger. However, Carter had no other alternative. He was trying hard to convince the Israeli prime minister and the Egyptian president to accept comprehensive negotiations in which he himself would be both organizer and arbitrator at one and the same time. He decided to send Vance to the Middle East to invite Sadat and Begin to a meeting at Camp David. Though aware of the hazards involved, the situation was becoming increasingly worrisome and Carter feared that Sadat might trigger off a crisis in October as he had repeatedly threatened. The Arabs were pressing him and he could no longer resist. He was compelled either to join them or to find a way out.

Carter sent invitations to both of them with Vance during his Middle East tour. They accepted with enthusiasm. Sadat asked to have the meeting in September after the feasts. It was decided to announce the news in August in the three capitals simultaneously.

The First Day of Camp David

It was obvious that Sadat wanted a comprehensive solution and Begin definitely wanted a limited one. Carter seemed to respect Begin's strength and courage but did not have absolute confidence in him. But as Sadat was resolved and determined to succeed, he was more anxious to see Carter convince Begin than to have Carter on his side. Sadat's primary objective was to sign a direct agreement with Israel but he believed that if this was not possible, concluding an agreement with Carter would be an equal victory; Begin could not reject this without facing fierce condemnation.

President Sadat's plane arrived just after 4:30 P.M. that day, 5 September 1978. After proceeding to the back terrace of the house, Sadat immediately said that he had come to sign a peace and not to prepare for further negotiations. He expressed his belief that Begin did not want a real peace and was doing his best to obstruct and delay. He added that he had—in his pocket—a comprehensive plan and was ready to make compromises over any point except the two concerning the return of land and Arab sovereignty.

He explained that he was ready to include a provision for the establishment of diplomatic relations between Egypt and Israel and ending the economic boycott of Israel, on the condition that Begin came into the negotiations with good intentions, but Sadat had many doubts about this possibility. He demanded an Israeli withdrawal from all Egyptian territories and the inclusion in the final agreement—if reached—of an item on the Palestinians and the West Bank concerning negotiations between the Israelis and their other neighbors. He left it to Carter to outline the details.

Two hours later Begin arrived. Begin drew Carter's attention to the fact that Egypt and the Jewish state had not concluded any agreement for over one thousand years and that this meeting was unprecedented, a historic event. Begin was just the opposite of President Sadat. He wanted to limit the objectives of the meeting to an agreement on general principles that would constitute the basis for subsequent negotiations on controversial issues by the foreign and defense ministers of both countries.

Carter strongly opposed this idea and explained to Begin that if no decision on an agreement was reached at Camp David not one of their assistants would be able to pull it off later on. Carter told Begin that they should prepare themselves to cope with all the sensitive issues and not avoid them.

Work at Camp David took thirteen days and ended on Sunday 17 September 1978 with the ceremonial signing of the Camp David Accords in Washington, which was televised live to millions of people around the world. In Egypt we were anxious to know the content of the agreement and its official text. However, the news that caught our attention at the time was the resignation of Foreign Minister Muhammad Kamil who was in the negotiations and had resigned while still in the United States, before the agreement was signed.

The Camp David agreement marked the end of a stage in the Middle East conflict. At the international level, the regional conflict between the two superpowers—triggered in 1956, reaching its zenith in 1967, and resolved in 1978—was settled in the favor of the United States.

At the Arab level, the Camp David agreement removed Egypt from the arena of the Arab–Israeli conflict, thereby weakening the Arab position both politically and militarily. It put Israel in a stronger strategic position, gave it freedom of action to swallow up the rest of Palestine in the short term, and to expand at the expense of its Arab neighbors in the future.

At the national level, the agreement and the subsequent peace treaty between Egypt and Israel resulted in the recovery of Sinai, but with powerful restrictions that gave Israel a stronger strategic position and brought to an end a stage in the conflict between Egypt and Israel. This stage had started with the October 1973 war, was followed by the visit to Jerusalem in 1977, and ended with the Camp David Accords in 1978. It became clear according to the text of the agreements, and later the treaty, that a new stage in the history of the region had begun which would have deep repercussions on the two superpowers in the Middle East. The repercussions would also be felt in the Arab homeland, and chief among them was a change in the security of the region, which became a 'Middle East security system' with the United States playing the major role.

Two weeks after the signing of the Camp David Accords, President Sadat informed me of the new stage which had started in Egypt and which required comprehensive changes in the state machinery.

PART VI

EL-GAMASY LEAVES THE MINISTRY OF WAR

Egypt is going through a new stage, so I've decided to make comprehensive changes in the state institutions and machinery.

—President Sadat

39

In the Service for Life

President Sadat asked to see me at the barrage resort on Tuesday 3 October 1978 at 11:00 A.M. Since the meeting was at his request with no specified agenda, I took my portfolio along with briefs on all major subjects related to the armed forces and the military situation, having assumed that these would be the major concern after the Camp David Accords.

The president received me in the spacious garden and immediately inquired about my wife's health, as she had been suffering from kidney failure for two years and was receiving treatment at the Ma'adi Armed Forces Hospital. The doctors there had recommended treatment at the Lyon Hospital in France hoping to stop her deteriorating condition.

After this brief exchange, the president shifted to domestic politics. He said that Egypt was going through a new stage, and said, "For this reason I've decided to make comprehensive changes in the state institutions and machinery. Mamduh Salem's government will be changed. The speaker of the People's Assembly, Engineer Sayyed Mar'i will be replaced by someone else and a new military leadership will be appointed."

He went on to say that he had already entrusted Dr. Mustafa Khalil with forming the new cabinet which would take the constitutional oath on Thursday 5 October 1978, adding that he had decided to appoint me as his military advisor, while Lieutenant General Kamal Hasan 'Ali would assume the ministry, whose name would be changed from the Ministry of War to Ministry of Defense. He had also decided to appoint Lieutenant General Muhammad 'Ali Fahmi as his military advisor and Major General Ahmad Badawi as chief of staff to replace me. I made absolutely no comment on his decisions and returned to my office.

On the way back, I thought carefully of ways to hand over the armed forces' command to Kamal Hasan 'Ali and the responsibilities of chief of staff to Ahmad Badawi in such a way as to avoid any vacuum in leadership for even the shortest time.

When I arrived at my office at the Ministry of War, I found Muhammad 'Ali Fahmi who had just returned from the Suez Canal zone and was still in his ceremonial uniform. He had been attending a final rehearsal of the military parade scheduled for Friday 6 October 1978 in the canal zone.

The annual military parades marking the October 1973 victory were usually held in Cairo, but the current political climate with Israel had not been favorable for this. Sadat had been scheduled to leave for the United States in September for the Camp David talks. Furthermore, the UN Emergency Force mission in Sinai was scheduled to end in October. At a meeting with the president in Isma'iliya, before his departure for the United States, I had proposed either canceling the military parade or limiting it to the canal zone with a reduced force which the president would inspect on the spot. The aim was for our forces in the canal zone to keep close to the positions they would need to take up in the case either of an emergency or an unexpected development should negotiations in the United States fail. The president had agreed to limited maneuvers in the canal zone.

While he was in the United States, we had been revising our military plans at general command. It had been essential to be ready for any contingency. After the Camp David agreement was signed in Washington, and before returning to Egypt, the president had asked for a full military parade in Cairo.

I had deferred, saying that time would not allow for the transport of heavy equipment, especially tanks, from the canal zone to Cairo for the rehearsal needed for an appropriate parade.

That same day, 3 October, I informed Muhammad 'Ali Fahmi of the changes in the military command. He received the news quietly and said something like "thank God for having granted us success in the line of duty in the October War and up to the present day. This has been the crowning of our military service." I also issued orders to Ahmad Badawi transferring the responsibilities of chief of staff to him as of that day. I added that I would continue to head the armed forces until Kamal Hasan 'Ali took the constitutional oath. Dr. Mustafa Khalil's cabinet took the oath on Thursday 5 October 1978 and that brought both my service in the armed forces and my public functions to an end.

I thanked God for having granted me success in the service of Egypt and the armed forces. I had served to the best of my ability, and I wished continued progress and success on the forces. They were my larger family with whom I had spent all of my life.

I had started my military career when I joined the Military Academy. I was then seventeen years and twenty days old. After graduation, I had served on the frontier in the Western Desert, between Sallum in the north and Siwa oasis in the south, where I had been a witness to the Italian attack from Libya on the British and the triumphant British counter-offensive in the battle of Sidi Barrani which had led to the withdrawal of the Italian forces.

The problem of Palestine emerged in 1948 with the establishment of the state of Israel. Our attention turned eastward to face the new menace. Numerous wars followed—the Palestine war in 1948, the Tripartite Aggression against Egypt in 1956, the June 1967 war, the War of Attrition, and the glorious October War in 1973. Our armed forces had spent thirty years of military conflict with Israel. I was one of the few who had taken part in all the stages of this conflict, except for the Palestine war in 1948 when I was on a training mission abroad.

In the preparations for the October War, I had been appointed to head the Armed Forces Operations Center in the first week of January 1972 and had as a result been promoted to chief of staff in mid-December 1973. I was among those who had been accorded the most recognition by the People's Assembly with my promotion to the rank of Lieutenant General. This was the highest honor achieved in my life, and made a deep impression on me that I will never forget. What more could a military commander ask for in military victory? I had hoped that chief of staff would be my last position, and had it been so I would have left the service satisfied.

But God had willed the course of my life to be different. Minister of War Field Marshal Ahmad Isma'il had died in hospital in London after several courses of treatment abroad. I had been shocked and saddened because we had had a close strong relationship during hard times. We had been in the service together in Sinai during the June 1967 war and had drunk the bitter cup together. We had been together in the canal zone during the War of Attrition and we had had to repress our anger and together take the sweet with the sour. We had served together in the October 1973 war and together we had tasted victory. I was among those senior officers who stayed up all night to organize Field Marshal Ahmad Isma'il's funeral before the arrival of the body from London, and it was then that Ambassador Hasan Kamil—head of the presidential office—phoned to say that I had been appointed minister of war and that I was expected to take the constitutional oath at 4:00 P.M. on the following day, two hours after the funeral ceremony.

This is how it goes in war. One fighter falls and another takes over.

Thus I started a new—and final—stage in the service of the state and the armed forces. At this point I had a political role by virtue of my ministerial post and a military one as general commander of the armed forces with the rank of general as of the end of December 1974. Naturally enough, military responsibilities took first priority both for me and for the entire armed forces. Fighting had ceased but the war with Israel had not ended. We had to work hard and in the spirit of the October War to preserve our gains and to translate the lessons learned into better organization, planning, and discipline.

I did not want—either for myself or for the armed forces—to live in the euphoria of victory and post-war slackening. On the front in Sinai, we were only a few kilometers away from the enemy, separated by an emergency force which would not be able to prevent either party from triggering a war at any time. We had to raise combat ability in the face of an enemy that believed that might was right and relentlessly improved its combat ability. Above all else, part of Sinai was still under occupation and we had to liberate it, either by force or through political means—which too had to be backed by effective military power.

I had expressed this frankly and clearly to members of the People's Assembly committees on 15 March 1977, and the statement was subsequently published in the press. I said,

> The armed forces are well aware that a precious part of our land is still under occupation. Consequently, our battle with Israel will not stop before the liberation of all our land. In light of this, our armed forces continue to conduct themselves in the spirit of the October 1973 war. They neither boast of their victory nor do they underestimate the enemy, and keep in mind that the sustained and intensive political effort to find an equitable solution must be supported by a capable and developed military.
>
> Since the October 1973 war the armed forces have worked to raise their combat ability and to develop their military competence. The task has been hard and the problems many and varied. We have solved them in the absolute determination to keep our armed forces

> able, at any time, to carry out their strategic tasks against an enemy that had not stopped building up its military capability since the October War. While the enemy has been speaking about peace in terms that contradict the essence of justice, it has been preparing for war and has never stopped these preparations for even one second.
>
> Despite its bitter experience in the October War and the high price it has paid, Israel still believes in the power of might. Instead of seeking peace as a source of security it continues the race for arms and military strength. No sooner had it caught its breath from the war than it set out to rebuild its military capability and to add to it and improve it using all the means available.
>
> Though the October 1973 war accomplished a great deal and is still yielding results, this should not leave the armed forces with the impression that peace is at hand and that the war has ended. We must hold to this belief or else we will be doing wrong to ourselves and to our homeland.
>
> We want Israel to understand that there can be no peace with the occupation of land. There is no safety or security in an arms race. We know that even though the path to peace is a long one, requiring tremendous will and effort, the road to war is the hard one. Thus, if we want peace we must be ready for war.

This was the reality in which the armed forces lived from the October 1973 war to the signature of the Camp David Accords in 1978.

An Invitation to the Military Parade (1978)

As I have already mentioned, the morning of 5 October 1978 marked the end of my service both in the armed forces and in public works. On the evening of that day, Minister of Defense Kamal Hasan 'Ali came personally to my home to invite me, on instructions from President Sadat, to the military parade in the canal zone the next morning, Friday 6 October 1978. He told me that a helicopter would be waiting at the Almaza military airport to take Prime Minister Mustafa Khalil, the minister of defense, and myself to the grounds. I thanked him but turned the offer down. I did not attend the parade that year.

I was annoyed and dismayed at the choice of the date 5 October to introduce changes in the military command, thereby denying the old leadership—those who had played a major role in October 1973—the privilege of taking part in the armed forces victory celebration on 6 October 1978.

Would it not have been better and more appropriate for the changes to have taken place on any other day except the one when Egypt and its armed forces had achieved a victory to which we had had the honor to contribute?

It is the prerogative of the head of state to appoint or to change the cabinet or the military high command as he sees fit, but I wished the choice of an appropriate date had taken into account the moral considerations which are so very important in the life of a soldier.

In the Service for Life

I had never had the least doubt that the day would come when my services to the public and in the armed forces would end, despite Sadat's declaration that I would remain in the service of the state for life.

He had said that on the occasion of the appointment of a vice president. The president had summoned me to his barrage resthouse where he had explained in detail the domestic situation and the system of rule in Egypt since the 23 July 1952 revolution. The outcome of this one-hour review was a decision to appoint a vice president from the "October generation."

The president told me what he thought of Admiral Fuad Zikri and General Muhammad 'Ali Fahmi, then he said what he thought of me and of Air Marshal Muhammad Husni Mubarak, going through the list in the order I mention. When my name came up he paid tribute to my accomplishments as head of operations, chief of staff and minister of war, saying, "You're Egypt's Grechko. You must remain in the armed forces for life. This is my will." He concluded by announcing that he had chosen Muhammad Husni Mubarak for the post.

The newspaper ***Akhbar al-Yom*** of 3 May 1975 (which reflected Sadat's views) came out with the news under the headline "Five Candidates for Vice President. Egypt's Rule Has Become Civilian and Will Remain So. Sadat Never Wants Gamasy to Leave the Armed Forces." Sadat had asked me to tell Air Marshal Husni Mubarak that he would receive him at noon that day. I contacted him by telephone to inform him of the meeting without disclosing anything about its purpose. Then I took the measures necessary until he assumed the post of vice president.

President Sadat had also decided to honor the military commanders of the October War and to use the experience of those who had survived, and had issued Decree 35 of 1979 for this purpose.[1]

The decree's explanatory memorandum said:

> Large countries with a rich heritage in soldiery and its principles honor those military leaders who have brought them victory in battles that have determined their fate. The honors must match their

deeds to express the people's gratitude and appreciation of their sacrifice and achievements. There are many examples, west and east, of honoring senior commanders and of benefiting from their experiences for life.

With regard to Egypt, the October 1973 war was a historic turning point at the national and Arab levels. It was the first real confrontation between the Arab armies and Israel in the various stages of the Arab–Israeli war. The results have paved the way to the liberation of the occupied Arab land and the establishment of peace based on justice in the Arab region. It is therefore deemed appropriate to present a bill expressing the people's gratitude to the armed forces and their leaders.

As well as expressing gratitude to and honoring the leaders of this triumphant war, this decree also aims at putting their unique experience at the disposal of the armed forces and the state for life. It is an experience acquired through long service, as the armed forces have become a modern force which has progressed and developed through the many battles waged. This experience has been crowned with the proof of their high ability in the arts of leadership and combat in the October War when they assumed grave responsibilities in the preparation, planning, and management of combat operations—with total efficiency and competence.

The bill was submitted to the People's Assembly and approved, and went into effect on 26 May 1979. Among other things it provided that "officers who occupied the most senior posts in the armed forces, in operations, and as commanders of the main branches of the forces in the 6 October 1973 war shall remain in service in the armed forces for life."[2] It also provided that

these leaders shall offer advice and opinion—when requested—on military subjects of special importance. They will remain military advisors for life, loyal to the armed forces. They shall not occupy military posts in the organizational structure of the armed forces so that honoring them and benefiting from their valuable and unique experience will not run counter to the principles of renewal and continuity while giving those second in command an opportunity for promotion to the higher command posts with the same capabilities as their predecessors. There is no doubt that our armed forces will be capable of producing another generation of commanders who, with experience and practice, can attain the abilities and the efficiency of the previous generation.

This was the idea behind 'service for life' which was provided for by law but which was never implemented.

RAISING THE FLAG AT AL-'ARISH

In civilian life and since I left the ministry, I had been used to reading and writing and often visiting my family in the village of al-Batanun—in Manufiya governorate—where I was born and grew up.

In the winter of 1978–79, at the time when I was officially a strategic consultant to the president, I was informed by the president's secretariat that I would be accompanying him to Aswan the following day where he would be taking some rest. He spent winter there every year.

I was put up at the resthouse belonging to the Ministry of Irrigation and spent my time reading. At the president's invitation, I had dinner with him more than once and this we always followed by watching feature films.

The Shah of Iran arrived during my stay, after his expulsion by the Iranian revolution and Khomeini. As he came off the plane he looked haggard and uncomfortable. He was accompanied by his wife and a small number of Iranians. Sadat received him warmly and cordially at the airport.

The president's conversations with me had revolved around the situation in Iran. He had expected the Shah to return to Tehran after the Iranian army had put down the Khomeini revolution and demanded—by force—his return to rule. Sadat was full of admiration for the Shah. He considered him one of the strongest and most competent rulers in the region who had played a major role in the politics of the Middle East. He also believed that his influence in the region had been imposed through his power and his political discretion which had made the United States pay him special consideration. Sadat was sure Washington would endeavor to bring him back to power as it had done during Musadaq's revolution. He went as far as imagining that when the Shah returned to his homeland he would propose stationing part of his air force in Egypt.

But I had a different view. I believed the Shah would not return in the face of a revolution of a religious nature and the people's desire to get rid of an autocratic ruler with an iron fist. Besides, the Iranian army and air force would not be able to face this revolution because it came from the people and not by an individual or a group. I told him that I had paid an official visit to Iran during which I had visited the Iranian forces (army, air, and navy) and returned—as I had told the president at the time—with the impression that their polish was deceptive. They actually lacked real power and combat ability. I had reached this conclusion after making specialized visits and after putting some tactical and technical questions to some senior commanders and men to test their real mettle. The Iranian armed forces had large quantities of advanced weapons but the men were not qualified or capable of using them properly in a war. I discovered that to make up for this deficiency the Shah was using a large number of US experts in every field I had visited. After having listened to my views, Sadat commented that the army's loyalty to the Shah was beyond any doubt, and that he expected the United States to try to make the Iranian forces restore the Shah, who would consequently be in a stronger position than before.

The Iranian revolution proved that the Shah—with all of his power and unique authority—had been living in an ivory tower, isolated from his people who were suffering terrible living conditions and who had been desperately waiting for salvation. After spending several days in Aswan and seeing Sadat a few times, I took leave to return to Cairo. The president had not raised any important issue on Egypt's domestic front, on foreign policy, or on the military strategies of Egypt, Israel, or the two superpowers in the region.

Naturally I followed developments after the Camp David Accords and the steps leading to the conclusion of a peace treaty between Egypt and Israel, which were then being discussed. The time came to celebrate the return of al-'Arish and to raise our flag after a long absence. When I received the invitation to attend the popular celebrations there, I found myself spontaneously wishing to take part in the celebrations marking the return of a part of our land for which thousands of soldiers had sacrificed their lives. Al-'Arish—and indeed every grain of sand in Sinai—held a world of memories both for me and for all the men who had offered their sweat, blood, and spirit for long years in the defense of Egypt.

I felt that Egypt had started to reap the fruits of the October War victory. I blocked out the contents and limitations of the Camp David agreement and the peace treaty—with all of their negative aspects. I now found myself among the invitees at al-'Arish.

I attended the celebrations and had the honor to kiss the Egyptian flag as part of the ceremony and watched it rise high in the sky of Sinai. I immediately returned to Cairo to revive many memories of years long past. The question I was preoccupied with was whether the October War was the last of wars. The solid fact before me was that the October war was not the last war.

At about 8:30 P.M. on the day of the celebrations, the late Hamdi al-Gammal, editor in chief of *al-Ahram*, phoned me to congratulate me on the recovery of al-'Arish and to wish me well on my promotion to the rank of field marshal. I had not been informed of this yet.

A short while later, the news was confirmed in a call from the Presidency. President Sadat was requesting my presence in Port Said the following morning for a cruise from Port Said to Isma'iliya. This was the first and last time I wore military uniform in the rank of field marshal. We boarded the yacht *al-Hurriyya* ('Freedom'). Also on board were Vice President Husni Mubarak, Minister of Defense Kamal Hasan 'Ali, and a number of officers and men wounded in the October War. During the cruise we spoke about war memories and, as we sailed past them, the ruins of the Bar-Lev line, the positions of the pontoons set up by our armed forces, war memories, etc.

We had made a similar trip in 1975 on the occasion of the reopening the Suez Canal but on board a destroyer belonging to our naval forces and at a time when our armed forces were on maximum alert. However, this time we were on board a presidential yacht. Egypt had moved from war to peace.

In Isma'iliya I shook hands with the president and returned immediately to Cairo.

That was my last meeting with President Sadat.

The Resignation

Almost one year before, I had submitted my resignation to President Sadat. In it I said,

> Since graduation from the Military Academy on 1 November 1939 I have been in the service of the armed forces, believing in its mission and completely loyal to it. That is why I chose the military as a profession—out of faith and conviction—and I have done nothing else in my life.
>
> Throughout my life's journey—with its wars and revolutions and its sweet and bitter experiences—my faith in the importance and honor of this national service has never wavered. I thank God for his blessings and for having given me the opportunity to occupy the highest military positions and to carry the most senior military rank in one of the most sensitive and critical stages in the history of our country.
>
> I have remained in service for forty years during which time I have not spared myself in the line of duty. Now I feel—with a clear conscience—that it is time to step down. I trust you will accept my resignation from the post of consultant to the president for military affairs.

It has been customary in Egypt for the minister of war to be accorded special status by the head of state, and history has taught us a great deal in this respect. The power struggle between Field Marshal 'Abd al-Hakim 'Amer and President Nasir was so acute that it ended in the 1967 defeat and 'Amer's suicide. There were differences of political and military opinion between President Sadat and Ministers of War General Muhammad Fawzi and (later) General Muhammad Sadeq, both of whom had felt the repercussions. It was believed that restrictions had been imposed on me after leaving the ministry for similar reasons. A number of friends, as well as Egyptian and foreign journalists, came to my home to make sure for themselves that it was not the case. This is a fact for the record.

I have been a professional soldier throughout my service. I am proud of this because I believe that when politics enter the army they corrupt it. My term in office as minister of war and general commander of the armed forces was a period of military conflict with Israel. The war had not yet ended when my service came to an end.

About two weeks after the signature of the Camp David agreement and a few days before the beginning of negotiations on an Egyptian–Israeli peace treaty, I had withdrawn from the ministry and from state affairs.

Some time later I was informed that my resignation had been accepted. I was happy that the decree of 11 November 1980 announcing my resignation included a phrase I had wished and wanted, namely that it was a resignation "at my own request."

MAPS

SINAI

◆

THE INVASION AND CROSSING ON 6 OCTOBER 1973

Map One • Sinai

Sinai is a peninsula consisting mostly of desert and mountains. Its northern section is bordered on the east by Israel and on the west by the Suez Canal.

Three principal roads traverse Sinai: the north coastal road, the middle road, and the south road. The north road extends from al-Qantara on the Suez Canal to al-'Arish to Rafah on the eastern border. The middle road extends from Isma'iliya on the Suez Canal to al-Maliz to Abu 'Uwigla to the Egyptian–Israeli border. The Khatmiya Pass controls this road. The south road extends from the city of Suez to al-Tamad, al-Kuntala, and Taba to the border. The Mitla and Giddi Passes control this road.

These three principal roads are axes for advancement for any Egyptian military forces moving from the canal area through the interior of Sinai and to the Israeli borders. The mountainous Khatmiya, Giddi, and Mitla Passes control the movements of military forces from east to west or west to east. During the June 1967 war, the Israeli forces advanced on the north and middle roads in their attack against the Egyptian forces in Sinai. During the October 1973 war, the Egyptian forces advanced—after crossing the canal—on all three roads to continue their attack against the Israelis.

The southern part of Sinai is bordered by the Gulf of Suez and the Gulf of 'Aqaba. Sharm al-Shaykh is considered the most important city in southern Sinai because it controls the Straits of Tiran, through which ships must pass from the Red Sea to the Israeli port of Eilat and the Jordanian port of 'Aqaba. Egypt's closure of the Straits of Tiran to Israeli shipping was one of the main causes of the June 1967 war.

Mediterranean Sea
Jerusalem
Dead Sea
Gaza
Deir al-Balah
Rafah
Khan Yunis
Port Said
Port Fuad
al-'Arish
al-Shaykh Zuwayd
Baluza
Bir al-'Abd
Mazar
al-'Arish Airport
al-Qantara
Israel
al-Sirr Airport
Abu 'Uwigla
Isma'iliya
Khatmiya Pass
al-Hasana
al-Maliz Airport
Giddi Pass
Tamada Airport
Mitla Pass
Suez
al-Kuntala
Jordan
Ras Sidr
al-Tamad
Eilat
Taba
al-'Aqaba
Sinai
Nuwayba'
Abu Rudays
Gulf of Suez
Gulf of 'Aqaba
Saudi Arabia
Dahab
al-Tor
Straits of Tiran
Sanafir Island
Sharm al-Shaykh
Tiran Island
Ras Muhammad
Shadwan Island
Red Sea

Sinai

Map Two • The Invasion and Crossing on 6 October 1973

The Egyptian Armed Forces began their attack on the Israeli forces in Sinai at 2:05 P.M. on 6 October 1973. The Egyptian forces operating on the Suez Canal front consisted of the Second Army, which operated from Port Said to Isma'iliya, and the Third Army, which operated from south of Isma'iliya to Suez. The Second Army consisted of three infantry divisions, one armored division, and the forces of the Port Said sector. The Third Army consisted of two infantry divisions and one armored division.

The Israeli forces occupied the fortified Bar-Lev line on the eastern banks of the Suez Canal. This line of strongpoints and defensive positions extended from east of Suez in the south to east of Port Said in the north. The Bar-Lev line was composed of three sections, each of which had its own headquarters. Situated east of the line, extending into Sinai from the Suez Canal, were the Israeli reserve forces.

The 1973 war began with an initial air attack by the Egyptian forces against a number of Israeli targets in Sinai. More than 200 Egyptian planes attacked three Israeli airports, ten Hawk anti-aircraft missile bases, three headquarters, and a number of radar stations and long-range artillery bases. The attacking planes took off from various airports, flew at low altitudes along pre-determined flight paths, and hit all targets simultaneously.

Protected by an umbrella of fire from the Egyptian artillery forces—over two thousand guns and a large number of land-to-land missiles—

and in the face of the constant fire from the Israeli forces occupying the fortifications of the Bar-Lev line, the forces of the Egyptian Second and Third Armies stormed the Suez Canal in continuous waves the length of the canal.

The Egyptians climbed the high sand embankments of the Bar-Lev line using rope ladders, the commandos crossing first in order to occupy the platforms and fortified positions behind the line. The Israeli forces fought back fiercely, sheltered by their fortifications, as their armored tanks from the special reserves rushed forward to face the attacking Egyptian forces. During the critical stage of the battle, Egyptian infantry troops used anti-tank missiles in difficult fighting against enemy tanks.

Egyptian forces crossed the canal using dingies. Eight thousand fighters landed on the east side during the first few minutes, and their numbers increased rapidly; by 7:30 P.M. approximately 33,000 soldiers had crossed.

Before sunset on 6 October, as the fighting continued on the east bank of the Suez Canal, a number of Egyptian commando units were dropped from helicopters into the middle of Sinai to terrorize the rear positions of the Israeli forces and prevent the reserve forces from moving toward the canal.

While the land battles raged several kilometers east of the canal inside Sinai, a large number of engineers crossed the canal in rubber boats. They carried with them not only their own arms but also their technical engineering equipment, including many powerful water hoses used to cut through the sand embankments and materials for building bridges and operating ferries on the eastern side of the canal.

The accomplishments of the engineering units on 6 October were stunning. They managed—after eight hours of combat and under constant attack from Israeli forces—to build eight heavy bridges, four light bridges, and to prepare and operate thirty ferries. Tanks, guns, and other supplies were transported across the Suez Canal on ferries and on the the bridges as soon as they were built. All the bridges and ferries were fully operational by 10:30 P.M.

The air defense forces successfully protected the attack day and night by providing the necessary shelter for the bridges and the crossing of the forces. Anti-aircraft missile batteries played a major role in defending the Egyptian forces east of the canal.

On 6 October the Egyptian naval forces fired on enemy positions east of Port Fuad (east of Port Said) and Rumana on the north coast of Sinai. On the Red Sea, Israeli positions in Sharm al-Shaykh were hit.

During the first day of operations, about fifty naval units participated in the Mediterranean and Red Seas.

By the morning of the next day, 7 October, the Egyptian forces were successful in attacking and crossing the Suez Canal, an extremely complex water barrier. They quickly destroyed a fortified defensive line and established five bridgeheads six to eight kilometers long in Sinai with the help of five infantry divisions and the forces of the Port Said sector. The bridges were constructed after five successful combat attacks. The Egyptian flags were hoisted over Sinai.

NOTES

CHAPTER 1 • THE ROOTS OF THE JUNE 1967 WAR

1. Ahmad Baha' al-Din. *Wa tahattamit al-ustura 'ind al-zuhr: qissat 6 Uktubar 1973* (Cairo: Dar al-Shuruq, 1974).
2. As reported by Muhammad Hasanayn Haykal in *Milaffat al-Suwes: harb al-thalathin sana* (Cairo: Markaz al-Ahram li-l-Targama wa-l-Nashr, 1986), 266.
3. Haykal, 368–69.
4. Quoted in Musa Sabri, *al-Sadat: al-haqiqa wa-l-ustura* (Cairo: al-Maktab al-Misri al-Hadith, 1985), 367.
5. Reported by the editor in chief of *Akhir Sa'a* magazine, Cairo, 8 June 1988.

CHAPTER 2 • ON THE ROAD TO WAR

1. Anwar al-Sadat, *al-Bahth 'an al-dhat: qissat hayati* (Cairo: al-Maktab al-Misri al-Hadith, 1978), 224.
2. Interview with the editor in chief of *Akhir Sa'a* magazine, 8 June 1988, on the occasion of the twenty-first anniversary of the June 1967 war.
3. Muhammad Fawzi, *Harb al-thalath sanawat 1967–1970: mudhakkarat al-fariq awwal Muhammad Fawzi, wazir al-harbiyya al-asbaq* (Cairo: Dar al-Mustaqbal al-'Arabi, 1984), 71–72.
4. Fawzi, 72.
5. Mahmud Riyad, *Mudhakkarat Mahmud Riyad (1948–1978)* (Cairo: Dar al-Mustaqbal al-'Arabi, 1985), 46.
6. Riyad, 46.

7. Sadat, 224–25.
8. Moshe Dayan, *Qissat hayati* (Trans. State Information Service. Cairo: Ministry of Information, n.d.), 343.
9. William B. Quandt, *Decade of Decisions: American Policy Toward the Arab–Israeli Conflict, 1967–1976* (Berkeley: University of California Press, 1977), 50.
10. Quandt, 57.
11. The complete texts of the US messages and the oral exchanges are published in Mahmud Riyad, *Mudhakkarat*, 47–66.
12. Riyad, 47–66. passim.
13. Yitzhak Rabin, *The Rabin Memoirs* (London: Weidenfeld and Nicolson, 1979), 76.

CHAPTER 3 • WAS EGYPT PREPARED FOR WAR?

1. Quoted in an interview with *Akhir Sa'a* magazine, 8 June 1988.
2. Kamil 'Abd al-Muhsin Murtagi, *al-Fariq Murtagi yarwi al-haqa'iq: qa'id jabhat Sina' fi harb 1967* (Paris: al-Watan al-'Arabi, n.d.), 58–60.

CHAPTER 4 • WAR

1. Rabin, 61–77, passim.
2. Murtagi, 144.
3. "An Answer from Husayn al-Shaf'i," in *Uktubar* magazine, No. 565, 23 August 1987.
4. Sadat, 227.
5. Fawzi, 132–33.
6. Fawzi, 124–26.
7. Fawzi, 144.

CHAPTER 5 • THE GENERAL WITHDRAWAL FROM SINAI

1. Murtagi, 164.
2. Murtagi, 183.
3. 'Abd al-Latif Bughdadi, *Mudhakkarat* (Cairo: al-Maktab al-Misri al-Hadith, 1977), 288–89.
4. Quoted in Mahmud Riyad, *Mudhakkarat*, 91.

CHAPTER 7 • REBUILDING THE ARMED FORCES

1. Riyad, 94–105.

CHAPTER 8 • THE ARMED STRUGGLE DURING THE BUILDUP

1. Riyad, 131–32.

CHAPTER 9 • THE WAR OF ATTRITION

1. Rabin, 118–19.

2. Rabin, 129.
3. Rabin, 132.
4. Fawzi, *Harb al-thalath sanawat*, 317–18.
5. Rabin, 130.
6. Riyad, 236–37.
7. Muhammad 'Ali Fahmi, *al-Quwa al-rabi'a: tarikh al-difa' al-jawwi al-misri* (Cairo: al-Hay'a al-Misriyya al-'Amma li-l-Kitab, 1977).
8. Rabin, 137–38.

CHAPTER 10 • AN EVALUATION OF THE WAR OF ATTRITION

1. Riyad, 130.

CHAPTER 11 • PLANNING FOR WAR

1. Riyad, 410.
2. This section closely follows the format of my presentation at the "International Symposium on the 1973 October War," held in 1975 at Cairo University.

CHAPTER 12 • THE ROAD TO WAR

1. 'Abd al-'Azim Ramadan, *Harb Uktubar fi mahkamat al-tarikh* (Cairo: Maktabat Madbuli, 1984), 41–42.
2. Sadat, 419–35, passim.
3. Egyptian Ministry of War, *al-Rijal wa-l-ma'raka: Uktubar 1972–Uktubar 1974* (Cairo: n.d.), 9–10.
4. Egyptian Ministry of War, 11–22, passim.

CHAPTER 13 • ARAB NATIONALISM AND THE STRUGGLE

1. This report was distributed to all Arab League member states at the time of the meeting. I have provided only an excerpt here to clarify its most important points.

CHAPTER 15 • THE NECESSITY OF WAR

1. Muhammad Hafez Isma'il, *Amn Misr al-qawmi fi 'asr al-tahaddiyat* (Cairo: Markaz al-Ahram li-l-Targama wa-l-Nashr, 1987).
2. Sadat, 382.
3. Isma'il, 267–69.

CHAPTER 16 • THE TIMING OF THE WAR: EL-GAMASY'S NOTEBOOK

1. Sadat, 326.
2. Rif'at Fuda, *Min mudhakkarat jiniral David Ili'azar* (Cairo: Dar al-Ma'arif, 1979).

CHAPTER 17 • THE DECISION FOR WAR

1. Isma'il, 302–3.
2. Sadat, 331.
3. The full text of the directive is published in its entirety in President Sadat's book *al-Bahth 'an al-dhat: qissat hayati.*
4. The full text of this directive is published in Sadat, *al-Bahth 'an al-dhat,* 444.

CHAPTER 18 • WE SURPRISED THEM BEFORE THEY COULD OUTWIT US

1. Fuda, *Min Mudhakkarat jiniral David Ili'azar.*
2. Dayan, 520.
3. Dayan, 365–68.
4. Quandt, 165.

CHAPTER 19 • 6 OCTOBER: THE CROSSING

1. Fahmi, *al-Quwa al-rabi'a.*
2. Trevor N. Dupuy, *al-Nasr al-muhayyar: al-hurub al-'arabiyya–al-isra'iliyya 1947–1974* (Trans. State Information Service. Cairo: Minstry of Information, 1988), 417.
3. Fuda, *Min mudhakkarat jiniral David Ili'azar.*
4. Bahgat's article was published in *al-Ahram* on the tenth anniversary of the October War.

CHAPTER 20 • 6–7 OCTOBER: DAYAN AND THE WITHDRAWAL

1. Henry Kissinger, *Mudhakkarat Kisinjar fi-l-bayt al-abyad, 1968–1973* (Trans. Khalil Frigat. Damascus: Talas, 1985), 263–66.
2. Isma'il, 313–14.
3. Kissinger, 263–66.

CHAPTER 21 • 7 OCTOBER: THREE BATTLES ON LAND AND IN THE AIR

1. Sadat, 238–39.
2. Kissinger, 293–94.
3. Dupuy estimates Israeli losses to have been even higher, claiming that by 7 October Mindler was left with little more than a hundred tanks.
4. Ben Porat, et al. *'Id al-ghufran* (Trans. State Information Service. Cairo: Ministry of Information, 1984). In this book, written by seven Israeli journalists who had participated in the war on both the Egyptian and Syrian fronts, the number of Israeli losses quoted for 6 October is 500 dead, 2,000 wounded, and tens of prisoners taken. In the Six-Day War of 1956, there had been a total of 850 dead, while 180 had been lost during the Tripartite Aggression.
5. Isma'il, 317–19.

6. Kissinger, Section IV, passim.
7. Kissinger, 317.

CHAPTER 22 • 8 OCTOBER: ISRAEL IN DANGER

1. President Sadat has said, "This exceptional performance was by a commanding officer from the new generation, and his name is Abu Sa'da." (*al-Bahth 'an al-dhat,* 341.) After the war, Hasan Abu Sa'da was transfered to the Foreign Ministry with the rank of ambassador.
2. Fuda, 449.
3. Muhammad 'Ali Fahmi, 178–80.

CHAPTER 23 • 9 OCTOBER: THE 'SPECIFIC MISSION' IS ACCOMPLISHED

1. The text of this press conference appears in Porat, et al., 161–75.
2. Kissinger, Section IV, 332.
3. Kissinger, 320.
4. Isma'il, 321–22.
5. Isma'il, 322.

CHAPTER 24 • 10–13 OCTOBER: THE LONG WAIT—A TACTICAL HALT

1. Isma'il, 325.
2. Kissinger, 345–47.
3. Sadat, 384.
4. By "academically" he means in the context of the "International Symposium on the October War," held at Cairo University on 17–31 October 1975, in which he did not participate.
5. Sa'd al-Din al-Shadhli. *Harb Uktubar* (Paris: al-Watan al-'Arabi, 1980), 248.
6. The interview appears in *al-Rijal wa-l-ma'raka: Uktubar 1972–Uktubar 1974*, published by the Egyptian Ministry of War with the approval of General Ahmad Isma'il, which includes all his press interviews after the October War.
7. He means the tank battles that took place on 14 October during the development of the offensive east toward the passes.
8. Isma'il, 323.
9. The data and statistics on the airbridge are taken from the "Report of the US Inspector General on the Airbridge to Israel in 1973."

CHAPTER 25 • 14 OCTOBER: THE DEVELOPMENT OF THE OFFENSIVE

1. Muhammad 'Ali Fahmi, *al-Quwa al-rabi'a*, 181.

CHAPTER 26 • 15–20 OCTOBER: THE BREACH

1. Sadat, 348.

CHAPTER 27 • 25–31 OCTOBER: THREE RESOLUTIONS FOR A CEASEFIRE

1. He means the night of 20–21 October.
2. Sadat, 347.
3. He means 20–21 October.
4. Sadat, 350–51.
5. Isma'il, 346–47.
6. Isma'il, 348.

CHAPTER 29 • THE OCTOBER WAR IN THE STRATEGIC BALANCE

1. Isma'il, 360.

CHAPTER 30 • FIRST MEETINGS AT KILOMETER 101

1. Isma'il, 358–59.
2. Isma'il Fahmi, *al-Tufawud min ajl al-salam fi-l-sharq al-awsat* (Cairo, Maktabat Madbuli, 1985), 64.
3. Isma'il Fahmi, 81.
4. Isma'il Fahmi, 85.

CHAPTER 31 • THE SIX-POINT AGREEMENT

1. Isma'il Fahmi, 90–91.
2. Isma'il, 373.

CHAPTER 32 • PROBING INTENTIONS IN GIANACLIS

1. Weisman says in his memoirs, "El-Gamasy appeared to hold to a firm stand. The man is calm, given to much thought, and pleasant in speech, but he is very strict. He did not show any readiness to make any compromise, however small."
2. According to Weisman, Sadat and Begin had reached an understanding on the subject in Jerusalem.

CHAPTER 33 • AN UNHAPPY BIRTHDAY

1. Ahmad Baha' al-Din, *Muhawarati ma' al-Sadat* (Cairo: Dar al-Hilal, 1987).
2. Baha' al-Din, *Muhawarati ma' al-Sadat*, 166–73.

CHAPTER 35 • THE SETTLEMENTS AND THE AIRPORTS ONCE MORE

1. Muhammad Ibrahim Kamil, *al-Salam al-da'i' fi Kamb David* (Cairo: Kitab al-Ahali, 1978), 93.
2. Kamil, 108.

CHAPTER 39 • IN THE SERVICE FOR LIFE

1. The law was decreed after the signing of the peace agreement with Israel. I had left the Ministry of War on 5 October 1978. Officially, I

was appointed advisor to the president of Egypt. He had not accepted my resignation yet, but he did so in 1980.

2. This applied to Air Marshal Mubarak, Lieutenant General 'Ali Fahmi, Admiral Zikri, and General El-Gamasy.

BIBLIOGRAPHY

al-Badri, Hasan, Taha al-Magdub, Dia' al-Din Zuhdi. *Harb Ramadan: al-jawla al-'arabiyya al-isra'iliyya al-rabi'a, Uktubar 1973*. Cairo: al-Shirka al-Muttahida li-l-Nashr wa-l-Tawzi', 1974.

al-Bughdadi, 'Abd al-Latif. *Mudhakkarat*. Cairo: al-Maktab al-Misri al-Hadith, 1977.

Baha' al-Din, Ahmad. *Muhawarati ma' al-Sadat*. Cairo: Dar al-Hilal, 1987.

———. *Wa tahattamit al-ustura 'ind al-zuhr: qissat 6 Uktubar 1973*. Cairo: Dar al-Shuruq, 1974.

Dayan, Moshe. *Qissat hayati*. Trans. State Information Service. Cairo: Ministry of Information, n.d.

Dupuy, Trevor N. *al-Nasr al-muhayyar: al-hurub al-'arabiyya–al-isra'iliyya 1947–1974*. Trans. State Information Service. Cairo: Ministry of Information, 1988.

Egyptian Armed Forces. *al-Nadwa al-dawliyya li-harb Uktubar 1973 allati 'aqadit bi-gami'at al-Qahira al-mudda min 27–31 Uktubar 1975: al-qita' al-'askari*. Vol I. Cairo: Idarat al-Matbu'at wa-l-Nashr li-l-Quwwat al-Musallaha, 1976.

Egyptian Ministry of War. *al-Rijal wa-l-ma'raka: Uktubar 1972–Uktubar 1974*. Cairo, n.d.

Fahmi, Isma'il. *al-Tufawud min ajl al-salam fi-l-sharq al-awsat*. Cairo: Maktabat Madbuli, 1985.

Fahmi, Muhammad 'Ali. *al-Quwa al-rabi'a: tarikh al-difa' al-jawwi al-misri*. Cairo: al-Hay'a al-Misriyya al-'Amma li-l-Kitab, 1977.

Fawzi, Muhammad. *Harb al-thalath sanawat 1967–1970: mudhakkarat al-fariq awwal Muhammad Fawzi, wazir al-harbiyya al-asbaq.* Cairo: Dar al-Mustaqbal al-'Arabi, 1984.

Fuda, Rif'at. *Min mudhakkarat jiniral David Ili'azar.* Cairo: Dar al-Ma'arif, 1979.

Haykal, Muhammad Hasanayn. *Milaffat al-Suwes: harb al-thalathin sana.* Cairo: Markaz al-Ahram li-l-Targama wa-l-Nashr, 1986.

Insight Team (Sunday Times). *Insight on the Middle East War.* London: Times Newspapers Ltd., 1974.

Isma'il, Muhammad Hafez. *Amn Misr al-qawmi fi 'asr al-tahaddiyat.* Cairo: Markaz al-Ahram li-l-Targama wa-l-Nashr, 1987.

Kamil, Muhammad Ibrahim. *al-Salam al-da'i' fi Kamb Divid.* Cairo: Kitab al-Ahali, 1978.

Kissinger, Henry. *Mudhakkarat Kisinjar fi-l-bayt al-abyad, 1968–1973.* Trans. Khalil Frigat. Damascus: Talas, 1985.

al-Magdub, Taha. *Hazimat Yunyu: haqa'iq wa asrar.* Cairo: Dar al-Hilal, 1988.

Murtagi, 'Abd al-Muhsin Kamil. *al-Fariq Murtagi yarwi al-haqa'iq: qa'id jabhat Sina' fi harb 1967.* Paris: al-Watan al-'Arabi. n.d.

Porat, Ben, et al. *'Id al-ghufran.* Trans. State Information Service. Cairo: Ministry of Information, 1984.

Quandt, William B. *Decade of Decisions: American Policy Toward the Arab–Israeli Conflict, 1967–1976.* Berkeley: University of California Press, 1977.

Rabin, Yitzhak. *The Rabin Memoirs.* London: Weidenfeld and Nicolson, 1979.

Ramadan, 'Abd al-'Azim. *Harb Uktubar fi mahkamat al-tarikh.* Cairo: Maktabat Madbuli, 1984.

Riyad, Mahmud. *Mudhakkarat Mahmud Riyad (1948–1978).* Cairo: Dar al-Mustaqbal al-'Arabi, 1985.

Sabri, Musa. *al-Sadat: al-haqiqa wa-l-ustura.* Cairo: al-Maktab al-Misri al-Hadith, 1985.

al-Sadat, Anwar. *al-Bahth 'an al-dhat: qissat hayati.* Cairo: al-Maktab al-Misri al-Hadith, 1978.

al-Shadhli, Sa'd al-Din. *Harb Uktubar.* Paris: al-Watan al-'Arabi, 1980.

Index